March 26, 202?

Dr. Vinson,

Thank you for
your contribution to
the Louisville Community

Happy Reading

Peter M. Grew, Ed.D.

TEACHER JOURNEYS

*Memories, Reflections, and Lessons from
20th-Century African-American Educators*

Rita Gilbert Greer, EdD

Archway Publishing books may be ordered through booksellers or by contacting:

Archway Publishing
1663 Liberty Drive
Bloomington, IN 47403
www.archwaypublishing.com
1 (888) 242-5904

Because of the dynamic nature of the Internet, any web addresses or
links contained in this book may have changed since publication and
may no longer be valid. The views expressed in this work are solely those
of the author and do not necessarily reflect the views of the publisher,
and the publisher hereby disclaims any responsibility for them.

Cover Photo by Dr. Bernard Minnis

Scripture quotations are from the ESV® Bible (The Holy Bible, English
Standard Version®), copyright © 2001 by Crossway, a publishing ministry
of Good News Publishers. Used by permission. All rights reserved.

ISBN: 978-1-4808-8799-2 (sc)
ISBN: 978-1-4808-8798-5 (hc)
ISBN: 978-1-4808-8800-5 (e)

Library of Congress Control Number: 2020905628

Print information available on the last page.

Archway Publishing rev. date: 4/20/2020

TEACHER JOURNEYS

Memories, Reflections, and Lessons from 20th-Century African-American Educators

Rita Gilbert Greer, EdD

ARCHWAY
PUBLISHING

Archway Publishing books may be ordered through booksellers or by contacting:

Archway Publishing
1663 Liberty Drive
Bloomington, IN 47403
www.archwaypublishing.com
1 (888) 242-5904

Cover Photo by Dr. Bernard Minnis

Scripture quotations are from the ESV® Bible (The Holy Bible, English
Standard Version®), copyright © 2001 by Crossway, a publishing ministry
of Good News Publishers. Used by permission. All rights reserved.

ISBN: 978-1-4808-8799-2 (sc)
ISBN: 978-1-4808-8798-5 (hc)
ISBN: 978-1-4808-8800-5 (e)

Library of Congress Control Number: 2020905628

Print information available on the last page.

Archway Publishing rev. date: 4/20/2020

Dedicated to

My Mother, my Sister, and my Daughter; my Friends and Colleagues who are Outstanding Educators with whom I have worked over the years; those Great Teachers today who keep coming back to their classrooms, day after day trying to make a difference in the lives of the students whom they teach; as well as to the Great Teachers of yesteryear who shepherded me through James Bond, William H. Perry, and Dunbar Elementary schools; Jackson Jr. High School, and Louisville Central High School. My Teachers taught me that "Intelligent" means you know stuff. "Smart" means you know how to use the stuff that you know, and you realize that you do not know everything.

The After-Fore Thought

The COVID-19 Pandemic struck while *Teacher Journeys* was in production. Out of fear and caution, this single event shuttered businesses, colleges, universities, and K-12 schools across the nation for weeks upon weeks. Many K-12 students were left to navigate new, unchartered territories for "school" as their primary educators struggled to design "reduced risk" systems of schooling without real books, without real lessons, and without real teachers as we've come to know them. While the full impact of COVID-19 is yet to be determined, I trust that when the eyes of the nation become unglued and open, the value and impact of America's teaching force will again be revered. Hopefully, the loss of America's teachers standing at the doors of classrooms greeting students with a smile, encouraging students to think, providing students with opportunities to be creative and dream, and guiding instruction and learning will perpetuate an enhanced value for our nation's teaching force. It is our teachers who again must step up to the plate and help students strive and achieve even higher levels of academic excellence in their new world that may change the way we view, perceive, and appreciate education and educators.

CONTENTS

Part 1: Memories of Inspiration

Part 2: Reflections of Initiative

Part 3: Lessons and Insights

Part 4: Legacies and Legends

Part 5: 21st Century Teachers and Teaching: Who Wants to Teach?

PREFACE

IN 2014, I SAT QUIETLY AT THE END OF A SOLID WOOD PEW listening to the eulogy of my second-grade teacher, Ms. Hughlyn P. Wilson. As I swiped at the tears ruining my once perfect make-up and collecting at my chin because I was crying so hard that I could not catch them fast enough, I thought about Ms. Wilson and my other teachers who had made such a profound difference in my life—the four-year old whose father was killed in an accidental stabbing, who lived in one room in an alley, who shared a bathroom and kitchen with other families that lived in one room in the shared house, and whose mom, a single parent, insisted that "where you live does not define who you are or who you can be." At that point in time I decided that I wanted to write a book about African-American teachers. I did not know exactly what I wanted to write about, but I knew I missed the chance of talking with Ms. Wilson about her amazing career and the things that she had done to support African-American educators, including me.

Later that year, this book began taking shape as I sat beside my mother's hospital bed while she travelled her final journey on this earth. Over the next several years, my personal, peaceful recoveries from breast cancer and a stroke were often agitated as I thumbed through research reporting dismal statistics about teacher recruitment in general and the lack of interest in teaching among African-American high school and college students. At that time, my many years of personal work and dedication flashed on and off through brain fog and memory recovery. Furthermore, the number of educators' funerals that I had attended over the last several years strengthened my resolve to do something. I am too old to travel to the 38 states and 100 plus college campuses that I visited each year during my prime, but I can talk and write. ***Teacher Journeys: Memories, Reflections and Lessons from 20th Century African-American Educators*** is a product of my remembering, talking, writing, and a little bit of researching.

The primary goal of this book is to recognize some of the outstanding African-American educators who may be highly notable and others who are unsung heroes. The contributions that they have made to the profession and to the lives of the children that they taught are all important. Originally, the book was also an invitation for African Americans and others to think about teaching as a career, *if* they have the heart, commitment, and caring attitudes to deal with today's students. However, the 800-page missile was considered too lengthy. So, I am focusing on my primary goal—recognizing some really great educators while being a little underhanded—helping you to remember those educators who impacted your life with the hope that you will encourage those around you with the needed aptitude and attitude to consider teaching as a career.

My school district, the Jefferson County Public Schools (JCPS) in Louisville, Kentucky, is among the thirty largest school districts in the nation. The home of more than 150 schools and 100,000 students, kindergarten through Grade 12, JCPS carries a checkered history like many large urban districts that were segregated; forced into merger or desegregation; and plagued with economic and social issues of the times.

A school district recognized across America twenty years ago as progressive and cutting edge, JCPS has solid historical foundations in the dedicated public educators who touched untold numbers of students matriculating through the hallowed halls and acquiring knowledge, skills, and attributes of character that have thrust them into leadership, service, and social and political positions across the world.

However, today, school districts across the country, including JCPS, are being bombarded with poor reviews; legal challenges; apathy and indifference within their student populations; and questions regarding the value and competence of the educators who teach in their schools. The vision and value of today's public schools, and more importantly today's public school teachers, are continually questioned. Large, urban districts with diverse student populations and teaching staffs seem to bear the brunt of criticism, dissatisfaction, and innuendo about teachers not being paid enough or too much for the jobs that they do.

On any given day, as you pick up the newspaper or listen to newscasters expound upon education, some parents and various community members would have you wonder about the stability of public schools and public school teachers. If you did not have an historical frame of reference, you would think that school districts are fraught with poor, uncontrollable slews of students, guided by teachers who are uncaring, unprepared, and indifferent about academic excellence. You might believe that student progress and the overall well-being of the system need a different type of leadership and different organizational rules for operation.

The pictures sometimes painted are of schools with children who remain "low-achieving" year after year because students are not kindergarten-ready due to teachers' lack of skills to make it happen. You might hear that teachers cannot "move the needle" toward student academic excellence in spite of additional support, more equipment, smaller class size, and more adult bodies in the classroom. You might believe that schools with the latest technology, according to research, should make a difference but have made no difference because student achievement has flat-lined for poor and minority students. The reason or explanation given is that teachers lack training and could not use the resources appropriately. You might see data that indicate the achievement gap between Blacks and whites and "haves and have-nots" continues to grow, spiriting a case for charter schools on one hand and state takeover on the other, mainly because teachers cannot do their jobs.

This is not the first time that urban school districts have tackled the issues and challenges of disproportionate educational attainment or non-attainment—a more accurate description. The nuance comes with today's technology. The media broadcast "Report Cards" touting schools as excellent that are high-achieving and labeling schools as failures that continue to struggle by not meeting their academic goals. The shame of a "failing" school is front-page news in the newspaper; it is a ping on cell phones as breaking news or a morning briefing for everyone to view; and it holds the top spot on the evening TV newscast to be relived and reviewed day-by-day, especially by those seeking to divert funds from public education. Imagine how teachers in struggling schools feel when test scores are made public and open to the world, with naysayers shouting, "Incompetent, incompetent, incompetent!"—supporting the relegation of members of the teaching profession to substandard, unnecessary, and mediocre at best.

A cursory review of teaching staffs across the country indicates that it is becoming more difficult for school districts to find adequate numbers of certified teachers to meet student enrollment needs. Teacher shortages occur in general in some areas of the country as well as in particular subject areas in other locations. In addition, the number of minority teachers, that is Black teachers, continues to decline at the same time the number of Black students or mixed-race Black and other students is on the upswing. Statistics indicate that the percent of Black college students electing education as a college major is steadily shifting negatively. White students are not electing teaching as a career as well. Schools and colleges of education are rethinking teacher training programs and are creatively incorporating other non-traditional areas like sports medicine and art therapy under the "education" banner in order to keep staffs intact and to meet budgetary quotas.

Furthermore, when we lose more than 270,000 Black teachers in fewer than ten years, we are adding fuel to a growing supply-demand inferno. Black teachers are rarely found in schools of rural America. Their numbers are limited in urban America as well where school districts support tokenism rather than true staff integration. Let me be clear. I do not believe that teachers should be selected because they are Black or minority. However, they should not be denied an opportunity because they are Black or minority as well. In addition, staff diversity done the correct way is valuable to Black as well as non-minority students. Diversity is the way of the world. All students should have an opportunity to experience the real world in the schools that they attend.

Overall, there is general agreement that education does not hold the same value for today's students as it did in the past in my generation—and not in my daughter's generation either. Schooling is not seen as

a way out of poverty when the differences between socioeconomic groups appear so monumental. The teaching profession and teachers are not held in esteem. Today, I can name every teacher that I had for every class that I took, kindergarten through Grade 12. I asked a group of twelve "smart" ninth graders, Black, white, and other, to name their elementary teachers. They could not.

Finger-pointing; declining respect for the profession; lack of understanding of the service that teachers actually perform for students and the community; lack of recognition for their accomplishments; issues of salary compared to the cost of preparation and training; and complicated certification requirements that vary from state to state along with the availability of jobs in other professions that are less stressful and more rewarding monetarily, have created a conundrum that may broach an educational catastrophe.

As the interest in teaching as a career in general and among minorities in particular continues to wane; as enrollments in teacher education programs across the country continue to decline; as public school student enrollments increase; and as competition for "brain power" escalates within districts, among states, and between countries; the need for knowledgeable, competent, outstanding teachers to direct instruction and help students develop academic knowledge and skills becomes paramount. Without a highly skilled, diverse, knowledgeable, and qualified teaching force, we have a crisis in the making!

For over fifty years, I have been engaged with teachers and the teaching profession. I have taught middle and high school students; identified and recruited perspective K-12 teachers; designed and implemented school-based teacher recruitment, professional development, and certification programs; taught and trained teacher education majors; hired and placed teacher candidates; chaired state committees for designing teacher standards; evaluated teacher education programs at colleges and universities; and monitored and lamented ideas and theories for enhancing the teaching profession. My thinking has always centered on teacher efficacy—developing knowledge, skills, and talents to make good teachers better so that they can grow and develop the knowledge, skills, and talents of their students.

The education arena is a confusing mess with even more confusing claims: teachers do not make a difference; teachers cannot teach; teachers do not care; teachers are not paid enough; anybody can teach; and smart people should not go into teaching. This rhetoric fails to recognize the struggle of African Americans and poor children to acquire an education; the need to promote learning among all races and classes; and the conundrum of where we will be as a society if we do not value education and those providing educational opportunities. This rhetoric also fails to recognize the demeaning connotation thrust upon teachers in the field who struggle every day to make a difference in the lives of children, or the depression among educators when they are continuously confronted with negativity about their profession and presses the question, "Why should I even try to make a difference?"

Teacher Journeys is divided into five parts. Parts 1 through 3, **Memories of Inspiration, Reflections of Initiative,** and **Lessons and Insights,** are stories primarily in the voices of the twentieth century educators themselves. **Inspiration,** Part 1, includes stories from teacher professionals who were educated by twentieth century teachers and who were *inspired* to become educators in the twentieth century. Their stories reflect the **Inspiration** that propelled them to choose teaching as a career and to support the profession. In a time when interest in teaching as a career is declining among all populations for a myriad of reasons, these stories share the "heart" of being a teacher and an African-American teacher in particular. These *Journeys* speak to **Inspiration** because of the aspiration provided by teachers and others who valued education.

Part 2, **Initiative,** shares the *Teacher Journeys* of another group of educators who experienced hardships along the way. Stories depict drive, determination, gumption, and resourcefulness that made teaching as a career come to fruition. Stories also share many of the accomplishments of these educators who fought for positions in the profession. Journeys of **Initiative** provide examples of struggles that many African-American educators of the last century endured. The ingenuity required to overcome many of the obstacles cast before them by circumstances of birth, upbringing, or societal ills is sometimes breathtaking.

Insights is Part 3 of *Teacher Journeys.* The stories related in this section sometimes touch upon Inspiration and Initiative. However, the key elements found here are the wisdom, understanding, and savvy about teaching; relationships with students and parents; and the values, perceptions, and visions of the profession. These stories address issues and challenges that teachers faced yesterday and overlay them with today's rhetoric and scenarios that offer understanding, guidance, direction, and food for thought. Stories highlighted in **Insights** provide clear, defined expectations of what good teaching is about—then, now, and in the future. The personal characteristics of good teachers are undeniable according to these educators. *Teacher Journeys*, both humorous and heart-wrenching, are honest memories and reflections that provide examples of dedication, determination, and stick-to-itiveness as well.

Part 4, **Legacies and Legends,** recognizes seven outstanding educators whose works are continuously recognized by the Louisville community. Six of their *Journeys* are shared through writings, public records, and the words of their relatives, friends, their students, and spouses because those individuals are deceased. Only one member of this group tells his own story, Dr. Sam Robinson. This is the same Dr. Robinson whose general counsel I sought early on when I began pondering and actually researching and writing this book. I asked Dr. Robinson if a book of this nature would be something that he would read. He asked me clarifying questions, helping me to get my "head straight."

Part 5, which I wanted to entitle, "They Never Promised Us a Rose Garden," allows the author to pontificate and share some final thoughts. The actual title of Part 5 is **21st Century Teachers and Teaching: Who Wants to Teach?**

On a final note, I would like to extend my appreciation to Yvonne Jackson, my editor and friend, for her professionalism, expertise, and guidance in creating this work. Yvonne added the commas, question marks, italics, and critical eyes, highlighting rambling thoughts and run-on sentences that I could not catch even when I tried. It was through discussions with Yvonne that decisions about terminology and consistency were made. On that note, I would like to give a little background for a decision that we made regarding terminology.

Many readers are familiar with scenarios that "people of color," that is, people of African descent have faced over the decades. What should we be called other than the offensive "*N*" word has been pondered on many different fronts as *Colored, Negro, Black,* and *African American* were all used in twentieth century America to describe "us."

When Yvonne and I put on our professional hats for grammatical consistency and continuity, the hats did not fit. The voices of the storytellers demanded flexibility in the terms used to describe who we are at any given time, locale, and/or circumstance. Hence, *Colored, Negro, Black,* and *Africa American* are used interchangeably in this manuscript rather than our being static and selecting one term to use throughout.

Colored, Negro Rita Greer is the same *Black, African-American* Rita Greer, except she may be older with a little more gray hair and a littler shorter because she didn't always take Vitamin-D when she was supposed to.

Thank You and Happy Reading!

ACKNOWLEDGEMENTS

TIME IS FILLED WITH SWIFT TRANSITIONS, ISSUES AND challenges that we do not always anticipate or know quite how to handle when we are embarking on a new journey like writing a book that you hope is meaningful. It is in those moments that individuals step forward to fill in the gaps; offer words of encouragement; give a quick "of course I will help you;" call to check on your progress; tell you it is O.K. to go slowly; send back information that you forgot was already returned; and give you the benefit of their knowledge, expertise, and talent just because you ask them to.

I have experienced a large cadre of individuals who have done all of the above and have been with me as I mulled over writing and re-writing *Teacher Journeys*. I want to take this opportunity to express my sincere gratitude to each of them. Also, my story tellers opened up their homes to me, met me in locations across the city, and spent hours on the telephone recounting experiences; sharing their inner thoughts and personal dilemmas; reviewing my transcriptions for accuracy; and filling in the blanks as my mind hiccupped.

I truly must acknowledge the spirit, expertise, and devotion of Yvonne Jackson who edited, re-edited, and cross-edited page after page as she tried to help me maintain focus and direction. Additionally, I appreciate the input of my former doctoral students, Dr. Yvonne Austin, Dr. Lynn Reynolds, Dr. Lemuel Jordon, Dr. Gwen Goffner, and Dr. Georgia Hampton who reviewed and critiqued portions of my manuscript and gave such meaningful feedback. Also, I am grateful for Dr. Sam Robinson for his overall guidance.

In addition, I must enunciate my appreciation of my family members for their support and encouragement throughout this venture. Their patience, enthusiasm, and positive attitudes helped me remain vibrant and persistent. A special acknowledgement goes to my sister, Olivia, for her listening ear, her no-nonsense critique of my writing, and her technical support when I did not know where to begin to crop a picture; to my granddaughter, Alyssa who helped me organize crates of interview materials and references; and to my husband, James, who understood that writing this book was something that I had to get out of my head and gave me the time and space to work and write.

My heart-felt **THANK YOU** goes to each of you, again and again. You have added to my blessings.

Teacher Journeys:

Memories, Reflections, and Lessons from 20th Century African-American Educators

INTRODUCTION

Teacher: One who imparts knowledge, educates and shares the meaning of information; one who develops individuals' skills through coaching, demonstration, training, and instruction; one who gives direction and intellectual, social, and moral instruction in general or in a specific field. One who cares, coddles, connects, and convinces that you can be anything that you want to be and supports your efforts to do so. One who plants the seeds of dreams and gives you the food and water to make them grow.[1]

Rita's Teachers

TEACHERS HAVE ALWAYS BEEN AN IMPORTANT PART OF MY life. Yes, my mom, my cousin Virginia, and my sister, Olivia, were all my first teachers, but they were not professionals; they were family. "Teachers," as I recall, were my "school teachers" and began with Ms. Harrison, my kindergarten teacher at James Bond Elementary School (currently Dan C. Byck) in Fall of 1953. How excited I was to finally go to school! I know that I was probably jealous of my sister going to school, having her own school books, doing homework, and having her own teachers that she talked about all of the time. I remember mumbling about wanting a reading book and getting a spanking for hiding Olivia's so that she couldn't read it. I also recall insinuating myself into Olivia's homework time when Mama or Virginia were going over lessons with her to make sure that she could fluently read a passage, spell the words on her spelling list, or compute the math problems on her take-home page of the frayed arithmetic book that had seen better days and lots of use. I do not remember watching Olivia learn to print, but I did watch her learn to write in cursive. Mama had a special practice that Olivia had to do every evening— making ten continuous circles on top of each other without lifting her pencil until the end swiggle.

Olivia was partially tasked with helping me practice my A-B-C's, learning my numbers, and learning to spell words from a list that Mama created. It was not today's Dolch Sight Words, but it came pretty close. As a result, I could read, print the alphabet, spell lots of words, count, add, and count money at a very early age. I entered kindergarten in the "Bluebirds" group and stayed ahead for most of my schooling. First Grade was a breeze. I could write my own signature and knew my 2's, 3's, and 4's "Times Tables" because Olivia knew hers.

Similar to the reflections in many of the journeys that you will read later, I loved and respected my teachers. They were kind, smart, and caring. They knew "stuff" and always wanted me to learn "stuff." It never occurred to me to be disrespectful, distrustful, belligerent, or to sass (my mom would have killed me). I wanted to please my teachers! I did what they expected me to do. They were "my teachers" who wanted me to learn; who helped me explore and discover; and who expected me to achieve.

Unlike Bob Coleman whom you will also hear from shortly, my teachers did not live next door or down the street, nor did they visit with my mom or come to my house. However, the care, consideration, and high expectations that teachers of my time showed their students is undeniable. "Haves" versus "Have-Nots" was not the dominating force in my schooling. In my neighborhood schools, we were all very similar in economic circumstances—different degrees of poor. What set students apart was their intellect. Because Olivia and I were smart, we schooled with the brightest and played with the smart, the not so smart, and the questionable. The other difference of note is our friends and our foes recognized that we were "smart" and respected us for being so.

As children, we never fought because I was in the Bluebirds and someone else was in the Redbirds. Our arguments and disagreements were over whether the softball bounced in bounds or was a foul ball;

who crossed the finish line first in the reoccurring foot races that began in kindergarten and ended about Grade 8; whose cake rose highest or whose tomato aspic came out of the pan easier in Ms. McCarley's home economics class; or if you were trying to steal someone's boyfriend or girlfriend. Our dress, our shoes, our hair, where we lived, or what our parents did for a living were rarely food for ridicule among students. In addition, if our teachers noticed something askew, we as students did not know that they did. Our teachers hugged us, patted our shoulders, proudly stood us in front of the class to recite, and whispered quietly in our ears to supervise, guide, and encourage.

Being poor may have meant something to some students. However, for me, living in Reed Alley, sharing a kitchen and bath with two other families, or living above the shoe shop on Walnut Street had little if any impact on my intellect and I never knew that it was supposed to. To emphasize this fact, to this day my sister tells the story that she never knew she was poor until she went to college (Knoxville College) and they told her so. Neither her teachers nor my teachers allowed students' poverty to determine what students could or could not have an opportunity to do or at least try. Those decisions were made outside of the teachers' wheel-houses.

Bob Coleman is not a teacher and lived in a different part of town than where I grew up. He experienced teachers everywhere in his upbringing. Bob's experiences with teachers offer another perspective of teacher-student relationships. Although a bit older than I—and, he says, a bit wiser—Bob speaks through the lens of being a teacher's child. Regardless of our differences in age and circumstance, we both share experiences with great teachers whom we remember and cherish.

Bob Coleman: His Story

It really is funny what a person remembers when looking back and thinking about one's childhood and education and what went on back in the day. For me, education has always been a focal point in my family. My mom and dad both graduated from Kentucky State (K-State) College. Going to school and going to college were taken for granted. In my neighborhood, everyone was college-bound and every neighbor checked progress toward getting there.

I am not an educator; however, I can certainly tell a little about my family and my childhood neighborhood that was flooded with educators teaching the importance of education. First, my mom, Dorothy Coleman, was a teacher. When DuValle Jr. High School opened, she was on its faculty. My dad, William S. Coleman Sr., was the executive secretary for the YMCA at Tenth and Chestnut streets. He had also been director of the USO and superintendent of the Civilian Conservation Corps Jobs Program at Mammoth Cave. Dad attended K-State on a football scholarship. J. Waymon Hackett, later principal of Central High School, played on the football team with my dad and was a friend of the family. My Aunt, Mable Coleman, was principal of two "Colored" schools. Hughlyn Wilson, later Assistant Superintendent of Human Resources for Jefferson County Public Schools, was a good friend of Aunt Mable's. Aunt Mable raised James Coleman, who later earned a doctorate in education and became another renowned educator. I also have known the Kean Family all of my life. Coach Kean of basketball and football fame in segregated schools across the South, was a friend of my dad's. Milburn Maupin, who later became a superintendent in Louisville Public Schools, worked for my dad at the YMCA during summers while working toward advanced degrees.

I was born in Louisville and lived at 3225 Dumesnil and went to Virginia Avenue Colored School. In my neighborhood there were educators everywhere. I could count nine school teachers close to our home and seven or eight more as I walked to school. Principal Cooper lived down the street. Ms. Preston, my fifth grade teacher, lived behind me, and the Price family that owned Mammoth Life Insurance was in our circle. When young people walked the neighborhood, they saw teachers, spoke to teachers every day, and had no choice but to say "yes sir, no sir." Teachers in the neighborhood asked students how they were doing in school and asked to see their report card. They could not hide their grades, and if they needed help in any subject, there were people right there to help.

Living in segregated neighborhoods meant growing up with everybody. The community's infrastructure was not there. Cotter

Homes and Southwick were housing projects but not like they are thought of today. Those students from the projects went to DuValle as well. Everybody contributed to the neighborhood. People were entrepreneurs because they had to be. Mrs. Minnis opened a Seventh Day Adventist school on Dixie Highway. Two fireman who lived on my block were the first to have a television. We could go in their house and watch TV. We learned how to make a wireless radio as well. Mr. Winstead, whose wife was a school teacher, opened a gas station at Thirty-fourth and Young streets to serve the Black neighborhood.

My mom's club, "Mother Dears" that later became Jack and Jill of America, taught us social graces and etiquette. Ms. Louise Reynolds taught us the value of politics and voting. Her husband, Elwood Reynolds, was a policeman. He taught us what we would not or "better not" do. We had teachers' husbands who were chauffeurs and waiters. If we were broke, we borrowed from the waiter. Gene Hunter, husband of a school teacher, was a barber. My dad helped people get jobs. Doris Furman was a substitute teacher. Mr. Furman worked for International Harvester and helped with jobs as well. Nobody got divorced. If someone was going to the park that person loaded up the car and took us all to Chickasaw Park. We respected our neighborhood and we respected our neighbors. Furthermore, school teachers had status in the community.

I was a good student and people thought I was smart—my brother and sister were smart. I could play the piano by memory. I participated in cultural things that we thought were a part of education. What no one realized was that I had a reading problem. I could memorize anything, but I never learned to spell phonetically until high school. I could do math computation, but not word problems.

I graduated from Central High School in 1959. I had gone to Madison Jr. High for two years and the newly built DuValle Jr. High for one year. I was in the first group, Post-Brown vs. Board of Education that could go to any school, and I was asked to attend Shawnee. I did not want to get involved. I remembered the stories about Emmet Till. At Madison, Ms. Wilhite stands out. She had a knack for encouraging a person to improve. We also had the Plymouth Settlement House where teachers were available to help students who needed help. The

Black community was education-minded. Teachers supported parents and parents supported teachers. They worked together to decide what children would do.

I cannot talk about education in the 1950s or education at Central High School without talking about Lyman T. Johnson. Mr. Johnson prepared students for the real world. He taught American History, Civics, and Economics. I went from a "C" student to an "A" student because of him. We had seminars, read certain kinds of books, participated in demonstrations and sit-ins, and debated Integration on the radio. Mr. Johnson taught us that during the debate, we could never call anything a lie. We had to use the word "fallacy." He also taught us the difference between being impressive and being smart. What we read made us smart.

There were other teachers and other events that stand out as well. Mr. Ramsay, whose wife had tried to get me to go to Shawnee, taught me trigonometry. Mrs. Rabb was right there beside Mr. Johnson when we were prepping for demonstrations or debates, including the Fourth Street demonstrations over serving groups of Blacks in Woolworths and Walgreens stores. She also helped organize a program where different corporations took students for exposure to careers like working on oil rigs. I also ate dinner in the dining room of the Seelbach Hotel in 1958. Also, I will never forget Ms. Cox who taught English and gave us survival skills on the side. Her message to the class: "If a boy gives you underwear for Christmas, he wants to see them on New Year's."

In spite of everyone assuming that I was going to college, I had no intention of attending. I had a taste of Walnut Street and wanted to walk up and down the street from Blues Joint to Jazz Joint. I finally decided to go because several of my friends went. I majored in history and political science—remember Lyman Johnson and remember "great memory." I loved the atmosphere although my first setback was having to take Remedial English because I lacked the writing skills. My professor said, "If you cannot spell it, I cannot read it." I could not spell it then and never could. My memory saved me. The other issue that comes to mind is if people do not pronounce things correctly, you may not spell it correctly; take for instance the words "specific" and "pacific" or "president" and "precedent."

I managed to stay in college for three years before I was drawn back into the money market. You see, at that time, I could make more money working at International Harvester without a degree than my mom made teaching with years of experience **and** a degree. And that brings us to issues and challenges of recruiting and retaining teachers today. One of the main issues is salary. When my mom died in 1972, still a teacher at DuValle, I made more money than she did and I was a non-degreed factory worker. What we ask and expect of teachers and what we pay them do not mesh. When we are competing with engineering, technology, and medical careers, we will not get the best teachers like the ones that I had, knew, or lived down the street from who had limited opportunities but taught with knowledge, pride, and conviction.

Families have changed. Neighborhoods have changed. If you live in Louisville west of Ninth Street, students no longer walk down the street expecting to greet their teachers living next door. If you are a Black student, you may graduate from high school without ever having a Black teacher, a role model who shows you that you can be a teacher yourself. We have to change our thinking about the work and the worth of teachers if we want to get great educators in our schools so that all children get a chance to learn. I had great teachers. I want children today to have great teachers.

Great African-American Teachers

Bob and I, and many others like *Journeys* demonstrate, were blessed to have great African-American teachers in our lives who educated, molded, shaped, developed, and guided us. However, today's African-American youth may not be afforded similar opportunities. The lack of African-American teachers is near crisis proportions compared to the percentages of African-American students in today's schools. Blacks, like others, have increasingly migrated from teaching as a career toward other professions which appear more prestigious, more lucrative, and less stressful. At the same time the Black, pre-school to Grade 12 population in public schools continues to rise, recruitment efforts among smart, potentially qualified African Americans who value education and may also possess the caring spirit essential for great educators are coming up short-handed as these individuals are not responding to the call. This was not so in the previous century.

Over the next several pages, readers will have the opportunity to travel *Journeys* with twentieth century African-American educators who continue to believe in the value and worth of education in general and teaching as a career, more specifically. These educators share their beginnings, upbringing, families, personal situations, educational opportunities and beliefs; and they share their dreams of yesterday and hopes for tomorrow. Readers will discover what prompted individual career choices as well as the motivation, hardships, and nuances of foresight that propelled their careers and kept them faithful to the profession. They also share wisdom from their experiences that might guide, direct, and/or influence others who are thinking about teaching as a career; those who have already made teaching a career choice and may be second-guessing themselves; and those who have never considered becoming a teacher.

Teacher Journeys include stories from home-grown Kentuckians as well as stories from others who matriculated from various parts of the country. The commonality is each educator eventually taught in the Louisville/Jefferson County Schools and continued on various career paths that allowed them to fulfill their calling and commitment to the education of youth under their charge and contribute to the education of youth overall in their community.

It is important for readers to understand that each *Journey* shared has its own context. The general educational landscape of the twentieth century was a historical masterpiece. The puzzling pieces of education of African Americans; the development of teaching as a major career choice for them; and the changing events in the education arena were daunting. Again, locale and circumstance impacted issues, challenges, and conditions of education and opportunities embodied in each narrative. We begin *Teacher Journeys* with Part I, **Memories of Inspiration.**

1

TEACHER JOURNEYS

Memories of Inspiration

Teacher Journeys: Inspiration

Inspiration (noun): Something that gives courage or confidence, boost, exhortation, motivation; Inspire (verb) To arouse the emotions of, impassion, inflame, to stir to action, trigger, prod, provoke, to be the cause of.[2]

Inspiration has several definitions and a variety of synonyms according to Webster's Dictionary and *the American Heritage College Thesaurus.* I remember the first time I was formally introduced to the word *inspire* in second grade as one of my spelling words. Ms. Wilson, my second-grade teacher, assigned several of us words from the third-grade book. Our class had gone to the library to use the dictionaries. I remember climbing upon the step-stool to use the "big" *Webster Dictionary.* I liked the big dictionary because it was big and had lots of pages. The problem was, other students liked the big dictionary also. So, in Ms. Wilson's infinite wisdom, groups of two were assigned to use the dictionary together. One person read the definition and the other wrote the definition on paper. Each pair had three words and was given five minutes to use the dictionary. My partner Bobbie, my best friend, was the writer and I was the reader. As the reader, I had to decide the two definitions to dictate. I do not remember the other words that we had to define, but I remember "inspire" because I could not make up my mind which definitions or synonym to choose and we ran out of time. Another pair was waiting. I remember Ms. Wilson saying, "Rita, what "inspired" you to work so slowly today?" I responded, "I couldn't make up my mind." About fourteen years later, when Ms. Wilson asked me a question about my inspiration, I had a more mature answer. The story that follows speaks to the beginning of my inspiration.

What's Love Got to Do with It?[3]

OVER FORTY YEARS AGO, I BEGAN ON A REMARKABLE journey. As I reflect on my years as an educator, several memories flood my mind. These I would like to share in hopes that someone will understand the message and pick up the gauntlet to continue the charge.

In the Beginning

I was in my junior year of college and planned on becoming a lawyer. As a political science major, I was steeped in politics, debate, and all of the rhetoric that went with seeking a career in a nontraditional field, for example, **not** teaching or nursing.

Because I was astute in reading a schedule and I did not mind eight o'clock classes, I found myself void of classes on Tuesdays and Thursdays. My sister, who had recently begun a career in a traditional field, high school mathematics and chemistry teacher, suggested that I try substitute teaching. Since $20.00 per day was an enticing amount for someone accustomed to working for $1.50 to $2.00 per hour, I used my sister as a "hook-up" to get the necessary paperwork completed to get started substitute teaching. I did not give up my afternoon job at

Sears because, after all, substituting was for some quick extra money, not for real income.

My first assignment was an English class at the now-closed Russell Junior High School, formerly Madison Junior High. When I got the call, I was nervous as could be expected, but I was not excited. "Just a day's work," was my attitude—nothing more or nothing less. Upon arrival at the school, I was told that the teacher had left plans in the room for me to follow. I was given a key and told which hallway to follow to find my room.

Since we were not given any orientation or training on how to be a good sub, I relied on my experience as a student to guide my actions as the sub. Only three years previous, I had been a high school student. I had encountered twelve years of great professional African-American teachers and knew how I was supposed-to look and act. It did not matter that I was stopped three times in the hallway and asked if I needed help to find my homeroom; or did someone in my family die, since I had on a Black suit; or would I like to go out on a date, since I was a new girl in school.

When I finally got the door unlocked, I was swamped by 18 ninth graders of all sizes, heights, and hues. Several young ladies wore miniskirts while others wore mini-miniskirts. Males wore "high water" pants as well as blue jeans from various Consolidated Department Store designers. Converse tennis shoes were still the rave with a rainbow of colors: red, gold, or Black.

My encounter with my homeroom that morning was memorable. It seemed that no one remembered his or her name. Several of the young men answered multiple times while others never responded. The young ladies did not respond at all. Several of the young men answered for them as well. As a result, I had not a clue as to who was present or absent. With my hackles up, I announced to the class the names of whom I was turning in on the morning report as absent. I also announced that "I did not give a fat cat if it was right or wrong" since they didn't seem to care. The outrage and indignation were echoed throughout the room since every girl on the roll was listed as absent.

After several outbursts, threats, and warnings the class decided that I needed to call the roll again to make sure that I had the right people listed. I reluctantly agreed but only by stipulating that everyone had to be quiet until I finished or I would send in my first report with no more discussion. It was agreed to readily. By the time the monitor picked up the report, I was pretty confident that it was accurate.

Day 1, Period 1 was the class that all teachers dream of having. Every child said good morning upon entering the room. They knew where to put their homework. They were orderly, mannerly and attentive. They followed directions; did not misbehave; worked independently; did not hit, bite, or spit. This Tuesday/Thursday work was going to be a breeze for the rest of the year with classes like these.

Day 1, Period 2 was "ditto" of Period 1. I needed to remember to bring my book with me on Thursday so that I could work on my policy report that was due in two weeks.

By the time Period 2 ended, I was pretty cocky. I had told my two classes about my dreams and aspirations to become a lawyer. They had told me how admirable they were. I had given a short expository on how Blacks need to aspire to be doctors and engineers; of how women could be anything that they wanted to be, including scientists and mathematicians. I recall saying that "Blacks today do not have to be "just" teachers, nurses, ministers, or mailmen. They can be on the Supreme Court if they wanted to be." The students agreed wholeheartedly. We had connected. They were college-bound, Advanced Program freshmen and the world was their oyster. They were like me.

Third period was Planning Period and first lunch. I was to meet my fourth-period class outside of the cafeteria and escort them to class. This should have been a warning to me, but being as green as grass, this potential problem did not register.

As I rounded the corner, my stomach did a nose dive. Pushing and shoving, hitting and kicking, gum-chewing and nail polishing were my morning 18 students—my homeroom. Ten minutes later, the last of the 18 found his way to his seat, towel paper in hand to wipe the bloody nose from the latest elbow thrown two corridors back.

This class was Period 4 and Period 5. Students had assignments using the newspaper; parts of speech from an English grammar book, and oral reading from a literature book. They also had individual novels that they were allowed to read independently if they finished their work early.

"O.K., let's get started. Everybody pay attention. Here's what you are going to do today."

To my surprise, the class quieted. Most got their paper and pencils out and began working. Several decided that they needed naps after lunch and put their heads down to snooze. By the end of Period 4, we were moving and grooving. After the break, I decided to start the literature lesson. I called the class to order and told them to open their literature books. All H__ l broke loose. It was as if I was raw meat in a lion's den. Students shouted at me, threw paper wads, told me "H__ l naw!" I was operating in a stupor. How dare they treat me this way!

Being who I am, it was no way that these 14, 15, and 16-year-old students were going to rule me. After all, I was 21. In a split-second decision, I called out the tallest boy in the room who had slept most of the last period and who had been the most vocal. I told him to lean over and touch his toes. I was going to spell H__l on his butt. The young man uncurled and stood about a foot and a half above me. He also outweighed me by approximately 75 pounds. This large-boned, dark-skinned young man with a menacing stare, said, "If you've got nerve enough to use that paddle, I've got nerve enough to bend over." He did and I did. That got their attention.

The literature book was old, one that I had used in junior high school. I don't remember the story, but I do remember the activity—round-robin reading, with random calling on students. The first three girls were volunteers and read well. The next boy who read volunteered. He also read well. The second male volunteer muddled through the text with help. After him, no more hands were raised. The first student that I called on tried, but needed lots of help. The next student refused to read. He put his head down on the desk and pretended to be asleep. After some prompting, one of the girls told me that "he never reads" and that several others didn't either.

From somewhere deep inside, I began to put two and two together and I was appalled. You see, I didn't know any children that were in junior high school and could not read, did I? I had grown up in a school system where students were tracked. College prep/Advanced Program students didn't have classes with the others. We did not mix and mingle. We ate lunch at "Our Tables" and they ate at their tables. We were the leaders, the movers and the shakers. They followed, sometimes excelling in sports. We had our teachers and they had theirs and everybody knew the difference. And, we did not worry about them. We were the chosen ones. Everyone had high expectations for us. We had high expectations for ourselves. Colleges had been handpicked for us. We had been groomed to lead. We were expected to compete with the best, Black, white, or other. But they could read, couldn't they?

I remember sitting on the end of the desk and my body slumping. I wanted to cry, but I couldn't, not in front of the class. Instead, I took a deep breath and said something like, "O.K., new rules. Everyone is going to read, but no laughing or making fun of one another. We are going to help one another. Close the door. What goes on in here stays in here. Agreed? I'm going to read first. Then, we will start on the back row. Volunteer or I will call on you. Now let's get started."

For the remainder of the period, we read. Some read a sentence, others a paragraph. Some found the passage that they were going to read and practiced the entire time until we got there and they could read it. The majority struggled, but not one kid laughed or made fun of another student.

When the bell rang for the period to end, no one jumped up to go, no one cheered that the period had ended; no one closed his/her literature book. The person who was reading continued and another started when he finished. At two minutes before the tardy bell, I told the class that we had to stop. There was a collective groan. To my surprise, one of the students that had napped during Period 4 said, "I wish you could be my teacher." To my utter shock I responded, "I wish I could too."

Dr. Gladys Louise Byrd

Teacher, Musician, Author, Highly Skilled Educator
and District Achievement Gap Coordinator for
Kentucky Department of Education

Dissertation: *Arts Integrated Schools:
Case Studies "I Can Hear You Now!"*
Author House - August 2013 - 44 pages SBN:
8.5x11 Paperback (978-1-4817-6635-7)

I WAS BORN IN WINSTON SALEM, N.C., in 1944 to parents who never finished high school. My mom married when she was sixteen years old and my dad only completed eighth grade. Being next to the baby in a family of five children, with a father who was a factory worker and a mother who did not work outside of the home, I did not know that I was poor until much later in my childhood. My parents were always supportive of their children, encouraging us to try new things, take chances, and use our talents. They also were strong supporters

Christine Howard Photographer

of education. I remember my parents saying to me and my siblings constantly that we had to get an education, have a career, and make our own money.

Although we were encouraged to be risk takers, we also were protected and safe within our environment. I was kept under my parents' and brothers' and sisters' wings. During my childhood in the '40s, we had to be obedient and respectful to our parents as well as older siblings and/or any adult. Sunday was a favorite time for the family. After church and dinner, we would pile into the car and go for a ride. We would top the ride off by stopping to get ice cream. Strong family ties were the building blocks for neighborhoods and communities, and as children we were accountable to and respectful of all the adults around us. They, in-turn, watched out for us and others in the neighborhood.

Being the second child from the baby, I spent a lot of time watching and listening. I was always quiet, but I paid attention to everything going on around me and learned from others' mistakes and/or successes. Our homework table in the living room where we had quiet time was also a listening time as Dad explained concepts that my older sister and I had trouble understanding. This opportunity was truly quality time with my father for us. My mother kept us busy. She said, time and time again, that an empty mind got you in trouble. I believed that, so I was always involved in school and church activities. To keep us further engaged, we took instrumental music lessons. Mom, a singer, never took lessons or taught us to sing, but she had a lovely solo voice and was asked to sing solos often. Since mom sang spontaneously, we just got up and sang too without any reservations.

My elementary school, Carver Crest, enrolled students in Grades 1-5. I was quiet and obedient; I followed directions and made good grades. Our teachers were our role models, well-dressed and well-respected. Everyone stopped and spoke to them as they walked the neighborhood or in church. They lived in better homes; their hair was always perfect, and they expected their students to learn. My fourth-grade teacher, Mrs. King, was my favorite elementary teacher. She was strict and had high expectations, but showed love for her students. Also, she took time to teach us practical things like which fork or spoon to use, how to cut with a knife, and how to sit at the table because during this time Blacks were fighting for their rights to eat in any restaurant. She took us to her home, on outings, and was not afraid to talk to parents if we were out of hand. I loved elementary school.

Paisley Junior High School, for students in Grades 6-8, was a different experience and a specific teacher spoiled it for me. She said, "You are never going to be anything," and I never forgot her saying those words. I knew that I was going to college, even when I was still in elementary school. I did not understand why this teacher, a Black teacher—in fact all of my teachers were Black—would say this to me. When asked, she said that I was too sociable. My whole attitude changed. I became compliant and quite reserved. Junior high school was just school, nothing special. When I became a teacher, I vowed that I would never make a child feel like that teacher made me feel. I felt not valued or appreciated as a student. When I went to our graduating class's fiftieth reunion, I tried to find this teacher, but I was unsuccessful.

My teachers at Paisley High School were wonderful! Our success was their success. They were positive, kind, and firm. They paid attention to individual students' needs and expected excellence. Mr. Foy stands out as a favorite teacher who was beloved by students, friendly with parents, and proficient as a teacher. He stood out among the rest of the teachers because we knew that he cared about us. The highlight of my high school year was when I became the leader of the Girls' Jazz Band. All of our teachers wanted us to go to college and took time preparing us for the new world that we would encounter as college students in an integrated society.

As students, we were not excited about integration because there was so much violence and hatred surrounding us. During high school, one or two students went to white schools for one period a day and would then come back to their regular school for the remainder of the day. Blacks could not go to white schools full-time. The students' experiences were guarded. Students were dropped off and picked up by a school official and taken to the assigned white school. I remember my classmate standing outside the principal's office with her notebook under her arm. She had no smile or no frown, just a strange facial expression, a "straight face." She didn't move or sway, simply standing at the door waiting to be summoned that her bus ride was there. When summoned, her body jerked. She would walk toward the open door, holding her breath.

My classmates would tell us what went on in their classes, how they were treated and/or isolated. Going to an integrated school or college was not appealing, but we had to be ready if we had to go. Teachers spent after-school time and Saturdays prepping us on manners: how to sit, how to order from a menu, and general etiquette—getting us ready. Teachers visited our homes, told parents how we were doing, and helped us plan for college. Our high school counselor kept us on track and helped with funding, for example, finding scholarships and grants. Amazingly, I thought that this was the model for how teachers supported their students.

When my time came to enter college, I chose North Carolina Central, a Historically Black College/University (HBCU) and chose a music major. I could sing and play the piano and saxophone. I enrolled in chorus and participated in the college concert and marching bands. Music brought me to life! When I was four or five years old, my dad told me to go sing in front of my first large group and then on the radio. I chose a career in education because of the impact my teachers had on me and I have never regretted my career choice. The same positive behaviors, attitudes, and beliefs about teaching that they demonstrated, I implemented as a part of my practices as well.

My first teaching job was in a consolidated K-12 school in LaGrange, North Carolina. As a first-year teacher, classroom management was not an issue. The challenge was older teachers who wanted the first-year teacher to stay in the box. "Oh, we do not do it that way here." In my classroom, I did what I wanted. Students danced, sang, played instruments, and did not sit in straight rows. I never screamed. I did what my teachers did for me. I let my students know that I cared, learned their names, spoke softly to them, greeted them with a smile, visited their homes, called parents, and had them engaged in the classroom.

My next two teaching assignments before coming to Kentucky were in an integrated school in Cincinnati, Ohio, and an inner-city school in

Chicago, Illinois. Again, I did not have discipline problems. Students followed directions, performed and were engaged. Since children were my main focus, I spent a great deal of time planning and collaborating with other teachers. I had high expectations, highlighting my students in the classroom as well as when they performed. When students feel that the teacher really likes them, they work with the teacher. When the teacher highlights the children, parents embrace the teacher!

After these very successful years of teaching, imagine my surprise when I applied for a teaching job with the Jefferson County Public Schools (JCPS) in 1976 and was told that I was not qualified, and that my credentials were not transferrable to Kentucky. My only recourse was to return to school for a master's degree. While completing it, I worked at St. Martha Catholic School—all white students and the only Black teacher. My first semester there, I received many complaints because students told their parents that I was too strict. I had a parent who supported his son's telling me that I should go back to Africa by removing his child from my class. I was not offended. I invited parents to come to my class and look at what I was doing. By the end of the year, I could "walk on water" because children's performances were exceptional and the school was highlighted in a positive way. Surrounding schools would attend our performances. Children performed classic shows like *Snow White, Cinderella, Wizard of Oz, Oliver, Hansel and Gretel,* and more.

In 1978, with a master's degree in hand, I finally got a job with JCPS as an elementary itinerant music teacher. Years later, I was standing in a Sears Department Store when all of a sudden I was picked up and spun around in a circle. When I landed back on my feet, that child who had been removed from my class apologized saying, "I am so sorry." I cried. It is always important to do the right thing, even when people are irrational or unreasonable.

I love teaching, children or adults, and I love school. While teaching at several elementary schools in the JCPS District from 1978 to 1999, I completed my Doctorate of Educational Leadership at Spalding University and was afforded the opportunity to move from the classroom to Highly Skilled Educator for the Kentucky Department of Education that same year. A job change was a difficult decision for me in that I would be leaving my students. In the back of my mind, I could still hear Dad encouraging me to step on the stage and sing. So I took the risk and I am glad that I did because it provided a deeper learning opportunity and helped me to become a leader. Students today send cards, letters, and sometimes visit to share their memories and fun times we had in the classroom.

It's funny how I surrounded myself with the right people who guided, supported, and mentored me sometimes without my being conscious that it was taking place. I did not know that until I was thrust into an extremely difficult situation as a Highly Skilled Educator in the Northern Kentucky area and had to deal with people who saw color before credentials and knowledge. This experience was a refining period that taught me much about people and life. I learned that in the tough times, God always sends a person (ram in the bush) to rescue and comfort you with words of wisdom and a listening ear. Since I couldn't make a difference there, I was provided a great opportunity in Louisville. By contrast, in the same position, working with JCPS schools, principals listened, strategies were implemented, scores improved, and I made a difference.

Over the years, I served in several other positions working to improve student academic achievement. I served as District Achievement Gap Coordinator, one of five in Kentucky; District Coordinator over Highly Skilled Educators in Hardin County; a member of many Scholastic Audit Leadership Teams; as well as a member of the School Cultural Audit Leadership Team after my retirement in 2010. These positions gave me numerous opportunities to observe and work with teachers, principals, and district leadership. Again and again, my theories about teaching and teachers were supported within the districts. For effective teachers to make an impact, they must have high expectations, make students feel loved and cared for, have structured classes, and provide a positive learning environment. As a result of my experiences in leadership, I shared in conferences and workshops around the Commonwealth of Kentucky.

However, my favorite teaching experience was in Chicago's West side. I was told that the students and parents were crazy and violent and would make my life miserable. As a risk taker, I was willing to at least try. My plan was simple: I set guidelines on Day 1, told them what I expected, how it would be measured, why and what we were doing, and how we were going to do it—including having fun. This experience was the most fun time that I ever had with students. Parents were thankful and appreciative. They knew I loved their children because I would tell them. Those students needed me and regardless of circumstances, I had to give them unconditional love. How could I not love a child who was coming to me for knowledge, the knowledge that I had because someone helped me obtain it?

The difference between good teachers and great teachers for me, brings to mind my fifth-grade teacher Ms. King. She had high expectations; we knew that she cared because she would stand at the door and say wonderful things to each of us as we came in. She showed us respect—never calling us out. We would cry if we disappointed her. She was data-driven; therefore students redid work until it was proficient. She could tell each student where they were socially and academically. When she spoke, parents and students listened. When she entered a room, everyone would get quiet to hear what her directions were and demonstrate respect. Above all, we knew she didn't play. We were going to complete all assignments. It made no difference whether we were rich or poor; she made it a point to know our parents and siblings. She celebrated our achievements and successes. She had the entire package and was the real deal.

In today's educational environment, the real deal is hard to find. There are so many issues and challenges faced by schools, students, parents, and teachers, but God has blessed America. Therefore, we have the tools at our deposal to turn this situation around. There is no need to lose a generation of children. We must get parents involved in the education of their children. Some parents are not parenting, while some students lack the basic skills that widen the academic gaps. Unfortunately, some students are not valued, appreciated, or loved, and some teachers have given up on children because of their negative behaviors. When achievement gaps among African- American students are increasing, not decreasing, yearly, we definitely are not doing the right things. In sports, when students are not performing, the coach takes them through the basics. In education, caring is basic.

Unfortunately, there are no tools that help schools identify caring teachers before teachers are hired. We always encourage teachers to stay in the profession, but sometimes we forget that teaching is a calling. You must love the children you serve. Teaching should be considered a ministry; therefore, teachers should love unconditionally and do the right things by giving students what they need to be successful. Maybe school districts need to have a three-month probationary period before signing a contract to make sure that teachers have the loving and caring pieces of the equation. I like the idea for rehiring teachers at the end of the year proposed by the late Phil Schlechty who worked with JCPS for several years on professional development for teachers. Dr. Schlechty always told us, "Let the students hire the teachers. They can tell who is getting the job done."

It is getting more difficult to attract smart African-American students as well as smart white students to the profession. I had excellent role models who wanted to teach and encouraged me to become a teacher. A few questions come to mind regarding these concerns which are as follows: Are we encouraging smart students to become teachers? Are we sharing the beauty of teaching? Do we show students that we hold the profession in high esteem by looking and acting like professionals in word and in deed? As educators, do we truly believe that all children can learn?

Teaching is a wonderful and rewarding profession that requires giving all your heart and mind or willingly doing whatever it takes to help children achieve. As greatly as teachers are needed, if a person doesn't love children, that person should not come into our profession and mess it up. If teaching is a work of love, continue on the road to making a difference and be encouraged. Dispel the myths that surround teaching by being an ideal example!

Dr. Byrd also has been instrumental in implementing an after-school reading program—a partnership between JCPS, the Metro Leadership Foundation, and several churches—which provides mentors and academic support for more than 125 low-performing students in selected JCPS elementary schools. She credits her husband as being her main supporter. Dr. Byrd has one son.

Verna Cahoon

Teacher, Resource Teacher, and Principal

LIFE HAS MANY PURPOSES. LIFE HAS varied surprises, but Faith, Hope, Empathy, and Compassion make life purposeful and rewarding. My immediate family consisted of my father, mother, and brother. They are all deceased. I have many reflections of life in my hometown, Brunswick, Georgia, a small coastal seaport town. Our African-American community had its own theater, parks, etc., and we thought our beach area was the best! We had pride in our community and never felt deprived of anything, regardless of the segregation era

Cahoon Family Photo Collection

that we lived in. When I was five years old, two of my best friends and I attended Mrs. Harrington's in-home kindergarten. We sat on wooden stadium benches. Lunches, prepared by our families, were in brown paper bags. A variety of learning experiences took place in that room.

The elementary, the junior high and the high school were all on the same spacious campus, but in different buildings. Eventually, a new high school was built at another location. The teachers attended the same churches and activities and lived in our communities along with the rest of us. Ms. Atwater, my first-grade teacher, always had some special program in which students were encouraged to participate. Developing skills to speak publically was important and encouraged throughout our elementary school years. We practiced at church and school for holiday programs. We did daily readings aloud from books (*Dick and Jane* series), recited poetry and time tables, individually and in groups. My elementary teachers made students want to succeed. Students were recognized for what they did well and were encouraged and praised. Also, students were immediately corrected when they were out of order. More importantly, students expected to be corrected by their teachers and any other adults. No back lash from students or their parents ever occurred. I loved being with my friends and enjoyed school.

What I remember most about junior high school, aside from the daily routine, is an incident that involved a classmate who told a lie on me. Even though I was proved innocent, my mother used this instance as a life learning tool. She felt that I needed time to reflect on how to choose "good friends." During this time of reflection I was not allowed to listen to favorite radio programs or to eat dinner with the family for one week. The lesson that I learned is that you may have lots of acquaintances, but you have only a few friends whom you should choose carefully.

My high school years were all about preparing for the future. The course work and the teachers focused on one objective, making sure that students were ready for college or that they had skills to be employable in the workforce. My favorite high school teacher was Ms. Ruth Lovelace Williams, a graduate of Spelman College. When we were seniors, she walked us to the courthouse to register to vote. A well-educated and classy woman who continued her studies during her summer breaks, Ms. Williams was the favorite of many students.

I thank all of the teachers throughout my school years for being role models and encouraging students to become achievers. I was an honor student, secretary of the Senior Class, and a member of the high school choir. I participated in various clubs at school, was chosen as the "Friendliest Girl," and was selected to be one of four speakers at my high school graduation. My speech to my 113 class members included these words from the poem, *Myself,* written by Edgar Albert Guest:

> *I never can hide myself from me,*
> *I see what others may never see.*
> *I know what others may never know,*
> *I never can fool myself and so*
> *Whatever happens I want to be*
> *Self-respecting and conscious free.*[4]

I have never forgotten these words. They are the ethics of sharing, giving and helping, but doing it in a way that you know is right. My eight high school girlfriends from kindergarten through high school recall those words as well. It is something that we have tried to live by. Our group has met for 20 years straight, except for the year of the September 11 New York bombing. We have never closed the chapter from being in that small coastal Georgia town and the knowledge, skills, and hope that our teachers instilled in us. We always remember our roots.

When I began thinking about a career, I planned a career in nursing. Two of my mother's sisters were nurses and my mother became a private duty nurse. They were my inspiration for choosing a career. The Grady School of Nursing was my goal. As part of the admission process, applicants had to complete a test at the school, that is, a "Profile" to determine compatibility. To my surprise and disappointment, my Profile indicated that teaching, not nursing was my main career composite. Over the years, I had taught Bible School, Sunday School, and Vacation Bible School—working with children, but I never considered teaching. When I had to decide upon another college and another career, I decided on Tuskegee Institute with a major in English since I loved to read.

Tuskegee is a Historically Black College (HBCU) that provides a family culture. Students were made to feel that it was an honor and a privilege to be on campus. You felt exceptional. You worked hard and you played hard. I enjoyed college life and I remained on campus for three years until I moved to Louisville, Kentucky with my new husband who worked for the Atlanta Life Insurance Company. I enrolled at the University of Louisville where I encountered only a few Black students since it was a private institution at that time. I changed my major to Elementary Education and began working on teacher certification. We lived in an apartment owned by Mrs. Lena Warders, principal of John F. Kennedy Elementary School. I also completed my student teaching at her school.

My initial teaching experience in the Louisville Public Schools was short. In 1968, I began my first year of teaching in a third-grade classroom at Henry Clay Elementary. We moved to the county and I began working for the Jefferson County School District, becoming a fifth-grade teacher at Newburg Elementary School. Mr. Walter Logan, an African-American male, was principal. The county was seeking African-American teachers and several young African-American teachers were at Newburg with me. We were all excited about teaching but were bombarded with many changes. After two years of working the regular curricular program, I was recommended for a new teaching position at Slaughter Elementary School in a new instructional program, the Stoddard Program, where social studies and science instruction were taught via television. Projects and follow-up activities were part of the learning process.

The next several years of my career included teaching all third-and fourth-grade students at the school and creating projects to support television instruction. When this instructional program ended, I taught fifth-grade students in a departmentalized teaching setting. Through the years, as the Jefferson County and the Louisville school systems merged, I taught in various summer programs; conducted and participated in workshops to develop strategies to help with student academic achievement; worked in JCPS Summer Camps for students; served on elementary social studies and reading textbook committees; completed a Master's Degree with Reading Certification at Eastern Kentucky University; completed Principal Certification at Western Kentucky University; and served as a Science Resource Teacher in the Learning Choice Program. Engelhard Elementary and Shelby Elementary emphasized special math and science curriculum to help students excel in those areas. Other elementary schools had different areas of concentration, for example, Montessori or technology education. Tom Johnson was the program director. I worked with excellent teachers, was supported by strong administrators, and learned from some of the best educators in the school system. Naturally, a few disappointments occurred along the way, but persistence was the key to survival and success.

As my career progressed, I was selected for the Lyman T. Johnson Fellows Program, a district initiative under the Jefferson County Public Schools Human Resources Department, to identify and train potential administrators for future principal positions. The program taught the basics of becoming a strong and dynamic administrator with vision. Participants had to be dedicated, knowledgeable, forthright, and serious about wanting to make a difference. Johnson Fellows also had to be supportive of one another becoming administrators, not stepping on someone else to move ahead. The program also emphasized this: "You cannot achieve alone. You need helpmates in your life's journey."

Selection by the Site-Based Decision Making Council to become principal of Wellington Elementary School, their first African-American administrator, was a rewarding experience. With the majority of the school's student population and staff being white and the community also predominately white, negativity was surprisingly minimal. A white male counselor was also a part of my administrative team. I attribute my success to intentional, deliberate bonding with the staff and creating a school culture that was open, inclusive, and sharing as a team. "We" were together, good or bad, even if we disagreed on the final decision. A fondness and connection always prevailed. The faculty and staff tried hard to let our students and families know that we supported them and strived to provide the best educational experience possible. Our motto, "We are a Wellington Family," dictated putting out fires with dignity, and helped us retain faculty because my teachers "wanted" to be there. We came together to find the best way in and the best way out with parents providing their support as well. We agreed to disagree and to come to solutions that we could all live with. When Wellington was awarded dollars for students' achievement, the faculty and staff, including classified employees, shared the monetary award, everyone going home with something. We were family.

I made a decision to retire as principal in 2001. However, JCPS needed experienced principals to support and mentor new principals. The universities also needed experienced principals to observe and supervise potential teachers in traditional and alternative certification programs. I worked with the JCPS ACES Program; the Kentucky Teacher Internship Program for first-year teachers with the University of Louisville; and Spalding University's Alternative Teacher Certification Program.

During my time in those classrooms, I watched school goals changing and evolving as testing and test results moved to the forefront. I also watched teachers' creativity disappearing because of the focus on content preparation for testing. Being penalized for performance on tests impacts the entire school and does not adequately recognize or credit other school achievements like decreased student suspensions; increases in student attendance; higher teacher retention; and increases in parent satisfaction, involvement, or engagement. It was incumbent for mentors to help teachers and administrators deal with the new landscape and continue to put children first. I always practiced and encouraged others to be compassionate. I also believe that second chances are due anyone to give them a chance to improve, whether they be children or adults.

When I think about great teachers, I see my mother as the greatest teacher of all. Mom did not preach; she led by example. When she was completing her correspondence course, she worked all day and studied late at night, never complaining. She was a hard worker and tried to provide us with all of the necessities. Mom was proud and generous, sharing when others needed help. She and Dad wanted us to do better than they had done, and Mom was the encourager, reminding us what should be done because "actions speak volumes." She always stood up for what she believed in and held her ground. She was strong in her faith like her mother, my grandmother, who prayed for her children and grandchildren and "all children to come." I know that I have my sense of self because of my mom. Also, my other "first great teacher" was Dad. He was the example of a strong work ethic as well as ethical behavior. For me, my family has been the hallmark of my being and my teachers helped support and develop my knowledge, skills, and character.

When I think of the teaching profession, going from good to great, among the generalities, I see good teachers having the following attributes: being prepared for lessons; able to deliver instruction for all children to understand; having compassion for kids; and striving to provide every student with the tools needed to be successful. Great teachers are very compassionate. They embrace children regardless of background or ethnicity; they strive to communicate with all of their students; and they have another sense that allows them to identify and communicate with those one or two students who need additional help and love.

Excellent teachers should be committed to helping all children reach their potential as productive citizens in our society. Opportunities and offerings must be available to African-American and other minority students to reach their potential as academic achievers. Without knowledge and skills, opportunities cease. The burden of developing and imparting the knowledge and skills has been placed squarely upon teachers, regardless of how unfair and lopsided it seems. If anyone is thinking about becoming a teacher, he or she must understand that this profession makes the biggest imprint of any occupation in society. Excellent teachers want their children to be successful and are seen as the core of life's aspirations for their students. For those thinking about becoming teachers, be sure that this profession is what you really want to be part of and that you have the love, understanding, compassion, and commitment to the children that you may end up teaching.

Finally, we must lay the groundwork for smart African-American students to consider teaching as a career choice. We should begin asking them what kind of ambassadors for life that they would like to be and talk about being that ambassador—sharing their academic expertise; helping children succeed; experiencing the joy of seeing the eyes of students light up when they finally understand a concept that they have tried to learn; helping a young person realize that effort, studying, and achievement are three important ingredients for their life's journey. They can be ambassadors for change, helping other children reach the pinnacle of joy, happiness, and achievement in their lives by becoming excellent teachers. I am blessed that I have had the opportunity to continue being an ambassador.

On this life's journey I pray children, family, and friends will find joy and happiness in all their endeavors. I feel that I have been blessed and I am ever thankful that my home foundation provided positive roots to declare that God is the center of my being.

Verna Cahoon retired from JCPS in 2001 after 34 years of service. She has three children, two daughters and one son, five grandchildren— an aspiring psychologist at Northwestern University; an aspiring special education teacher at U of K; an aspiring lawyer at Howard University, an undecided major at U of L; and a 16-year-old grandson. Verna is a member of Eta Omega Chapter of Alpha Kappa Alpha Sorority, Incorporated. She is a life member and past president of the chapter. She is also past president of The Louisville Chapter of Jack and Jill, Incorporated and a member of the Louisville Urban League Guild where she is co-chairman of the Scholarship Committee. Verna serves as a licensed Lay Reader, Chalice Bearer, and Sunday School teacher at the Episcopal Church of Our Merciful Savoir where she is a member. Having the City of Louisville proclaim Verna Cahoon Day—December 2, 2002, in honor of her service and retirement as principal is among Verna's most cherished recognitions. She is also a Kentucky Colonel (2003) and recipient of the National Council of Negro Women 32nd Anniversary Bethune Recognition Program Award for Loyal and Faithful Service (2006). In addition to travelling, community engagement, and her continued service to her sorority and various social clubs, Verna is also active with the Louisville League of Women Voters.

Ernesteen
Chislom Greer

Elementary Classroom Teacher

I KNEW VERY EARLY THAT I DID NOT want to clean toilets and wash coal dust off of walls for the rest of my life. Born in a tiny little Eastern Kentucky town, Liggett, in Harlan County where Tennessee, West Virginia, and Kentucky come together in the Appalachia tri-state area, my dad was a coal miner and Mom stayed at home to take care of my brother, sisters, and me, the second oldest girl. Mom died following child birth when I was six years old. Of course, no one wanted to take another bundle of children, so different family members volunteered to

E. Greer Family Photo Collection

take "onesies." My father would not hear of it and kept us together with a different arrangement. One aunt took the new baby. She lived three doors down the street. Every night we slept at home, dressed in the morning before going to school, went to her house to eat, went to school and then came back to her house for dinner. That evening, we went back home and went to bed.

We lived in the Upper Camp. Down the hill was the main store and areas where whites lived. In the early years, we walked to the one-room elementary school that had an outhouse. In later years, we rode a bus. All of the students through Grade 8 were together with the same teacher, Clara Woolfork. We had a chalk board and inherited used books from the white school. The older students helped the younger children. They read to us and helped us learn to read and to count. Ms. Delaney was our school bus driver.

In addition to regular school, we had "Little Camps" in the same one-room schoolhouse, taught by missionaries. We read Bible stories and learned Bible verses. If you learned 200 Bible verses, you got to attend Camp Nathanial, a Christian camp like today's Vacation Bible School. Our missionary in charge was Nancy Johnson whom we called Aunt Nancy. She had a big Bible with pictures and small booklets about different stories; she used a flannel board with cut-outs as a teaching tool. That same technique, flannel board with cutouts, was one of the most effective teaching strategies that I continued to use over the years.

Julius Rosenwald High School closed in 1963 and my senior class was the last segregated class to graduate. Located in the city of Harlan, Kentucky, we rode the bus to school. Again, we had used books from the white school with pages torn out, marks and writing over important information, but we managed. We didn't know anything better. My senior class had fewer than 40 students. Some of the elementary students did not go to high school. Some went to the military and others took jobs. The first time that I had physical education was in high school. Dad was reluctant to spend extra money for us to "go play." He was accustomed to what we did in elementary school where we had recess, not a formal physical education class.

High school was a window into a new world. I loved geometry with Mr. Clements and typing with Ms. Rogers. Ms. Curry taught home economics and sewing. We had to follow our patterns, cut, sew, and model three pieces for the Spring Style Show, a cotton piece, a silk-like piece, and a wool piece. The teachers taught more than academics— comb your hair, put on deodorant, pull up your slip. They told us to watch who we courted and to pay attention to how our children might look.

Teachers talked to us about making something of ourselves. We didn't always know what "something" meant. Dad was strict, and we could only attend day time school and social events. We had no car and used our neighbor's phone in emergencies. We still took baths in #3 tin tubs. I "drowned" myself in reading and had a glimpse of "something different" through books.

When I was a junior, I took a summer job in Wildwood, New Jersey, a place where my cousin and sister worked summers as well. I was a "chamber maid," a glorified housekeeper who cleaned toilets for the rich and spoiled. I wasn't washing down soot-covered walls, but a toilet is a toilet. However, I did experience something different—carpet, shiny hardwood floors, colorful walls, plush furnishing, tables set with china and silverware—things that I had read about and seen pictures of in books and magazines.

When I told Dad that I wanted to go to college, I don't know if I expected him to help me. My sister began college at Kentucky State, but did not graduate. She left home, moved east with another aunt, and got a job. Nothing or nobody came to mind as a "helper." I was not a cheerleader. I had no money. My parents were not professionals. I was not an athlete. I filled out my own paperwork. I saved my money from working in the summer. I did not get any scholarships to attend college. My saving grace was Aunt Nancy, the missionary. We had moved to Harlan, Kentucky, and another student and I carpooled with her, driving back and forth each day, sometimes even taking classes together during the two years that I attended the University of Kentucky Extension in Cumberland, Kentucky.

I moved from Harlan to Lexington, Kentucky, to attend the University of Kentucky and complete my bachelor's degree. A number of people moved to Lexington from Harlan. Several of the local homeowners rented rooms to students for $10 per week. I never lived on campus but rented an attic room with another student. I was in walking distance of the buildings where my classes were located. I still did not own a car and originally got to U of K's campus on the Greyhound bus. I had a National Defense Student Loan, did Work-Study at the Education Library, and chose elementary education rather than social work, business, or nursing as a major. I remembered where I came from and wanted to make a difference.

Over the two years that I was an undergraduate at U of K, I had no real social life and no campus life. I never had a checking or savings account until my landlord's husband took me to the bank to open an account. I always kept my money with me, even when I worked in New Jersey. I pledged Alpha Kappa Alpha Sorority, Inc. in 1966. My sister sent me the $40 initiation fee, and ladies in the community allowed us to meet in their homes to conduct sorority business. I worked with a professor in the College of Education who lectured at Kentucky State and rode to class with her weekly, serving as her teacher assistant and earning a few dollars.

I was on track to complete student teaching and graduate in 1967 when I received another blessing. A friend of mine received a fellowship to complete her master's degree but decided to travel to Europe. She offered me the fellowship to complete my master's at no cost. I accepted the fellowship, spending another year at U of K, graduating and beginning my first teaching assignment at Brandeis Elementary in Grade 6 in Louisville, Kentucky, with a Lifetime Teaching Certificate effective August 1968.

My first assignment as a new teacher for the second half of the1968-69 school year was a learning experience. More experienced teachers who were master teachers, like Mattie Harris, helped new teachers, my friend Sharon Brown and myself, with lesson plans and would come to our room to check on us. We had a music teacher who would come to our room, model a lesson, and leave lessons for us to teach as follow-up as well. Gloria Smiley and Rosemary Bell, master teachers, were super helpful to all of us. Student discipline was not a major issue. Students were generally orderly and respectful. However, one of my lasting memories about that year was the shock at seeing students throwing eggs at teachers' cars on the last day of school.

When I transferred to Carmichael in 1971, I was part of the team who worked with Teacher Corps participants, non-education majors aspiring to become teachers, as part of Focus/Impact. Because I already had a master's degree, I was a mentor teacher. I was only at Carmichael for one year before going on maternity leave. When I returned from leave, I was assigned to Bloom Elementary where I spent the next ten years of my teaching career.

Bloom's student population was mostly white and there were only a few Black teachers on staff. Parents were not always comfortable with Black teachers and we were aware of their feelings. Bloom had elementary teaming, and I remember arriving early and staying late to plan for my Grade 4/5 split, to make sure that I had everything ready for my class and my ability to teach well could not be questioned. One year there was a straight fifth grade opening that I wanted. There was a Black teacher in fourth grade. Parents did not want their child to have two Black teachers in a row because they thought, "It may set their children back." However, I did get the fifth-grade assignment.

I was more aware of prejudice at Greathouse Elementary than at Bloom although seventeen years of service at Greathouse supported my reputation as an excellent teacher. Over the years, I saw my students out in the community and they recognized me and spoke. I had a student who called me each year. I have an African-American student who attended Greathouse, who now attends my church and calls me "Mama." I have another African-American student who worked with Congressman John Yarmuth in Washington, D.C. However, I cannot forget the parent who saw me in the shopping Mall and crossed over to keep from speaking. She had been in my room smiling and trying to incur favor for her child a few days before.

After my retirement in 1999, I worked with Dr. Bernard Minnis and Dr. Cheryl Walker creating bulletin boards at VanHoose Education Center and researching, writing, and editing news articles for a department newsletter. My talent is with visuals, and I have used them in every aspect of my teaching, including working with children at church.

It has been awhile since I have been in public schools because my four grandchildren go to private schools in Lexington. However, I do remember the transition that schools were going through as I was winding down my employment. Schools at one time were a "Safe Place." Students were not overtly harassing and bullying other students and drugs were not the front-burner issue. Today's schools struggle to be safe places. An example is when I worked with Dr. Walker in Compliance and Investigations. A principal thought children were smoking "pot" in the building. It was a teacher. We also had an instance where a teacher was drunk at school. These are the people who are to create the culture of a "Safe Place." In addition, I encountered situations where students told teachers, "You cannot touch me. I know my rights." So, teachers who are trying to do their jobs and maintain discipline in the classroom are hindered by students' sense of what teachers can and cannot do.

I am puzzled as to how we can get parents to help us bridge the academic gap between students. We have a tutoring program at church and we continually strive to keep our parents knowledgeable of what they can do to help their children. Bussing kids away from their community does not help to get parents involved with their children's education, but neighborhood schools may not be as well-equipped as others, based on the school's location. I am concerned about the high academic expectations for some students at some schools and the low expectations for other students at other schools. I know that many of our babies start out behind the curve and they struggle to catch up. Their parents cannot pay for the private schools with expectations of "you get what you pay for." I see the book reports, projects, current events, vocabulary list, journals, and essays that my grandchildren work on throughout the summer and wonder how we can get student, parent, and teacher buy-in so that all students have a level of engagement throughout the year, including summer vacation. The unanswered question is, "What must we do to create that inner drive within each child, regardless of where they come from?"

I came out of a coal camp. My aunt led me to the Lord. Books in my school library gave me a vision of the world beyond my surroundings. My dad helped me understand the value of working and being independent. Mr. Walker, my history teacher; Ms. Watts, my science teacher; Ms. Buckner, my French teacher; and Mr. Woods, my high school principal helped me dream a dream that did not include making up beds and scrubbing toilets. When I attend my high school reunions, I am especially grateful for the past that gave me the drive to create a different future, and I thank God for His blessings, His grace, and His mercy throughout the years.

Ernesteen, the only college graduate among her siblings, has been married to Joseph Greer for over fifty years. They have two daughters,

Jevonda, who works for the Kentucky Department of Education, and Joy, a doctor, whose "first pay check was more than my (Ernesteen's) monthly retirement check." Ernesteen has continued working on various projects with her church, Zion Baptist Church, and has spent time working with her grandchildren to assure their "kindergarten readiness." She is an active member of Alpha Kappa Alpha Sorority, Inc., and has worked with Black Achievers and other community projects. She and Joe enjoy travelling across the United States and having fun as they age gracefully.

Shirley Fuqua-Jackson

Elementary Teacher, Guidance Counselor, Principal, and University Supervisor

SCHOOL WAS MY SAVING GRACE. IT got me through some very difficult years during my childhood. I was born in Louisville, Kentucky, grew up in a poor family, and dreamed of a better life than my parents who were from Alabama and had only an elementary education. Mom was an only child. Her parents were sharecroppers in the Greenbriar/Athens area. Dad was one of thirteen siblings and was from the Rogersville/Huntsville area. His family members were sharecroppers, also. He and Mom met and married in Alabama, then moved to Louisville when my Mom's parents decided to relocate there.

Rhonda C. Dunn Photographer

In Louisville, we lived at 2612 Reed Alley in a three-room shotgun house with an old coal stove and initially, an outside toilet. Eventually, we had an indoor bathroom addition built onto the house. We once had a boarder who lived with us for a short period of time, so my sister and I shared the same pull-out sofa bed in the living room, and my brother slept on a cot. Dad, who was a World War II veteran, worked at the

Redstone Arsenal in Alabama for a time then did seasonal construction work in Louisville when we moved. Mom worked at the Seelbach Hotel as a maid. Later she worked at the original Cunningham's Restaurant in Old Louisville where my grandmother was a cook. Mom took the job of dishwasher.

In 1958, I began school at F.T. Salisbury Elementary School. The student body was integrated, but I had all white teachers first through third grade, Mrs. McNearny in both first and second grades and Mrs. Skaggs in third grade. When the new Dann C. Byck Elementary School was built, I was transferred there in Grades 4 through 6. Beaulah Sykes in fourth grade was my first African-American teacher. Mrs. Brown taught fifth grade and Harry Ropke taught me in sixth grade. Both were white. I remember painting a large colorful mural of a coffee bean when we studied a unit about products of countries in South America in fourth grade. It was hung on the hall bulletin board. I was so proud of it! In Mrs. Brown's fifth-grade class, learning was fun. We often had spelling bees and games to help us learn our state capitals and math facts. We received neat prizes for doing well. In sixth grade, Mr. Ropke gave me the job of reading the Bible scripture in front of the class each morning before we said the Pledge of Allegiance to the Flag. I felt so special. He had a funny sense of humor and used to do silly tricks like making his elbow swing as if it were on a hinge or making his thumb disappear. He used to make us laugh.

In seventh grade, I met my best friend, Rosa Gail Walker Sanders, at Harvey C. Russell Junior High School where I attended through ninth grade. Gail's father was a math teacher at Russell. He taught me algebra and geometry. Gail and I were bosom buddies who looked like "Mutt and Jeff" side by side. She was barely 5 ft. and I was 5 ft. 10 in. tall. I was a good student and took advance classes with other students whose parents were professionals and were considered middle class Blacks.

My Dad became an alcoholic during that time. It was hard on our family dynamics and it was embarrassing to me. We never owned a car and had to walk, ride the city bus, or take a taxi everywhere. Whenever I had to participate in after-school activities like Dance Team practice, I'd have to walk ten blocks home afterwards. Gail's Mom would also give me a ride home after some school events when I was in junior high and high school.

My favorite teacher at Russell was my seventh-grade English teacher, Mrs. Macklin. She was young, tall, and thin like me. I really admired her. Mrs. Barbara Stringer was my eighth-grade English teacher and drama teacher, as well. She spoke so eloquently. I remember her using the phrase "various and sundry things" quite frequently. I learned to sing my favorite song, the "Negro National Anthem," in Mr. King's music class.

I was in an after-school Reading Club at the Main Library at Fourth and York streets. Mrs. Barbara Miller, the librarian, made books come alive for me. I remember reading the book, *A Wrinkle in Time*, and thoroughly discussing it with the group. I loved checking out books and taking them home to read. Mrs. Jones, our librarian at Russell, made it possible for me to purchase my own set of blue-covered *World Book Encyclopedias* to use at home.

While at Russell, a representative from Lincoln Institute, an all-Black boarding school in Shelbyville, Kentucky, visited Russell to recruit students. I was told that I was eligible to attend. I did not go. Mom did not allow me to attend, since I was needed at home to look after my younger sister and brother in the evenings when she was at work.

I was a member of the Red Cross Club at Russell and continued during high school at Central. I volunteered to wrap blood bottles and worked as a Candy Striper at the hospital. I spent two summers attending Red Cross Camp at Camp Crescendo in Lebanon Junction, Kentucky. I took swimming lessons each summer, but just could not float, kick, breathe, and stroke all at the same time! As a teen, I never learned how to swim or skate either.

At Central High School, I participated in the Future Teachers of America Club, the Red Cross Club, and the Co-Ed Club; worked as a student-aide to the Spanish teacher; was initiated into the National Honor Society; and was president of my senior homeroom class. My favorite teacher at Central was my math teacher, Mrs. Rosa Crumes. Again, she was tall and thin like me. She dressed in tailor-made suits and heels. She always looked divine. I wanted to be just like her. As a result, I took sewing classes at Central in order to learn how to make my own clothes. Surprisingly, I got really good at sewing!

When I told my mom that I wanted to go to college, she told me she could not afford for me to go. My friends were going, and I truly did not know what I'd do if I could not continue my education because school was my life and my way out of poverty. I assured her it was possible through applying for financial assistance. I was accepted into Western Kentucky University (WKU) in Bowling Green, Kentucky, in the fall of 1970. I had only received a $300 Dare to Care Scholarship from Central's PTA and I was also granted a work study program at WKU.

I was so excited to be able to go to college! I was the first person in my family to graduate from college! I remember that a friend of my mom's drove me and all my belongings to WKU in an old mobile home. I was blown away by the beauty of the campus! I worked in the concession stands during the basketball and football games. Later, I became a resident assistant in my dorm, which helped pay for room and board; I did not have to repay any money back after graduating.

Selecting elementary education as a major was easy. I used to play school as a kid with my sister and brother. I was the teacher and they were my students. This gave me a good deal of practice. I remember my junior high school counselor, Mrs. Geneva Hawkins, who had students to begin thinking about career choices early. I chose teacher, secretary or nurse. It seems those were the typical careers for women then. Narrowing my choice to teaching was not a difficult task.

In college, one of the biggest challenges for me was the enormous amount of reading assigned in every class every day. I was not prepared for it. We never had that much reading assigned in my high school classes. One thing that I did take advantage of in college was taking electives for fun—Swahili, piano lessons (which required too much practice), tennis, and dance. These classes were of interest to me and provided me different experiences.

I also joined a sorority at WKU. I was initiated into Alpha Kappa Alpha Sorority, Inc., number 15 of the 15 pledges. We pledged from September 1971 to February 1972 and we were called "The Fine'N Foxy Fifteen." We were expected to dress alike while pledging and we needed to have coats during the winter. I used Mom's old portable Singer sewing machine, which she let me take to college, to help make pink and green crushed-velvet maxi coats for me and my line sisters. I also made my own formal for the "Pledges on Parade" program in which we participated. Another memorable experience that I have of my college life was participating in a Sit-in at the Administration Building with 300 Black students, including student athletes. We were protesting because we wanted a Black cheerleader. We were successful. We got one!

I did my student teaching my senior year in Bowling Green, Kentucky in a third-grade class in a low-income school, Parker Bennett Elementary. My father had died when I was a sophomore. After his death, I was able to receive money from his Social Security pension. I bought a used car for $700 from money that I had saved. It was a blue Chevrolet Chevelle. I used the car to help me get to my assigned school while student teaching. The car really burned a great deal of oil, so I learned how to change the oil and always kept a case of oil in the car. It was important that I finish student teaching and graduate on time.

My Supervising Teacher was Ms. Hall. She was a white female who had an integrated class of students from low-income families. I could easily relate to the students and Ms. Hall was extremely helpful to me. She modeled what good teaching and classroom management looked like. I kept a binder of notes and lesson plans I felt would prepare me to manage my own classroom. I maintained good grades while doing student teaching and was on the Dean's List. After I graduated, I was hired for my first teaching job in 1974 in Louisville at J. B. Atkinson Elementary School in the Portland area. The principal was Harry Ropke, my former sixth-grade teacher at Dann. C. Byck Elementary School. He was happy to have me on his staff.

I taught second grade with a team of teachers who were all white and offered little to no help to me as a beginning teacher. However, one of them did finally reach out to me and became a mentor to me that first year. I will always be indebted to her. Teachers at that time were expected to teach all subjects, including art, music, and physical education. We did not have itinerant teachers who specialized in these areas to teach our students.

Atkinson was a school participating in Project PAD, a Sullivan Programmed Reading Pilot that included Portland, Atkinson, and

Dolfinger Elementary schools all located in the Portland area of town. Teachers in this pilot were expected to teach students who rotated from teacher led reading groups, centers, and seatwork after the spinning of a wheel to indicate when students were supposed to move to each. Much preparation was required. Teachers taught from sixteen program-leveled reading books. We had to teach to the middle ability level in group-reading time. However, students could read at their level and complete as many books as they were capable of. I did not have math books for the students and had to develop my own lessons. A supervisor/coach from the Project PAD staff came regularly to observe me teach. He would provide both positive and negative feedback, with suggestions for improvement. I would arrive at school early to make sure that everything was in order each morning before the students arrived.

I remember Katie and Troy who were two of my highest achieving students. They were good readers and were eager to learn. Also, they were able to help other students in class. I guess I was doing something right as a new teacher because I was interviewed by Monica Kaufman, a prominent black local news reporter and was featured on WHAS TV, highlighting my first day of teaching. That year, I was also featured in a *Louisville Defender* "Best Dressed" photo shoot. A letter was mailed to me at my school from a prison inmate who saw my picture in the paper and wanted to hook up with me. Of course, I ignored the letter!

The next year, in 1975, when the city and county school systems merged, I was transferred to Slaughter Elementary School in the county to teach third grade. Slaughter was exempt from busing because there were enough black students who resided in the school's attendance area. During my eight years at Slaughter, I met outstanding teachers, mentors, role models, and administrators. Verna Cahoon and Jean Clemons were the first teachers to welcome me and they soon became friends.

Fonrose Wortham was my first principal at Slaughter, followed by Virginia Cheaney and Marjorie Staten. Alice Cooper, a third-grade teacher colleague, was in an adjoining classroom. We could open the wall to do team teaching. She was a wonderful mentor. She invited me to her home and even brought me souvenirs from a trip she took to Scandinavia. After she retired, Linda Cunningham moved into her classroom. Linda and I had a great relationship, team-teaching social studies and science lessons. When studying a lesson on New Orleans, we cooked jambalaya, ambrosia, and pralines for a culminating tasting party for the students. We often did this at the end of units of study. This was fun for our students and something different to keep them interested and engaged. I taught third grade for eight years at Slaughter.

Sometime during my tenure at Slaughter, I became restless and considered leaving the teaching profession. I thought I wanted to do something different, like pursuing a new career as an airline stewardess or something more exciting. I even went to the University of Louisville's Career Center to explore other careers, thinking about free travel and seeing the world as a stewardess. But, in any case, I didn't go there. Mary Keith Todd, the guidance counselor at Slaughter at that time, talked me out of it, reminding me that I had a Counselor Certification for the elementary and middle school levels. She encouraged me to think about applying for an elementary counselor position. I decided to do it. Linda Cunningham, my team-teaching partner, decided to apply as well. We both got hired as counselors! She got a position at Cochrane Elementary School in the city and I was hired at Bates Elementary School in the county.

Bates was an excellent fit for me. The staff was just like family. I knew the parents, students, and the neighborhood. The teachers worked together and sometimes took trips together. I had my own classroom, and students came to my room for classroom guidance, group counseling, and individual counseling. The counseling program was excellent. Bates hosted a Young Author's Tea that Superintendent Donald Ingwerson visited every year. When he came, my principal, Rita Johnson, used to tell him that I was going to be a principal. She was really a great encourager! I implemented a mentoring program called "Project Amigo," pairing faculty with students who needed an adult friend to show them that they cared about them and to provide encouragement and support. I also implemented a Study Skills Unit to help students get organized and get in the habit of studying. I shared information about it at principals' meetings and at counselor conferences. I received the Outstanding Guidance Program Award from the Kentucky Department of Education.

Rita Johnson encouraged me to apply for a principal position and I finally did. I received the call at the AKA Boulé that I was attending in Los Angeles, California, notifying me that I had been selected to be the principal at Whitney Young Elementary School! It was located in the West End of Louisville. On my very first day of work at Whitney Young, I got my hubcaps stolen off my car. What a welcome to the neighborhood!

I spent two tough years at Young, fighting the resistance of Advanced Program (AP) teachers who thought I was micro-managing them because I checked their lesson plans and another group of teachers who were resistant to trying anything new and did not want to come back to school to participate in evening PTA programs or activities. However, I persevered. Young's enrollment was more than 700 students. Some white students were bused from the Story Ave. area and others from the Dixie Highway area. Many of the Black students who were enrolled lived in the neighborhood. We had a large number of needy students, but we only had one counselor. The staff did agree on becoming a Learning Choice School while I was there. We wrote a grant and became an International Studies School.

After two years, I was transferred from Young to Garland S. Cochrane Elementary School in Jeffersontown. I was there for twelve years. It gave me the opportunity to grow as a leader. Cochrane was traditional in nature, and the staff actually wanted to become a Traditional Magnet School. However, the Board of Education would not approve the change. Cochrane was a small school with approximately 300 students. Byck Elementary was head of our school cluster. Because we had extra space, we were assigned overflow students from Byck, which was overcrowded. One day shortly after school had started, we welcomed two bus-loads of rambunctious students who rode across town each day. The faculty really did not know the challenges these students brought with them. I remember calling the counselor, Family Resource Center coordinator, and Home School coordinator into my office to pray before the students arrived, asking God to give us wisdom and strength to make a difference in their lives.

Neighborhood issues resulting in students' fussing and fighting on the bus and home problems sometimes spilled over into Cochrane's classrooms, changing the dynamics of the school. Again, there were teachers there who were resistant to change and had to re-think their classroom-management strategies. Changes in the local community, parental involvement in the school, and expectations for student achievement by the state were all challenges for Cochrane teachers who struggled to keep scores up but were still reluctant to try new approaches. I remember the day that the Twin Towers in New York came down. I was in a Site-Based Decision Making (SBDM) meeting trying to convince teachers to try a new reading program.

The small neighborhood feel of Cochrane continued during my tenure there. We were able to get a Family Resource Center which we shared with Jeffersontown Elementary School, and our PTA and SBDM Council were strong. However, Cochrane's faculty was divided: those who wanted change; those who only wanted to remain set in their traditional ways; those who willingly went the extra mile for the kids; those who only wanted to do the minimum; those who wanted their classrooms to be fun, exciting, and welcoming; and those who were satisfied with a sterile classroom where students sat in straight rows and were expected to be quiet.

Fortunately, the small clique of negative teachers were outnumbered by the outstanding teachers on staff, like Excel Award winning first-grade teacher, Myra Malish, who made science fun as she made it come alive for her students. She wore a lab coat and did many creative activities with her kids, including having Mary Ann, the class pet guinea pig who wore ribbons in the school colors (blue and orange) in her hair. She was adored by the kids. She also made class quilts with her students and I always enjoyed visiting her active, hands-on learning classroom.

In addition, there was that wonderful Alternative Certification teacher, Nannette Smith-Jones, a young Black woman who left her job in the business field to teach. She had a quiet, firm demeanor, and a loving spirit that touched all students whether in the classroom, in the hallways, or in the cafeteria.

I officially retired in 2002 from full-time work, but I continued working at various schools as a part-time sub-administrator, a guidance counselor, an ECE ARC chairperson in both elementary and middle schools. I also worked every year since my retirement for the University of Louisville as a supervisor for student teachers.

I have always loved my job as an elementary guidance counselor because getting to know the students and providing guidance lessons and activities were fun and rewarding. I also attempted to get my doctorate degree in Educational Administration at the University of Louisville but failed to finish it after being overly busy as a principal. To this day, I remain ABD, (All But Dissertation), my biggest personal disappointment.

Over these past seventeen years while working in schools, I have seen the number of ECE units increase; an overload of required paper work for both teachers and counselors; limited guidance and counseling given to students before they are sent to alternative schools; and disproportionate numbers of Black students identified with an Emotional Behavior Disability (EBD). I have noticed the breakdown of the family; young single parents who did not have good experiences in schools whose kids were not having good experiences; kids with so many issues – "Crack" babies, no structure in the home, and changes in morals and values. I have been in cultural shock watching kids run over teachers, using profanity, showing disrespect, screaming, using the N-word and the B-word. I have seen counselors so overwhelmed with paperwork and testing requirements that they cannot sponsor Career Days, organize small-group counseling, provide mental health counseling, or have hands-on involvement with the kids—fundamental duties of my day.

Because my vision is cloudy, I am not sure how we will continue to recruit caring, knowledgeable teachers who can work effectively with parents, build relationships to gain the respect of students, and help them acquire the skills they need to meet assessment expectations and standards; at the same time teachers are faced with pension issues, discipline issues, respect issues, and, don't forget, pay issues. My teachers made school my saving grace. I just hope and pray that we continue to have individuals who care, want to teach, want to help students dream and be their saving grace.

Shirley Fuqua-Jackson is married to a retired educator, Willie Jackson, who, she says, has a no-nonsense but caring manner that has evoked respect and recognition from students across the District for well over 30 years. She is actively involved as a Greeter in her church; as a lifelong member of her sorority, Alpha Kappa Alpha Sorority, Inc., where service to all mankind is important to her; and is a member and volunteer for the Louisville Urban League and Guild. She stays busy, traveling, cooking, reading, dancing, modeling, and quilting.

Lonnie Johnson

Teacher, Coach, and Community Volunteer

The love and laughs of my students and their parents were my rewards, and they gave me a lifetime of worth.

I AM NUMBER 15 OUT OF 16 CHILDREN born in Campbellsville, Kentucky, to my parents who were hard workers. My father worked at a cooperage company and my mother was a housewife. My older brothers were like a father, buying me things—a bicycle, baseball gloves, sports equipment. My older sisters, on the other hand, bought me things and took care of me, especially after Mom died when I was ten years old. Mom had a fifth-grade education and Dad had an eighth-grade education. My dad remarried when I was thirteen. My second

L. Johnson Family Photo Collection

mom, a seamstress with two sons who were added to our family, never attended school, but was the wisest woman that I have ever known.

Our house was always filled with people, lively but peaceful. We did not have drama or confusion. All of us knew what we had to do. Dad was the anchor and passed his work ethic to all of us—go

40

to work, be on time, and do your job or go to school, be on time, and do your work. When I went to segregated Durham Elementary, I went to school, was always on time, did my work, and received a solid education. I liked all my teachers, but Ms. Watts was special, energetic, and nice—a good person who treated us all the same and made each of us feel important. Mr. Graves, later Central High School's Coach Graves, was my seventh-grade teacher and he was a good model.

When we moved to Lebanon, Kentucky, my second mom was counselor to the community. A strong Catholic woman, she counseled with her priests who would sit for hours talking to her while she worked. Our home was happy, and the children were well-disciplined. I attended an integrated high school with all white teachers and white students who argued with teachers, something unheard of in the Black community. Although I played basketball and baseball, and the white teachers were "nice," I had no role models or motivators unlike my older brother, Elwood Johnson, who completed Durham High, played basketball for Coach Rodney Ivory, received a scholarship to Jackson State, and later taught in Jefferson County Public Schools, or my sisters who attended Western Kentucky Vocational School in Paducah.

My high school experience was uninspiring, but I did learn. I remember my history teacher, Mr. Biswick, telling the story of the Buffalo Soldiers leading white troops through Indian country and the Indians questioning "why they were fighting with them when they should be fighting with us." My graduating class had five Blacks out of the 100 students. In later years, only two of us returned for reunions.

My journey to college was somewhat unusual. When I graduated from high school, I worked at the local grocery store for about a year and a half. One afternoon, a man from a civil-rights organization came to our house selling tickets for a car raffle for Homecoming at Kentucky State (K-State) College. I stood on my front porch talking to him about wanting to go to college. I had written to several colleges, but not K-State. He gave me some information and contacts. With the Vietnam War in full swing, I was admitted to K-State, and two weeks later I was drafted. I went to Ft. Knox and passed all the tests, then proceeded to the local Draft Board where I presented my letter of acceptance to K-State. Two weeks after that, I received a deferment letter, so I could go to college. In the winter of 1968, I began college at K-State and one of my dreams came true.

My brother who had attended Jackson State, had graduated. He sent me to see Luscious Mitchell, his former basketball coach who was now at K-State. Coach Mitchell, a man of strong character and a strict disciplinarian, hired me as basketball manager, a position which provided a full athletic scholarship, free summer school, summer job opportunities, and my same room in the dorm during the summer. I only paid $250 for my first semester at K-State; my job paid everything else.

I had no academic problem with coursework at K-State. I liked college. I majored in history because of Dr. Henry Chaney, a total historian who taught me the History of Blacks in Kentucky. I fell in love with history. Other professors were motivators as well, and my internal motivation was to stay out of the Vietnam War where I would land if I flunked out. Coach Mitchell was a character builder and hard worker like my father. He stressed teamwork. Our basketball team became the best in the nation, winning three national championships in 1970, 1971, and 1972. I also met my wife, Azalene, a business major from Alabama who eventually taught in JCPS for more than 35 years.

I never had any doubt that teaching was for me. I liked kids and I liked working with youth. My student teaching was in Frankfort, at East Elementary School in Grade 8. I loved it. In the middle of my practicum, my mentor teacher left to cut tobacco. I took the class, handling things until he returned. After that, I had no doubts. I knew I could do it. I could teach!

For some people it may be hard to believe that their steps are guided, but not for me. I finished coursework for certification in December 1972, but I did not march until Spring of 1973. I came to Louisville to pay a quick visit to my brother who was teaching at Shawnee High School. I was wearing my brother's Army jacket when I walked up to the desk in the office. Someone said, "Hi, Lonnie where have you been?" When I turned around, it was John Whiting, my brother's former basketball coach and now Shawnee's principal. We talked. He asked me if I wanted a job. Two weeks after Christmas Break I was a social studies teacher at Shawnee High School where I remained until Merger of the city-county school systems. I was also the boys' basketball coach from 1973 to 1975. I was transferred to Stuart High School when the Louisville and Jefferson County schools merged.

Stuart High School in the Dixie Highway area was different. On my way to find out where Stuart High was located, the WLOU "Soul" radio station faded out. I said to myself, "Man this place is really in the woods." The racism at the school didn't bother me because I had gone to a white high school, but Stuart was in the Dark Ages compared to Shawnee. The school was not progressive. Teachers were not energetic. I loved the kids, but I expected more from the school. Black and white kids were disciplined differently. The overall attitude at Stuart was, "The Black kids are here, but we will not deal with them." Kids walked the halls. The school was out of control. Shawnee had had a much stronger system of disciplining students. I believe that kids do as much as they are allowed to do. Discipline was not a problem for me because I knew how to relate to teenagers. The black and white students seemed to be getting along but it seemed that the Black students were having problems with their teachers.

In October, a big fight broke out. Black kids getting off buses were met with white students marching in the courtyard carrying signs, "Niggers Go Home." When my students came to class that morning they told me that I should go to the gym because a big fight had broken out. Actually, all my students had come to class on time that morning. None of them had been involved in the commotion. My kids were in class sitting quietly, not saying a word when I returned from the gym. The commotion had died down by the time I got to the gym. The protest lasted for about two weeks longer. There were several proposed interventions to help Stuart's faculty and students. We started a Human Relations Club that I directed. We talked things over and sponsored several activities during the year. By Derby weekend of 1976, we had the Black and white students dancing together in the courtyard instead of fighting. Things had smoothed out and we ended the year on a high note. I continued coaching basketball but was overstaffed from Stuart at the end of my third year as the number of students in the District declined because families were moving out of Jefferson County.

I taught at Shawnee High School again from 1978 to 1985, at Seneca High School from 1985 to1987, and at Pleasure Ridge Park (PRP) High School from 1987 until 2007. Shawnee was my number one school, but PRP was a close runner-up. It had the Shawnee feel, and the principal, Charlie Miller, made everybody feel at home. Black students were welcomed and included on the baseball, football, and basketball teams and other extra-curricular activities. Teachers at PRP wanted to be there and students at PRP wanted to be there. Everybody—clerks, lunchroom workers, janitors, support staff—wanted to be there. PRP showed how a neighborhood school could be, even though most of the Black students were bused in. PRP had that neighborhood flavor that Shawnee had had before busing! Charlie Miller was a great principal. He was a people person, and, yes, a politician. He walked with, greeted, and talked to all of us. At the end of announcements, he always said, "Have a happy day."

Motivating students has always been important for teachers. John Whiting and Charlie Miller were great motivators. My style was like that. A teacher must be real with kids, building trust and letting kids be kids. A teacher must treat them right and talk to them. Teachers should never get in kids' faces because they don't know their backgrounds, where they came from, or what they have gone through that day. The teacher-student relationship sometimes makes the difference if students are successful just as students being a part of the group or click. Both instances help students feel that they belong.

Student-teacher relationships also effect discipline in the schools. Discipline is different because respect is different. At one time, children came to school with a level of respect and a degree of self-discipline because of expectations from "home." Today's children are not disciplined at home and do not respect the adults that they live with. They do not get paddled at home and a teacher cannot paddle them at school. When we talk about the education of poor, Black children, we have an adult family problem, not a teacher problem, not a school problem, but a family problem. Real love begins with mom, dad, aunts, uncles, grandparents, that is., family. While teachers may love from a distance, they are not family and cannot replace family, but they help their students feel better about themselves when they show their students that they care about them.

Caring, again, helps with relationships and with discipline. If teachers have a positive relationship with a child, they can discipline that child and that child will accept it. If you do not, that child will rebel. I saw a teacher snatch a hat off a student's head, and the kid reacted, causing the teacher to write a referral that sent the kid back to Buechel where the kid was later in a fight with another kid and received a serious injury. This all could have been avoided had the teacher had a relationship with the student and approached him in a caring manner.

Teaching is challenging but rewarding. A teacher must have a certain personality to be a good teacher. A teacher also needs a strong foundation and discipline. It is fun to see students progress and come back to thank you or to tell their friends about being in your class.

For instance, I was riding my bike along Poplar Level Road and heard this guy hollering at me, calling my name. He knew me, but I did not remember his being in my class. He was standing outside a whiskey store with his friends. When I stopped, his friends asked me if he had passed my class and before I could respond, he said," Yes, I passed Mr. Johnson's class! I got a D-"! We all laughed. I slapped them five and rode on!

Schools correlate with society and society is what effects kids. Depending on the environment that I was in, I might be dealing with sagging or dealing with crack or students who did not value education or who could care less about going to college. These are real social issues that kids deal with. Kids have not changed; we have.

Busing did not help the education of Black kids. It was cruel and unusual punishment to put a kid on a corner waiting on a bus through snow, rain, cold, and heat. I believe in neighborhood schools; keeping young students in their area schools would improve their education. Later, they can choose their high school. I am not the type who thinks you must sit beside another race to succeed.

Bad fruit does not come out of good trees and good fruit does not come from bad trees. We must continue to plant good trees—responsible parents, supportive families, a society that does not discriminate, positive expectations for all students—to get good fruit—equal opportunity for all. And, we must continue to pray for our teachers and our students.

Lonnie Johnson coached basketball for more than ten years, his teams winning various tournaments. He exchanged his coaching career to be more engaged in raising his children, Candice and Gregory. Lonnie received an award from the Jefferson County Public Schools for raising the most money for the United Negro College Fund, leading the county in raising funds for three years. He is an avid reader and is in the process of writing a book to support his family legacy. He is active in his church, Community Missionary Baptist Church, serving as Trustee for several years.

Sherrie B. Lyons

Teacher, Middle and High School Counselor, GED
Instructor, Community Program Director, and
University Administrator

MALCOLM X SAID, "EDUCATION IS THE key to the future; tomorrow belongs to those who prepare for it today." My parents, Calvin and Ann Butler, constantly emphasized the importance of education to their children and made sure we all had the opportunity to attend college after high school. My father came to Kentucky as a result of his Army assignment to Fort Knox; he served and fought in World War II. My mother came shortly after to be close to her husband. Both of my parents were born and raised in Alabama. I have three siblings

Lyons Family Photo Collection

and we were born in Louisville. After the war, my dad worked as a welder at International Harvester; after multiple strikes, he took on a temporary seasonal job as a mail handler for the U.S. Post Office. This temporary job became permanent and a check mark on educational opportunities for the Butler children. My mother worked evenings cleaning offices at the Starks Building and on weekends doing hair at Lucille's Beauty Nook on 32nd Street. (I found her degree from Madame

CJ Walker's School of Beauty Culture several years after her death in 1993.)

We lived on Twenty-Ninth Street and Virginia Avenue; a tree-lined neighborhood where blue- and white-collar African Americans lived side by side. Mrs. Emma Ford, her husband George, and Mrs. Barlow, her mother lived next door. We referred to Mrs. Ford as Aunt Emma; that was a time when neighbors were like family. Principal Evelyn Jackson; Dr. Alexander, a professor at Kentucky State College lived across the street; Mr. Brown, a well-known math teacher at Central High School and his family lived a few houses away. His wife was my first piano teacher.

My family attended Brown Memorial C.M.E. Church located on Eighth and Chestnut streets. The ground-breaking segment of my educational journey began with my parents. The cement was poured, solidifying my foundation, by my exposure to outstanding women who taught my Sunday School class, directed the Easter and Christmas plays, taught African-American history, and directed the children's and youth choirs at our church. These women were Mrs. Maude Brown Porter, Lela Tate Blakey, Evelyn Waldrop, Katherine Lowry, and Alice Lucille Martin. All of these ladies were trail- blazers in their own right and consistently promoted the concept of excellence without excuses. We always memorized Easter poems and Christmas play lines, and they expected good grades and stellar behavior. There were no exceptions!

In elementary school, I liked all of my teachers, but two ladies come to mind, Ms. Edna Calhoun, my fourth-grade teacher and Mrs. Virginia Higgins, my fifth-grade teacher. Mrs. Calhoun was very loving and caring; Mrs. Higgins a strong-willed woman, harsh sometimes in her approach, prepared us well for sixth grade. We worked on public speaking and did all kinds of science experiments in the classroom. I remember an experiment with white mice and a step-by-step process to make cottage cheese. We were given meaningful assignments that built our confidence and improved our academic and social skills. Mrs. Cleopatra Gregory and Mrs. Helen Smith were beautiful female teachers with very high fashion sense for women, especially in the 1950s and early sixties. They were always super sharp sisters; in my eyes they were glamorous.

My memories of Parkland Junior High include Mr. Clifford, the principal, an individual who seemed angry most of the time; he was actually a nice man. I also recall my seventh-grade English teacher, Mrs. Whiteside, who required our class to memorize and recite an assigned poem in front of the class every six weeks. I remember the experience of my first gym class where we dressed in blue, one-piece suits and were required to shower at the end of each class. I was in the choir where Ms. Hollis introduced us to songs like, "Give Me Your Tired Your Poor"; taught us descants to almost all of the Christmas carols; and prepared us for our spring concert performance. I loved the chorus, not so much the instructor. I also loved to read and travelled to many places through books. The Street Library was my summer home. It was located on the corner of Twenty-Eighth Street, one block from our house; I was allowed to walk there unaccompanied.

Our house was a place where everyone was welcomed. After church on many Sundays my friends would come over for dinner. There was always enough food for visitors. Our home was a place where we could listen to music, sit on the front porch swing, and watch cars go by on a Sunday evening; we would discuss the events from the weekend or coming events of the next week.

My brother, sister, and I attended Louisville Male High School, and in the sixties students were tracked. There were definite issues of discrimination. I was in a college-prep English class in my freshman year; I got out of the class second semester. However, I returned to the college-prep English class during my junior and senior years. I had a friend who was a cheerleader; we were in U.S. History class together. We competed with each other for grades. Our teacher was a football coach; my friend dated a football player. If I got an *A* she got an *A+*. If my paper was an *A+*, she got an *A++*. We both knew what was happening with our grades.

During my first years at Male, Blacks could be in the Glee Club, but not in the Choir. I had taken piano lessons for years; I sang in the choir in junior high school, so I knew how to read music. I performed with a musical group, auditioned and performed on the television show called "High Varieties," and sang with a group at monthly USO shows. This changed before I left: however, I decided the choir was not the place for me. I auditioned with the group in Cincinnati and was offered a contract to go on tour, yet I could not be in the Male High Choir. (Mom said no to the contract. "You are going to college.")

My older brother graduated from Morehead State, received his master's degree from the University of Maryland, and earned his Doctorate in Clinical Psychology from Howard University. My sister and I attended and graduated from Western Kentucky University with both our undergraduate and Master's degrees. Our younger brother graduated from the University of Louisville. While in college, I was on the Student Government Board activities committee, a Charter member and secretary of Epsilon Zeta chapter of Alpha Kappa Alpha Sorority, Inc., and vice president of National Association of Collegiate Secretaries. I always wanted to be a teacher and business education was a fit. After taking a course in children's literature, library science became my minor.

When I applied for a position with the old Louisville School System, I was hired as a librarian. I was assigned to Roosevelt Elementary School; I was there for one semester. In January I reported to Louisville Male High School where I replaced retiring business education teacher, Mr. Brown. I quickly adopted the teaching style of the strong Black teachers from Virginia Avenue. This was beneficial because it helped differentiate me from the student body that I still resembled. Male had changed from the school that I attended. When I graduated they selected the first black cheerleader. When I returned four years later, there was only one white cheerleader.

For the remainder of my career as an employee of JCPS, I served as a counselor, first assignment Russell Junior High School then Western Junior High. I witnessed poverty, pain, progress and pride, people who cared and loved their children. I have seen students not able to attend school during the first weeks because they were working in the tobacco fields helping the family that still lived on the farm. While working at one school, I was invited by a colleague to ride through the community to get a front-seat view of the community we served. This individual is someone I will always remember as an example of a true educator and mentor. There were beautiful homes with manicured lawns; homes that were small but well-kept, some small quaint cottages, and some structures that looked as if they were waiting for the demolition ball to strike. However, most of those homes, whether large or small; manicured lawns or overgrown with weeds; were filled with loving parents and happy children.

After merger of the city and county school systems, with the onset of busing, I was assigned to a middle school where I witnessed what I call "blind discrimination." This school continually had errors in the Black/white student count required for Board of Education documentation. The error was found to be caused by teachers who did not count Black children who lived in the neighborhood in the Black student count; they only counted Black students who rode the bus from downtown as Black. As a result of this discrepancy, during the first month of busing, the Black/White count at the school was totally incorrect.

In 1981, my family moved from Louisville and I found myself in an educational setting that I never expected, teaching GED to inmates at East Moline Correctional Center in Illinois. This classroom was no different from any classroom I had entered because I was in charge of the educational outcome of the students. In the two years I worked at the institution, every student I submitted to take the GED test, passed. I returned to Louisville after two years. My new assignment was Central High School. I truly loved working at Central. I only left because I was overstaffed due to seniority.

I also enjoyed my tenure at Eastern High School, my next assignment. For ten years I worked with students from ninth through twelfth grades and eventually with just juniors and seniors in an effort to better prepare our students for college admission. Ninety percent of our students applied and were accepted to colleges and universities. It was not unusual to assist students in completing applications to schools like Yale, Harvard, Centre, Transylvania, Vanderbilt, Penn State, and West Point.

I also read applications for the National Merit Foundation in Evanston, Illinois, for three years. I learned what was important when applying for scholarships and saw what really counted in the college admission tests. Students earned stellar grades, but fell short when applying for top scholarships. Generic letters of recommendation, little or no service hours, limited or no leadership positions can be detrimental to acquisition of certain scholarships, especially National Merit ones. Students become candidates for National Merit as a result of scores on the PSAT; they become National Merit Scholars based on a total score calculated after completing the application packet and it is reviewed by a committee of readers.

During my tenue at Eastern, Central, and Western, I encouraged African-American students to participate in The YMCA Black Achievers Program. In 1991 Eastern had eleven students receive more than $650,000 in scholarships from that program alone.

Since my retirement, I have remained active as an educator. In 1986 I started working as a counselor with Project One, an organization that focuses on meaningful summer job opportunities and training for youth. I served as a counselor/Dean in this program for more than ten years. I received the *Outstanding Woman of the Year Award* from this organization in 1999. My association with Project One opened doors to several of the positions I held after retirement. I was Director of the Louisville Youth Opportunity Network, a city grant designed to provide high school graduates opportunities to develop skills to improve their job readiness and life skills. As associate director of the Governor's Scholars Program, I encouraged qualified juniors around the commonwealth to complete the application process for this prestigious program. I received a grant and directed The Career Academy at St. Stephen Church. We partnered with CW Johnson XPRESS trucking company; provided recruitment, and testing and assisted with funds for CDL permits. The focus was to assist individuals with criminal records gain meaningful employment through training and additional support.

I describe my last position, Director of Academic Advising at Kentucky State University, as my bucket list opportunity because I always wanted the experience of working in a college dedicated to supporting African-American students, for example, an HBCU. I loved the flow of the campus, the feel of community, and the compassion of the staff.

My parents were not college-educated, but they wanted us to have every opportunity to achieve and reach goals we set for ourselves. They

accomplished this by encouraging us to appreciate the importance of hard work and always doing our best. Poor children do not have to stay poor. Poor is not forever. Education is the No.1 resource out of poverty, and we must have good teachers providing that education. We cannot invite people—smart people, Black people, and white people—to join our profession if they come to the table as the invited guest but end up the main course on the menu—disrespected, underpaid, unwelcomed, under-resourced and unappreciated!

As educators, we must continue working to get our educational system back on track in order for all children to benefit. The atmosphere of the school impacts self-image, expectations, and attitude. Educators must be intentional in creating that atmosphere, putting their eyes back on the prize—bright, curious, and open-minded, successful young people with the knowledge and skills to be successful adults in the real world. We do this by "striving for excellence; caring more than others think wise, risking more than others think safe; dreaming more than others think practical; and expecting more than others think possible."

Sherrie Lyons is married to Joseph Lyons, a retired educator who graduated from Louisville's Central High School and who is in the CHS Hall of Fame. A former football and basketball coach, Joe and Sherrie's blended family includes five children; all attended and graduated from Jefferson County Public Schools (KY). All five are college graduates. They have nine grandchildren. Two of their children are educators, one in Florida and the other in Louisville, KY.

Patricia Pointer

Substitute Teacher, Teacher, Drop-Out Prevention
Coordinator, and Administrator for Title I Programs

I CANNOT REMEMBER WHEN GET-
ting an education was not emphasized in my
house. Born in Paris, Tennessee, I was the
oldest of four with one sister and two brothers. We were all expected to go to college, although my grandparents who raised us did
not complete high school—my grandmother
completed eighth grade, and my grandfather completed fifth grade. The elementary
school that I attended was a one-room, all
Black, country school with twelve students
in the class for Grades 1-5. We each had a
desk and a set of eight books. Ms. Bennet,

Douglas Pointer, Jr. Photographer

our teacher, was stern and structured and talked about college. Every
day she asked us, "Tell me what you want to do when you grow up,"
and every day we told her, "We want to go to college."

Let me back up a minute and share another part of my story
that I have not told before. When I was nine years old, I witnessed
my father being shot six times by a white man who was his friend.
My father was mixed or bi-racial. His mom was white and his

father was Black. My mom opened the door and invited his friend into the house, not knowing that there had been an argument or confrontation earlier that day. When my father came to the door, he was shot again and again. He ran outside, falling by a tree in our front yard. My sister and I ran to a neighbor's house and asked them to call the police. That is all that I remember. I went blank. Mom lost the baby that she was carrying, had a mental break down, and was hospitalized, never to raise any of her existing children. My white grandmother and Black grandfather took over, even though my mom's family was willing to take us if dollars were involved. My father's parents were embedded in the community. Grandpa was superintendent of the Sunday School and we attended church regularly, sometimes most of the day on Sunday. We were taught to put God first and foremost in our lives.

Even though those were emotional times and we did not have a lot of money, we were not poor-poor and we survived. We lived in a three-bedroom house with a living room, dining room, kitchen and huge back yard. We had a garden and lots of land. Grandpa farmed as well. He also worked for the railroad and Grandma did not work. They nurtured us even though they had raised four children on their own and were up in age. Our neighbors up the road had horses and were always generous to my grandparents. They gave my grandfather $1500 when I graduated and went off to college.

I attended Grades 6-12 at the Central High School in my hometown and my favorite teacher was Ms. Lewis who taught algebra, geometry, and trigonometry. She was an inspiration because she always dressed sharp **and** because she was smart. She wore suits. We said the Lord's Prayer every morning and we said the Pledge to the flag. When we walked through the door, there was a problem on the board that we copied and worked in our notebook. Algebra was easiest, and I had to study for geometry and trig. Ms. Lewis planted the idea in my head that appearance has a lot to do with learning. Ms. Morris, an older teacher who taught me in high school, also left an impression. Students had to keep a notebook and we had to conjugate verbs, adjectives, etc. She also dressed fabulously and gave me the idea that I wanted to major in English.

In 1966, I graduated as salutatorian of my class of 70 Black students, having a .5 difference in grade-point average from the valedictorian, my best friend. Some thought that the difference was not real, but that the advantage was given to her because her father was principal and her mother was a teacher. I never felt that way. Her father listened as we both practiced speeches for graduation. We both did well and remained friends.

Although my grandmother thought that I would do better in an integrated setting, I wanted to go to a historically Black college. Murray State College in Murray, Kentucky, was only fifteen miles from home. Nashville, where the nearest HBCU was located was 85 miles from home. Also, two of my girlfriends were going to Tennessee State University (TSU). I received an academic scholarship from TSU that provided books, tuition, room and board, and some spending money. That was my choice. Our pastor, Rev. Ward, and grandma took me to college, unloaded my stuff at the Women's Resident Center and drove back home. I cried for two days. It was scary being away from home and standing in those long registration lines going from table to table. Not knowing quite what to do was unnerving even though my uncle worked at TSU. (*That is why it is so important today that we get students out on college visits, tell them what to expect, and do freshmen visitation and summer-prep programs.*)

College was fun with lots of parties, and college was serious business with teachers who were dedicated to helping students **earn** their degrees. As an English major, I had excellent teachers who took pride in preparing their students for careers, many of whom would be teachers themselves. They cared about their students and when a student finished with Dr. Lindsay or Dr. Hudson or Dr. McDonald Williams, that student knew that she had a strong knowledge base. These teachers did not play and they expected excellence. Sometimes getting a "B" was excelling. Teachers taught well; they were dedicated; and they were there for you at all times.

After four years of study under caring and knowledgeable teachers, after listening to an outstanding band, watching football games from my dorm room, eating whiting fish at the Fish Place, picking through the "mystery meat" in the school cafeteria, and opening the food boxes that my grandma sent, I was ready to graduate with a major in English and a minor in French. My plan was to move to Detroit to continue my education and get certified as a teacher. Instead, I got married on June 6, 1970, graduated on June 7, and moved to Louisville, Kentucky a short time later.

My new husband's employment at B.F. Goodrich allowed us to get an apartment on our own. We moved to the Algonquin area, across the hall from Shirley Merriweather, an elementary teacher who encouraged me to think about substitute teaching to get my foot in the door and to meet new people. I thought about it and decided that I would try it because it gave me flexibility. I could work on the days that I chose. From 1971 to 1973, when my first child was born, I was a substitute teacher, working in Louisville's West End schools, including DuValle and Parkland Junior High schools and Central High School.

Substitute teaching gave me the opportunity to meet new people, to get an inside view of schools and classrooms, and to see Black children at their best and worse. I substituted for a number of teachers who left clear, concise instructions and directions, whose lessons engaged their students even though they were not present. I saw administrators walking the halls and checking on classrooms to make sure that students and teachers were on task. I saw administrators and teachers (who looked like teachers) in control of the school, and students and parents supporting and respecting teachers and their authority. I saw teachers teaching, not babysitting, and demanding that students try—no heads down and no sleeping in class. This was not at one school, but at all schools in which I substituted prior to the Merger of city and county schools.

For the next several years, including 1975-76 school year, I substituted then became a homemaker and mother, waiting for my daughter to go to elementary and then my son. She was bused in first grade to Blue Lick Elementary because of our Oregon Avenue address. I remember following the bus to Blue Lick. This was too far for any first grader to ride at that time of the morning, then or now. My daughter did stay at Blue Lick for about six months before transferring to Audubon Elementary. My son followed her footsteps from Audubon to Male High where they both graduated.

I returned to full-time teaching as an English teacher at Moore High School in 1986. This was a great experience, working with students, teaching the subject that I loved, English. Although I never did student teaching, my substituting experiences and the teacher role models that I had as a student got me through. I knew the content and I knew how to treat students to get the best out of them. I also knew how I was supposed to look as a professional. I remember one of my students telling me that I looked nice, "but you always look nice," he said, reaffirming that students still paid attention to what teachers wore and how they looked.

I stayed at Moore for eight years, teaching English and as Drop-Out Prevention Coordinator in The Partnership Program, a collaboration between Jefferson County Public Schools, the Louisville community, and the city government. The program focused on providing academic support, teaching students self-awareness, job skills and interviewing skills, and dressing for success. Mayor Jerry Abramson, Marty Bell, and various community leaders were actively involved with the project to improve graduation rates and employability of high school students.

In 1994, I became a Coordinator I of Title 1 Programs where I supervised a staff of Home-School Coordinators in seventeen high schools. Our job was to improve attendance, decrease the drop-out rate, and provide students with support for academic problems as well as providing students' parents, grandparents, and guardians with workshops, information, and strategies to help keep students in school progressing toward graduation. Our data showed success—a positive impact with increased graduation rates and a decrease in drop-outs. I retired in 2009, but continued to sub until 2018.

As I substituted in the more recent years, I noticed differences in teacher attitudes and interactions with Black students and white students. I have seen teachers bribe Black boys or "give him an A if he sits down" or if he will "be quiet and don't say anything." I have seen teachers, both Black and white, afraid of Black boys and the boys know it. The teacher tells them something to do and the boys just look at the teacher, totally ignoring the request. The teacher says nothing more. I have seen students running the school and teachers and administrators allowing this to happen. There was no learning going on.

I have encountered issues where students want to do the right thing, but because of teacher shortages and changes in substitutes, students have not received accurate information. For example, I had a senior math class where students had not taken the ACT because the teacher had resigned six months prior and no one at the school recognized that these students were "left out."

I have also seen the decline of parental involvement over the years and I do not know why. Because these are high school students? Maybe, but parents come to football games and basketball games in the high school, so, why won't they get involved in their children's education?

Because we need teachers, schools sometimes look at certification and not the person or their beliefs about children and education. We know that there is a gap between college training and real classroom teaching. Something is wrong that needs to be fixed. Until we fix it, we will have a hard time developing great educators who go above and beyond their duties, take internal interest in their students, are knowledgeable, and are dedicated. I have had great teachers where I felt the love. The harder they were we knew they cared. They took a personal interest in us that went beyond teaching as their job. When I had trouble with trigonometry, Mr. Lewis took his time after school to work with me. When I finally got it, we both celebrated. Furthermore, great teachers understand the inequities in learning and in how students learn. They use their talent and skills to close those gaps and level the playing field.

As I close, I must address one final issue, how many of our teachers look or dress as professionals. When entering into a high school, a visitor cannot tell the teachers from the students because they are both wearing jeans with holes in them, flip flops, and T-shirts. That is a problem! Teaching is a profession and teachers should look professional. That does not mean wearing suits, heels, and dresses every day. However, it does mean that teachers should dress for their roles as leaders, motivators, care givers, and knowledge brokers. Teachers want to look their best when outsiders are coming to visit the school to take pictures and share with other people who maybe do not care. So why wouldn't professionals want to look their best every day for perhaps visitors, but most certainly their students that they care about? How you look may remind that one student that you took the extra time to look like a teacher and may cause that student to give you that little extra respect that makes your day and lets you into his or her mind.

My primary experiences have been with high school students. I think if I were starting out today, I would try working with elementary students because there are habits and beliefs that you can instill early that carry on through a child's life and impacts behavior and decisions. I have enjoyed my career with JCPS and I am always gratified when I hear from my students, read about their successes and their children's successes. I am blessed to leave a professional legacy that has positively impacted students and demonstrated my love for them and for education.

Pat Pointer has been married to her college sweetheart for nearly fifty years. They have a daughter, Selena Rogers and a son, Christopher Pointer. Pat, her sister, Clairene Tibbs, her sister's husband, and their daughter are all graduates of Tennessee State University. During her career, Pat was presented a Certificate of Award in honor and recognition of her performances with the JCPS Mentoring Program. She received the JTPA Annual Award for Outstanding Business and Education Partnership Programs presented by the Louisville Education and Employment Partnership. She was presented the "Champion for Children Award" by JCPS for her outstanding commitment, time, and service to the students of JCPS; and she was given an "Award of Excellence in Recognition of Outstanding Leadership" by Dr. Charles King, CEO and President of Project One, Inc. for her contribution to the youth in the Louisville community. She continues working at Zion Baptist Church as a member of the Senior Usher Board.

Mary Loretta Stewart

Teacher, University Counselor, Business Education
Specialist, Instructional Assistant Principal, Assistant
Principal, and Educational Specialist

I WAS FIFTEEN YEARS OLD WHEN I graduated from high school and nineteen years old when I graduated from Kentucky State College with a degree in business. Born in 1941 in Paducah, Kentucky, the fifth of nine children, I had a wonderful childhood. My parents, Birdie and George Reeves, owned a large farm and employed several workers. Even though they had only an elementary education, they wanted their children to become educated and worked hard to see that we had what we needed in that one-room school house that I attended

Author

in Grades 1-8. Class does not necessarily come from economic status. My mom was a true country lady. She was witty and creative and she had a knack for making things. Her wash was the whitest and her work ethic was evident. It was important that her girls learned how to take care of themselves. She was also religious. Every Sunday morning we would all pile in the car and go to church. We also had Bible class and a treat afterwards.

Dad, on the other hand, never went to church but he was a good person. He was an overseer of sharecroppers on our land. He made sure that they had a nice place to live. To make money, he bought livestock and sold it at a profit. All of us children worked on the farm that our grandpa had first owned, raising tobacco, soybeans, and tending vegetables that we sold out of the back of our car. We worked hard and played hard, sometimes just walking and looking to see how thing grew, building playhouses in the woods, playing hop-scotch— taking a break and coming back to work to get finished before Dad got home. He was truly a hard worker and a human calculator. In spite of his limited education, he knew math and calculated in his head. He gave me that same talent—I gobbled up math.

Because I was the middle child, I had the opportunity to live with all of my sisters and brothers, older and younger and to attend school with some of them. We had the best elementary teacher, ever. Ms. Mae Anna Britt, my first teacher, was smart, creative, and could write. She taught us everything we needed to know and do. School was fun. I loved going to school. We were never bored. Education to us was fun things and fun learning, from making great paper outfits and decorations to learning how to use a sheet on the wall for a movie screen as we spent Saturday night, movie night at school, with hotdogs and popcorn. Eighth graders were in the 4H club and learned to sew aprons, blouses, and skirts. Since we were all in one room together, things spilled over as we watched. I could even sew like my mom.

I was heartbroken when Mrs. Britt was transferred from our one-room county school with 30 students in Grades 1-8 to the city school with more children and more than one classroom. She was so dynamic. Her gift to us when she left was a puzzle of the United States where we learned the states and their capitols. This came in handy as I skipped the sixth grade and missed geography lessons. Her replacement, my second teacher or substitute, had no charisma. She whipped the children and really could not teach. She was terrible. It was the knowledge and work ethic that Ms. Britt had instilled in us that kept us moving forward and learning on our own.

My third teacher in Grades 7 and 8 was a dreamboat. We all had crushes on him because he was so good-looking. Since school was three miles away, he sometimes picked us up in his car. Other times we walked. However, because of this teacher, we had an appreciation for music. He introduced us to jazz and we loved it.

Lincoln, my high school, Grades 9-12, was located in the city. I had a wonderful principal and wonderful teachers. We were exposed to cantatas, band, basketball, typing, literature, and vocal music—the works. In the high school, there were two teachers from Tennessee State University (TSU); one taught business. That teacher made me think about going to college because of what she told us about TSU. My vision had been to finish school, get married and have babies—no thinking about college—until that teacher sparked a flame. Western Kentucky Vocational and Junior College was known to everyone around our area and was referenced when people talked about college in general. However, Ms. Williams, who taught bookkeeping and majored in business, was the encourager. She was well-dressed, knowledgeable, and an excellent teacher. She made the difference in my life and the lives of several others in the class of 1957 from which five students went to Kentucky State (K-State) College, one to TSU, and one to Southern Illinois University.

As one of the K-State group, I was told that I was third in the senior class based on grades. I also was class president, an unusual feat for someone from the county since discrimination in this all-Black school was based on city vs. county, with students from the county being looked down upon. I earned a $100 scholarship toward the $400 cost of attending K-State for one year. And, at fifteen years old, I knew that I should have been valedictorian but I was denied the opportunity because of a fraction of a grade-point average based on a grade in band class. However, for my family, being the first of the nine to attend college, that situation hurt but did not matter. What mattered was my family working to get the money for me to go to school, my mom, dad, little sister, and little brother driving on back roads from Paducah to Louisville on Highway 62 and Louisville to Frankfort on US 60 to get me to K-State.

I entered college at age sixteen, scared, homesick, and begging to return home. Mom told me to "think about it." There was never a question about my major, business, or my profession, teaching. I worked part-time to help pay tuition and was elated to get a few extra dollars from home to buy food, sandwiches, and snacks. That first year was also difficult because I was so young. My classmates were knowledgeable about the world and many of them had grown up in the city. I had a complex about being young and had to adjust to make it and stay. I had no real social life although I did learn to play the card game Bid-Whist.

One of the great things about K-State was the activities on campus—cultural entertainment such as Marion Anderson, Duke Ellington, and Butterfly McQueen who performed in person. The Lyceum Committee brought well-known artists in music, dance, and cultural arts. There was a library booth where you could listen to Martin Luther King flying from New York to California. Langston Hughes read poetry to me. I was sitting at his feet. The administrators understood that as Black students in a segregated society, we needed enhanced cultural experiences and they made every effort to provide them.

College was a challenge for which I was not totally prepared in that I never had to study in high school, and I thought college would be somewhat the same, but biology taught me early on that I had to put in the hours; I had to study. My work ethic, inherited from my family, kept me going and helped me make the Dean's List and graduate in 1961 at 19 years old with certification in business after student teaching at Lexington Dunbar High School in Lexington, Kentucky. I was the first of the nine siblings to complete college, and I was slated to begin work in the fall at K-State as secretary to the Dean of Students. However, when the Dean discovered that I had a boyfriend on campus, the job offer was rescinded and I resorted to looking for employment in my field, teaching.

My career as an educator was a whirlwind. My first offer of employment was in Middlesboro, Kentucky, in the mountains at an old dilapidated school. I said, "No, thank you." The offer that I accepted was at Douglas High School in Murray, Kentucky, teaching business,

English, and math. At 20 years old, many of the high school students were close to my age. They were also some of the smartest math students that I have encountered. I had to re-learn how to diagram sentences and study all over again to stay one day ahead of them. One of those students became a renowned medical doctor. There were six of us teachers in the high school and several lived in the boarding house across from the school. During the summers, I attended Murray State working on my master's degree although I went home every weekend for the two years that I taught at Douglas until it was closed in 1963 and I got a job teaching in Paducah back at the high school from which I had graduated.

Lincoln High School had several new teachers, including the man that I would eventually marry, George Oscar Stewart, who had been sent to Lincoln by the Placement Office at Hampton University. On August 7, 1964, I received my master's degree from Murray State University. On August 8, 1964, I was married in a beautiful wedding gown that I had made myself, and a few days later, Stewart and I drove to Louisville to apply for jobs as teachers with the Louisville system. I did not get a job because there were no vacancies in business, but Stew was hired. As a result I was unemployed for three weeks until I was hired as an English teacher.

My tenure as a teacher in Louisville began in 1966 as a math teacher at Shawnee Jr. High School with 57 teachers. That assignment was followed by a half year at DuValle Jr. High School, replacing Gloria Talbot. I was returning from maternity leave and she was going on maternity leave. I enjoyed teaching and seeing my students make progress. I had to work hard at times to engage students. We used typewriters at that time as well as other business machines. Schools were not in the forefront with new technology. As a teacher who fluctuated between business and math, I had to understand math for everyday use and math for business applications and adapt to the student population as needed. Learning to integrate the math functions helped me help students.

My next venture in this whirlwind came in 1969 when I left the Louisville system to become the Director of Tutoring and Counseling in the Office of Black Affairs at the University of Louisville (U of L).

Don't ask me how I got there, but I assisted with recruitment and was the intermediary between students and professors. I taught shorthand in the College of Business while tutoring students; counselled them on course selection and majors; and ran interference for them when problems arose by meeting with professors and clarifying issues. One of the challenges that I faced was attitudes and perceptions about poor, Black students that were sometimes dominant among white faculty who had no experiences with poor, Black children. "Black kids are not all dumb kids," was a reminder that had to be repeated on several occasions and was reinforced by the students as their grades improved and "C" students who had been "A" students in high school became "A" students in college. (Rita Greer was one of those.)

Prior to Merger of the two school systems in 1973, I was devastated as my husband became ill and I had to make a career decision to stay at U of L, which meant returning to school for a doctorate in higher education, or returning to the District. I chose to return to old Louisville city schools as Supervisor of Business Education and to pursue my Rank I Principal/Supervisor Certification

When Merger came in 1975, WOW! There were two of every administrator. As a Specialist in Business, I had a counterpart from the county who had never ridden in a car with a Black woman and who considered me his assistant rather than his equal. The first two months were difficult, to put it mildly— with lack of cooperation and insensitivity. The quiet, soft-spoken woman who smiled and didn't rattle learned to speak up for herself as she had spoken up for students over many years. I did not raise my voice, but there was no doubt that I would not be ignored, pushed around, or stepped upon.

Dr. David DeRusso's appointment as superintendent of the merged Jefferson County Public Schools brought an unexpected resurgence to my career. With all duplicate positions being eliminated, I was assigned a teaching position at Moore High School. After two days at home crying and talking to the powers that be, I reported to Moore. It was absolutely wonderful being back with the kids, having direct responsibility over their program, seeing their growth, and being the everyday role model for those high school students as my two high school teachers had been for me. Coupled with my knowledge from my university experience, I was even more prepared to navigate and support students to pursue going to college. The technology transition which was underway meant that I had a new learning curve as well.

Between 1981 and 1991, I worked at Stewart Middle School, was assigned as an instructional assistant principal at Moore High School, coordinated the Academic Vocational Project at Fairdale High School, got my old job back as Business Specialist, and served as assistant principal at Lyndon Vocational School until it closed. I became the assistant principal at Central High School from 1991 to my retirement in 1999. Truly, my last job was the best job of my career. The principal of Central, Harold Fenderson, shared my philosophy—schools are about kids and our job was to help students take pride in their school to engender pride in themselves. He and I both worked toward getting students to believe that they could be anything that they wanted to be. I suspect that I got the job because in the interview I talked about what my teachers had incorporated in me and how I approached teaching—having high expectations, knowing the basics, being career ready, not boring or dull, making learning fun, and instilling a can-do attitude. We produced some phenomenal students that I still run into—doctors, lawyers, judges, teachers, other legal professionals, and business professionals—many who are impacting this community today. Retiring from Central was one of the hardest decisions of my career, but family circumstances dictated that I needed more home time than the assistant principal position allowed.

My career provided opportunities to observe teachers and students in a variety of settings, from all-Black schools in Western Kentucky, to Louisville, to integrated schools all over the JCPS district for well over 35 years. I saw outstanding teachers who could teach any child in any school, who were dedicated professionals, encouragers, and desirous of making a difference. However, in more recent times, what troubled me most are three things. First, good teachers who appear to care about kids seem to assume that even their top students cannot perform well enough to go to four-year colleges and recommend community college or schools like Spenserian for continuing education/training. This may be related to another phenomenon where I saw kids being moved on when they still did not have the basics.

Secondly, I noticed that lots of teachers only looked out for certain kids, invariably not low-income and not Black students. The focus was on college-bound students, not those who might have been interested in a trade or vocation (even though that trade may have paid $38.00 an hour—like welding). Thirdly, as Black teachers began disappearing, increasing numbers of Black children had no African-American teachers over their entire twelve years of schooling; therefore, these students had limited role models, limited encouragement to consider teaching as a career, and fewer teachers who were likely to give the students voice in situations where their voices needed to be heard.

With my observations in mind, I have to say that regarding the education of Black children and poor children, we are missing the boat. Too many are falling through the cracks when high school students do not know the basics and cannot read, write, and do math. Too many new things are introduced; however, when students do not have a solid foundation, we are crippling them. We must work toward making every educator a great educator—who desires to make a difference in the life of each child; who wants nothing but the best for all children; who takes pride in being a role model; who loves kids and is willing to obtain the knowledge, skills, and training necessary to make a difference in a child's life, even under the most challenging circumstances.

Finally, it must be said that if we want great teachers, we must work to re-build the profession. Teachers have to be positive about teaching. We must highlight successful role models and share our success stories; we must work on pay and retirement issues; we must encourage teachers to seek promotional opportunities and assure that they will be treated fairly in the selection process; and we must look like professionals that students will want to emulate. There is no better feeling for teachers than when they see their former students who tell them how they impacted their lives and then say, "I am a teacher because of you." To my teachers, I am a teacher because of you, and there is no other profession that I would have chosen. Thank you.

Loretta Stewart worked with the Lincoln Foundation for five years after her retirement from public schools. In later years she returned to JCPS as a retired administrator to assist with the School to Work

Program. She and her husband also owned and operated Madeline's Flower Shop with her daughter serving as a designer. Loretta, the mother of two children, Kevin and Angelique, who are second-generation college graduates, served on the Governor's Research Committee on Women in Kentucky and the Kentucky State University Foundation Board of Directors. She is a member of Alpha Kappa Alpha Sorority, Inc. was chairman of African American Heritage Weekends, a delegate to Zonta International Conference, Sydney Australia, and has been recognized among the 100 Outstanding Graduates of Kentucky State University as well as Lincoln High School where she is in their Hall of Fame.

Emma McElvaney Talbott

Elementary/Middle School Teacher, Reading Specialist,
Adjunct Professor, Alternative Certification Teacher
Educator, and *Courier-Journal* Op-Ed Contributor

Author: *The Joy and Challenge of
Raising African-American Children*

BORN IN LOUISVILLE, KENTUCKY, TO hard-working parents who were old enough to be my grandparents, I have lived in Louisville all of my life with the exception of one year when I lived in Atlanta, Georgia. I was born in the Limerick neighborhood but moved to the California neighborhood at the age of three, and I am the youngest of seven children. Both Mom and Dad grew up in rural Kentucky towns and finished eighth grade, which was the end of formal schooling by the Common Schools of Kentucky. This was the equivalent to the general knowledge base of a high school education today. My dad owned a hauling business and worked as a chauffeur to support the family. My mom finished school at the top of her class and had

Talbott Family Photo Collection

dreams of attending Kentucky Normal School; however, those dreams were not realized when her father reneged on his promise to help her attend college.

I remember all of my school teachers from elementary at Phyllis Wheatley through high school at Central. One of my favorites is Ms. Harriett Porter Baker, my kindergarten teacher. She was focused on making sure that each of us was prepared for first grade. She was energetic, creative, and very kind. Anna Pittman Swan, my first-grade teacher, was a world traveler. She told us about places she had visited all around the world. I could not have imagined that I would grow up and get to visit some of the places that she talked about. I was excited about being in her class and felt the pressure to be a good student since she had taught some of my siblings.

Mr. Dunbar Hannibal was my sixth-grade teacher and my first male teacher. He had his own style and own way of encouraging. I was chairman of a reading group in his class, an honor because of my academic knowledge and ability. I remember one of his sayings, "Some of you are going to take a college course and some of you are going to take a cottage course," meaning some of us were going to college and others were going to be homemakers.

Most of our teachers were knowledgeable and caring and had the best interests of their students at heart. Because of segregated housing patterns, all of our teachers lived in the neighborhood. Sometimes they would walk home with us and come to our door to speak with our parents if there were issues or concerns. I remember one of my brother's teachers walking behind him all the way to the front door where she knocked and spoke to Mom about his behavior that day. We revered and respected teachers and classroom disruptions were unacceptable by teachers and parents.

I loved reading, spelling, and social studies. After a time, my classmates expected "the two Emma's" to be the finalists in the Spelling B contests. The other Emma in my class won more than I did. Recitation was an important part of our curriculum. We learned poems, songs, and passages from historical documents. I was asked to recite the "Gettysburg Address" from memory before the entire school during Negro History Week. Although I was quite nervous, I was honored that I had been selected. I also took piano lessons from Emma L. Minnis from Grade Four until graduation from Central High. I liked to sing and always looked forward to learning new songs in elementary school, as well as high school where I was a part of a select girls' singing group named The DeNalls. Ms. Carpenter, the music supervisor, made teachers a little nervous when she visited because she expected students to perform with precision. When we went to Making Music Concerts, we were not allowed to sit down front at the Armory Building at Sixth and Walnut streets (Now Muhammad Ali Boulevard). We sat in the back in the corner and watched white students talk, play, and be disruptive. We knew better than to "act out" because misbehaving was not tolerated.

I attended DuValle Junior High School the first year that it opened. A year earlier, my sixth-grade teacher told us about the Supreme Court decision to desegregate schools, so after one year at DuValle, the school district reworked the boundaries and many of us in the California neighborhood were assigned to Manly Junior High School. My time at Manly was a very unhappy experience. Most of the white teachers did not want to teach Black students, and the majority of the white students did not want us in "their" school. Overall, we were unwanted, unwelcomed, and not graded fairly by many of the teachers, with the exception of two English teachers and maybe two others. A different culture existed at the school as well. I remember more than one parent coming to school signing for their daughters to get married at the young age of 14-years old. This was unheard of in the Black community where most of us were not allowed to date until we turned sixteen.

I chose to go to Central High School although I could have attended other high schools. I fell in love with Central when I was four years old and one of my sisters carried me to school with her on several occasions. Many of my friends chose to go to Male High and they still remember the poor treatment they received. Many of them harbor negative feelings toward Male and duPont Manual to this very day. It was also during my high school years that the Civil Rights Movement came to Louisville. Black leaders recruited us to participate in the sit-ins to push for open accommodations. I was very much involved in this struggle and looked forward to the daily demonstrations on Fourth Street.

Dad died when I was 11 years old and we struggled to survive economically. When I started tenth grade, Mom moved us to Beecher Terrace Housing Projects, where I could actually walk to Central at Twelfth and Chestnut streets. Even though the projects were different then because the residents respected the property and each other, it was still the projects, a government-subsidized housing project for poor people.

My focus was getting some skills, graduating, and getting a job to move my mother out of the projects. I loved going to school and had perfect attendance for three years, although I was not recognized in the yearbook. I took commercial classes—bookkeeping, shorthand, typing—so that I could get a job as a secretary or in a law office because I thought I wasn't going to college even though I was in the National Honor Society. Mrs. Frazier, who taught shorthand, was one of my favorite teachers at Central. Mrs. Cecilia Horton, Mrs. Thelma Tilford, and Mrs. Mildred Griffin also were excellent teachers, and I have fond memories of them.

I wanted to go to Tennessee State, study, and party, but I had no funds to go there. A small scholarship to Kentucky State College was one of my life's blessings. With the Work-Study Program, student loans, and a small scholarship, *I was able to go to college, a dream come true!* In the fall 1961, I enrolled as a business administration major. I worked in the bookstore where my earnings were paid toward my school bill. It was a struggle. There were no extras. Mom sent a few dollars now and then when she could. In my second year, I switched majors because I did not like the business curriculum, and the job opportunities for business majors were limited. My alternatives for a major were music or elementary education. I chose elementary education. Working in the summer and taking additional courses, I was able to complete all coursework for elementary education, except student teaching, in three years. In the fall of 1964, I began my senior year doing student teaching at Stephen Foster Elementary School under the supervision of Mrs. Carrie Evans in fourth grade. This was a premier placement and I learned so much.

The old Louisville School System was desperate for teachers, and after a year at Virginia Avenue Elementary School teaching second grade, I transferred to my second teaching assignment. I did not like the work atmosphere at Virginia Avenue and threatened to leave the Louisville Public School System if I were not granted a transfer. I had a job offer in hand for a teaching position in Indianapolis, Indiana. Believe it or not, I asked for and was assigned to Stephen Foster to teach in the very same classroom where I had done my student teaching. Ms. Evans was promoted to a position in Central Office. I was in heaven teaching fourth grade at Foster from 1966 to 1969. Fourth grade is my favorite grade to teach because students learn new concepts. Students spend the first three grades of school learning to read and when they transition to fourth grade, they use those skills of reading to learn subject matter. They are a bit more mature and can understand a little humor, not like the blank stares of third graders.

Question: "Do you think you are capable of teaching white children?"
Answer: "I can teach all children."

When I returned from maternity leave, I was assigned to fifth grade at Clark Elementary School, just off Frankfort Ave. The administrator in charge of teacher placements questioned whether I was "capable of teaching white children." Three Black teachers at the school helped integrate the faculty. My students were hard workers and we had a great class. I know that my students went home and talked about the things that we were doing in class. Most of the parents assumed I was "White" and looked visibly shocked when they came to school and realized that I was Black. Kids did not care and were not thinking about race. They were thinking about the fun things that we were doing.

Over several years, I earned a master's degree at Indiana University, Bloomington, Indiana. I continued my studies at University of Kentucky, Western Kentucky University, and University of Louisville. After attaining the Louisville School system's Rank I status, I continued my studies and earned an additional 64 semester hours acquiring certifications as an Elementary School Administrator, Supervisor of Instruction, and Reading Specialist. I taught at Gavin Cochran, Phyllis Wheatley, Laukhuf, and Goldsmith elementary schools, as well as Myers Middle School as a regular elementary teacher, a reading specialist and as a middle school language arts teacher. During my nine years as Reading Specialist, I supported the work of classroom teachers, creating a model reading center where other new reading teachers shadowed me to learn how to design and implement effective reading centers at their schools.

One of the positions that I wanted was Curriculum Coordinator, but in order to attain this positon, I needed to transfer to a middle school. However, as soon as I transferred to middle school, the Curriculum Coordinator positions were phased out. I stayed with middle school because I liked working with that age group, and teaching language arts for Grades 6 and 7.

In 1992 after 27years of service, I retired without celebration. I chose not to tell anyone of my decision because I felt this would not be a "full retirement" but only a pause in the road while I decided what I would do next. As I continued my journey, two of my goals were to write a book on raising children and to find a way to speak truth to power.

One thing is certain: You do not stop being an educator because you retire from everyday classroom teaching. JCPS Alternative Certification in Elementary and Secondary, ACES Program, gave me an opportunity to help adult teacher candidates learn teaching skills as well as elementary content to pass the PRAXIS examinations. I tried to give candidates insights into classroom management as well as what good teachers do to engage parents, work with all students, and push students toward higher expectations. I helped the ACES students develop effective strategies for teaching reading and language arts.

Over the years, I have served as an adjunct professor at several universities, including University of Louisville, Spalding University, and Clark-Atlanta University. It has been gratifying watching many of the university students excel as classroom teachers. Quite a few have become school administrators, and several have continued their studies and received their terminal degrees.

Because I love expressing and sharing ideas, I became a *Courier-Journal* Forum Fellow. When I applied, I had no idea that I would be selected. My interest in all things political was driven by my parents who always talked about the issues of the day and never missed voting. I spent a two-week internship sitting in Editorial Board meetings, listening and interacting with the editorial writers. I then began penning opinion editorials for *The Courier-Journal*. I had much that I wanted to say. Editorials by and about Black people and Black issues had always been limited. The history of the newspaper revealed a pattern of writing many negative and disparaging stories about Black people. Though *The Courier-Journal* was improving in its outlook toward Black people, I wanted to have a voice in addressing African-American concerns and concerns of other citizens as well. My goal has been to make a difference, to be a voice for the voiceless, and to fight injustice with my pen.

My husband Cecil and I have also tried to make a difference by assisting African-American students who want a post-secondary education. We established the David C. and Emma Wilson Miles McElvaney Memorial Scholarship through the Community Foundation of Louisville. Funded solely by contributions from our family, the scholarship fund has awarded many scholarships since May 2006. The first scholarships were awarded through The Lincoln Foundation. After a few years and in order to reach a broader base of young people, the scholarship fund was transferred to The Community Foundation of Louisville. The Talbotts have invested more than $100,000 into the scholarship fund.

There is no simple answer as to how to improve the education of poor/Black children in today's society. In many instances, parents do not know what their role as parents should be. They see their job as providing food, clothing, and shelter but do not ask the question, "What else do I need to do for my child?" They leave it up to the schools. School efforts may be a good thing, but we lose so much when children are not reaching their potential. We know that schools have an unequal distribution of resources and there has never been an equal playing ground. As a nation, we need to do things differently to train teachers to be great educators who inspire and help students dream often bigger than they think they can. We must level the playing field to help all children reach their potential, giving more credence to the gray matter in their heads instead of the color of their skin.

Emma considers her parents and other ancestors who've gone before as her foundation and credits them with any success she has had. As a first-generation college graduate, she feels indebted to the many strong, competent, and caring Black teachers who laid a solid educational foundation for her. After publishing her first book, The Joy and Challenge of Raising African American Children, she has continued her pursuit of writing by working as the Parenting Editor for Family Digest Magazine and Family Digest Baby Magazine (Danville, California) for seven years. She has authored a second book of historical fiction, yet to be published. In 2018, her essay was included in an anthology of writings by women of color, All the Women in My Family Sing, by Nothing But The Truth Publishing. Henry Louis Gates, Jr., writes that this book is "essential reading." Emma has received several awards, such as JCTA Schoolhouse Award, The Links Service to Youth Award, Chestnut Street Family YMCA Volunteer of the Year Award, awards from Omega Psi Phi Fraternity and Delta Sigma Theta Sorority. She feels deeply honored to have been a 2018 inductee into the Central High School Distinguished Alumni Hall of Fame. She and her husband Cecil have been married for more than fifty years. They have two sons, Cecil Jr. (Chip) and Chad, both college graduates. She attends Brown Memorial CME Church.

Gail Jeanette Taylor

Teacher, Director of Pepsi Generation Singers,
and District Administrator for Options
and Magnet Programs

I WAS BORN IN LOUISVILLE, KENTUCKY, the third from the youngest of eight children, three girls and five boys. My dad, Jessie Taylor, was the first Black homicide detective in the South. Dad's first ambition was to be a fireman, but he was turned down because he was too short. My dad became a policeman in the Louisville City Police Department. Even though the department was integrated, dad's partners were all Black, so there still was segregation within the force. My mom, Jeanette, worked with pastries and salads at

Taylor Family Photo Collection

Howard Johnson's Restaurant. Because of segregation, she entered a door marked "Colored" to go to the rest room even though she entered the same back door with white employees to go to work side-by-side.

Dad was known in the community and was powerful in the corrections arena. He was particular and precise about law enforcement. He told us the story about trying to clean up Walnut Street, the Black community's center of night life, entertainment, gambling, and shady "good times." Because he was stepping on the wrong toes of the money makers and they complained, his duty was changed. He was transferred to patrolling Chickasaw Park for a short period of time.

The principal at Central High School loved Dad who had attended Lincoln Institute and whose family taught in the old Louisville school system. When Dad was on patrol and saw students cutting class, walking the neighborhood, or sitting at Pages, a local soda shop, Dad put them in the squad car and escorted them back to school, sometimes taking the long way around so that he could lecture them about not wanting to be in the back seat of a police car "for real."

After living with my grandparents at Thirteenth and Jefferson streets for several years, we moved. For five years, we lived in Cotter Homes or "the Projects." Our Projects housed families where both parents worked and strived to get ahead. They were relatively new, clean, and free from paper and litter; the grass was cut and the parents of children who lived there had high expectations for them. The children were not disrespectful and any adult sitting on the porch could correct anyone else's child without fear of the parent getting angry or cursing them out. The Projects were not your forever home. They were a step up while parents saved money to buy that house and move their families to another step-up.

While we lived in Cotter Homes when I was in kindergarten, I was bused to the old Dunbar School while a new school was being built to serve the children in the area. My favorite elementary teacher was Gladys Carter. She had personality and loved children. She was caring but she had structure. She would show students, "This is where we want you." She would raise her arm, "I want you here." Ms. Carter became ill and the class was assigned a substitute who was a nightmare. I went home crying and traumatized. My parents had me moved to another class until Ms. Carter returned. We later found out that the substitute teacher's daughter was dying and that may have explained her behavior.

I really got the "three Ds" in school, everything that I did or said was placed under a magnifying glass. Also, some Black teachers were not always kind. Dad's job as a policeman caused issues for us. When we moved from Cotter Homes to a house, I transferred to Carter Elementary. I had a teacher whose nephew had been locked up by my father. Not a good situation! I transferred back to Cotter. Dad sometimes brought home gangsters who had fled back to Louisville. He worked on some tough cases, including working on the Alberta Jones unsolved death mystery. However, he always made time for us. He always attended our programs, took us to the programs when our siblings were performing, and took the neighborhood kids under his wing as well. If the children were running late for school, he would put them in his police car and take them to school. And, if the young men were shooting dice in the alley and saw his cruiser coming, they would leave money and dice, running because, "Here comes Jessie Taylor."

I began playing the piano by listening to my grandmother play by ear. My parents realized that I had a talent and a love for music. Emma Minnis, my cousin, would ride the bus to our house to give me piano lessons, and Dad drove me to Smoketown for lessons from Mary Elisa Smith who taught piano at Grace Presbyterian Center. I was the only "chick" into music. In fourth grade while in elementary school, I began playing for any of the school programs that needed a piano assist. In sixth grade, I had my first white piano instructor at Shackleton's Music Store where my Aunt Evelyn took me every Saturday to work with top music students.

When I attended DuValle Junior High School in Grades 7 through 9, I accompanied all choir performances for all programs under the direction of Mary Elisa Smith, my former piano instructor. To this day, I remember her for always being dressed professionally, for her skills and talents, and for the unbelievable sounds that she would get out of her junior high students. By far, she was an inspiration that helped shape me and my teaching.

When I attended Central High School in the tenth grade, Patsy Ford was the senior organist and pianist under Ms. Alice Holden, and I was the assistant pianist. When Patsy graduated, Ms. Holden needed someone who could step into her spot. My parents, impressed with my musical talents and determined to develop those talents, had purchased from Shackleton's an organ that transferred from piano to organ for $1,700. Its cost was more than the cost of a brand new car. They paid for the piano-organ for many years, and I kept it for well over fifty years until it was damaged when my home was flooded. Having played that piano-organ not only allowed me to step in as the senior organist, but also solidified my next step as a music major at Kentucky State College.

My life was built around music. I played for community functions as well as my church family. When I was eight years old, my church bought a piano just for me to be able to play in church for the Buds of Promise children's choir, the Youth Choir, the Gospel Chorus, and the Senior Choir. While I also played an old pipe organ on occasion, my aunts had me playing for all kinds of venues, community events at my grandmother's nursing home, and at any event that the teachers who lived around me called me to do, including weddings and funerals.

I auditioned and received a partial scholarship in music from Kentucky State College. However, when I began this journey, my focus was on becoming a concert pianist. It was my music teacher, trained at Oberlin College, who steered me toward music education, with the constant reminder that having talent was only one part of the equation, but "the right person has to give you a break." As I took different courses in music education, I learned so much about music and how to extract those "sounds" from students while travelling with the Concert Choir and Dr. Carl Smith, director for four years.

After completing student teaching, split between Central High (A.M.) and DuValle Junior High (P.M.), I met John Whiting, one of my former high school teachers, now principal, while shopping in Kroger. He hired me to teach music at DuValle Junior High School, effective November 1, 1970. Totally different because of the Focus-Impact Program, Mr. Whiting, wearing a dashiki, told me that "he wouldn't answer if I didn't call him John." From "Sensitivity Training" forward, my teaching career took off in a whirlwind with my trying to meet expectations for music instruction, meet the needs of my students, and do the "right thing" for both.

Day 1 story—Gayle Ecton, assistant principal, contacted the music supervisor to give me procedures and to demonstrate how to get students up and motivated, singing. She directed the students to sing a song, "Home on the Ranch." A student sitting next to me says, Ms. Taylor, who is that red-headed B____? The supervisor begins crying while the students laugh and carry on. I get up and bring the class to order and begin directing. When my supervisor goes to report to Mr. Ecton, she says, "Ms. Taylor is going to be all right."

Teaching music called for me to use my creativity and my humor. For example, when students were not singing and I asked them what they wanted to do, they said play cards. I made eight decks of cards with music symbols and notes on the cards and created a card game. I told the students, "If you play and win, then you will be able to use the music books to sing and you will know the notes and symbols." They played to win. I also changed or enhanced the songs that students learned to sing. I added relevance to the traditional at Principal Whiting's suggestion. I taught my students to sing "To Be Young Gifted and Black," and other nontraditional songs so they could go out and sing with others in their community. Some of these were popular songs of the day and some were spirituals.

I never had to spank a child or discipline a child in a harsh manor. I always hugged them and spoke kindly to them. They knew I was their friend, but I was their teacher as well. When a child said, "Ms. Taylor, can I talk to you?" I stopped working at the piano and listened. Once, I had an eighth grader who stole money from a restaurant. He robbed a store at gun point and told me. I called my father; then I told the principal. Dad got the money and the child to Children's Center. I went to court with the child and kept in touch for years. He never got in trouble again.

I was afraid of teaching high school, but I went with Mr. Whiting to Shawnee High. Again, I taught songs that were meaningful and current. I established a gospel chorus and a choir at Shawnee. We visited other schools, competed in District festivals, and participated in community festivals.

Year 2 Story: One day during practice while singing, "Reach Out and Touch" and "On a Clear Day," a female student began crying. I walked her outside and asked what was wrong. She indicated that she was having back pain. When we went down to the nurse, the nurse discovered welts on her back. I called my dad. We later discovered that the student had been sexually assaulted and beaten by her father since eighth grade. In the end, a teacher took the student in when her father was sent to jail. That student graduated from Western Kentucky University and is doing well.

The boys in Shawnee's Choral Music class were "big boys"—tall, hefty football player types. I told my students on Day 1 that "My hands are registered" and that "I have the black belt." I demonstrated how and where they were supposed to stand if they were coming to my desk—stand in front, not on the side or behind me. I had a male student who kept telling me that he wanted to marry me. I told him no thanks, I did not want to marry. The story goes that this student was having some mental issues. He asked his parents if he could use the car and they said no. He got angry, killed both parents and borrowed the car. He came to school every day and came to class, smiling, still wanting to marry me. When a family member had not heard from his relatives, he went to their house and discovered their bodies. The police picked up the student who was riding around in the car without a care in the world. I just hoped that he hadn't told the police to go find his fiancé, Ms. Taylor. (By the way, I was on jury duty sometime later and who should appear, but my student from Shawnee? I asked the judge to be excused from that case before he had a chance to see me sitting there. The judge granted my request before the student had a chance to say, "Oh, there's my wife.")

During Year 3, I am playing the piano and the students are singing when I get a note, "Ms. T., I think my baby is coming." I get up, leave class, and escort the girl to the nurse in a hurry since the girl is about to have a baby in my classroom. When the ambulance arrives, the student insisted, "I want Ms. Taylor to go." Ms. Taylor said, "No!"

One of my most heartbreaking stories happened during Year 4 to one of my chorus students who also played football and was bound for Tennessee State College upon graduation. The young man went to Kentucky State College for homecoming activities. As the story goes, someone put LSD in his drink. Although his mind never fully came back, the Shawnee faculty was determined to get him graduated. The teachers at Shawnee pulled together and worked as a family. He made it. He graduated.

I learned by letter that I was being bused to Doss High School at the beginning of the 1975-76 school year when busing began. I was still building confidence and had some fear of teaching in the newly integrated setting. My Aunt Madeline and Frances Saunders took me to visit Doss. Principal Pittinger gave me a tour of the beautiful building and the music suite. When school opened, there were soldiers and guns everywhere and everyone feared that the students, Black or white, would not get on the bus to travel.

The school environments were also different. While I had to sign in and out at Shawnee, there was no sign-in at Doss. "We know that you are here or your sub is here," is what I was told. Furthermore, once keys were issued, they were not returned until the end of the year, rather than leaving them on the peg each afternoon. To my surprise, there were no Black students in any of my music classes. Class officers checked roll and students lead the warm-ups and devotional. My extracurricular assignment included an eight-student barbershop quartet that I was not prepared to teach, as well as a group of RC Singers that sang in Kroger and at the RC factory. I was unfamiliar with the groups and their songs. I was also given an edict from the principal to "get some Black students into the music classes," including band because I was Chair of the Music Department. Another difference was that in the old Louisville school system, students used band instruments and were not charged. Cheerleaders received uniforms and were not charged. However, under the Jefferson County system, cheerleaders paid $300 for camp and outfits and students rented or bought their own instruments. So, for the Music Department, recruitment of a diverse group of students to be infused into all of the groups, choirs, band, etc., the identified mission was hampered by additional dollars that participants would have to pay and possibly could not afford.

Building an integrated program was not easy, especially when there were other dynamics occurring that we did not know about. First, the band director and I were assigned part of the day to middle schools because there were not enough teachers for some of the student populations at the middle school level. Next, our groups only performed on limited occasions and were not recognized throughout their own community or outside of their community. Thirdly, there were issues with sponsorship being handled by the principal that were unknown to us, so as we recruited for RC Singers, later, the RC contract was voided.

Our plan was simple: get out, get known, and get diverse numbers. I began by not changing the initial group but adding students and going different places to perform. I took the choral music group to the middle schools who would be sending students to Doss. We gave counselors information about opportunities to participate in musical events and activities. We had students on display, performing every chance that we could get, at school and in the community, with the students putting on a good show. The payoff was in growing numbers, diverse participants, name recognition, and a new sponsor, the Pepsi Cola General Bottlers (PCGB) supporting a new group of student performers, the Doss High School Pepsi Generation Singers (PGS).

PGS was officially formed in 1978 as a 40-member vocal group. I believe that every school should use the talents of its students. We did not have to be a performing arts school to perform and do it well. However, the rule was that you had to be in choral music class or the Instrumental Music program to audition for PGS. I built the program looking at the individual child and received universal support from the Board and the school's administration and staff as well as the community. When children auditioned, I always asked myself, "Why does this child need the group?" They were not always the best singers to begin with, and a parent would sometimes complain that students were moving their mouths and not singing, which was true. However, I would tell my students at times that, "The group needs you and how you carry yourself; I want others to see that." This built their confidence and eventually they could sing with the group.

Over our twelve years of existence, from special education students to the school's valedictorian were members of the Pepsi Generation Singers. We sang on Fourth Street, in hotels, and as half-time entertainment for various University of Louisville sporting events. PCGB established an annual Christmas performance on WAVE television. One of our Christmas shows was "Christmas in the Air" performed on the 25th Floor of the Humana Building. Another Christmas show highlighted the City of Louisville Airport in the

"I'll Be Home for Christmas," performance. We participated in Tree Lighting ceremonies in Downtown Louisville, in the Kentucky Derby Festival Parade, and in the "Christmas Around the World Festival" in Chicago sponsored by the Chicago Museum of Science and Industry.

I was blessed to have Principal Stan Whitaker who gave me full support for the music program at Doss. I love the fact that my students learned music and were successful as singers, but I also love the fact that they learned discipline, self-confidence, poise, and self-esteem in addition to the social skills that they will need to be successful in life after high school. Pepsi Singers gave students an opportunity to participate and grow regardless of color, parental involvement, finances, or lack of finances. It was about the students. However, in looking at issues surrounding the education of black and poor children today, I believe parents and family members who love their children and give understanding and discipline so that the child can be a successful student are vital. Care for the child has to start at home. Another consideration—the school's culture has to show caring about the students' wellbeing, never treating the student as an outsider.

It is hard to tell someone to love somebody, but if you are a teacher or want to become a teacher, you must care about children, be able and willing to share your knowledge, and sometimes your dollars; you have to want to take students to levels that they did not know they could achieve; encourage them; understand them; and respect them.

In 2016, my former principal, Stan Whitaker organized the Pepsi Generation Singers' Reunion. Nearly fifty students returned to Louisville from all across the country to join in the celebration. There were doctors, sheriffs, lawyers, housewives, judges, prosecuting attorneys, teachers, policemen, firemen, mechanics, and ministers among the group. The students performed one of my favorite songs, "Let There Be Peace," and talked about their experiences "during their Pepsi Years with Ms. Taylor." I listened as my now adult students talked about how students know good teachers—they want to be there and they care about their students. They also talked about how good teachers instill a confidence level where students feel that they can conquer whatever comes about. I am proud that my students honored me as one of those good teachers.

Gail Taylor served 42 years with the Jefferson County Public Schools, 21 teaching and 21 as an administrator in the District's Options and Magnets Program where her primary focus was assuring that schools followed policies for selecting students and monitoring protocols for exiting students. She retired in 2013. She is a volunteer at several senior citizen nursing homes and volunteers as a music consultant for music programs throughout the City of Louisville.

Guy Wesley Wigginton, Jr.

Elementary Teacher and Assistant Principal, Federal
Reading Program Coordinator, Elementary Principal,
Elementary Executive Director, District Ombudsman,
and Elementary Principal Liaison

I AM AN ONLY CHILD, BORN AND bred in Louisville, Kentucky's West End. School for me began in the first grade when I was four years old because of my mom's insistence after teaching me to read, count, and color. My dad was a postal worker while Mom was a homemaker. Both parents were graduates of Central High School, and we attended Plymouth Congregational Church with lots of teachers and leaders in the Black community. It is reported that my dad was a great tennis player; however, he never taught me the sport, but his friends did.

Wigginton Family Photo Collection

Virginia Avenue Elementary School with principal Clyde Liggin was my home for elementary grades. Ms. Payne, my favorite teacher, taught me in first grade. She was always calm—nothing seemed to upset her. She always held everyone's attention. By the way, she was also a member of my church. My fifth- and sixth-grade teacher, Ms. McGruder, was dynamic! She had her fingers on the pulse of every student in that classroom, including me. She was sure of herself, had gorgeous handwriting like calligraphy, and paid attention to those of us who did not want to pay attention. My mom was always in "cahoots" with my teachers. Ms. McGruder, like Mom, always tried to keep me under tight control.

My age was always an issue in my mind. I was always in the top group or "Bluebirds," but I wanted to be in a group with more boys since this group was always full of girls, but I had no choice. There were other things that I would rather do than read books and study, but again, I had no choice. Mom was also the encourager and asked my teachers to do likewise. She knew that I was uncomfortable about my age, although the other kids really did not know how old I was. It was not until fifth and sixth grade that I began to like school "a little bit" because of the extra things that you got to do in Ms. McGruder's class.

I loved Madison Junior High School. We changed classes, could actually talk in the hallways between classes, and had kids from everywhere instead of the same students that you had gone to school and played with all of your life. We also had new and different recognitions for success, like the "Triple Honor Roll": *Academics*, A or B in all classes; *Conduct*, A or B in all classes; and *Perfect Attendance*. I loved English and math and made the Triple Honor Roll several times, but my conduct grades were not always acceptable. I was talkative, playful, and somewhat socially immature. Mom would say, "Guy Wesley, I don't know what I'm going to do with you. You act so strange at times."

The new DuValle Junior High School opened for my ninth-grade year, and I was sent to DuValle because of where I lived. The beautiful new school was a total disappointment for me. The friendly, easygoing atmosphere of Madison was not present at DuValle. I spent lots of time in the counselor's office because I could not relate to some of the teachers, even though most of the teachers tried to relate to me. Mr. Robinson, the counselor, helped me get through the year. It helped that I liked gym; my gym teacher, Mr. Lewis, was one of my favorites. Ms. Baker, my English teacher, was perplexed by my B-C grades, but high test scores. She worked with me after school to help me get my grades up.

Children in my neighborhood were assigned to Shawnee for high school during the first year of school integration. Shawnee was all-white at the time. My mother was not having it. Mom went to the Board of Education to have me transferred to Central High School. Her argument was that we had a family legacy of attending Central and that was where she wanted me to go. She won her argument. I enrolled in Central after the school year had begun and was assigned to Home Room Class 4. At that time, students at Central were highly "tracked." The smartest, college-bound students were in 10-1 through 10-5. As the end number got higher, students were classified as general academic or more skill-focused, that is, focused on cosmetology, business and typing, tailoring, woodworking or auto mechanics, etc., but not college-bound. Because of my delayed enrollment, I was assigned to 10-4, Ms. Lucille Madry's homeroom and period one English class. It did not take Ms. Madry long to say, "You do not belong in this class." As a result, my schedule was changed. I stayed in Ms. Madry's homeroom, but was farmed out between the 10-2 and 10-3 class schedules.

I liked high school, especially the tenth and twelfth grades. I either walked to school from Thirty-six and Greenwood streets or caught the city bus, often with another student who would become world famous. Sometimes I thumbed rides, but I did make it to school. I knew many of my classmates and I had a cousin who attended Central as well. I made decent grades and overall was in the top third of my class. Ms. Madry, who remained my English teacher at a different period, called me a "wild weed" because I generally acted as if I didn't care or laid back as if I didn't know. She was demanding and required the class to do a variety of readings. I liked Ms. Madry and I always came prepared for English class, acting as if I weren't listening or simply "playing dumb." Ms. Madry wanted us to understand sentence structure. When she was frustrated with other students who just didn't get it, she would call on me and I would go to the board, diagram the sentence, and get it right.

Although Atwood Wilson was principal at Central, Maude Brown-Porter was the disciplinarian, and I saw her on more than one occasion.

During my junior year when I was assigned to library or study hall, I ducked out. I spent my time in the auto shop or downstairs in tailoring class. I was reported for cutting class several times and had to see Ms. Porter. She really wasn't hard on me. I reported after school and wrote essays on subjects of her choosing. By the time I left her office, all of the kids were gone and I would be at the bus stop alone.

During my senior year, I developed another interest and it was not at Central where I spent homeroom to Period 4 and disappeared during periods 5 and 6, later showing up at Shawnee High School. Sometimes I actually sat in on classes at Shawnee, the teacher knowing that I was not in her class. I participated with the other students who also knew that I did not belong there. They never said a word.

Attending college was never a question. The issues were where I was going and what I was going to be when I grew up. Honestly, I really did not care as long as I got away from Louisville and did not go to Kentucky State College where my parents wanted me to attend. Dad wanted me to pursue a medical career and Mom pushed toward something in music since I had music lessons early on and played the E-flat Alto Saxophone. It so happened that Mom and Dad knew the Kean family, Henry Arthur, Willie Lee, and Sister Kean who had ties to Tennessee State College. When I graduated in 1960, I enrolled at Tennessee State with a partial band and work-aid scholarship. The band members reported early when the football players reported and we worked on "practice makes perfect" throughout the summer.

The Marching 100 was the "aristocrat of bands" and the entire state of Tennessee knew that. When President John F. Kennedy was elected, there was an argument over which band would represent Tennessee in his inaugural parade. Some high school band, not of color, was selected over Tennessee State. We were disappointed, to say the least. I don't know what happened, but miraculously Tennessee State got an invitation to perform in the parade. We were dead last in line to perform. It was freezing cold and snowy, and we had been there most of the day. People began inviting us into their homes to warm up and gave us hot coffee and cocoa. When we were signaled to line up, we were ready. When we marched past the viewing stand, President Kennedy was still there. He saw us and we saluted him.

I left Tennessee State at the end of my sophomore year. It wasn't that my grades were bad; I just wasn't ready. I did not know what I wanted to do with my life or what I wanted to be. I bummed around for almost three years, taking on odd jobs and trying to clear my head. I knew that I did not want to be a doctor or do anything in the medical field. At the same time, I discovered that I wanted to help others. Finally, it came to me that I wanted to be a teacher, not just any teacher, but an elementary school teacher. My dad was truly disappointed. He was a licensed mortician and embalmer and tried to get me to move in that direction. I said, "No." Finally, Mom came around because she wanted me to finish school and do something worthwhile. Dad never got over my choosing teaching over medicine. However, he did end up being very proud of his only son.

There were six males in the Elementary Education Program at Kentucky State where I enrolled. We did the heavy lifting, moving boxes, books, and materials. We worked on all of the extracurricular activities like setting up for parades, dances, and campus speakers. We also decorated floats for parades, all part of our work/study program. The professors in our Elementary Education Program were strict and demanding, and each wanted it his or her way which actually turned out to be positive. We had to learn creativity, flexibility, and structure and when, how, or if to apply them to which system. I had favorite teachers like Ms. Simpson, Ms. Regal, and Rev. Sampson who each had his or her own formal systems for doing things, systems that you did not change. It had to be done their way if you wanted to pass their classes.

When I returned to Louisville to student teach at John F. Kennedy Elementary School under principal Lena Watters, I was prepared and ready, almost "too sure." The negativity of my family spurred me on. I wanted to be successful. I was determined to be successful. When there was a problem with a group of sixth-grade boys, my supervising teacher, Ms. Davis, agreed to take the boys into her class for me to work with. These were Housing Project kids and the Projects had changed. Living there was tough, and poverty was the root of most of the problems that the children were encountering. I knew the brothers or sisters of three of the students that were reassigned. That helped. The other thing that helped me work with these students was reflecting on me. I wasn't poor, but I had been "bad" and I could have been worse. I became creative, looking for ways to pull these students into the mainstream. With the help of Anna Huddleston, an art teacher, I created fun projects that the students could work on, provided they did their other work. The students loved the art projects and stayed out of trouble. I began practicing some of what I had been taught and some of what I had internalized from my own behavior as a student.

My first job after graduation was a new teacher's dream job. I began teaching for the Louisville Independent System in 1966 at Shawnee Elementary School. My classroom had been set up for a premiere teacher who decided to retire about the same time that I completed my student teaching. Mrs. Rowland, principal, said, "You are going to be in a classroom where you are going to be successful." She was absolutely correct. My fifth-grade students, half of them white and half Black, were extremely bright, undoubtedly the smartest single group of students that I ever taught! One student from this class later became valedictorian at Shawnee High School and another became salutatorian. I only had two small problems that the District supervisor had to bring to my attention—how to complete the "Bird Book" that was the attendance record, and how to spruce up my classroom. I remained at Shawnee Elementary School for three years before volunteering to transfer to a Focus-Impact school. During those three years, I proved to myself and my parents that I would be successful as a teacher.

Dr. Newman Walker was the reason that I became interested in Focus-Impact. He sold me on what he wanted to do when I heard him speak, and again, I thought about myself as a student. I was assigned to Coleridge Taylor Elementary as Team Leader for Grades 5 and 6 under the great principal, Lillian Henderson. I had only three years of teaching experience. Ms. Henderson's mentorship was vital for my understanding of the program's philosophy. Still, I remained somewhat traditional. I had three interns to quit because I would not let the kids run wild and kept some structure. The idea of letting students investigate and have "free will" was a program standard, but I felt students were expected to learn and teachers were still expected to teach, and I had to create an environment that made that happen.

During two cycles or four years of Focus-Impact, I completed my master's degree and began on Rank I at the University of Louisville. My wife Marva was teaching in the reading program at Shawnee Elementary when I became assistant principal (AP) there under Forrest Turley. City elementary schools had to have a certain number of students to get an AP and there were no APs in elementary schools in the county.

In 1975 while serving as AP, I received a call from the Personnel Office to report the following Monday to Engelhard Elementary as interim principal. My first thoughts were "WOW," this is something good! That lasted until I pulled into the parking lot that Monday and walked into the building. There was a house of prostitution across the street, Hell's Angels headquarters down the street, parents fighting in the hallways, students with head lice, and racial problems in the building. When I could catch my breath, I found the one Black teacher that I knew who could help me understand the overall situation at the school. It was that teacher who told me point blank that I needed to get the all-white Hell's Angels under control. I said, "WHAT!"

On Day 2, I walked down the street to the Hell's Angels headquarters and knocked on the door; I did not get an answer. I knocked again. Finally, I saw someone peak through the window shade and heard them say, "Some N_____ out there knocking on the door." The door cracked and someone asked, "What do you want?" My response was, "I got a problem and I need your help." I was told to come on in.

When I entered, I said, "I'm the new principal down the street." I saw men and women sitting on the floor, and the "Boss" sitting in a chair at the table. To my surprise, the "Boss" was "Junie," who lived in the same neighborhood as I did as a child, at Thirty-six and Greenwood. He was as surprised to see me as I was to see him. After speaking with Junie in the "language of the streets," I told him that I needed the fighting to STOP! When I left the house, I let out a breath and went back to school. The next day when I arrived at Engelhard, there were two people sitting on the steps in front of school. From that day on, there were no fights, no arguments or parents screaming at each other in the halls and the teachers thought I had worked a miracle. Other teachers on staff helped me get everyone on board so that we could get the school on track. I remained at Engelhard for several months until the permanent principal's injuries were healed.

In the years that followed, I received several phone calls detailing my new assignments or telling me where to report next. I was called to Central Office at the Brown Hotel to be told about coordinating a new Elementary and Secondary Education Act (ESEA) program. I did not know what ESEA was, except that the program would have thirteen reading specialists, a three-million-dollar budget and a focus on improving reading. I managed the teachers in thirteen different schools, handling all problems before they escalated. I saw that the teachers got the materials and supplies that they needed and told them if they had problems to call me first. We identified students who needed extra help and those who were below grade level. We helped improve their grades and tested to measure their progress. I told my teachers if a kid needed help and was not in the program, they should help the child anyway. That extra effort kept principals happy and the program worked well.

My next call was about a job as elementary principal, a positon that I had had sights on for a long time. I was discouraged from taking the position because I would move from a 12-month employee to a nine-month position and would lose salary. Mr. Beams told me that, "I have to offer you the position, but I think you shouldn't take it." I wanted the job and took the position as principal of Kerrick Elementary School where I remained for nine years. I had a great core group of teachers and an influx of new teachers who were also really good. Our focus was teaching reading and each of my teachers had his/her own system. I attended "Effective Schools" workshops and appreciated the work of Earlene Minton and Madeline Hunter and began implementing their methods at Kerrick.

I believed my job was to combine the multiple systems so that we were all moving in the same direction. Teachers bought into the idea of a structured program, and I became the "Poster Boy" for the West Region, being asked to demonstrate live lessons for principals. My fellow principals originally were tense and not receptive. This made my teacher/co-presenter nervous. The teacher left the room and I did not realize it when I began the demonstration. I was giving my spill and turned around to an empty chair. I continued talking to the chair. The principals began to laugh when they realized what happened. That broke the ice and the presentation went well after the teacher returned. "Effective Schools" research became an important part of Jefferson County's overall approach for improving student academic achievement.

The other challenge at Kerrick that was important to me was the lack of Black students in the Advance Program (AP) at the school. Central Office administrators drafted requirements for admission to AP and were reluctant to change or amend requirements for placement in the program. As a result, AP participation was all-white at Kerrick. My teachers and I agreed that there were Black students who may not meet the cutoff score for the test, but were more than capable of doing the work. We agreed to put students in the program whose scores were one to five points below the cutoff score. This allowed us to recruit several Black students into the program. They were able to do the work and did well in the program. I did not make friends at Central Office for implementing this change, but I did inspire some of my students.

Our new superintendent, Don Ingwerson, brought a new system to the District, eliminating regions and creating executive directors at each level—elementary, middle school, and high school. I had no plans to apply, but I was called to the side at a West Region meeting and "told" to apply. I applied at the last minute with no references and was the last person to interview. I learned that I was to be one of three elementary executives at a principals meeting at the University of Louisville. I really hadn't explored the ins and outs of the job. Bottom line, we would be in schools listening and looking at problems that we were to solve. We needed a briefcase and the District was to provide us with a car. We were to keep our fingers on the pulse of each school that we were assigned, and it would be a real problem if issues made their way back to Central Office. I lasted longer than my two counterparts, moving to a new position after four years.

My next position was District Ombudsman, reporting to an assistant superintendent on paper and directly to the superintendent in reality. I was the "handler." The superintendent identified problems and I fixed them. I was in everybody's business and heard myself talking in my sleep, "Do not call the superintendent!"

I continued as problem solver, fixer, and supporter over my final years with the District as elementary principal liaison. Again, I dealt with issues and challenges, both internal and external. My reach affected administrators, teachers, parents, students, and sometimes the general community. I had to be a creative problem solver, make tough decisions, and sometimes establish the bottom line—this is how it's going to be, no discussion. Through any situation, I had to have a calm face and keep my finger on the pulse, something I learned from my elementary teachers. I also had to be conscious of what was best for the education of children in the District, knowing that individual situations sometimes conflicted with the big picture.

Deciding to become an elementary teacher instead of a doctor was the best decision that I made for myself. Of all of the positions that I held, teaching was actually my favorite. It was the most natural for me. Being principal was next. Having summers off to play tennis and travel were factors, but the main attraction of these two positions was the ability to work directly with kids. I could see, hear, and respond to the needs of kids every day and sometimes make a difference immediately. I could also work with other teachers to help them make a difference.

Today, as a seasoned educator in the community, I hear about the current challenges like the achievement gap and its impact on poor, Black kids, or discipline problems in schools. This is not new. We have always had students who needed academic support and those who were considered "tough" kids. However, ownership of the problem began at the top. Today's schools must have student-centered leadership whose mission is to tell the people on staff that "I want results" and work with them to provide the tools that they need to get the results that they want. Principals must establish clear goals and objectives with their staff and bring in the outside resources to help them if necessary. You cannot send the tough kids home. You must make it a priority to have someone get in there with them to get an understanding of their particular issues and challenges and find creative solutions with the kids, for the kids. Furthermore, school leaders must understand the politics of the profession. Teachers have union protection and school leaders must work within those guidelines, understanding that without teachers working with you, you will accomplish nothing.

There is a constant need for good teachers, but you hear lots of negative things about the teaching profession—low salaries, bad kids, no power. However, we must give a clearer picture of what teaching is really about. Good teaching begins with the mindset, "I want to make a difference," or "I want to help others." It is followed by dedication and understanding what the profession is really about, that is being honest about what teachers face day to day. It is supported by a university training program that provides real-life experience and a broad knowledge base for teaching skills that students need to be successful—sometimes basic skills, sometimes more advanced skills. It is complimented by training to assess individual student needs and practice using different strategies to address those needs. Good teaching culminates in an individual who faces the day-to-day challenges; does not give up on kids; understands that "bad" is not new, but seeks ways to turn bad into good; continuously strives to help all students be successful; and does not quit the profession because they know that they are needed to make a difference in some child's life. Some thought that I was a bad kid. I had good teachers at all levels who cared, even in the days of segregation and exclusion. Those teachers did not give up on me, like my junior high school counselor, Mr. Robinson, whom I met out of the blue on campus at Tennessee State. He called me by name; reached in his wallet and handed me a $10 bill; told me to keep it up; and said good luck. Teachers made a difference in my life. I was inspired to make a difference in another child's life.

Guy Wigginton has been married to another educator, Marva Wigginton, for more than fifty years. Since his retirement from JCPS in 2002, he says he has been "fully retired." Guy is an avid tennis player, a sport that he picked up in high school from the auto mechanics teacher, Arthur "Dribble-Drive" Johnson, whom he cut class to visit and later saw on the tennis courts at Chickasaw Park. He plays tennis two or three times a week, year round. Guy has received several awards and recognitions, including professional awards and tennis trophies that are "carefully packed away in a respectful manner." He says that he "would rather look to the future than to the past." He and Marva have two children and one grandchild that Guy says is "so much like his daddy and me, that it is scary."

Dr. Daniel W. Withers

Math Teacher, Athletic Director,
Assistant Principal, and Principal

Dissertation Title: *A Study of At-Risk Youths Who
Attended Residential Education Programs*

ALTHOUGH BOTH OF MY PARENTS were from the Louisville, Kentucky area, I was born in Chicago, Illinois, the city that they fled to when they were prohibited from marrying in Kentucky in the 1940s because Mom was White and Dad was Black. When my parents later separated, my brother and I werc raised in Louisville by my father's sister, Aunt Mable Evans. We lived on Thirty-six Street between Virginia and Hale avenues with lots of teachers around us, but I do not remember being close to any of the ones in the community. However, I was close to

Withers Family Photo Collection

teachers at my elementary and junior high schools and an aunt who taught at the high school I attended.

I attended Virginia Avenue Elementary but was often absent and fell behind in first grade because I was infected with ringworms. I struggled with reading because of missing so many of the basics in first grade. However, it was my sixth-grade teacher, Ms. McQuinny, who helped me catch up. She went the extra step to find out what I was interested in and worked around my interests to help me improve my reading and comprehension. *Alexander the Great* was one of the books that we used because I loved history.

At DuValle Junior High School, my uncle was the plant operator, and those junior high years were rough. Older kids bullied the younger students and those who were quiet like me. I accelerated in math under Ms. Calhoun and Mrs. Martin. My favorite teacher was Mr. Lewis, the gym teacher. I didn't play sports, but I worked on body building and strength training. I had friends at DuValle, but those years were nothing outstanding.

At Central High School, my favorite subject was Algebra 1 taught by Mrs. Carroll who was my favorite teacher. She noticed that I did not often raise my hand or speak up, even though I had the correct answer on my paper. She encouraged me to speak out and talked to me to help build my confidence. I participated in track, was on the football team but was not an outstanding athlete. However, in tenth grade I was named Mr. Physical Fitness of Louisville, my work-outs and body building bringing me some recognition. Central High was a great place, like a big family. There was no more bullying. Teachers accepted you and students accepted you for who you were. I loved biology with Mr. Forbes and, of course, I liked all of my history teachers. I did not like English because I did not like writing, and again, I loved math!

Because we were poor, I really did not plan to go to college. As a senior, I hoped to attend United Electronics and had begun classes there after graduation. Then an opportunity for me to attend Allen University in South Carolina materialized. My Aunt Emma who lived in Philadelphia was somehow connected and arranged for me to participate in the Work-Study Program at Allen. In 1964, many people said that the best jobs for Black men were teaching, being a postal worker, or serving as a waiter. When I began at Allen, I was thinking that physical education would be a good major.

Later in my freshman year, teaching became more of a choice for a career. The college algebra course that I took was a repeat of my high school Algebra II course. I had the third highest score on the Math Placement Test, often fell asleep in algebra class but still did well and was encouraged by Dr. Marcos to major in math. I fell in love, worked in the cafeteria, played football, and switched my major to math with a minor in physical education. My plan was to later join the Teacher Corps to get certified.

I was drafted into the military in May 1968 right before completing my senior year and graduating. The one good thing that happened was the extension of my reporting date so that I could finish my coursework. The Vietnam War was in full throttle and I objected to the war. I attended Officer's Candidate School for a short period of time, but in good conscious could not lead a troop into battle in a war that I was philosophically against. I went to Vietnam in 1969 as an enlisted soldier in the Army, then received a month's early discharge in June 1970 because I had been accepted to graduate school. I attended Miami University in Ohio for about six months before dropping out. I had contracted malaria.

Married and trying to get my career on track, I worked with a sheet-metal company in Cincinnati, Ohio, while exploring ways to get teacher certification with a degree in math. I applied for jobs as a teacher in Louisville, but had to take two additional education courses. Finally, after completing the courses at University of Cincinnati, I was hired as a math teacher at Shawnee High School, beginning January 2, 1972, the beginning of my 44-year career as a professional educator.

With merger and desegregation taking place in Louisville, I was transferred from Shawnee to Pleasure Ridge Park High School in 1975 and remained there until I transferred back to Shawnee in 1980 where I was athletic director before becoming assistant principal in the 1982-83 school year. From 1983 to 1991 I was assistant principal (AP) at Fairdale High School, a time when I knew of only two black families who lived in the Fairdale community. The central focus of the community appeared to be the athletic programs. The "N" word was used frequently. I went to Fairdale because Hughlyn Wilson, administrator over the Personnel Department, insisted that Jefferson

County needed strong Black male representation in that community. Later, I became interim principal for one year at Iroquois High School. I was AP at Emerson Teen-Age Parent Program for one year before becoming AP at Central from 1993 to 2002 when I assumed responsibility as principal until I retired in 2015.

I cannot count the number of teachers that I have worked with or the number of classrooms where I have observed. I have seen all kinds of high school teachers, some great, some good, and others not so good. The best classrooms, however, where students are engaged and learning is taking place, are characterized by teachers having content knowledge and a passion for their content regardless of the area. It is evident that the teacher enjoys being with kids and is comfortable speaking with and reacting to their students. They are trying to make a difference, pushing students to give a little more or think more critically, which goes to expectations. They are organized and enjoy what they are doing. On the other hand, kids in those classrooms are respectful, receptive, and responsive or eager to learn and demonstrate their understanding of the subject at hand.

When I was a student, my teachers were the cream of the crop. We were a segregated system with highly educated Black teachers. We took pride in our school as students and our teachers took pride in us. Our teachers were professionals who dressed professionally and expected students to act respectfully. They were in education for the long-term. They took their jobs seriously. A change has occurred that says education is unimportant; teaching is not for the long-term; and teaching is just a job. When the systems were segregated, we had to hire Black teachers. With integration, we no longer had to hire Blacks. I think that was a problem. The percent of Black teachers should equal the percent of Black students. Granted, one reason it is difficult to get minority teachers is because there are more job opportunities for minorities than when I was young. Another reason it is difficult to get Black students interested in teaching today is because they do not see people teaching who look like them.

My teachers were motivators that I sometimes emulated. It was the little things—knowing the students, not only being friendly, but wanting them to be successful. Motivation includes being a disciplinarian and having contact with parents. Years ago, teachers sometimes did home visits. That is more difficult to do today, but relationship building is important. Students are more likely to listen to a teacher if they have a relationship with the teacher. Sometimes, that relationship was as an older brother, as a father figure or as a grandfather figure. That relationship also helped me to figure out ways to present information to students. I thought about my students when I did lesson plans so that I could get the content across. What I knew about them impacted the examples I used and the assignments I gave them. I used what they were interested in to help me teach the content.

One of my favorite teacher stories happened when I was a poor, first-year teacher. I dressed well even though my clothes were sometimes older. We were in class and I was going to the board when a student raised his hand and said, "Mr. Withers, where do you get your clothes cleaned?" I said, "Why do you want to know?" The kid said, "I just want to know so that I can get my pants shined like that." We laughed. The leisure suit had some age. My kids called me, "Dapper Dan, the Ice Cream Man." That was OK. We had a positive relationship and discipline was not an issue in my classroom. Those same students would do anything that I asked them to do and worked hard to learn what I was teaching them.

As an administrator, building relationships with the faculty is important. Knowing that you are a good teacher helps build respect. You must also demonstrate that as an academic leader, you know what is important. I was genuinely honest with my staff and communicated in terms so they knew what needed to be done to support the mission of the school. I was fair and friendly with staff and treated them with respect.

Administrators must build relations with teachers if they expect to establish and maintain academic progress for students. Teachers and administrators should have a clear understanding of the need for assessments to determine how well students are doing. Assessments are points of comparisons to help guide us, not to cast blame. I do believe that the ACT or SAT is the best assessment for comparisons. The problem that schools are facing today is so much emphasis on testing; teachers are focused on teaching to the test rather than emphasizing the chronological and sequential skills, the basics that students really need. When students do not do well on the tests, the blame game begins. That is not to say that all teachers are doing their best to assure that students are successful.

We must be intentional about who we place in classrooms. Education is the most important profession. Education is critical for students to be able to prosper and teachers must find ways to inspire children. Everyone cannot be an effective teacher, Black, White, or other; therefore, we must give sound, honest advice when a child says, "Dr. Withers, I think I want to be a teacher." I always talked about teaching as a great profession and what it had done for me. I give them things to think about—that they must identify content where they are strong and must enjoy working with that content. I also advise that they must make sure that they like children and the age range of students with whom they prefer. I also tell them that teachers go beyond the classroom. They step forward to help students with weaknesses caused by the environment. They deal with students from different communities and home situations. They may be role models or tutors because some students lack role models in their homes and communities and may need extra academic support. Teachers sometimes have to provide finances to support student needs, and they must always show students positive ways of doing things. I also tell them that the problems in education today are not Black vs. White, but socioeconomic—haves and have nots. I then say, "Think about it and go for it if teaching is your dream and you have the passion for it." I have had several of my students who have become teachers.

When you have been active in the profession as long as I have, thinking about what you could or should have done differently comes to mind from time to time. As a student, I think that I would have studied more in elementary and high school or I might have taken graduate courses earlier. As an administrator, I could have been more rigorous in my evaluation of teachers. I was probably more lenient because a person was a good teacher and I let them get by with other "stuff." However, the one thing that I have never questioned is my teaching. I realized early on that I had a real passion. I enjoyed figuring out ways to get information across to students. I know that I would still be an educator regardless of the other occupational choices available. It was my profession that kept my life together through personal trials and tribulations. I cannot see myself as any other professional than being an educator.

I was the only high school principal at a predominately Black school, and I thought that I would not be acceptable in high school as a principal. I wanted to be at a school where I could make a difference and Central High School was that place. Sometimes, I had to battle for things for my school that I would not have had to fight for if I were at other schools, like the swimming pool that it took ten years to repair so that we could open it or issues with the physical plant like the leaky roof that was continually patched and not replaced. However, overall, I have enjoyed being an educator. A part of my legacy is I did no harm to students. I helped and inspired kids to be whatever they wanted to be, and I modeled compassion for others.

Dr. Withers received his doctorate from Spalding University in 2000. After his retirement in 2015, he has continued working as a retired administrator for JCPS, sharing his skills and talents when called upon. He continues to travel throughout the world, including South Africa, Spain, Portugal, Hawaii, and Australia. He is a member of 100 Black Men of Louisville and the Ye Old Esquire Club. Dr. Withers has received numerous awards and recognitions throughout his career. In December 2016 the swimming pool area at Central High School was named "Dr. Daniel Withers Aquatic and Athletic Center" in his honor. He is most proud of being recognized as the Outstanding High School Principal of the Year – 2011. Dr. Withers has been a member of the First Virginia Avenue Missionary Baptist Church for more than fifty years. He has taught Sunday School in the past. At present, Dr. Withers drives the church bus for Sunday School and church services. He has been married to Valarie (Terrell) Withers for 31 years. Dr. Withers has five children and three grandchildren.

2

Reflections of Initiative

If, Only You Knew: Rita's Journey Continues

Initiative: The power or opportunity to act or take charge before others do; the ability to assess and initiate things independently; an act or strategy intended to resolve a difficulty or improve a situation; a fresh approach to solving your problem.[5]

DEALING WITH HARDSHIP, CHALLENGES, ISSUES, AND conflict was nothing new for me. When you are the child of a single parent who dropped out of high school, and when, at age four, your father dies in a court-declared accident, but neither you, your mother, or sister get one dime from his $10,000 insurance policy, you learn to deal with injustice and disappointment. You also learn to respect and cherish the person who makes sure that you never go hungry, you are never dirty, your clothes are always clean, your hair is always combed, and you always have a roof over your head. So, when my mother said, "Have you lost your mind?" I began to wonder if she might be on the right track. Had I lost my mind?

Making the decision to switch career focus from law to teacher education was a monumental task for me. Three days and three nights of torment had ensued after my substitute teaching experience with junior high school students who could not read. I tossed and turned and debated, over and over and over again. Lawyer-lawyer-lawyer. Teacher-teacher-teacher. I had fluctuated back and forth. I went to class in a stupor, blurry-eyed and hungover without drinking a drop of alcohol. I couldn't pay attention and do not remember anything that my favorite political science professor said. My normally bright eyes were red-rimmed with dark brown circles underneath. However, the most revealing indication of my unrest was my mouth. I didn't open it. I was quiet and never said a word, totally unusual for the girl with the gift of gab.

My stomach churned and I could not digest my food. At night, I tried to sleep or pretended to sleep so that I would not disturb my husband, Jim. I would slip out of bed and creep down the hall to our living room, taking up residence on the orange leather sofa that was rock solid and unforgiving, regardless of who sat or slept upon it. On the third night Jim found me there, hugging a pillow as silent tears streamed down my face while I hiccupped, unable to catch my breath. He sat beside me, but never hugged me. He looked down at his hands that he rubbed against his pajama-clad thighs. Finally, he looked up at me and said, "Do what you want to do. It's your call, your career." When I began to say something, he held up his hand as a stop signal; shook his head, no; then got up and walked back down the hall toward our bedroom.

It was my call and I had to make it. I also knew I would have to live with it. Jim would support the decision that I made, either way, lawyer or teacher. We had married after my first year at college and we had an understanding. He always said that he was neither a scholar nor a teacher, and I was smart enough for the both of us. My career was my career and he would be there for support, not direction. (And he has been for more than fifty years.)

My mother was the first person that I told of my final decision to change majors. Her reaction was somewhat expected and somewhat unexpected. You see, my mother was the youngest of five siblings whose parents were both deceased by the time Mama was nine years old. Raised mostly in Louisville by their Aunt Gee and Uncle Joe, she and her siblings attended Louisville City Schools, including the old S. Coleridge-Taylor Elementary, Madison Junior High, and Central High schools. They always told us stories about school and the outstanding teachers who taught them, Blyden Jackson, Mr. Tisdale, Ms. Matthews, Lyman Johnson, Ms. Holt, and Doc Whedbee to name a few. So, Mama and our entire family highly respected teachers and appreciated education because, "Education is something that no one can take away from you"—another idiom that we often heard.

Mama and her siblings, the three sisters in particular, also had plans for their children. My mom and my aunts were very close and they had children who were stair-stepped. The sisters observed, discussed, and sometimes issued edicts to their children. My sister, Olivia, is the oldest of the line of 22 first cousins, the children of the five siblings. I am number three. Based on family observations, evaluation of talents and skills, discussions, and close scrutiny, each of those 22 first cousins was assigned a career goal.

My sister was outstanding in mathematics, won a national math contest, and was steered toward teaching math. She is a math teacher, certified in Tennessee, Kentucky, and Indiana. Number 2 in line was cousin Bennie. He loved science, dissected animals, and was the family's go-to person when signs and symptoms of illnesses appeared. He always had some kind of medical book or magazine in front of him and could trace every system in the body by the time he was in eighth grade. He was designated to become a doctor. He is currently a licensed medical doctor in five states. Number 3 was "motor mouth," the one who could talk-talk-talk and could argue with a brick. I debated about anything and everything and could present a convincing argument on either side of a given issue. My teachers, Carrye Evans, John Miles, Jr., James Mosby, and Lyman Johnson made sure of that. I was slated to be the family lawyer and the first female with a doctorate. Part of this slate for the future was to be wiped clean if I chose teaching as a career.

I could continue on, one-by-one from here, but I will summarize career achievements of the 22. Of the first twelve cousins, ten of them successfully entered and maintained the professions identified for them by the sisters. Careers include chemist, nurse, engineer, secretary, teacher, military officer, and military enlisted person. Cousins 13 to 22 did not readily conform as the first group. Times, circumstances, as well as opportunities changed.

My mom was one of the smartest women that I know because of her breadth of general knowledge, her creativity, and her analytics. She was an avid reader and could cook most any dish. Mama kept abreast of current politics; she could recite poetry, explain the Amendments to the Constitution, and display handwriting that rivaled the best calligrapher's writings. She taught herself how to repair televisions and wrist watches. She also helped design and pilot one of the first insurance billing coding systems for the federal government. Even though Mama never graduated from high school, she retired as Director of Patient Accounts for Louisville's Park DuValle Neighborhood Health Center.

When I walked into Mama's living room that Thursday evening, I could hear my heart beating in my ears. My hands were sweaty and I had a strange taste in my mouth. Mom was standing in her bedroom when I stepped in the doorway and blurted out, "I want to be a teacher."

She turned, looked at me in a way that I knew indicated she was gritting her teeth, and said, "Have you lost your mind? You are supposed to be the first woman in the family with a doctorate. You're going to law school. What are you talking about, teaching? We already have a teacher in the family and it is not you!"

I was both crushed and torn, but not surprised. On the one hand, I was not living up to my family's expectations. On the other hand, my heart was no longer into going to law school. I really wanted to be a teacher. I had debated over and over again in my mind and had come to the same conclusion. There were so many unknowns for me, like who did I want to teach? What did I want to teach? How many of my hours would transfer from Arts and Sciences to Teacher Education? How long would it take to become certified? What would be the additional cost? I was a National Merit Scholar and my full tuition was paid at the University of Louisville with those funds. However, I had to graduate in four years.

Finding a Way to Make It Happen

As I stepped into the Personnel Office at the Louisville Board of Education at Fifth and Hill streets, I rehearsed my spill again in my head. My sister had told me about something called a Professional Commitment and I wanted one of those. She had been enthusiastic about my becoming a teacher and offered some direction. Now, I had to build the strategy to put the pieces together. I knew Step 1 was getting the school system and the university to accept me as a program participant.

When the secretary opened the door to the director's office and said, "There is a young lady here that wants to talk to you about teaching careers." The person on the other side of the door said, "Send her in." The secretary told me to go in. I smiled, said "Thank you," and waltzed through the door with all of the confidence in the world, my game face that I had acquired long ago already in place. When I heard the words, "Why are you here, Rita?" I recognized the voice as well as the body image behind the desk. Sitting in a comfortable high-backed office chair, with hair cut a bit shorter, a small mix of gray around the temples, and a few pounds added to her upper torso was Hughlyn Wilson, my second grade teacher.

I slid dumbfounded into an oversized chair facing Ms. Wilson's desk, unable to speak. My game face transformed into one of awe! I was surprised that she still knew my name after so many years. She said again, "Rita, what brings you to the Board?" I blurted out, "I want to be a teacher."

Ms. Wilson drew in a breath, never taking her eyes off my face as I stared back at the teacher who, many years ago, had stood at the back window of her classroom with her arm around my shoulders as I cried that I didn't want school to be out and to leave her class. I was going to another school the next year because my family had moved. I remembered Ms. Wilson telling me that I would be fine regardless of the school I attended because I already did third-grade work. "You just have to keep working hard and learning everything that you can learn," were her words.

Ms. Wilson brought me back to reality with the next question, "Why do you want to be a teacher? What is your inspiration?" I blinked, then blinked again, remembering my second-grade dictionary assignment. Ms. Wilson remembered, too. She smiled and I smiled, my jitters evaporating in an instant.

For the next hour or so, we talked, Ms. Wilson telling me about her teaching experience over the last several years and my bringing her up-to-date on my school and college experiences over the years. She listened, nodding her head, taking notes now and then, often smiling, and sometimes laughing at some of my antics that I shared. "So, you see, the University of Louisville has offered me a Professional Commitment. Now, all I need is a job."

Ms. Wilson's expression froze, her left eyebrow cocked higher than the right, and her mouth twitched just a little. She turned her head to the side, giving me that critical eye, the same way that she did in second grade when a student said something far-fetched. "So, U of L has placed you on a Professional Commitment and you need a job. Are you sure?"

"Yes, I'm sure."

"Professional Commitment is a difficult program that requires lots of initiative, but I see you've already begun." Ms. Wilson knew that I lied and I knew that she knew. She shook her head, smiled, picked up the phone and called the dean of the School of Education at U of L. You see, you could not be on a Professional Commitment if you are not degreed and I had not graduated.

For the next several months I had to learn how to marry two different systems very quickly. I strategized so that I completed every class that I needed for admission to the Professional Commitment Program by the August graduation date. I asked lots of questions; I spent time on campus taking day and evening classes, working part time in between; and I acted as a go-between for Dr. Morgan, my social science advisor, and Dr. Jones, my political science advisor. I was persistent. This was a new venture for the professors because normally a student seeking a Professional Commitment had already graduated with a major in a content area. The two professors pushed and goaded each other as well as compromised so that in the end, I had two academic majors for teaching, political science and social studies, instead of a major and a minor.

Mama was happy. I graduated and I had a job, almost. A couple of months prior, I had placed an application with Ford Motor Company—just in case. While I was waiting to hear from Human Resources about a job with Louisville Public Schools, I got a call from Ford. They offered me a position in their Human Resources Department.

I had worked part-time at Sears for several years selling fur coats in the summer, and guess what—working in Human Resources. The job opportunity paid almost $3000 more than I would earn as a beginning teacher and I would be in an office, not on an assembly line. The offer was more than tempting, but, I said, "No thanks." When I told Jim that evening, he looked at me, shook his head, smiled then said, "It's your career. Do what you want to do. It's your call." And I did what I wanted to do. It was my call. I am a teacher.

The stories that follow depict many of the trials and tribulations that storytellers experienced on their journeys to become educators and to persist in the profession. The variety of challenges, and the strategies employed to overcome those challenges take readers down many side-roads that ultimately lead back to the main highway—-individuals having the grit and fortitude for becoming professional educators.

LeRoy Anderson, Jr.

**Lead Teacher and Special Education Teacher,
Elementary and Middle School**

I HAVE LIVED IN LOUISVILLE, Kentucky, for nearly fifty years although I was born in Savannah, Georgia, a total surprise for my parents, LeRoy, Sr., and Johnnie Mae Anderson who were in their 40's. My older brother and sister were 22 and 19 years older than I, respectively. My ability to work with anybody and my passion for cleaning comes from my mom who had an eighth-grade education and was a domestic worker, cleaning homes of more affluent whites. I sometimes went to work with her and helped. She talked to everyone and

Clinton Bennett Photographer

everyone talked to her, seeking advice, asking her opinion, or just greeting and inviting her to have a nice day. Mom taught me never to compromise my values or when cleaning, never do less than my best! If you are cleaning the room, move the dresser out from the corner, clean the back of the dresser, clean the floor, wipe the baseboard, and clean the wall behind the dresser before you push it back in place. Then start on the front, sides, and under the dresser; then clean the floor. Not only was Mom meticulous about cleaning, she was an accomplished pianist. She actually could put her leg up on the piano and play it as Little Richard did. My brother, who also was a musician and singer and sometimes called "the Black Frank Sinatra," inherited her musical talents. I loved singing, but never associated singing with my future career.

My dad was a painter by trade and worked for the Housing Authority, teaching younger guys how to paint and supervising their work. Dad did plumbing, electrical work, bricklaying, and roofing on the side. He worked all over the city for whites who told their friends about the quality of his work and the fairness of his pricing for his excellent work.

We lived in a two-story house that went through lots of renovations when I was a child. At one time, we lived on the second floor, and the first floor was a knick-knack store with a jukebox. At another time, Dad converted the first floor into an apartment and rented it out. Later, Dad added a bathroom to both floors and we moved down stairs and rented the upstairs. He was very creative and his work always exceptional. He even tinkered with cars. I remember working with him to overhaul the engine of a '57 Chevy. As talented as my dad was, he could not read and did not go to school past the second grade. However, his ability to count and estimate was phenomenal. He could look at an area and tell you exactly how many gallons of paint it would take to cover it or how many bricks it would take to build a wall. When I asked him how he learned to do so many different things, he said that he watched people then tried to do it himself. If he couldn't do it or get it right, he would ask them how to do it.

I was a quiet child. You could sit me in a corner and give me something to play with and find me in the same spot three hours later. That did not last when I went to school. I loved to talk and socialize. I enjoyed kindergarten that was taught by a holiness lady in her home and her backyard. I did not consider kindergarten as school because we played and had so much fun learning. Elementary school was different. I went to a Catholic elementary school in Savannah, along with Supreme Court Justice Clarence Thomas. We were in the same classes at St. Benedict for our first five years of grade school. Later on during my high school years, I lived in Liberty City near Clarence Thomas's grandfather. Clarence lived with him while continuing to go to Catholic schools.

Most of the white nuns who taught me at segregated St. Benedict were like robots, unfeeling and devoid of caring. It was not until third grade that I had a teacher that I could relate to, finally understanding that teachers could be nice people. She was a young, pretty, Italian woman who would look at your paper and pat you on your shoulder to encourage you rather than hit you across your knuckles with a ruler to embarrass you because of a wrong answer. Grades 4 and 5 were better for me. I was involved in singing with a chorus and was a show-off. On one song that we sang, my solo part was "Give them children some shortnin' bread." I was innocent and did not understand the ramifications of what I sang.

In Grades 6 through 10, I attended a Seventh Day Adventist school, Ramah Jr. Academy. Adventism was a legacy from my mother's family. My grandfather, her dad, was an Adventist and Mom had been raised in the religion. She left the faith as an adult because she felt it was too restrictive. She returned to Adventism when I was about ten years old because of a dream and a revelation that she experienced. I was mixed up and confused about my religious beliefs that had influenced me by being Presbyterian, attending Catholic schools, and then becoming Adventist, and then changing my sacred day from Sunday to Saturday, the same day that all of the fun activities and "stuff" were going on, including Boy Scout activities.

It was common among Adventists for African-American high school students who could afford to attend boarding school to attend church schools. My older sister, a registered surgical nurse in Philadelphia, could have been a support to me if I had attended Pine Forge Adventist School in Philly where my parents also wanted me to go. I did not want to go. Instead, I persuaded my parents to allow me to attend public schools for Grades 11 and 12 and remain in Savannah. By this time, we had lived in two other areas of Savannah before settling in Liberty City on the outskirts of town where we had a house built.

Beach High School was similar to Louisville's Central High, segregated. I took advanced classes because of my prior preparation in the Catholic and Adventist school systems. I knew all of the gangs in the school because I had lived in different parts of town. I made a little pocket change by using Dad's equipment to sharpen the gangs' knives at 75 cents per blade. I repaired bicycles as well. Also, instead of eating lunch, I helped kids who were having problems with their classwork. I did not charge them for tutoring. As a result, kids would tell other kids, "LeRoy will help you." The number of students meeting me in the library steadily grew. I loved high school because my teachers were very professional teachers. I was always respectful, and I wanted to impress them, so I always did my work and I always had my homework.

I planned to be a teacher and I pursued a teaching degree at Oakwood College in Huntsville, Alabama. Two of my teachers left profound impressions on me and influenced my career choice. Sister Hill who was my second teacher at the Adventist school, was a real inspiration for me, continuously trying to teach us something new, taking her time, not criticizing us when we did not understand. She was invariably the same person, whether at school, in church, on a program, or during activities; she was herself in any event. She was perceptive as well, moving my desk closer to her desk and giving me the encouragement I so desperately needed when I was sorting through Adventism, Catholicism, and the Presbyterian faith. Her demeanor and style and her caring were models for me. Ms. Dean, a high school teacher, was another inspiration. Not as personable as Ms. Hill, Ms. Dean loved her subject and did not want to see her students fail. If you did not do well on a test, you could retake the same test after you had more time to study. Ms. Dean was my high school social studies teacher. I would sit in her class during my free period and watch her teach. It didn't hurt that she was also good-looking and a true lady.

In order for me to graduate with teaching credentials from Oakwood, I had to complete two student-teaching assignments. My majors were social sciences and psychology. I student taught in middle grades at Oakwood Academy, the campus school, and at the integrated Edward White Jr. High School. At the Academy, it was like being the real teacher. I had to prepare lesson plans, teach lessons, test the students over the material that I taught, tend to discipline, take students to lunch, and act like the real teacher. At Edward White, things were totally different. I had to sit and observe the white teacher teaching to the white students in the front of the room while the Black students whom she had placed in the back of the classroom were basically ignored. She never walked back to see what they were doing or had written, and she never asked them if they understood. Both Black and white students took the same tests, and, of course, the Black students did not do as well as the white students. So, as I sat in the corner toward the back of the room, I began writing notes to students who looked puzzled and asked them if they understood. I would try working with those students when they were doing seat work. The teacher did not like my "interference."

How I found my way to Louisville, Kentucky, after graduating from Oakwood is a story unto itself. When I graduated, I applied for certification in Georgia, Alabama, and Kentucky. It just so happened that when I was in Catholic elementary school, my teacher talked about the "Bluegrass in Kentucky." I asked if she was telling the truth about the grass being blue and she said, "Absolutely." I made up my mind that one day I would see the Kentucky bluegrass. When I was a bit older, I road my bicycle all over Savannah. One of the main streets that I often road on was "Louisville Road." Also, Savannah was serviced by the L&N Railroad. I finally learned somehow that "L & N" was the abbreviation for Louisville and Nashville. In addition, Muhammad Ali was someone that I followed. He was a loudmouth talker who was called the "Louisville Lip." I always argued that he may have talked too much, but he won his fights. Finally, I liked horses and loved watching the Kentucky Derby. When the superintendent for Adventist Education called to tell me, "Boy, do we have a job for you," I asked where. He said, "Louisville, Kentucky." It made no difference what the job was; I was going to Louisville!

My first job was overwhelming. I was principal/teacher at Emma Minnis Academy where I taught all subjects for middle school, handled discipline for the entire school, evaluated the three teachers on staff, took care of all finances, managed the day-care program, managed the kitchen, and cleaned the building. At the end of the year, I knew

I had had enough. My calling was working with kids, mainly in the classroom. I wanted to motivate and support my students and help them to progress, removing all barriers and ceilings so that they could be and do whatever they chose. I looked for a teaching job that allowed me to focus on kids and found a position at Russell Junior High School from 1971 to 1975 where I taught English and drama and organized the talent shows, giving me opportunities to have fun with kids as well as teach them in a critical area.

Those four years at Russell also allowed me to become grounded as a teacher because I learned about good teaching and how to deliver services to students individually. I became a good listener as well as a good "looker." I listened to and watched how my students reacted as I taught. I could look at them and tell if they were understanding what I was saying. I had an easygoing style that helped students relate to me, and I never embarrassed or harassed any child. Because of the type of teacher that I had developed into and my number one priority was to help children, venturing into Special Education areas seemed automatic.

With the merger of the Louisville and Jefferson County school systems, and desegregation came another teaching assignment for me at Highland Junior High School where I was to teach the remainder of my career in Jefferson County—more than 24 additional years. I loved working with special-needs children and earned certification for teaching Educable Mentally Retarded as well as Learning and Behavior Disorders and Emotionally Disturbed. I worked as a self-contained teacher and as a resource teacher, in addition to teaching Advanced Program, predominantly teaching students in Grades 6 through 8. I also taught summer school and in State Agency Schools, including Home of the Innocents and Maryhurst. Teaching for me was more than the content in the book. I helped kids learn to think, question, and understand that it is important to set goals and work hard to achieve those goals. With my students, I also used the scenario about planting seeds and watching them germinate over time as a partial description of the role of teachers.

I often told my current students a story about a former student that I had run into. The student said to me, "I remember you. You always encouraged me to do better. I decided when I got out of jail the last time that I was going to do what Mr. Anderson told me to do, and I did."

Another story that I recall is about David, one of the few students that I ever told to sit down and don't move. David, a white student, went home and told his mom what I said, stating that I was picking on him. His mom came to school the next day angry and cursing up a storm. "Where is the little N_____? I'm going to kick his a__." The office staff was waiting to call the police when I took that parent into the conference room. I let her vent, then showed her his work. I asked her if there was something that David was really interested in doing at school and she said he would like to be a teacher's aide. I called the librarian to see if David could work in the library, helping with moving boxes and books. His mom said, "I called you everything and you are still willing to do something for my son." We finished our conversation talking about cars and fishing. Much to the office staff's surprise, we walked out with her arm around my shoulders. Years later that same David brought his daughter to Highland and insisted on her being placed in Mr. Anderson's room.

A final story that I will share involved a home visit. I had been warned that the worst kind of parent was one who belonged to the Ku Klux Klan (KKK). One of my young female students told me that her father belonged to the KKK and did not allow "N_____" in their home. When the student's father finally allowed me into their home and I shared his daughter's work and my plan of action to help his child, the father said, "You know, da_____, for a N____, you're all right." That was his compliment.

During my teaching career, I also embarked upon another career that put my teaching skills to use; I joined the U.S. Army Reserves. When I was at the bus station, on my way to Oakwood College, I ran into a group of my classmates going to Viet Nam. It never left the back of my mind that they were going to war and I was going to college. In high school I had thought about joining the Marines, but Mom reminded me that I was going to college like my older brother who had attended Savannah Sate College and worked in the insurance industry.

The Reserves allowed me in some ways to make up for not going to war with my classmates, several of whom did not return or returned in poor health, disabled, or mentally impaired. I also wanted my son, who was born in 1978, to be proud of me. The Reserves also provided a needed outlet for some of the personal tragedies that I had encountered, and training was teaching. I was a medic who worked with a number of younger recruits. One defining moment for me as a reservist and as a teacher was when my unit was set to go to Iraq in place of active duty personnel and I was given another assignment. I had been training those 17 to 28-year old troops over the years, and I knew to what degree they were going to be in harm's way, being a part of the first wave. I would not let them go alone. I volunteered for active duty and to be sent with my squad. I gave teacher-talks all the way as we flew across the ocean, reminding my troops of lessons learned. For me, this was "guided practice."

I still believe that teaching is the best job that you could ever find. Teachers are responsible for helping students achieve at their highest levels, and they do make a difference in the lives of their students. Sometimes it takes everything that you have to give to get a student on track. When I retired from JCPS in 1999, I was tired, not so much of teaching but of teaching and doing so many other odd jobs that I took on to keep myself busy after a messy family situation. I did not want to be a teacher who retired on the job while continuing to draw a paycheck.

My life took a different turn when I was asked by an older woman standing in front of my apartment complex, if I would give her a ride to her meeting that was to begin shortly. That woman was Senator Georgia Davis Powers, the first woman elected to the Kentucky State Senate and the first Black. Through my escorting Sen. Powers to various community affairs in Louisville and across the state, listening and talking about issues and challenges for Black America, I became more aware of the politics of education for Black children and even more adamant about the need for Black teachers.

It is going to take society, not money, to change the perception of the value of teachers. Pay is important, but for those contemplating becoming teachers, the reward is when you have twisted and turned that lesson upside down and finally gotten the kids to get it. Their light is your light.

Developing that interest in teaching as a career means starting early with activities like participating in Cadet Teaching programs; having elementary and intermediate students tutor primary and kindergarten students; providing community service credit for students mentoring other students; having seasoned retired teachers share experiences with high school and younger students; and allowing older teachers, including retired teachers, to mentor young prospective teachers in an organized manner.

When on campus at the University of Louisville, I saw a student with a big grin on her face. She walked up to me, called me by name, and said that I had been her homeroom teacher at Highland. You know, students change from when they are 12 years old to 22 years old. I did not recognize her, but remembered her when she told me her name. She began relating some of the things that I told the class during homeroom. She finished by telling me that I was always encouraging the students and lifting them up. She also said that she decided to become a teacher while a student at Highland. There is no better gift that a teacher can receive than a salute from a student, and you just never know when that salute is going to come.

LeRoy Anderson, Jr., re-entered the teaching force as a teacher in New Albany/Floyd County Consolidated Schools from 1999 to 2012. He also continued his military career, retiring as Master Sergeant, United States Army Reserves in 2003. His other affiliations include serving on the Jefferson County Teachers Association Board of Directors before he retired; serving on the Executive Board of the Louisville NAACP; serving on the NAACP Armed Services and Veterans Affairs Committee and as Chair. LeRoy has remained active as an Adventist leader, serving as School Board Chairman of the E. L. Minnis Junior Academy, as a New Life SDA Church Board Member, and as an Executive Committee member of the South Central Conference of SDA, Nashville, Tennessee. He is an Elder in his church and prides himself on being a man whose life has been dedicated to serving his family, his church, his students, and his fellow troops. He has one son, LaRon, and one grandson, Cade.

William Hiram "Bill" Donaldson

Teacher, Band Director, Musician, Songwriter, and Pianist

I WAS BORN JULY 10, 1934, IN BADIN, North Carolina, to a family of college graduates and musicians where everyone played the piano, sang, and performed on stage. Mom, a graduate of Bennett College and my first-grade teacher, actually taught for fifty years. Dad was a minister who loved music and joked that when anyone was born in the family, he or she had to give a concert the next day. If they did not pass, they would be kicked out of the family. He was proud of the fact that all of our relatives graduated from college, and they all taught

Clinton Bennett Photographer

school with the exception of my older brother, Lou Donaldson, a jazz musician. Both of my sisters, Eloise, and Pauline are teachers.

Music has been a part of my life forever and piano since I was four years old, when my lessons began. Our house was a studio. If someone was at home, there would be music—someone singing, someone playing an instrument, music from the radio, a group practicing for a performance. Music was everywhere and of every kind—church music, jazz, contemporary, children's music, opera, Bebop. Even though Dad went blind, he still played the piano. My family sang at church; Mom directed the band at school, and I could play all of the instruments. My favorite is the trumpet that I began playing in fourth grade.

School for me was just school. I was always around teachers; I knew what happened in school; I knew what I was supposed to do in school; so, school was just school. My favorite teacher was Hazel Taylor in second grade. She was always upbeat and pleasant and gave us inspiration—things to think about and dream about—life's possibilities. J. Lincoln Brown, another teacher, was "sharp." He always looked good, wore diamonds, and would go to the poolroom and drink beer some evenings with the dads. He was well-respected by the community. He was also the best English teacher ever, insisting that students speak correctly at all times.

My school building, West End Badin Colored School, had wings for various grades. On one side were Grades 1 through 4. Grades 5 through 8 were on the far side with the middle section assigned to Grades 9 through 12. I participated in music, basketball, and football and I learned to play golf by caddying at the white golf course. There was no such question as, "Are you going to college?" The question was, "Where are you going to college?" While I was in junior high school, I began to consider the answer to that question.

Eight boys who were in my senior class in high school were all assigned to home economics class for first period. Although the principal's wife taught the class, we simply refused to take home economics. We went to the principal and negotiated a deal. The principal understood our side of the argument and assigned us to the library with the school's librarian, the most beautiful woman that I had ever seen at the time. We all reported on time to sit around, laugh, and tell jokes. We didn't need to do homework or get ready for a class. That was already taken care of. Some of us were going to college and we knew where we were going. I was headed to North Carolina A & T College. On a Thursday in April 1952, two months before graduation, our principal came to the library with three letters from Kentucky

State (K-State) College in his hand and told us that the letters said that the college wanted "students good in music." I enrolled there reluctantly, with lots of push from my parents.

I had a good time my freshman year. K-State had choir, band, concert choir, and church choir, everything that I had been used to and had participated in. I could sing and I was good in music, not so in biology. I flunked it and almost didn't go back for the spring semester. But, I did after the head of the Music Department called Mom. When I registered, this same professor told me, "By the way, you know you are on scholarship now." My college life changed. Lots of people were in my corner. I had help and tutors and people to talk to. I forgot about North Carolina A & T, passed biology with a "B," and had fun. I was too ignorant to realize that I almost flunked out.

When you have been told from Day 1 that you are going to teach, what else can you do but be a teacher. I student taught in Lexington, Kentucky, at Lexington Dunbar High School under Charles Quillings, an outstanding musician, and graduated from K-State in 1956. My first fifteen or so years of teaching were in North Carolina. My very first teaching job was in Laurel Hill as music teacher for one year. I then moved to Clarkton, fifty miles from Wilmington, North Carolina, and taught for five or six years. I met my wife, Anita at K-State. She loved music, but she was a business major. She could play the piano, too. Anita and I taught in segregated schools in and around Wadesboro, North Carolina, for about eight years. We did not always teach in the same district, both driving our separate ways when necessary. We taught at Lislesville High School the same year. I taught language arts and Anita taught business. We thought that we would be at the newly built school in the area, but the new school did not open. I had selected all of the music equipment and Anita had selected equipment for the Business Department. However, the county refused to open the school as a segregated facility. We were both assigned to Anson County High School and we stayed for one year.

We got to Louisville in a round-about way. We have missed only one K-State Homecoming since 1952. One of my friends that I saw at Homecoming told me about a job possibility at K-State, so I began looking for jobs in Kentucky. We came to Louisville in 1967 without jobs. Before school started, we found out that Anita was pregnant and I was offered a job at Parkland Junior High School. Anita did not take a position until the fall of 1968. She taught Business Education at Central High School. My Kentucky story begins at Parkland.

I never had a problem with discipline or student misbehavior from the time I began in a classroom. I was not scared of kids and I was not unsure of myself. I had been around teachers all of my life, and I knew that I was supposed to plan, let students know what I expected of them, and explain how we were going to do things. I did that. I evaluated my students' skills and divided them into Beginners, Middle, and Elevated. I had students who I had to teach how to play an instrument because they knew nothing, and I had students who had played since elementary school. We did programs for school, and I intermingled with parents and met good people. I recruited students through churches and through the three to five elementary schools where I also taught that were "feeder schools." Students that come to mind are Leroy Brown, Fred Fishback, Leroy Jones, and Daryl Griffith. Regardless of how they came to me, by the end of the year, my students knew that they had learned a great deal and could demonstrate their talent.

When I hear about teaching today, what strikes me is who is in charge. Mom, my sisters, and all of my teacher family always believed that students had to know who was in charge—the teacher was in charge. I remember something I did at the beginning of the year when I first started teaching. Every day I placed a big "F" and a little "A" on the board. I would then ask the class, "What can we do to make this little "A" become larger and this big "F" become smaller? I told the students how they each would grow their "A" shrink their "F" by hard work and not playing around. "The more you do, the larger the "A" and the smaller the "F". We talked about cooperation and attitude and it was left up to each student to work *with* me to change the "F" to an "A" by "not doing what you want to do but doing what needs to be done."

Another lesson I learned being in the house with teachers was that you had to know how to bluff and you cannot let students out-bluff you. Two of my biggest bluffs were when it took being a fool, I had to be a fool. When it took being sedate, I was "Mr. Cool" and sedate. When it comes to a point where students run your class, you are in trouble!

Over the years, in addition to teaching at Parkland Jr. High, I taught at DuValle Jr. High, Male High School, and several elementary schools, including Rangeland and Jacob. Anita was transferred from Central to Westport High School when the city and county school districts merged. When Westport was closed as a high school in 1980, she was transferred to Butler High School and remained there until she retired in 1992.

My most talented student ever was a base drummer who played the big drum. While normally my no-nonsense female drum majorette marched out front and led the band, on this day the drummer told her that he was in charge that day. He walked front to back, laughing, carrying that big drum. He marched back up front, did two somersaults with that big drum and never missed a beat. He now has a Ph.D. in music.

Anita and I both enjoyed the entire time we taught. When we reminisce, Anita always talks about how rewarding it was to see kids learn. She once shared that she found that all children wanted to be loved, even in high school. She also had very few discipline problems. It was always difficult for her to see Black students getting off the bus at Westport, knowing that the majority of their parents would never come out to the school, and many didn't even know where the school was located. I remember the day that she came home so upset because she had witnessed a Black student in the hall, banging on her locker. When she approached the young lady and asked what was wrong, the student told her that she had been put out of class and that she had not been talking. When Anita suggested that maybe she should tell her mom, the student told her, "My mom said that she was not coming way out here for some mess like this." Anita was truly heartbroken. She wanted Black parents to take more interest in the school and to take time to see about their children who she felt, "Didn't always get a fair shake."

Anita also tells the story about her first class at Butler when she told the students, "I love each of you and I expect you to love me." She said that a young man came up to her desk and asked, "You mean you really love us?" and she said it again. She told him yes, she meant that she loved him. She always smiles when she says that he was the best student/friend that she had throughout the year and often wonders where he is today.

Just like new students coming into my classroom, new teachers coming into the profession begin at a point where they do not know all that they need to know about how to do their job. They must work hard to grow and learn what they need to know to help their students. Band is a performing activity and teaching is a performing activity. Be yourself and know how you made it this far. As you mature, the bigger the grade will be toward "A," being a good teacher, as long as you keep doing what "needs to be done" rather than what you want to do or what is easiest to do.

Bill and Anita Donaldson both retired from JCPS in 1992. Also, they have been married more than 60 years. They have three children, the oldest daughter a writer and public speaker; the youngest daughter a teacher and singer; and a son who is a singer and musician. They also have seven grandchildren and nine great-grandchildren. Bill, who is a member of Kappa Alpha Psi Fraternity, has been a Mason for more than fifty years and still attends meetings regularly. Anita, a member of Alpha Kappa Alpha Sorority, Inc., was the pianist for several churches over the years as well as a "Work from Home" secretary for over five years. They are members of Broadway Temple AME Zion Church.

Rothel Farris

Teacher, Counselor, Principal, Volunteer, and After
School Program Community Educator

CAN YOU IMAGINE WHAT CHILDREN
today would feel like knowing that they lived
in a place called, "The Bottoms?" Well, I am
a native of Louisville, Kentucky, who has
born at the segregated Red Cross Hospital
and who lived for a time in a four-room
shotgun house at Brook and Floyd streets,
and I lived in an area called "The Bottoms."
We lived in my mom's family home with
her parents, my aunt and cousin, Mom and
Dad, my sister, and me—nine of us! My
family slept in the same room. The family
group shared an outhouse for a bath room,

Farris Family Photo Collection

and a tin tub for bathing. Although my dad only completed eighth
grade, he was a hard worker whose work ethic eventually earned him
a position as foreman at Louisville Cooperage. He was my example,
getting up every day at the same time, even on Saturday, working in
church, and giving back (he was a trustee), and doing things right or
doing it over. My mom, a graduate of Louisville Central High School,
realized the importance of education and made sure that we were

readers. She took us to the library, ordered us the *Weekly Reader,* and sent us to camp in the summer.

My first and second grades of school were at "city" Cochran Elementary. In 1956, beginning the first year of integration, we moved to Garland Avenue, the second Black family on the block. Our house had indoor plumbing, a yard, and a garage, and I had my own separate bedroom. I attended Foster Elementary School from the third through fifth grades where I met my favorite teacher, Ms. Kaufman, a white teacher who believed in structure and in being courteous. I learned a great deal in her third-grade class and I began to try harder. She would praise us when we did things well and my being Black did not make a difference in the way she treated me. As an educator, I learned from Ms. Kaufman that you must get students' hearts first, show love, but discipline, that is "chastise with love."

At Shawnee Jr. High, I felt good about myself, never having experienced racial tension. Foster had many doctors', dentists' and lawyers' kids who attended the school, and this gave me a sense of cultural pride. Shawnee Jr. High in the sixties was very integrated; we had white students from Portland and Black students from Cotter Homes and Southwick. I played basketball in junior high under a white coach, Mr. Jones. I was an athlete in high school also. I never felt hate. I was part of the team. My high school psychology teacher was my junior high school coach Mr. Jones. He made me show him my grades. I did not want to disappoint him. I felt OK in an integrated setting, and my school settings taught me to deal with other races as an adult. I learned what you could and could not say around them.

I do not know when I began thinking about college. I do remember my minister, Rev. Herschel Martin, saying, "I cannot wait until you go to college." My parents got the message. Dad took a second job and Mom went to work. Shawnee High School counselors did not provide help and direction for any seniors striving to go to college. There were no mentors at the school and no scholarships that we knew of. I was scared to death when I went to Western Kentucky University (WKU) alone, on a train. I chose WKU because I played football and baseball at Shawnee and the one year that I was on the track team, we went there to run. It was the first college campus that I had ever visited.

Dad was a great mentor, but he did not have exposure. While he began driving late and really did not like to drive, he was a money manager. When I worked at Henry Vogt during the summer, Dad would take me to the bank and tell me how much I was going to save. Consequently, I was able to pay first semester for registration, books, and dorm from working summers, and Dad would pay for the second semester.

I had limited exposure to well- educated African-American men. I saw the preachers and teachers and Ernest Jasmine, an educated Black man, making church announcements, hands flying and knowledgeable of the Black community and capability of African Americans. I remembered that vision of him when I went to college. It wasn't until my sophomore year that I really decided on majoring in education, after taking general classes during my freshman year.

Learning early that playing Bid Whist instead of doing my classwork would cause dismissal from school, I tried my best to stay focused. What also helped me was pledging a fraternity during my sophomore year. The older guys (Kappas) took me under their wings. There were several Vietnam Vets who were mature and kept us in line. One frat brother was assistant dorm director. We bought groceries together to make our money stretch. I had a great college experience because I fell in with the right people. I knew when it was time to study and when it was time to play.

I was good at teaching. I learned that being a good disciplinarian was key to the job. I completed student teaching at my old elementary school, Stephen Foster. My brother who is 11 years younger than I, was in the sixth grade at Foster when I was completing my program.

My first teaching job, 1972-73, was at Phyllis Wheatley Elementary with 37 fifth graders in my class; we did not have enough of anything, including books and supplies. Carol Roberts, the teacher next door, took me under her wing and got me through Year One. Predominately Black, 600 or more students were enrolled at Wheatley and every classroom was packed. Principal Wiley Daniels was a master, supporting us and "putting out fires." I remained at Wheatley for three years until the beginning of busing and desegregation.

In 1975-76, Engelhard Elementary School was my assignment as the Math Plus teacher. I completed my Master's in Counseling at University of Louisville during the same period. Math Plus was a program designed to help struggling students acquire the skills they needed to get on grade level. Students were given specific help for the skills that they needed to develop. Whole-group, small-group, and individual instruction were included in the plan, but the focus was on the individual child.

Like so many other administrators with less seniority from the old Louisville system, we were put in positions and bounced around as the merged system began to downsize. I was a counselor at Roosevelt-Perry Elementary for the 1976-77 school year, then returned to Math Plus as a teacher at Paxton Wilt from 1977 to 1979; then I went back to counseling at Luhr Elementary from 1979 to 1989. Elaine Keller, principal at Luhr, was an excellent mentor. I learned from helping her, and she encouraged me to complete my Principal Certification. She also helped me understand the importance of developmental counseling, working hands-on with students helping them learn life skills, coping skills, and self-awareness. She also helped me further develop my leadership style of structure with compassion.

"This school has been a thorn in my side since I have been here. What are you going to do to clean it up?" Those were Dr. Ingwerson's comments to me when I accepted the position of principal at Whitney Young Elementary School in 1990, after two other unsuccessful interviews. Being at Whitney Young was God's plan, not mine. Marty Bell had told me that I wasn't successful at the other schools because I was not selling myself. It was only through prayer and conviction that I was successful over the next twelve years.

The school was a wreck! The Advanced Program teachers and parents had taken over the school. They had their own wing in the school! They had planned a school trip to Florida, and every student who could not go on the trip was Black. I called on my entire life experience in working with people in multiple settings to deal with the Whitney Young challenge. I began by turning staff meetings into Professional Development sessions. During Year One, I implemented only a few changes. Year Two, we implemented multiple changes as the staff bucked and rebelled. In Year Three, we worked together.

One of the most important things that I did as principal was to hire young, innovative teachers. I learned through the process that people won't tell the boss what they do not know. Furthermore, making a change requires teaching how to make the change. A "drive-by" lesson will not work. Demonstrating more than once is required. It took the fourth year to teach teachers that kids are kids and they learn from their cultural environment. White teachers had to recognize and accept their disconnection with Black students and learn a different dialogue and skill set to keep Black kids engaged. We had to teach kids Peace Education so that I could stop riding down Muhammad Ali Blvd. putting out fights. I had to stand up to parents and stand behind my teachers, emphasizing kids were on school time until they got home, while at the same time asking parents to work with us.

Over time, Young became an International School, but the community around Young was changing. There were days that I could not let the kids go on the playground because of shooting in the area. There were teachers who did not want to come to Young because of the changing neighborhoods. There were good teachers who taught at Young but did not want to stay after school because they were afraid of being in the neighborhood after dark.

Whitney Young became a successful school in rewards because of its dedicated teachers and with the assistance of Rosemary Bell, a retired administrator who worked with us. We set goals for kids and used multiple strategies and incentives for students to reach their goals. People work harder when there are goals and when they know they are getting paid. We set up a store in the school with prizes for kids based on points they earned. They read books and took comprehension tests at the end of the book. They got points. Top readers earned a pizza party: structure and strategies. I could stand in the hall, hold up two fingers and students would get quiet as a mouse. We gave incentives for hall traffic—tokens. The top three classes at the end of the week had a party.

Three of the best teachers that I ever encountered were Linda Dunn whom the kids loved; Traci Barber, who later became principal, had boys eating out of her hand because she could relate, was positive, organized and could be playful then jump back in line with business;

and Judith Caldwell, whom I hired to teach first grade. She was wired from the time she stepped through the door to the time she walked out the door for home. She was creative and positive and she praised the children all the time. She had creative songs, jingles and sayings and her students learned what they needed to know and loved learning it. I retired as principal in 2002 but remained active with the District in several capacities over the years, including screening African Americans for the Aspiring Principals Program.

When I think about the education of poor, Black children today, I think about the neighborhood currently surrounding Whitney Young. There are young Black moms who are babies themselves, trying to raise boys to men. They cannot do it alone. It takes a man to help a boy become the type of man we really want him to be. These children are coming to school behind socially and academically. Ray-Ray is living with grandma and does not know his real name, his address, or his ABC's, but educators still must make all children feel special regardless of where they come from.

Today in many schools, we have kindergarten students turning over tables, fighting, shouting, and cursing. They have a different mindset. In my day, there was no cursing and only a few fights. Today, there is little if any training at home. In my day, training began at home. Kids now do not go to church. We went to church regularly. Today, kids feel free to say anything in front of anybody. They lack respect for authority and do not care if they get suspended from school. We respected teachers, were raised by a village, and if I was acting silly on the bus, Mom knew it before I got home, and I was disciplined.

We as educators must continue using our skills to turn things around, and Charter Schools are not the solution to our problems. Over the past seven years, I have worked with my church, First Gethsemane Baptist Church, as an unpaid Director of Education to establish after-school and summer programs to support student achievement. We began as a homework help service to see which skills students did not know and to check their work. Our Center for Family Development (CFD) acquired 501C3 status for our programs. Since 2012, we have been writing grants and have received over $150,000 from various organizations to provide free after-school programs for

students in grades K-8 four days a week, using certified teachers. I have also directed Summer Program Camps where we incorporated a full academic program with four or five teachers who taught language arts, writing, computer, math, and a social emotional component from Metro United Way that incorporated circle time emphasizing respect, bullying, and how to treat others without cursing. We take students swimming and on field trips. Parents pay a small fee. We also have added a Coding class to our after-school curriculum and have three dozen computers available for student and community use. We work in concert with JCPS, not in opposition. My reward, and that of my co-director Edwin Fox, is the opportunity to give back and make a difference.

If I had to do it all over again, I would choose to be an educator. The power of the principal is to hire talent and to use their talents. The work is hard, but great educators learn as they go. They give credit to the team. I learned that this work is not about me. A principal cannot lead a school and expect it to thrive if he is not giving the staff opportunities to grow and not giving them praise for their work and treating them with respect. Everybody should be expected to work, but the leader should be good to teachers and support them, and teachers should be good to their students and support them.

My life's journey is driven by this biblical verse from the English Standard Version of the Bible, Luke 12:48—Everyone to whom much was given, of him much will be required, and from him to whom they entrusted much, they will demand the more.

Rothel Farris is married to a retired teacher, Gloria Farris. They have two sons, Gerard and Gerren, as well as three grandchildren, Jalen, Gerardi, and Nia. Over the years, Rothel has been recognized for his volunteerism with his church and community. He also works with Kappa Alpha Psi, a service fraternity. In 2015, Rothel was recognized as the Big Brother Volunteer of the Year for the Kentuckiana Service Area by The Big Brother/Big Sister Organization along with a Governor's Citation from Governor Steve Beshear.

Farris Family Photo Collection

Rothel receiving Big Brother of the Year Award

Farris Family Photo Collection

Rothel with Little Big Brother Jamil Haraday, receiver of
YMCA Award for Outstanding Community Service

Bernadette Hamilton

K-8 Teacher, ECE Resource Teacher, Gifted and
Talented Resource Teacher, and Director of Options,
Magnets, and Advance Programs

I WAS BORN IN AKRON, OHIO, TO a 14-year-old war bride, Agnes Gentry Chapman, but my grandmother, Anna E. Bishop, kept me in Tennessee until I was five years old. Consequently, for the longest time, I thought my grandmother, called Granny, was my mother and my mother, an older sister. We called our mom "Mother." She told us she never wanted to be called mama.

Clinton Bennett Photographer

I think it was due to the fact that she called our Granny, her mother, mama. Mother moved to Louisville, Kentucky, and had other children with her husband, Caldwell Chapman. Granny decided to return to Louisville to help Mother with her four new children. It was at this point in time that Granny explained to me that I was not her daughter. I never remember her telling me that I was her daughter only that I thought I was. Granny was orphaned at a young age and I believe this gave her the deep love for family. While she and I lived in Tennessee, I was always surrounded by her family members, Aunt Val (full-blood Cherokee Indian), Cousin Perry, and others. Mother was an only child and Granny, Aunt Agnes Ford, Aunt Rachel Gentry, and Mother's father, David Gentry gave her everything she wanted. I believe this is one of the reasons she had eight children. Mother always said there were enough of us, four boys and four girls, to play among ourselves. I Bernadette, am the oldest, followed by Betty Strasser, Cardell Smith, Caldwell, Jr., Deborah Hampton (deceased), Michael, Stephen, and John Marion Chapman.

I cannot remember when Granny did not talk about school and the importance of education. She would often go back to Tennessee to visit her relatives. When she returned, we would hear the stories of how the teachers would meet at Cousin Perry's house and have cocktails, play cards, or just visit. This was the beginning of the planting of the seeds of knowledge to "get an education." I attended first grade in a one-room school house in Portland, close to our home on Fifteenth and Jefferson streets. However, by the time I entered sixth grade, we had moved several times. I often teased Mother about being a nomad. I didn't understand the trials of being a single parent and divorced. I attended a real school, Virginia Avenue, for sixth grade. Prior to that, I had attended Salisbury (now an apartment complex); Mary B. Talbert (now on the national registry of preserved buildings, called Old School House and located on the corner of Sixth and Kentucky streets); and Stephen Foster Elementary (now Stephen Foster Traditional Elementary) schools. One of my lasting memories about school was third grade at Talbert Elementary and my teacher, Ms. Radford, who kept boxes full of puzzles in the cloak room. Every day I would rush to finish my work so that I could work the puzzles. I don't remember if my work was especially sloppy or what, but, on one particular day, Ms. Radford hit my hands with her ruler and called Mother. I was having reading problems. She told me and Mother that she thought I was not living up to my potential. In those days, children had to attend conferences with parents and parents came when scheduled. This was not acceptable to Mother or for the rest of my family. From that moment on, I was the best reader in the class. I did not want to be hit again.

We were a close family—Granny, my Aunt Agnes, Aunt Rachel, Mother and the eight children. We were a family of twelve, including the four adults living and working to feed and clothe us, which included granddaddy Bishop and stepfather, John Board. Every child had a job that rotated and included helping with the cooking, cleaning the bedrooms and toilets, waxing floors, polishing furniture, and keeping the house clean. All the brothers were given garbage and yard work. In those days housework was designated as either boy or girl work. Everybody valued education, and everybody read books from the library until each child decided reading was not the hobby for them. Mother went to nursing school and became an LPN. She was always an avid reader. As an only child, reading was her fun thing to do. She loved comic books as an adult, even *Mad Magazine*. Mother bought books like *Ben-Hur* for me to read and discuss. She realized early on that my hobby was reading and not sports. Even on the hottest days with no air conditioning, I would be in my shared bedroom reading a novel. During the Cowger-Miller years, Mother worked for the Republican Party. She was an Inspector for the City of Louisville, riding through alleys, ticketing residents when their areas were not kept clean. Aunt Agnes, who lived to age ninety-two, was a maid at the Post Office. Granny was a matron at the City Jail until the administration changed to Democrat. She was our stay-at-home mom during the early school years as well as our spiritual leader. Southern Star Baptist Church was the place to be every Sunday and throughout the week. When we were given the job to clean up the house, wash the dishes, sweep or vacuum a floor, whatever, we did not complain. That was our job and Granny always said, "Cleanliness is next to Godliness." Because we saw the work ethic in these women, working was a part of our make-up.

Junior high school years were difficult for me. I became a model student after third grade. I didn't talk much and I never went looking for puzzles in the cloak room after the parent conference, unless it was play time. I was always clean; clothes looked nice, hair was done (washed and pressed every two weeks), but I was not with the 'in-crowd." I didn't have many friends, but I had my group at DuValle. We were church members together at Southern Star Baptist. We were there for weekly choir rehearsals, Sunday School, and Vacation Bible

School. One teacher I was especially fond of was Ms. Calhoun, my Latin teacher. She was no beauty, but she was very quiet and pleasant. It goes to show that you never know what a person thinks of you. According to Ms. Calhoun, whom I met some years later, I "didn't turn out to be so ugly after all." I was shocked to say the least when she said this to me, but good manners prevented me from retaliation.

Fighting in school was not an option. I had to be pushed to the limit to defend myself. I was pushed one day by a larger girl, and I threw down my books and put the challenge to her. I think she was totally shocked when I challenged her in a loud voice about bumping into me every day at my locker for no reason. I was raised at home under the rule of no fighting or arguing among the brothers and sisters. If one of us did, Mother made us stand and face one another until we kissed the brother/sister on the lips and made up. We all hated this method of solving conflicts, but we don't fight each other physically or verbally today. When there is a conflict, we always settle it peacefully after arguing our point of view. Mr. Maupin was my favorite teacher at DuValle. I loved his biology class even when we dissected dead starfish and insects.

High school was a welcomed change. I took Latin, chemistry, geometry, and several Advanced Program classes, but I was not in classes with my homeroom members. I wanted to go to college, but there were no guarantees. I knew I had to work if I did not go to college, so I took some other courses. Ms. Griffin taught me how to sew and I continued sewing into my adult years. I never told my homeroom members which courses I was taking, even when they commented that they didn't see me during the day. I knew that I was on the college track and they were not. I didn't want them to think that I thought I was better, smarter. We all know how students form opinions. Therefore, I remained quiet, completed my work in all classes like any other student when I was with my homeroom group (in classes such as sewing, typing, shorthand, bookkeeping, and social studies) as I recall. I was taking geometry, chemistry, algebra, Latin, and civics, my college-prep classes, the remainder of the day. I ate my lunch with my friends due to the college-prep schedule.

I graduated from Central High School in 1965. During my senior year, I had sent applications to a number of colleges. One week before college started, I received an acceptance letter from Tennessee State College. I knew I couldn't go. Poor children do not have instant money or funds to pack up and go off to a college. Instead, I took a job working in the Voter Registration Office for a short time before working for the University of Louisville (U of L) under Dr. Eleanor Young Love-Alsbrook (Dr. Whitney Young's sister) as part of my work-study program. I don't remember how it happened, but Dr. Eleanor Young found out I had applied to U of L at the last minute. She had me tested and placed in classes for the spring semester. She was the first woman that became a role model for me. At that time, I did not know what the term "role model" meant. I began night classes with a major in biology (Mr. Maupin's influence) for certification in medical technology at U of L in January 1966. When I thought about all the test tubes of blood involved, I began thinking about other career choices that I might be suited for as I continued working at U of L's Night School office. I suddenly remembered how I loved playing school all summer, the joy I felt when my grades were an *A* or *B*. I could share my passion for learning with our community of Black children.

I married the love of my life, Edward N. Hamilton, on August 12, 1967. For the next eight years, I worked a variety of jobs while attending school: I was a key punch operator at the Census Bureau; a secretary at First National Bank for their Small Business Administration Division; as a bank teller on Mondays and Fridays at Thirty-fourth and Broadway; as an assistant for the law firm of Friedlander, Webb and Belknap; and in the legal department of Brown & Williamson Tobacco Corporation. Along the way, I decided that I wanted to be an elementary teacher and completed student teaching at Engelhard Elementary in the fall of 1975 before getting my first job with Jefferson County Public Schools on October 13, 1975, at Valley Elementary School under Principal Woodford Allen.

It was on my way to Valley that a group of white boys pulled up beside me in their car and called me the "N" word and I knew that there was no place in that community that I could go during a tornado warning. It was also at Valley that I confirmed my choice of teaching as a career. There was a contest where participants had to wear their shirts inside out. I had only been there for one week and the contest was sponsored by the PTA on Friday. On the day of the contest, my entire class came with their shirts turned inside out. We won and I cried. At that moment, I knew teaching was what I was meant to do. I was where I should be. However, I was released from my contract at the end of that 1975-76 school year, the first year of busing. I was not the only one.

As it turned out, the District had a need for Exceptional Childhood Education (ECE) teachers (special education) and had a surplus of elementary teachers. In my opinion, someone decided that the Black students were in need of ECE because of their behaviors of not listening all the time, not sitting still in class, and not paying attention and obeying the teacher. Surplus elementary teachers were told if we got six hours in ECE, we could be rehired. I knew nothing about ECE, but a colleague told me that Emotional Behavior Disturbed (EBD) would be better to work with than Learning Behavior Disorder students because the EBD students had higher IQs. I began that summer by enrolling in U of L for my first six hours toward ECE certification. It would take twelve hours to become certified.

Over the next several years, I switched between teaching ECE and teaching regular elementary grades. I taught at Valley Elementary (regular classroom); Mill Creek Elementary (EBD self-contained class); Layne Elementary School (regular class); and DuValle Middle (resource teacher EDBD class). I was motivated by the opportunity to pay off my college loan. If a teacher worked in a poverty area and special education, yearly deductions were available. I considered this as a gift, my "40 acres and a mule."

One of my most heartbreaking experiences was at Layne Elementary. We were producing a Christmas play and students had practiced and rehearsed to get their roles down pat. On the night of the play, one of my students from the West End missed the performance because her parents could not find the school. The child was devastated and so was I. The parents had never come to the school to visit. A child on a school bus does not realize that the landscape may not be easily identified in the dark. She arrived as her segment was ending. Due to my certification for ECE covering grades K-12, I left Layne Elementary

School to be closer to home. Layne is in Valley Station. DuValle was located in Louisville's West End.

I left the elementary classroom and decided to try middle school. I was the Emotionally Disturbed Behavior Disorders (EDBD) resource teacher at DuValle under Principal Willie Lewis. Over the five years that I taught at DuValle, teaching at DuValle was more complicated than being a student at DuValle. The change to an integrated student body and an integrated teaching staff was not, in my opinion, a plus for the school. As a student, I felt that my teachers were great teachers and I liked the school. As a teacher, I felt most of my fellow teachers did not want to be at DuValle. High school teachers were transferred to DuValle and they thought the children could do things that they really could not do; therefore, academics suffered. They expected them to take notes, read books, and give reports. The high school teachers would complain to us about how the students did not know what to do. The neighborhood had changed from my days at DuValle as a junior high school student. The area was "tough" and there were more textbook "career project kids" in the school. One student informed me that her mother and grandmother lived in the housing projects and she wanted to live in the projects too. I was shocked to hear that she had no ambition to go beyond the "project" world. The neighborhood parents, by and large, were not engaged in the school or with their children's academic pursuits. The PTA membership had one main parent, Mrs. Yarborough. With a few other parents, she was able to provide the teachers with special treats on designated school days.

Three stories about "attitude" remain with me: A white teacher got a hardship transfer because she complained, "I can't breathe. The air down here (West End) is so different"; a little white boy with braces started a fight to see if he could get hit in the mouth so that he could go back to his home school after a bloody fight; and during a home visit in the projects, when I knocked on the door, my student's mom came to the door with a butcher knife in her hand because she thought I was her boyfriend's girlfriend. At the end of year five, I transferred to Jefferson County Traditional Middle School (JCTMS), back to the regular program. I always thought I would retire from JCTMS if I didn't have the "I want to be a principal" call in my head. The first day

I arrived in the building, there were 20 or more people in the office. I thought they were teachers. No, they were parents ready and totally committed to every child in the building because their child was there.

I spent six years teaching language arts in Grades 7 and 8 at JCTMS before becoming a Districtwide Gifted and Talented (GT) resource teacher. Teaching at JCTMS was totally different from teaching at DuValle. Now, I was moving to the Traditional Program where traditional students and their parents held a reputation of having power and authority. Academic expectations for every child were high. Black parents were as engaged as white parents. Supposedly community influence and economics did not matter because this was a Magnet School with a random draw list.

I enjoyed my assignment as the Gifted and Talented resource teacher for Jefferson County Public Schools. I was employed with Robert West, the director of Options, Magnet and Advance Programs. I worked with Montest Eaves and Janice James for several years providing districtwide training for teachers and summer school opportunities for minority students that had been identified through the district's Cog AT testing as students with potential for success in the Advance Program in Grades K-8. Because of instructors like Dr. Nettye Brazil and the U of L Special Education Department, I knew about different intelligence tests, the processes for interpreting them, and the laws impacting placement of students, and any question a parent might ask I was prepared to answer. The district started a summer program entitled **Project REACH** (Realizing Effort, Achievement and Commitment Towards Hope). We used this as a teaching model for the selected schools. I supervised nine selected JCPS resource teachers. They were placed in high-minority population elementary schools and provided district or local school in-service for teachers. The District continued grappling with issues of disproportionate representation of African-American students in Advance Program classes in Grades K-12 until I retired in 2013. It is probably still an issue. Part of my role was helping teachers understand what the terms "gifted" and "talented" meant as well as developing programs and supports to assist teachers and students with identifying and developing their talents. The ultimate goal was to increase the number of African-American students who actually participated in the Advanced Program. We were able to increase African-American enrollment from 10% to 17% participation during my tenure.

I am particularly proud of the AP Prep program that focused on skill building and the Trial Placement Program that allowed promising students to participate in AP to see if they could do the work even though they did not meet all of the test score requirements. One of the things that I noticed while working with GT students was that when white families called about test results, we had to be prepared to give specific details about the child's needs and refer the parents to additional resources. When we talked with West End Black parents for the most part, they accepted the score report and never asked questions or gave any response seeking next steps or other resources. If an African-American student was placed in an Advance Program class/classes, we sometimes had to probe and give them the questions to ask in order to help them help their children. Getting assigned to Central Office during my tenure as the GT resource teacher was quite enlightening.

My final assignment with JCPS was as Director of Options, Magnets and Advance Program from 2000 to 2013. During this time, I discovered the benefits of networking: knowing the person needed in order to use a school site for testing; knowing who is in charge of all test scores for the District; and learning what is needed to get a list of AP students per school by grade level, including tests scores. The number of departments that intersected for meetings was amazing. For example, a meeting with the superintendent may include staff from the ECE Department, Advance Program, Transportation and Demographics if the topic was about changing school boundaries or opening a new unit for ECE or AP in a school. Computer lab training on new equipment and the necessary forms needed to request documents for information was important. Most important of all was the end-of-year budget meetings. Would losing a staff person or funding for supplies become necessary? In the regular school building, these things are decided by the principal and bookkeeper. Teachers were not included in the decision making before School Based Decision Making (SBDM) was established. The head of the department in the building or a fellow teacher had a small, short meeting and reported the amount for supplies available for your class or unit and that was it. This information is shared with supervisors who provided it to the principals who take it to the schools after the superintendent and all high-level people, including members of the Board of Education, have discussed it for days/weeks. The cardinal rule is to spend all the money received but **DO NOT GO OVER BUDGET**. I discovered that Magnet Programs provided white flight parents a reason to stay in a certain program and supported the district's integration and demographic plans.

Integration was the worst thing that happened to the Black community in my opinion. We all knew who we were. We had good teachers who pushed us and lived next door or down the street. They were the role models whom we saw every day. Our teachers were firm, stern, fair, and consistent and Black children were disciplined. As Black children, we were raised in homes where parents told each of us what to do. The rule was, "Do as I say do, not as I do. If I'm smoking, that does not mean that you can smoke." We never questioned the authority of adults. All of a sudden, Black children go to an integrated school and the teacher gives them a choice as to what they want to do or not do. It was shocking to adults in the Black community and a destroyer of young lives in the schools.

Maybe this was the white plan all along—to take away their desire to learn; to make them think it was too hard to take an AP class; to discourage them from thinking about their future success. All of these things needed to be nourished each day by an adult to and for children. It provides them with hope, security, and the knowledge that someone cares about what happens to them; that someone wants my school work to be on time; that they want work neat and clearly written. They want me to answer all the questions and they want me to think and discover resources to get information I don't know. I'm greeted with a smile and talked to respectfully. I never had a discipline problem as a teacher. I would establish rules for the classroom and post them on the wall. I had a three-finger rule to stop talking. I would hold up one finger at a time and say, "Don't let me get to three fingers." After about a month or less, all I had to do was hold up the fingers and I never reached the third finger. In my classroom, when Blacks saw that white students were held to the same standard, there was no problem. This is true in every employment situation. Fairness and equal opportunity are important issues. School is the first job for students.

As time went by, Black children experienced more negative differential treatment from unsupportive and unhappy white teachers, those who did not want to be in downtown schools, those who refused to teach Black students about slavery or understand the concept of African-American culture; those who wanted to file suit because there were "too many Black students in their class" or there were "too many Black students in our school." I feel that many Black children became impassive with low expectations, limited opportunities, and insecurities while many Black parents felt powerless even though they knew that many white teachers did not care about our children.

At the same time that Black children were experiencing crisis in the schools, Black neighborhoods in the West End were crumbling. Those who were financially stable moved out. Blacks left the Black community and abandoned homes. Uncut grass could be seen on every street; couches appeared on front porches; drive-by shootings occurred; purse snatching was common; and bodies were dumped in the alleys while the dope man owned any street that he chose. The community that I knew as a child was destroyed as good people felt they had to leave. This was a different type of flight, Blacks leaving the West End. After forty years in our home, we left our community, what was left of it, that is. I was heartbroken, and I felt at the time that we role modeled going to work every day, going to church on Sunday, and having parties that didn't interfere with others by the volume of the music. Whereas, a few good neighbors cannot change the culture of a street or neighborhood, a few bad neighbors can. What happened to the village?

In my opinion, many of today's parents do not want to be responsible for anything, and in many cases do not establish in their children the basics, beginning with the concept that learning is important. They may not take time or know how to establish a home where learning is going on. Their personal experiences may cause them to devalue education and to have little trust in the system. They may have dealt with racism, as a student and as an adult, and economic disparities as adults. It's like nothing has really changed for African Americans; we have not given up, but the pendulum is swinging backwards and we are losing our children.

However, I still believe what I was taught can make a difference. Mother's rules while in school: You cannot have a part-time job because you will be working all your life; don't babysit unless I know the parents personally; your job is to go to school! Reading is the most important basic skill that students need. The ability to read, comprehend, and make an inference about any subject, event, or person is fundamental. Having a library card and books to read is important for all children. Also, our first teachers are parents; our churches and teachers are secondary, in no specific order. We must guide our Black children to help them understand about the "future." Jobs as ditch diggers are gone and Hispanics hold a monopoly on hotel jobs. We must instill in our children to "be the best" at whatever they are doing and they must "put forth the effort and try every day," and they must ask for help when they do not understand, don't know, or can't do. Students need to realize and understand that not completing assignments, being late to classes, making excuses that are not valid, crying, and cursing do not make people respect you or want to help you.

When I began teaching in 1975, it did not matter what color the child was. I told them all the same thing, "They had to respect me not like me." I think that goes for today's teachers who are getting no respect, in addition to low pay and more issues with student discipline. Furthermore, 27 or 28 of our brightest or average students are too many for one teacher to handle. We must look at class size and consider reducing it to twenty students at every grade level. Finally, we might consider looking for areas of strength and extreme interest in students and use the basis of Individual Education Plans (IEPs) that are developed for special needs students to create similar academic plans for each child.

If I had to, yes, I could teach in today's schools. Because I had six jobs before teaching, I know that there are other things that I can do. But I like kids and I do not mind talking to people. I think that I could establish the rules and regulations in my classroom today and make sure that kids understand and follow them. Most important, I could still teach them how to read.

Bernadette Hamilton has received recognition and awards for her dedication to education. She has served as bookkeeper for St. George Episcopal Church since 1990; as ambassador for Maryhurst, a former member of Delta Kappa Gamma, an educational society, and as a member of the Board of Dare to Care. A member of Alpha Kappa Alpha Sorority, Inc., Eta Omega Chapter, Bernadette is also a member of the Louisville Chapter of the Moles, Inc.; The Louisville Chapter of Girl Friends, Inc.; and she formerly served on the Episcopal Diocese of Kentucky's Trustees and Council as well as serving as President of the Kentucky Association for Gifted Education (KAGE). She is married to the world famous sculptor, Ed Hamilton. They are the parents of two children, Edward III and Kendra.

Gwendolyn House-Cork

Second Career Elementary Teacher
and Community Volunteer

THE JOURNEY TO TEACHING WAS different for women of my generation. Born in the 1930s, it was somewhat unusual for a female to have two careers, each of which required a different college degree. It was even more unusual for a Black woman to accomplish this feat, becoming a teacher as a second career when one professional career was widely sought and many times unattainable. My background and upbringing may shed some light on my career transition.

*Christine Howard
Photographer*

Raised by my maternal great aunt and her husband, Uncle Charles, I was born to parents who were not married, and I became the "treasured child" of the family. Mom's and Dad's families were close. While Dad never had additional children, Dad's brother, Uncle Joe, had Michael and Sondra, my first cousins who were college graduates. Going back further, my great grandpa Andrew Hoffman, born a slave in 1862, was three years old when slavery was abolished. His father was a farm owner and his mother was a slave. Grandpa had twelve children, many of whom died before he died at age ninety-two. Those aunts, uncles, and cousins were a source of inspiration and support throughout my childhood.

My mother's family resided mostly in Tennessee. While Mom was usually employed as a domestic in private homes and Dad worked as an attendant in the men's rest room at the Brown Hotel, Mom's parents, my grandparents, Myra and George Nesbitt, were teachers in one-room school houses in country areas in Tennessee. Each summer they had to attend Tennessee State College in order to remain qualified to teach.

My dad, Thomas House, did not marry until he was up in age, but my mom married my stepfather, Harvey Hawthorne, and moved to Cleveland, Ohio, when I was six or seven years old. Harvey went to work for Chase and Brass Manufacturing Company. Mom and Harvey came to Louisville every Christmas, and I spent every summer in Cleveland during school break. I even had summer jobs in Cleveland when I was old enough to work. My Mom became pregnant with Harvetta, my half-sister, when I was 17-years-old. So, for many years, I was a cherished child of the House, Hoffman, Nesbitt, and Hawthorne families.

I lived with Uncle Charles and Aunt Doshie on Nineteenth Street between Walnut and Madison streets. We had a happy house where everyone read books and talked about the books that they read. My aunt walked me to school each morning. We were friends. Western Elementary School was great! Ms. Peters, my first-grade teacher, had reading groups, the Blue Birds, the Yellow Birds, and the Red Birds. No one told you, but you knew if you were in an achievement group or a group that needed help with reading. There were no advanced programs, but students knew if they were high- performing or "smart." I had a love for reading before I went to school and never struggled in that area. My uncle, my mother's brother Andrew, was the intellectual in the family, even though he received his diploma through night school. Later when he was in the service, he sent me a map of the world. In later years, he would order books and I would pick them up for him in a downtown Louisville bookstore. My aunt kept the books that I read as a child and I shared some of those same books with my children and grandchildren. I believe reading has always been an encourager for my entire family, all avid readers.

Madison Jr. High School's general classes where you read and used your mind were fine; however, I had a terrible time in sewing class. I liked the foods class and loved Ms. Ramsey and her husband who both taught me Math. I remember my greatest challenge in junior high was I had to climb a rope in gym, which I finally did with great effort. There was no bullying, name calling, or fighting like you hear about on the news in today's schools. I had buddies at school and at church, West Chestnut Street Baptist Church; was in a Scout troupe and bore the nickname "Bootsie," after a cartoon character in the newspaper called *Boots and Her Buddies*, said to fit me because I always had buddies. I almost did not remember that my name was Gwendolyn because everyone called me Bootsie, even most of my teachers. I became Gwen when I went to college.

Graduating from Central High School in 1951 is a story unto itself. My classes had always been with the "achiever group," which meant homework-homework-homework. One day another group of students questioned why we were doing this and that and all of that "homework" and they were not. This was an awkward confrontation, group-to-group since these students may not have been our academic peers, but they were our social peers.

Doc. Whedbee, Mrs. Lauderdale, and Mr. Davidson taught our college-bound group. No secret to our teachers or our counselor, we were all planning on attending college. In January of my eleventh grade year, we were told as a group that it would be to our advantage to graduate in June with the Class of 1951 rather than in January with the Class of 1951 ½. To their thinking, it would be better for us to enter college in September rather than in January. To graduate early, we had to take two English classes simultaneously for the "skip." Being in the upper quartile, we were "looked after" by our teachers and we took the advice that they offered. My group came out early and entered college in September of 1951. I received a partial scholarship to Central State College, entering my program without any financial worries, assured that my family would meet my needs as I was still their "treasure."

They knew, and I always knew, that I was going to college, and every family member who worked was willing to support me. Every Saturday I could count on getting an envelope in the mail with three one dollar bills for spending money from Cousin Anna Laura.

I had not planned to become a teacher when I entered Central State. My intentions were to follow in my cousin's footsteps, becoming a laboratory technician after completing a two-year program and one-year internship. My cousin from St. Louis had discussed her training at one of our family reunions that began when I was 13 or 14 years old. The children from all over the country slept on the floor on pallets in whichever home we gathered when we met. The older unmarried children talked about what they were doing in school, how things were going, and their careers. I felt lab tech was a good choice for me because it would not take too long and I loved science. What I did not know was the upper-level courses like bio-chemistry and organic chemistry, needed for the lab-tech program at Central State were unavailable to freshmen or sophomores.

Because I was adamant about the program I wanted and I talked to everyone at registration who would listen, I was finally allowed to register as a special student and take the courses that I needed, provided I made continual progress—no "F's." I did not have a problem, but, again, one of my teachers looked out for me. Mr. Lane, a biology teacher at Central State suggested that I consider medical technology, an emerging field rather than lab tech. He gave me information about the two colleges in the United States that offered a full degree in medical technology. Nazareth College in Louisville, Kentucky, was one of the institutions.

I did not complete my internship year at Central State, but transferred all of my coursework to Nazareth, today's Spalding University. The Med Tech Program at Nazareth was a five-year program, including a one-year internship that I completed at St. Joseph's Hospital. I worked as a medical technologist for fourteen years before transitioning to teaching in 1970.

Becoming a teacher was a selfish decision based on my wanting to spend more time with my three children. Med tech did not have off time, but worked year-round, some weekends, and some holidays.

When asked how can we recruit individuals to the teaching profession, I say remind them of the work schedule—9 ½ months with summers off. It worked for me.

My husband discouraged me from returning to school to become certified as a teacher. I continued working full-time while taking classes at night. To be honest, I was excited that my brain was working again and I had not embarrassed myself in classes where others were also working on master's degrees, but were much younger and had attended college more recently. When I later decided to return to school full-time, I chose elementary education as my major, even though I could have selected secondary education because I had a bachelor's degree with a major in biology and a minor in chemistry. My decision was influenced by the extra-curricular and after-school activities that secondary teachers were expected to sponsor or participate in, when I wanted more time with my own children. Also, committing to teach in Title I schools earned financial support to help pay tuition for the Master of Arts in Teaching degree.

I completed student teaching at the elementary school that I attended, then called William H. Perry Elementary. My actual teaching assignments were at Perry, Roosevelt, Atkinson, Booker T. Washington, and Breckenridge Elementary schools. I taught self-contained grades with 25 to 30 students for four or five years, then migrated to the Math-Plus Program at the suggestion of my principal. I then taught 80 or more students daily in Grades 1-6. My principal had watched the progress that I had made with my sixth grade self-contained students and felt that my skills would be useful to students struggling with math and teachers struggling to teach catch-up math skills.

Math Plus was an excellent program. It was structured and allowed students to acquire and/or build upon skills in a systemic fashion, moving from easy to hard. The program provided manipulatives, a structured curriculum, and structured assessments reflective of specific skills taught. For example, if we were working on division, we began easy with one-place divisors and moved to harder four-place divisors as students learned the skills and demonstrated proficiency. Friday was my "Move-Up Day" where students who mastered the skills for that week were given special activities and treats. I remember meeting one of my elementary students at a gas station. He had completed college, but he still remembered, Hard Add, Hard Subtract, Hard Multiply, and Four-Place Division. He was still a little miffed that I did not allow him to do five-place division.

My 20 years of teaching, most of which were in Title 1 schools, was an excellent second career for me. I raised my children, completed a 30-Hour Rank I Program, participated in activities sponsored by my sorority, Delta Sigma Theta, Inc., and I helped children. Student test results told me that my students made improvements in math knowledge and skills. Over the years, students themselves have told me how I made a difference in their lives. I have seen some of my students become teachers and have watched them impact the lives of their students. While teaching was not my first career choice, I am blessed that I made the right decision in selecting teaching as my second career and have had opportunities to positively impact the lives of many children.

Gwen House Cork retired in 1990 at the urging of her husband who had retired from postal management five years earlier. Married for more than 62 years, Gwen and her husband, Thomas Earl Cork, Sr., who received the Congressional Gold Medal for his military efforts in the Korean War, have three children who attended Jefferson County Schools before Merger. They have two grandchildren who also attended JCPS. Both their children and grandchildren all graduated from Ballard High School. Gwen, along with one of her colleagues, formed the Retired Educators group to work with Black Achievers. She and another friend put their postal retiree husbands to work in what became a third career as a small business owner. She still enjoys talking rather than texting or email. She loves oral history and continues to review and treasure documents from her ancestors, celebrating her heritage by contributing to efforts like purchasing memorial stones at the African American Heritage Museum. Gwen is also past president of the Graduate Chapter of Delta Sigma Theta Sorority, Inc. Gwen and her husband were both selected as Black Achievers, sponsored by Churchill Downs, and she has served on the boards of several community organizations. She also continues working with her church family, West Chestnut Street Baptist Church.

Dr. LeDita Howard-Hobbs

Teacher, Resource Teacher, Principal, Principal
Coordinator, Adjunct Professor, K-TIP
Coordinator, Program Director, and Pastor

Dissertation Title: *An Exploratory Comparative Study
of Behavioral Strategies for At-Risk Children from Two
Pre-School Classrooms in the Jefferson County Public
Schools in Louisville, Kentucky*

MY MOM, EDNA ROBERTS SMITH, taught business at Central High School and died when I was eight days old. I was born at the segregated Red Cross Hospital in Louisville, Kentucky and, I am a second-generation college graduate since my mom graduated from Wilberforce University in Ohio. As an only child, I spent my early years living with my grandparents, Fannie and Cliff Roberts. Their daughter, my Aunt Generia, and her husband lived down the street and visited every day.

Steven Hobbs Photographer

I had a wonderful upbringing even though I was not close to my father who lived away from Louisville. I lived on Greenwood Avenue, a predominantly white neighborhood at that time, and my family often travelled to California by train to visit relatives or to St. Louis to visit my cousins. Occasionally, I visited my Dad in Chicago. I remember the first spanking that I received because of those cousins. As two of my white neighbors walked down the street, my cousins called out "nigger, nigger, nigger," and I joined in. I was taught to never use that word again.

Ms. Brown, my kindergarten teacher, helped me to love school. She was kind and loving, always approachable with her gentle manner. However, my all-time favorite teacher was Gladys Carter, my third-grade teacher. She was loved by all. She challenged us and made learning fun. She was considerate, loving, and caring. She gave us hugs. Now my second spanking was because two other third-grade students and I attended Ms. Carter's mother's funeral after school. My grandmother did not know where I was, and it scared her to death that I did not come home right after school. In fact, all the parents were quite upset.

I cannot talk about elementary school without talking about my second-grade experience. The death of my mom and distant dad was common knowledge among some faculty since my dad now dated my school's secretary. For some reason, my second-grade teacher insisted that the quiet, reserved, shy, and sometimes nonverbal LeDita was suffering and not performing well because of her traumatic childhood and needed to be placed in another class. This teacher sent me to an ungraded special class in the basement without telling my parents. When I finally told Aunt Generia, all H_____ broke loose. Principal Liggins had no idea that I had been moved. To say the least, I was moved back into my regular classroom. However, I do believe that my short-term experiences with those "basement kids" left a scar that remained with me throughout my life and influenced my decision to become a special-needs teacher.

My junior high school years were another experience altogether. In 1957, I went from an all-Black school—teachers and students—to Shawnee Jr. High School with all- white teachers and very few Black students. My grandfather insisted that I go to Shawnee rather than DuValle Jr. High because he felt I needed to "assist with integration."

I knew that the students did not like me, and I had very few friends. The one white friend that I remember became my friend by accident. She was considered pretty, with long blond hair. I remember asking her if I could touch her hair. I stroked it, felt its softness, and stroked again. I asked her if I could comb it and she said yes, so I combed it. After that, Phyllis was always friendly.

I always loved music. My mom played the piano every day when she was pregnant with me. She told Aunt Generia that she was going to "mark" her baby. I feel that she did because I played the violin and was in band and chorus. One ugly incident that I've never forgotten happened at Shawnee in the music room. I can't remember why I went to school early, but another student and I were alone in the room early. I really don't recall what I said, but she turned around and slapped me so hard that I saw stars. The strange thing is that I did nothing. I did not retaliate. I didn't tell anyone. This was just an unpleasant flash in the music room that etched itself in my memory.

My grandmother died from breast cancer when I was 11 years old, and my grandfather, a waiter at the Kentucky Hotel, died six months later. I had my third mom and dad in junior high school, Aunt Generia and her husband Uncle A.B., an avid tennis player. They took over the chore of raising me. Aunt Generia worked as a teacher's assistant in the reading program and always thought that people were watching how she raised me. While she had not completed college, she was surrounded by college graduates, from our cousin, Dr. Fred Sampson, who was on the Louisville Board of Education, to teachers with whom she interacted daily and the teachers who lived in our neighborhood. She did not want me to make a misstep and she shepherded me through high school.

My high school days were totally different from junior high. You could still count on one hand the number of African-American students in my classes, usually no more than four. However, when I walked through the hallways, there were students who spoke to me— Ann Garrison, Marie Porter, Ishmon Burks, Danny Lawson—to name a few. Also, by the ninth grade, I had teachers who understood the children they taught. My physical education and Spanish teachers were my favorites. They were aware of students' strengths and shortcomings. My Spanish teacher made me love Spanish. She praised me when I did well and told me that "maybe someday you can go to Spain or a Spanish-speaking country." I took Spanish classes years after my retirement from Jefferson County Public Schools and, yes, I did go to Spain. Two other teachers, Mr. Johnson, history and sociology, and Ms. Hale, psychology, knew their content and taught it well. Mr. Johnson helped us understand Black-White relations and Ms. Hale gave us insight into our own psyche.

While I had only a few Black students in my classes, 20 Blacks out of 204 students, I reconnected with the Black community through my activism. I participated in the Civil Rights demonstration for freedom in downtown Louisville. I was arrested and rode in the back of a police car for demonstrating on Fourth Street for the integration of Blue Boar Restaurant, Stewarts Department Store, and the Marion Anderson and Ohio Movie Theaters. I was 1 of 265 students, including National Association for the Advancement of Colored People (NAACP) vice president, Raoul Cunningham, and my cousin Dr. Sampson, "locked up" that day. I was in the "Youth Choir" through the Chestnut Street YMCA at Tenth and Chestnut streets. I was chosen to work with the Human Rights Commission as a "tester." I went to Kresge's, a downtown five and dime store, and sat at the lunch counter to see if I would be served. I was sent to pharmacies/apothecaries with prescriptions to be filled. Later, the medication was analyzed to determine if it was what was actually prescribed. These were enlightening experiences. Also, the songs we learned and sang helped us to relieve stress.

I always knew that I was going to college and that I wanted to be a teacher because I wanted to follow in my mom's footsteps. However, the difficult classes that I had to take in high school made me question if college and teaching were for me. Aunt Generia, who exerted tight control over my social life, was the deciding factor. I wanted to get away from home, be on my own, and experience some of the things that my friend's sisters and brothers talked about. Murray State was as far as I could go and remain in state to keep down the cost, so I went to Murray State College. I kept down the cost.

My college years were tumultuous because of my first taste of freedom and falling in love. I had a great time going to Tennessee, going to Kentucky Lake, and staying out all night. My grades during freshman year were terrible. My advisor told me, "Maybe you need to go to Kentucky State where you can be with your own kind." I didn't go. I stayed out one semester, working in Louisville with Upward Bound, and later returned to Murray where I remained until my senior year when my fiancée and I broke off our engagement. I returned to Louisville to work as the children's librarian at Western Branch Library without a degree, my dreams of following in my mom's footsteps broken. I was crushed.

Through the heartbreak and disillusionment of young love, I finally fought my way back to my dream. I wanted to be a teacher and it was up to me, not my family or friends or teachers, to make my dream a reality. It was up to me. I had to make that difference for myself. I changed jobs, bought a car, and enrolled at the University of Louisville (U of L) for night classes. In 1975, I received my Bachelor's Degree in Elementary Education. The following year, I received a Master's in Education Degree f with certification in elementary education and Emotionally Disordered/Learning/Behavior Disorders, both degrees from U of L. Yes! I was certified to teach and had my first teaching job at Foster Elementary School.

Over my career, I can say that I loved teaching and working with teachers and parents of special-needs students. Dealing with this population was not easy, but it was extremely rewarding because at times, immediate results are realized, like talking an emotionally disabled child down from jumping off a ledge or teaching parents some simple strategies to keep their child from hurting himself and others. After leaving Foster Elementary, my assignment for six years was special education teacher at Keller Child Psychiatry, a medical model and partial hospital. Following that opportunity, I served as a teacher/consultant for JCPS for special education teachers for professional development and curriculum and instruction. Following that I became a principal for four years and principal coordinator at Dawson Orman Center and six special schools for eight years.

What made my career so meaningful was I learned as I taught. I incorporated methods and strategies and ideas from general education, from psychology, from medical professionals, and from curriculum gurus to find ways of helping my students or for helping my teachers help my students. We went beyond cookie-cutter methods of delivery because our students each had an Individual Education Plan or IEP that dictated individual attention and specificity in handling. We dealt with services for expanded classifications of special-needs students like Autistic classes for pre-school and for infants and two-year-olds. My teachers and I had to step up and continuously expand our knowledge and skills to help our parents and students.

One of the most important aspects of teaching and administering is building a culture of trust and respect in the teaching environment or where one is delivering services and understanding that one may need to use different strategies for differing environments. This may mean involving the community by knocking on doors and inviting parents into the school; asking other community organizations to join forces; adding programs to address specific issues like reading deficiencies; creating after-school programs to support student interest; providing resources to address social and emotional needs of parents and students; greeting students and calling them by name; recognizing students for their accomplishments; or doing something silly like dancing the Macarena with students or wall-climbing with teachers.

However, in the end, parents must trust teachers; teachers must trust administrators; and the children must trust all three. Parents want to feel that their children's teachers care about them, whether it is an Atkinson Elementary parent or Lyndon Elementary parent. Children want to feel that they can trust their teachers because their teachers know them and care about them individually. And, teachers want to know that they are respected by parents and administrators who support them and want them to be effective and successful when dealing with children.

I also have observed teachers, students, and classrooms in China and Japan to find methods that may be used to improve student achievement in our schools here. That has been difficult because we are transitioning cultures. What was outstanding in those countries was the degree to which students were engaged in their learning. Students were more musically inclined as music commenced with pre-school. Furthermore, students began the morning routine and guided the exercises and teachers were businesslike. While this model seemed to work for them, I still see teachers as being "called," meaning they are caring and loving and have a positive personal relationship with students, recognizing the importance of the role that parents play since they are the child's first teacher. That partnership between teacher and parent means parents should think "time out" when they are about to do something negative in front of their children, and good teachers should think "time in," as they create that partnership focusing on students' accomplishments and achievement.

Dr. LeDita Howard-Hobbs is the former director of the Minority Teacher Recruitment Program at U of L and the past president of the local chapter of Phi Delta Kappa. She has studied at the Presbyterian Seminary and Simmons University where she is pursuing a degree in religious studies. She holds a Doctorate in Education from Century University. LeDita, a breast cancer survivor, has published a number of articles and is in the process of completing her first book on Positioning Power. She is also an associate pastor at Zion Baptist Church, Inc. Since her retirement, Dr. Howard has continued to travel and found Cape Town, South Africa, and Rio de Janeiro to be her favorites.

Howard-Hobbs Family Photo Collection
Principal Hobbs celebrating Black History Month
with her students at Atkinson Elementary

Dr. Bonnie Nelson Marshall

Teacher, Program Director, Parent and Community Organizer, Adjunct Professor, Teacher Mentor, Teacher Preparation Program Consultant, University Supervisor, Program and Grant Writer, and Advisor to the Kentucky Department of Education

Dissertation Title: *The Attitudes of African American Males About Teaching: The Impact of Participating in Minority Teacher Recruitment Programs*

I WAS BORN IN GASTONBURG, ALABAMA, the oldest daughter in a family of four siblings, with two older brothers. My mom and dad, members of very large families, were extremely intelligent trailblazers and risk takers. Daddy was exceptionally good in math and Mama's strengths were reading and anything artistic. They attended one-room, segregated schools in very impoverished areas. Potbellied stoves, outdated books, and a single teacher for all grades were the norm for the time. Neither of them attended high school, but both were

Marshall Family Photo Collection

bright enough to complete two grades in one year on more than one occasion.

My parents were farmers who worked with their hands, crude machinery, and strong wills. They leased acres of land from a white landowner in a sharecropping kind of arrangement. However, after a time, the owner did not take his share from my father's sales. Instead, Daddy was responsible for reading about and growing new crops for the landowner. He was so successful with his responsibilities of raising new corps that when my father was drafted into the military, that same landowner told the Draft Board that, "Enoch is a good man and does not need to go to war." Daddy was given a military deferment while his brother and many other men in the area were drafted.

My family relocated to Louisville, Kentucky, when I was three years old. Daddy and Mama decided that they wanted a better life for their children than what sharecropping would provide. Daddy came to Louisville to find work before sending for us. When we arrived in Louisville, we moved in with my uncle's family for about six months. Uncle Bud, Daddy's brother, had been stationed at Ft. Knox and had invited Daddy to stay with them until he became familiar with the area and had secured employment. Later, Mama and Daddy rented a basement apartment at Thirty-six and Greenwood streets. Not liking the environment of the basement apartment, Mama and Daddy moved to a three-room rental house in the alley behind Thirty-Six Street and Hale Avenue prior to Daddy and Mama deciding that we needed a home of our own. City Hall approved the plans that Daddy drew for the house. He constructed our first home during the day while working nights at Atlas Plaster and Supply Company. Mama helped support the family by working as a domestic in private homes. Years later, when the City of Louisville purchased our home to make way for the construction of Interstate 264, the city inspector told my parents that our home should have been built in the Highlands because of its superior construction and the "stuff" that my parents had put into the home.

I was a student at Virginia Avenue Elementary throughout my elementary grades. When I think of those elementary days, I know they were about shaping students. Mrs. Cleopatra Gregory and Ms.

Laverne Smith were my favorite teachers. In second grade, Ms. Smith always had something special for me to do. I was shy and would sit back and not say anything. She drew the quietness out of me and made me become a leader by making me her assistant.

Cleopatra Gregory taught me in Grades 5 and 6. Her class did so well in fifth grade that the principal moved her with us to the sixth grade. I was excited and happy in Ms. Gregory's class. She emphasized how smart women were; she taught us to perform native and modern dances. We learned the Thirteenth, Fourteenth and Fifteenth Amendments and their importance to our lives. She pushed us to take tests, teaching us test-taking strategies that I use to this day when I train future teachers for taking the PRAXIS Test. She read Shakespeare's *Merchant of Venus,* and I learned how important it is to be exact in my dealings with others.

Our principal, Mr. Clyde Liggin, presided over student assemblies each month, discussing a variety of topics, including Black History, current events, and cultural issues. Sometimes he featured people we should know about and highlighted topics that supported what our parents were teaching us at home as well as major and minor issues related to our school and community. One of his legendary programs even addressed "bathroom etiquette." We were taught that, "once you use the bathroom, wash your hands and wash-off the soap so that you leave the soap clean." Mr. Liggin would walk up and down the aisles, asking questions and telling students, "Look me in the eye when you are talking to me." He would often stop us in the hallways and question us about what we learned in class and in assembly sessions. He praised us when we answered correctly and scolded us when we did not know. He would tell us to know the answer the next time we saw him.

Mr. Joseph Robinson, my counselor, was one of my favorite adults at DuValle Junior High where we had regular class counseling periods. We discussed social issues, drugs, our future hopes and aspirations, and college. We were grouped by ability or "tracked." Mr. Robinson invited sorority and fraternity members to speak to our class.

Mr. James Coleman was another junior high school teacher who taught us about peaceful protests. I remember how the class decided that we were tired of taking tests two or three times a week. One day, we refused to take the test he had prepared. He threatened us with our grades and with notifications to parents. Most of the class caved. Those of us who continued the protest were kept after class and praised for taking a stand. He first questioned our motives and then provided us with strategies that would have increased the effectiveness of what we were trying to do. He allowed us to have input on our class procedures while still maintaining his strong leadership role.

Principal Thomas Long would free-up teachers to talk to us about where they had gone to college. His message, loud and clear was, "You are going to college." I took French and Algebra I at DuValle. Our educators pushed us to excel; they were preparing us academically, socially and emotionally for life. I believe that my schooling prepared me better than the schooling my own children received because my children, Kenneth and John, did not have the scope of exposure and preparation that I had. They did not have the knowledgeable and caring Black teachers emphasizing and pushing them to be the "best and the brightest" as I had.

Central High School (CHS) was my favorite K-12 experience. Classes continued in academic tracks; we explored different career paths with our counselor, Mr. Lowery, and results of the Kuder Preference Tests guided our career choices. Two of my favorite teachers of all times were Thelma Lauderdale and Lyman Johnson.

Mr. Johnson taught history by telling fact-filled stories—just "crude" enough to capture the attention of inquisitive and mischievous teenagers. We wrote more notes in his class than we did in most college classes. We read, researched, discussed, and debated issues. He taught us to analyze information and discern important points. We would fold a piece of recycled paper in fourths to answer his test questions or to condense information into its major points.

Mrs. Thelma Lauderdale taught us to read a variety of materials, problem solve, think critically, speak effectively, question, express ourselves creatively, and be accountable for our actions. She was a strict teacher with high expectations from her students. She had a great sense of humor and would like to catch us making ridiculous mistakes.

I never had a choice about going to college. My parents knew that I was going; we just didn't know where. During the 1960s, students in my group were highly recruited and received early acceptance letters because smart, Black students were sought to integrate white colleges, and HBCUs did not want to lose their talented students because of integration. Mr. Lowery completed inquiry applications for most students in my class. For me, he completed applications to Marian University, Kalamazoo, Knoxville, and Central State colleges, all of which accepted me; however, my parents were unaware. I hid the acceptance letters because I was concerned about finances and the cost that my parents would incur if I attended. It never dawned on me about getting a scholarship.

When Mr. Lowery had not heard from me or my parents about my choice or next steps, he called my parents for a conference. When Mama and Daddy met with Mr. Lowery, Mama spread index cards with the names of the colleges where I had been accepted. She looked at me and said, "Pick one." I chose Knoxville College.

Oretha Norris, a CHS graduate who attended Knoxville, spoke to our group during English class with Mrs. Lauderdale. Her description of college life at Knoxville peaked my interest. I thought Knoxville was a fit for me even though I continued worrying about how my parents would have to work to keep me there.

In the end, my tuition, books, room and board were paid primarily by scholarship and my worries subsided. Several CHS students from my class enrolled at Knoxville and several from prior CHS classes were at Knoxville when I arrived. I initially chose Math Education as a major. While I did well in the mathematics coursework, it did not come easy to me, and I was intimidated by the genius of the head of the Mathematics Department, Dr. William Harvey.

Dorothy Kitt Howell, the head of the Elementary Education Department, taught several other courses that I took. There was something about Ms. Howell that attracted me to her classes which reminded me of Cleopatra Gregory's classes in elementary school. I switched my major to Elementary Education, leaving my buddies who were math majors.

When Ms. Howell took a medical leave the first semester of my junior year, I was asked to teach her classes. I was scared to death teaching my classmates. I wasn't paid to teach, but I received credit for the classes that I taught. I was honored when Ms. Howell told me, "I see something special in you." The second semester of my junior year brought my own medical trauma. I was diagnosed with tuberculosis and left Knoxville to be hospitalized in Louisville until my recovery. I returned to Knoxville the following August after full recovery, ready to complete my degree. Having communicated with several of my professors, I picked up where I left off and forged ahead. When I arrived on campus, I made a promise to myself that I was going to be the best I could be and not slack on my work or take my "talents" for granted.

I did not do traditional student teaching. Instead, when I was completing "Phase Work," a fourth-grade teacher at one of Knoxville's cooperating schools began maternity leave. I took her class as the teacher. Again, I did not get paid. I had frequent observations and evaluations, but I did not have that luxury of a supervising teacher in the room with me. A teacher educator from Knoxville College visited me every week to assist me with planning. She always asked, "What are you doing next week?" The principal kept tabs on me as well, visiting my class daily, talking to me and to my students. My "student teaching" was the real "learning by doing." At the end of my assignment, the principal sent letters to Knoxville College and to the Knoxville Board of Education's Human Resource Department praising my work with the fourth-grade class. In December 1968, my coursework at Knoxville was officially completed.

When I interviewed with the Louisville Independent Schools in January 1969, I was hired and assigned to replace a white first-grade teacher at Henry Clay Elementary School. Located at Thirty-Fourth Street and River Park Drive where a fire station currently resides, Henry Clay's teaching staff was diverse, with an equal number of white and black teachers. Only a few white students attended there. Our principal was a white male with a military background. I earned $6,000 annually and was paid monthly. I probably lived better back then than I do now.

When I began teaching, I had freedom to teach and integrate curriculum, using lots of creativity to meet academic goals. We used Basal Readers and workbooks to push reading comprehension. We knew where we had to be, that is, what students needed to know by the end of the grade. The only things set were lunch and the beginning and end of the school year. We had Board of Education supervisors who observed and provided feedback, helping us stay on track. Grace Champion was an invaluable supervisor for me. Henry Clay, an old school with wooden floors and big cloak rooms closed. Our staff transferred to the new school, Whitney Young Elementary, named for a Black civil-rights leader. The West End had changed and the Black community wanted a school named for an African American.

Teaching first grade was my most rewarding teaching experience. Seeing the change in my students from those who entered first grade, not kindergarten-ready and unable to read or write to those making academic progress, fulfilled a personal commitment and goal. I loved teaching and I loved my students.

I was transferred to Goldsmith Elementary when a court-ordered merger of Louisville Independent Schools and Jefferson County Public Schools began in 1975. While I began as the first-grade teacher, Principal Mary Dove asked me to move to third grade to teach students in the Advanced Program (AP). I taught AP for two or three years but requested to return to teach students in the Comprehensive Program (CP) because only one or two Black students were placed in my AP classes. I had the cream of the crop white students, but I wanted to share my gift with "my" people. Black children bused to Goldsmith were underserved in the CP and underrepresented in the AP. The climate of the school for Black students did not align with my beliefs about teaching ALL children.

Many of my first-grade students from Henry Clay went into AP when they were tested because of their brightness and their exposure to what was considered as AP curriculum. I taught them as much as I thought they could absorb. For example, I did not know that I wasn't supposed to teach them certain concepts and processes. I took them as far as I could take them and as far as they would go; yet, the Black students at Goldsmith could not make the cut for AP placement. While I have taught diverse groups of students, I have a special connection to Black students. Something happened when I looked upon their faces and they looked into my eyes. That "connection" was evident.

I moved from third-grade AP to fourth-grade CP. I was given the most challenging students in the school—little Black and white students who were some "Challenging Little Jokers." When I was at school, there were no problems. When I was absent, the students acted up. What many of my colleagues failed to realize was that those "jokers" were smart. Many of them outscored the AP class on the California Test of Basic Skills. Because my students scored so high, they were retested—thinking we cheated and sited "Irregularities" on the test. I was arrogant, cocky, and nasty when my students did so well. I had gone to the teachers' lounge during testing and let someone else administer the test. I told my students, "They think you are dumb and that you can't do it." They showed out. They did it! My students got even better scores and supported my belief that students will rise to the occasion if they feel you are going there with them. I remained at Goldsmith in the Comprehensive Program until 1988 when I became the Administrative Intern for the Minority Teacher Recruitment Project (MTRP).

I spent the next years of my JCPS career completing my doctoral degree at the University of Louisville under the guidance of Dr. William Husk while working as the coordinator of MTRP under the leadership of Montest Eaves, the first director of the JCPS Department of Equity and Poverty. Dr. Husk and Montest Eaves encouraged me to challenge the system, collaborate to maximize impact, make informative presentations, fund raise, supervise employees, interact with administrative personnel, and step out beyond my comfort level. I worked in a collaboratively supported position with the University of Louisville and the Jefferson County Public Schools. My responsibilities included recruiting individuals into the teaching profession and finding minority teachers for JCPS by working on a variety of education initiatives. I travelled to colleges and universities to identity prospective teacher candidates and prepare them to pass the National Teachers' and PRAXIS exams. I visited college and university bookstores to assure that candidates that we were interested in recruiting had exposure to the appropriate pedagogy that aligned with JCPS's progressive approach to teaching.

I designed the Middle School Teacher Awareness Program, the A-TEAM, Escorts to Success, and the Mathematics, Science,

Technology and Communications Programs to help create an early interest in teaching as a career among middle school students and the Tots-to-Teachers Program at a local elementary school to provide opportunities for students in elementary grades to learn about and respect teachers and teaching.

I had the opportunity to design Kentucky's first district-led Alternative Certification Program for Secondary Certification in collaboration with Kentucky State University. I worked with the Kentucky Department of Education to develop minority teacher, counselor, principal, and superintendent recruitment and retention programs for Kentucky. I also developed and managed the Career Paths and Project Rise Programs to support aspiring teachers who served in classified employee positions.

As I continued with minority educator shortage issues, I was fortunate to work on other concerns across the educational spectrum. I helped to write the charters for the Greater Louisville Alliance of Black School Educators and the Kentucky Alliance of Black School Educators. I identified ways to engage Black parents living in Lang and Cotter Homes in their children's education and designed a program to help to reduce the school district's middle school suspension rates.

I enjoyed this new focus and eagerly embraced the new opportunities. My role with the parent group that named itself "A Voice for Our Children" was to facilitate workshops and activities that assisted parents in understanding what "academic progress" meant for their children and what their roles in holding schools and teachers accountable looked like when they (parents and students) were doing what they were supposed to do. The Lang-Cotter Homes Parent Group became the model for the Parent Commission of the National Alliance of Black School Educators (NABSE). The group travelled across Kentucky on buses helping other parent groups get started. They became resources to help parents understand their rights, roles, and responsibilities.

My role in reducing suspension rates of Black middle school students was to develop the Broader Visions Program (BVP). This multifaceted program allowed students facing suspensions to spend up to five days at the BVP site to complete coursework assignments and participate in social and emotions learning sessions. It was my job to document trends and patterns in suspension practices for the Department of Equity and Poverty. Students participating in the BVP were not counted as suspended.

After retiring from JCPS, I began a second career as Director of Innovation at Spalding University. The College of Education (COE) needed ideas to get people into the COE and to get them to graduate. I developed an Alternative Certification Program for Spalding that included a large number of African-American males and resulted in a PRAXIS pass rate of 100% the first year and never dropping below 95%. The program prepared students to work in any school, both Catholic and public. The skills that were being assessed on state-required tests were incorporated in the coursework and in required and focused workshops. Students completing Spalding's alternate route teacher certification programs are current teachers and administrators in Bullitt, Oldham, Shelby, Meade, Hardin, Kenton, Henry, Franklin, Fayette, and Jefferson counties in Kentucky. I also designed a program with JCPS for instructors that allowed instructors to return to their classroom positions between completing student teaching and employment as a certified teacher.

Over the years, I have worked with the Kentucky Education Professional Standards Board as a member of the Kentucky Board of Examiners; as a State Trainer for the National Council for the Accreditation of Teacher Education (NCATE); and as a consultant for every state university in Kentucky, supporting the development of strong, effective teacher-preparation programs. I have maintained the belief that great teachers must have heart, a vision of where they want students to go, and a love for learning. Great teachers do not allow a child's status in the community to determine how that student will be treated. Instead, they pluck and propel them based on their abilities and talents--just as Ms. Lavern Smith, Ms. Cleopatra Gregory, Mr. Joseph Robinson, Dr. James Coleman, Mr. Lyman Johnson, Mrs. Thelma Lauderdale, Ms. Dorothy Howell, Dr. William Husk, and Mr. Montest Eaves did for their students. Great teachers keep learning, remain knowledgeable and love teaching. They do not run when it gets tough but continue to support their students over time. In addition, they do not use social, economic, or learning challenges as excuses for students not achieving. They understand and teach above expectation. They understand how to teach and how learning occurs, going beyond the "script" they are given, using their own "bag of tricks" and inserting their own creativity based on the needs of their students. They also understand that parents are critical components to the education partnership.

As I move into a "slow-down" phase as an educator, my focus reverts to supporting parents. When I began teaching, I visited with every parent, called them regularly, and easily related to them because we were close in age. As I developed parent programs in the community, I learned not to lead, but to sit back and follow. (Great teachers understand the value of listening to parents.)

As a retiree, I work with churches across the city helping parents understand what they need to know and do to help their children get kindergarten-ready. It disturbed me that 80% of Black babies do not have the knowledge and skills to enter kindergarten ready to learn, and, in many cases, parents do not know what their children need to know and be able to do. However, educators know that those babies will be on the slow track—behind for the rest of their school lives if interventions are not put in place. I believe that our churches are tremendous avenues for augmenting early childhood education by incorporating kindergarten-readiness skills in their religious education programs.

My compassion and heart for people are products of the training, development, beliefs, and faith put in place by my parents Ola Mae and Enoch Nelson. They taught me to care for people because they are people. My siblings (David, Samuel, and Annie), caring teachers and a supportive cast of extended family and community members have taught me the importance of building and maintaining positive relationships.

I understand the self-doubt of some people, but I do not condone it because I know they can overcome their fears and rise to heights they cannot imagine. I am thankful that I have been able to do my part to blend those belief systems together to positively impact teaching and learning in the Louisville community.

Dr. Bonnie Marshall enjoys support from a close-knit family. She is the proud mother and mother-in-law of four educators, John, Kenneth, Tiffany, and Nichole. All four are employed by Jefferson County Public Schools. John is the Chief Equity Officer for Diversity, Equity, and Poverty. Kenneth is the associate principal of a state agency school. Tiffany and Nichole are elementary principals. Bonnie's deceased husband Kenneth was a trainer/educator for the Kentucky Law Enforcement Council. Her family calls education "the family business." Bonnie has six grandchildren (Isaac, Arika, Kaden, Kendyll, Kennedy, and Kori) who attend or have graduated from JCPS. Her sister, Annie Harlan, was a high school mathematics educator for the school district with more than 30 years of service. Annie and her husband Joe, a retired associate director of programming for WAVE 3 television station, have one daughter, Jillyan, who also attended JCPS schools and completed her doctorate in pharmacy studies at the University of Tennessee. Bonnie's brother, David, and sister-in-law, Dorothy, are both ministers who retired from engineering and nursing professions. Bonnie and her family have created a scholarship fund to support educational attainment in Louisville's Black community. Currently, Bonnie's social, civic, and religious work centers around membership at Phillips Memorial CME Church, scholarship committee work with the Louisville Branch NAACP, facilitation of a Religious Educators Group, and membership on The Beech, Inc. Board of Directors. She has received numerous awards and recognition over her professional career; however, one recognition that means most to her is the recognition given to her by her former students in recognition of 30 years of service to education. She is appreciative of opportunities she has been afforded to serve.

Edward Anthony Newton

Secondary Teacher, Drill Team Coach,
Track Coach, and Counselor

I ALWAYS WANTED TO GO TO COL-
lege, but I didn't know how I was going to get
there other than being the best drum major in the state of Florida. When every day
of your young life you hear about, see, and
hear music and marching bands everywhere
you look and everywhere you go, music and
marching become part of you and part of
everything that you know.

I was born and raised in Liberty City, a
suburb of Miami, Florida. My parents, Daisey
and James Newton, were hard workers who
managed their own corner grocery store after

Newton Family Photo Collection

dad left his job with the railroad. Although my mom attended college,
she was a homemaker until they opened the grocery store where Mom
cooked the different foods that we sold. We were not poor, but we were
not rich either. My hard-working parents made sure that we had plenty
to eat and a decent house to live in by owning their own business.

Number two in the family, I had an older brother and a younger brother and sister. We all attended segregated Liberty City Elementary School for Grades 1 through 6 and Dorsey Junior High School for Grades 7 through 9. I began playing in the band in junior high school with Mr. Thurston, one of my favorite teachers. Everybody looked at my tall, thin, over six-foot frame and assumed I would play basketball. They didn't know that my idol was the drum major in Florida A&M's band. My goal was to lead the band, to be out front high-stepping, strutting, and showing those precise movements and turns that most people could not do, even with lots of practice.

When I was at Northwestern High School, which sat smack-dab next to the Housing Projects, I did practice and practice to be the best. Sometimes, I would see people in the Projects watching me. Mr. Pascal, the high school band director was impressed with my movement and skills. I auditioned and got the job as drum major my junior year in high school. Mr. Pascal had an unwritten policy that he followed. If a student was in band for four years, he saw to it that you went to college if you wanted to go.

For the four years that I was at Northwestern, I played trumpet in the band and was drum major. During my senior year, I received full scholarship offers from North Carolina A&T College, Mississippi Valley State College, Jackson State College, Tennessee State College, and Kentucky State (K-State) College. I had a difficult time deciding which college to choose because I had another goal—performing in the Orange Bowl. Jackson State was my first choice, but Jackson State had gone to the Orange Bowl the year before, and I believed they would not go two years in a row, so I eliminated Jackson State. Of the remaining colleges, Kentucky State added another incentive that made it stand out. Kentucky State agreed to give me *and* my brother who was in the band, full scholarships if I would accept their offer. My family did not have the money to send me to college or to send my brother. It was a no-brainer. I chose Kentucky State.

K-State did not have a real band when I got there. We were called "The Stumbling 30." It took four band directors before we got the right leadership, the assistant band director from Tennessee State, brought onboard by our new college president, Dr. Hill, who understood "showmanship," and we put on a show. By my junior year in college, there were more than 230 members of the K-State Marching Band, half from Florida and half from Tennessee. Our three drum majors were from Florida as well. We brought Florida A&M to Kentucky State. At half-time, the sports fans never left their seats because they waited for us to perform. I was living my dream and leading the pact.

During my senior year, I completed student teaching at Russell Junior High School and Central High, graduating on time in four years in 1966. Mr. Bobby Edwards, a great instrumentalist, was my cooperating teacher. My bachelor's degree was in Music Education, and more than anything, I wanted to be a band director, but I could not get a job as a teacher. I worked at Seagram's Distillery for a short time until a friend of mine, Charlie Roberts, a teacher, told me about a position at DuValle Jr. High School teaching vocational students and organizing the school's drill team. It was not a high school marching band, but it was a great start for me.

The DuValle Drill Team performed all over the city of Louisville, at Indiana University, during University of Louisville (U of L) basketball games, at Bellarmine College, and in several Derby Pegasus parades. I taught my team my basic belief as a drum major—when you show up, show out. My young ladies were proud, professional, and accomplished even though they lived in Cotter Homes and Southwick Housing Projects. They were respected in their neighborhood and at school. Mr. Long, our principal, treated the group as a prized possession. They had a practice area that was off limits to outsiders and the rest of the school. He welcomed and appreciated their parents. It was the students' mothers who actually made the uniforms for the team. Denny Crum, coach at U of L, allowed these girls to perform on his sacred basketball court wearing their "stomping boots." Over the years when I have seen my drill team participants, they recall some of their experiences and how those experiences impacted their lives and their future.

My first high school teaching experience was at Male High School. Male wanted an experienced drill team coach and an Occupation Work Experience (OWE) teacher. OWE students attended school for half a day and worked at jobs that I secured for them the other half of the day. Their work experience counted as credits toward graduation.

I observed students in their work environments, conferenced with their supervisors, and coordinated grading for the course. My student orientation was about work ethic, including teaching students about the importance of being on time, following directions, being respectful to their supervisors, dressing appropriately for their jobs, coming to work as assigned, greeting customers appropriately, staying on the job for their designated shift, and doing the job that they had been assigned to do. The work ethic that I preached to my students years ago appear to be challenges for today's workforce, according to several news reports.

I built the Male Drill Team for two years with half of my team members coming from DuValle. At that time, students could choose the high school they wished to attend. During my third year at Male, an unexpected twist affecting my future career materialized. I became coach of a sport that I knew nothing about, Track and Field, and my team won the State Track and Field Competition during my second year as coach. Now, for more than 40 years, I have coached track.

My coaching mentor was Coach Bob Thompson. Just like I could walk through Cotter Homes and Southwick without fear because everyone knew not to bother DuValle's Drill Team coach, Coach Thompson could walk through the Projects without worrying about his safety because he was the Track coach. He and I were both seen as supportive and caring for our "Project" kids. We did not have problems with parents, or with students, or in our neighborhood. I firmly believe this it was because we showed that we cared about our kids. We sometimes had to slip them a few dollars to feed them, and we did so without broadcasting to everybody that this child was hungry and broke. Anybody that I have ever coached will tell you that when you screwed up, I would say, "Take off my uniform," and threaten to make them walk home. They also will tell you that I followed my old band director's philosophy that Coach Thompson also shared, "If kids run for you for four years, you owe them an opportunity to go to college if they want to go." This was not about the 3.5 Grade Point Average (GPA) students, but the 2.3 GPA group of kids who were more athletic than academic. Time after time, I practiced my belief that if a kid ran for me, I had to find some place to send him or her after graduation.

Parents during that time depended on kids getting scholarships, not loans. As Coach Thompson put it, "There is a place for every kid. It is the coach's job to find it," and we did.

Prior to the Merger of the city and county school systems, I had outstanding female athletes who won state titles and went to colleges and universities with outstanding Track programs, including Tennessee with the Tennessee State Tiger Bells; Alabama A&M, and Western Kentucky University. In 1975 when the school districts merged, I remained at Male High. One of my favorite stories is about the twins and a friend who were assigned to Male for one year, but remained that second year instead of returning to Moore. There was no bus to take those students home from school. I would take the students home through the back streets and drop them off about three blocks from their house where they would walk the rest of the way. They were more fearful that someone might see me and do me harm than they were afraid for their own safety. We came in second in the State Track and Field competition. They graduated from Male, one going to the University of Kentucky (U of K) on a track scholarship and the other two going to college, but not for track.

I was at Ballard High School from 1979 to 1986, continuing to work with the OWE Program and coaching track. Two outstanding athletes were Donna Combs and Karen Johnson. Donna was a distance runner who eventually was inducted into the Hall of Fame at Ballard and into Kentucky's Hall of Fame for Track and Field. Karen was an outstanding runner as well and received several scholarship offers. In fact, from 1979 to 1986, every senior on our track team received a scholarship.

My last full-time school assignment was at Shawnee High School. From 1986 to December 1997, I served as a school guidance counselor, initially under Herold Fenderson. We enrolled 1300 students when I began at Shawnee. I loved Shawnee and principal Fenderson who had a vision and beliefs about how we could help our students advance and be productive wage earners with good-paying jobs. He looked for ways to partner with business and industry and made use of my business contacts through the OWE Program. He was innovative and forward thinking, traits that successful leaders must develop. He also had a dynamic personality that could sell kids, parents, and staff on an idea and get them onboard.

I liked working with OWE, but I could help more students being a counselor. As a counselor, principal Fenderson helped me hone my skills to "sell" our students, be they track students or others, to colleges and universities, making the number of Shawnee students being accepted into college multiply. I could sell the 2.0 students as well as the 3.8 students. I developed relationships with all of the colleges in the area, including, U of K, Berea, Morehead, Indiana University Southeast, and Kentucky State. I would put kids in the car and drive them up to a college when we were up against the clock for them to get scholarship dollars and acceptance. I thrived off getting students scholarships, especially if those students were "have nots." Aviation Program students sold themselves and Black and white students loved the program and did well. I was egotistical about poor Black students getting an opportunity to move ahead. Getting them scholarships fed my ego.

As I think about today's counselors, I see them as too regimented rather than interpersonal. Harold Fenderson required that counselors learn the names of every student in the building, and we did, even though it sometimes took us most of the year. It helped when you were on lunchroom duty and knew every child by face and by table. Can you imagine how students felt when you walked down the hall and called them by name, even though they had never been in your office, or when you went into a class to provide college and career guidance and you knew who the students were by name? This one little "trick" had a profound impact on student discipline because it was the foundation of interpersonal relationships between students and faculty.

My story as an educator continues to this day. While I am not managing a classroom or a counselor's office, I am in schools regularly, coaching track. I have seen my students and the children of some of my students become educators, both teachers and administrators. My son did his student teaching under one of my track participants, Marcia Cole, whom I had mentored and helped through college. I interact with students, teachers, and school administrators, and I have noted changes in school environments over time. Two things that I would like to say in closing: Every school needs diverse students—some "haves" and some "have nots" rather than all students from low socioeconomic status; some smart and some needing extra academic support; and some Black and some white. When children first walk through the doors of a school, they should be made to feel that the teachers and staff care about them and that there is a positive place for them at that school, and that the faculty and staff will help them find that place.

Coach Newton is known for his continued work with Track and Field programs throughout the community. Married to Patricia Newton for nearly 40 years, they have a son and a daughter who are both educators. Their daughter, Angela, also a Jefferson County Public Schools graduate, is an assistant principal in Baltimore, Maryland, while their son teaches in JCPS. Coach Newton and Pat spend summers travelling with track events and for leisure travel visiting relatives and friends. Coach Newton is a member of Alpha Phi Alpha Fraternity. He also works with various community organizations interested in developing a Track and Field footprint in the Louisville Community. He holds a master's degree and Rank I Certification as a school guidance counselor from Western Kentucky University. He has helped many individual athletes earn recognition and awards from the United States Association for Track and Field (USATF) and the Amateur Athletic Union (AAU). He was inducted into the Kentucky Track and Cross Country Association (KTCCA) Hall of Fame in 2009.

Faye Owens

Teacher, Coordinating Teacher Focus-Impact,
Instructional Coordinator, Staff Development
Specialist, Curriculum Coordinator, Principal, KTIP
Principal, Director of Whitney M. Young Scholars
Program, and Director of Lincoln Foundation
Educational Programs

*If you give teachers what they need, they
will teach and teach well.*

ALTHOUGH I WAS BORN IN ST. LOUIS, Missouri, I grew up in Alabama, being raised primarily by my grandparents who took charge while Mae (I called my mother Mae) worked and kept me when she moved to Washington, D.C. after my parents' divorce. I visited my mom every summer and was introduced to Howard University because Mae worked for the university. Mae attended college for three years in Urbana, Illinois, and talked to me about going to college for as long as I can remember, so college was always on my radar.

Clinton Bennett Photographer

I attended Central Girard Elementary School and walked to school every day past Ku Klux Klan Hill which was located between two churches and was where they burned crosses. I was generally the smallest student in the class and was a "goody-goody." I liked school, and Ms. Merriweather was my favorite teacher because she let us play when we finished our work. Also, studying for me was entertaining. I listened to soap box operas on the radio and spent my $1.00 per week allowance on ribbons and magazines. I loved dressing up in the clothes that Mae sent me and I was sheltered beyond belief. I skipped sixth grade and was valedictorian of my class in elementary school which was Grades 1 through 7. We actually wore red caps and gowns.

My junior high school, Grades 8 through 10, was in South Girard. I was always on the Principal's List and the Honor Roll. I was extremely shy. I liked a boy, but was so shy that when he walked me to the bus, I never said but two words, *hello* and *good-bye*. I liked exploring and always wanted to go places but was restricted. If Granddaddy, a presiding elder of the African Methodist Episcopal Church District and a contractor, or my uncle could not carry me or pick me up, I could not go. Neither could I attend any school events after dark, except for church, when I was with an adult, uncle, aunt, or grandparent. I had nothing else to do but study. I never wanted for anything, always had a home, food, and clothes, but I really wanted to live in the Housing Projects because children from the projects got to play and do things.

When I passed to high school, my aunt convinced my grandparents that I should attend the Catholic high school because she thought I would get a better education even though the students were still all Black, but the teachers were white nuns. My grandparents paid tuition for me to attend Mother Mary Mission Catholic High School where I graduated valedictorian in 1956, a shy, little Black girl, smart not brilliant, and still lacking self-confidence.

Can you imagine how I felt when I could not get admitted to Howard? It had been my dream and I liked how they sang. However, I did not try out for the choir. I hadn't talked about it. I just knew I was going, if not to Howard then to Tuskegee, but I had to get away from Alabama. My major was going to be math because I loved math. If not math, then marketing since Mae said that there were no Blacks in marketing. My third choice was business with a major in accounting. It was all in my head. Fortunately, a friend of Mae's pulled some strings and I was admitted to Howard although Mother Mary Mission was not accredited. I graduated from Howard in 1960 with a Bachelor of Arts in Accounting and was involved in many extracurricular activities there.

My first job was financial secretary at the Delta Sigma Theta Sorority Headquarters. My most heart-wrenching experience at that time was the death of my boyfriend the day after his twenty-first birthday, the week after I started my first job. By November of 1960, I was "pinned" to a friend from Howard's Law School and was married to him in 1962 after he graduated and passed the Bar. We moved to Oakland, California, and lived there for three years. In 1965 we moved to Louisville, Kentucky the hometown of my husband and the place where he began his law practice.

Once in Louisville we could not find an apartment, so we lived with his parents until new apartments were completed. I could not find a job in accounting in Louisville in the early 1960s. Because of segregation, I was told I was overqualified for the jobs. Because of this I enrolled in the University of Louisville (U of L) to work on teacher certification, an area where jobs were more plentiful.

I began my teaching career at Parkland Elementary School, teaching second grade under Principal Lilly after taking three education classes and student teaching in the summer. There were few minorities in education at U of L during that time, and I knew every time I went to class that the professor was going to call on me. I felt picked on and was shocked when I wrote a paper and waited for the professor to embarrass me by saying negative comments about my paper, but to my surprise, she said that was the best paper written in the class. As luck would have it, when I was hired by Jefferson County Public Schools, the professor was going to be my supervisor. So, I told her how blessed I was to have her. She turned out to be my mentor, taking an interest in me, helping me move up in the system. The Lord moves in mysterious ways. While teaching and raising a family, I completed a Master's Degree in Education from the University of Louisville with an endorsement as Reading Specialist; an endorsement as Supervisor of Instruction Grades K-12, Principal; and Lifetime Teacher Certification.

After my third year at Parkland Elementary, I applied for the Focus/Impact Program as a Lead Teacher, a new innovation being launched in the Old Louisville School District under Superintendent Newman Walker. From 1968 to 1975, I was blessed one more time. During the training, I was promoted to Team Leader. I was assigned to Roosevelt Elementary. This was truly a learning experience. I knew if I did not lose my mind in Focus/Impact, I would never lose it.

I enjoyed a wide variety of teaching experiences, including being a Team Leader for Focus at Roosevelt, Reading Specialist, Coordinating Teacher, Instructional leader, In-Service Specialist, Coordinator for Optional Programs, as well as serving as Field Coordinator for the University of Kentucky and finally, school principal Grades K-5, where I observed many new teachers taking their first steps into the profession. All of my many positions prepared me for being an elementary school principal.

Observations and evaluations helped me learn and grow and gave me insights to use later in my career. Over the years, I was also fortunate to work with excellent administrators and colleagues like Hughlyn Wilson, Genevieve Boone, Booker Rice, Rosemary Bell, Carlisle Maupin, Deanna Tinsley, and Patsy Brisbon. I also worked at Manly Jr. High, Noe Middle School, Carrithers, DuValle, and Stuart Middle as well as Kennedy, Coleridge-Taylor, and Gutermuth Elementary schools in a variety of assignments, including instructional coordinator, curriculum coordinator, and Summer School principal.

Every position that I held helped me and taught me something, including patience. I remember being instructional coordinator at Carrithers during Merger. There were only three Black teachers, and there were daily bomb threats while Black kids were getting off the bus, and white students acting crazy in the halls and classrooms in a school setting with very few walls. I was called on to help with discipline, especially Black students, because the administration did not feel comfortable working with Black students. With my little short self, I remember asking the students, "Why are you here?" That got their attention and started a conversation that helped us bring some order to the chaos.

I also remember Dr. David DeRuzzo and the cuts that he made as superintendent for that one year. Positions were eliminated. So many things and people were changed and uprooted. It took a while before the new administration brought calm back to the employees, teachers, and administrators. It was a sad time for me. I was cut and had to return to the classroom, but I still had to apply for positions that I knew I would not be able to get, due to my lack of seniority.

For many years, I wanted to be an elementary principal, but I was told that I did not have enough elementary experience. I also remember my competition, big men and "little old me." When I applied for principal, thirteen positions, elementary and middle, were available. All applicants had to interview with the thirteen School-based Decision Making Teams to be selected for principal. Back then, applicants met with the "big dogs," each asking questions and evaluating answers. Let me clarify something here. I was finally appointed as principal because I worked hard for it, not because of who my husband was and his political connections. I was asked why I should be selected to be a principal by one of the superintendents; my answer was "because I have an innate ability to motivate people to get them to do the best that they can do." To this day I think that answer helped seal the promotion.

When I was appointed to Mill Creek Elementary School as principal in 1984, I encountered seasoned teachers who had a passion for teaching and learning and who shared my beliefs. My focus was on the school as a whole. I had ECE units and BD students. I tried to give teachers what they needed and liked. I knew my staff and their talents. I cannot remember getting a *no* answer to anything I asked. The key was to know the staff and to ask teachers who had a talent or interest in shared goals. My biggest asset was my personality and ability to treat everyone as I wanted to be treated and make everyone feel important because they were. We had campers, singers, drama teachers, etc. We did what kids liked to do. My staff knew I cared because I called them when they did not come to school. I did not stand over their shoulders; I allowed them to do their job, but they knew I was there if they needed help. I had visions and told them what I'd like to see. I asked who could help make my vision come true. I walked the halls and did not stay in the office. If I ate, everybody ate. If I worked, everybody worked. I helped clean up when things needed to be cleaned. We were a team.

I never had a grievance and prayed two teachers out of my school, even though most of my teachers stayed with me. I had 50-50 Black/white students and was in the same cluster as Mae Kennerly. She and I would fight over money at cluster meetings, but we did not discuss anything about the money when we left the meeting. (I miss my buddy.)

My accounting background helped me manage the dollars. I had good relationships with everyone in my building, teachers and support staff and district support staff. When the HVAC on the roof of the school needed repair, the technicians came quickly because they knew I would feed them. When my kids and teachers had sleepovers, there were kids everywhere. I slept on the couch.

As principal, I had to motivate both students and staff, and I had to show that I appreciated each child, each teacher, and each parent. I did crazy things to reach out and show them that I was not above them, but was one of them. Parents really accepted me when I performed at the talent show as Diana Ross and when I danced on the roof of Mill Creek with Fred Cowgill, sport's announcer for Channel 32. I respected them and they respected me. Our scores went up; our parents were a part of our team; and our students did well when they moved to middle school.

When I retired in 1999, every class decided what they were going to do as part of our "Fifteen Days of Celebration." Students composed bulletin boards of what they thought I would do after retirement to celebrate my fifteen years at Mill Creek. The celebration went on for fifteen days. Our story was on TV; parents sent flowers and gifts; and a limo carried me to school on the last day. For Sunday's grand celebration, our school secretary sang "Wind Beneath My Wings." To this day I still meet with some of my teachers and I enjoy a rum cake that one of my teachers bakes and sends every year for my birthday and Christmas.

I could stop here, but my story would not be complete if I did not talk about my working with the Whitney M. YOUNG Scholars (WMYS) and the Lincoln Foundation from 2000 to 2018. I work only on Tuesdays. My teaching and administrative experiences helped me direct WMYS, whose mission is to help underprivileged students in Grades 7-12 with 3.0 grade-point averages who qualify for free and/

or reduced-priced lunch to graduate and get a degree from a four-year college. This non-traditional, year-round program includes many community partners. The program has three components. The first component is Educational Clinics, where scholars meet on the first and third Saturdays for classes. The classes are seventh-grade science at the Kentucky Science Center; eighth-grade math at Bellarmine; ninth-grade language arts at Bellarmine; tenth-grade conflict resolution /Shakespeare; eleventh-grade ACT preparation; and twelfth-grade college admission. The second component is the Parental Institute that engages parents to be advocates for their children. The third component is Summer Institute for rising tenth, eleventh, and twelfth graders. It provides opportunities for scholars to visit and stay on college campuses for two week. Other programs are Study Skills for eighth graders, Math and Science for ninth graders. The third component has two reading programs for Grades 1-3 at Portland and Western Libraries. The program engages students with hands-on activities, helps promote self-confidence, and builds interpersonal skills. Certified teachers who know and own the curriculum are essential to the program and to student success.

My success story for the years that I directed the WMYS is that my students are now at the point of being able to give back through their donations of money and time to mentor incoming students. They have stories that they now share with current students. That lets us know that we have made a difference in their lives.

As an educator for nearly 60 years, I am always grateful for my students' successes, and I am saddened to hear about test scores, test scores, test scores! Kids, in general, are smarter today than they were fifty years ago. Maybe we are using the wrong tests and maybe we are testing the wrong things. I do not know what the problem is that kids cannot read, but I believe that they think better. I suspect that teachers are not getting the knowledge and skills in their college and university coursework that they need to be able to teach students how to read.

We also must be careful who we allow into the profession. Some see teaching as a job with good retirement and they do not care about kids. At the same time, parenting skills are out the window. When kids misbehave, there is very little that teachers can do. Kids do not respect adults and parents want to be friends rather than parents. With shootings and gun violence, teachers are scared.

Home and school are not in sync. Parents are generally not cooperative and schools cannot do it alone. Poor parents when they are working have little time for children because they are busy working to put a roof over their heads. They may not have the skills to help with reading and there may not be conversations taking place at the dinner table. We have to acknowledge that economics makes a difference and the education of parents impacts the education of their children. And, there is a "race problem." We have come a long way, Baby, but we have a long way to go. Some Black students only see one Black teacher their entire K-12 student experience. What does that tell them about becoming a teacher?

When I talk to young people about teaching and new teachers about staying in the profession, there is some crossover. I say, "Treat children as if they are your own. Know your subject matter. Know where your students are and start from there." Understand that students may not all be at the same place in the learning process. Use the Madeline Hunter Method; it works. Tell, provide an example (guided practice); allow students to practice (independent practice); evaluate, reteach, and evaluate again using a hands-on approach. Also, make each student feel valued and loved even if their behavior is awry! (I don't like your behavior, but I love you.)

I have had examples of great teachers throughout my career. Mr. Fitzhugh, my business teacher, took interest in what we did and what we would become. He was caring and well-respected; he tried to give us all opportunities to be successful. At Mill Creek, I had many great teachers who took an interest in the whole child. They gave love. We were a hugging school. They were hands-on and could break a child in like you break in a horse. Great teachers know that all kids can learn, but at different speeds, and they must teach to the senses. Sometimes they must teach over and over again until the child gets it.

If we want to address some of the achievement issues of today's students, we might take another look at elementary grades and focus on teaching reading, writing, and arithmetic in addition to handwriting. Teachers should let their walls speak, displaying student work with pride and being a source of instruction as well. And, finally, we must give elementary teachers the skills and knowledge to teach different students with different capabilities and strengths and the ability to know the difference.

If I had to do it all over again, I would. I have no regrets. If I had to teach today, I could, but my patience level is not the same (but my passion for helping is stronger than ever as evidenced by my scholarship that is given every four years) and kids are not the same. Kids like me and respect me and I still have the personality where I make learning fun. Vacation Bible School has taught me that I have to be careful about volunteering because I would give away all of my time. I still fall in love with my kids and they still energize me and keep me young. I still have the passion and I still feel the joy when I see the lights go on in children's eyes when they say, "I got it," and when my students from Mill Creek see me and give me hugs and tell me how I impacted their lives.

Faye Owens continues to motivate students and adults as she recruits participants and teachers for the Whitney M. YOUNG Scholars Program. Over her career, she has received numerous awards and recognitions, including the Martin Luther King Award from the Kentucky Commission on Human Rights, the Louisville Defender Newspaper Professional Award, and the Kentucky State PTA Educator of the Year Award as well as the Outstanding Principal of the Year Award from Jefferson County Public Schools. She is a member of the Quinn AME Methodist Church, where she is a member of the Trustee and Usher Board, President of The Louisville MOLES, Life Member of the NAACP, a member of ETA Omega Chapter, Alpha Kappa Alpha Sorority, Inc.: The Girl Friends, Inc., and Pas Si Bete-Atomies Bridge Club. She has two children Deborah Owens Evans, Dedra Owens, and a son-in-Law, Ferguson Evans.

June Anderson Owens

Elementary Teacher, Intermediate Grades

I TAUGHT 11 YEARS AT SOUTHWICK and 20 years and seven months at Portland Elementary School, one of the longest reigns of an African-American teacher assigned to that school after the merger of the Louisville City and Jefferson County school districts. Natives of Louisville, Kentucky, my hardworking parents set the expectation that I would go to college, even when I was in elementary school. My mom worked occasionally, but mostly took care

*Anderson-Owens Family
Photo Collection*

of the home while Dad worked in the cleaning company that he owned and he served as night watchman at Tube-Turns. Prior to second grade we lived on Eleventh Street across from George McClellan Elementary School where I spent one and one-half years. While in elementary school, my father, a deacon at Calvary Baptist Church, along with two or three other members of the congregation who were skilled in construction helped build our house on Ormsby Street. At this time, I transferred to Phyllis Wheatley Elementary at Sixteenth and St. Catherine streets.

Throughout my early childhood educational years, many of our teachers lived in our neighborhood and some attended our church, so our parents were always informed of our conduct as well as when we had been corrected by them. At Wheatley, we had "Chapel" every Friday where students could recite poems, tell stories, and play instrumental music. Teachers that I remember from Wheatley were Miss Winston, who later married and became Mrs. Shelburne; Mrs. Sunshine Bullock; Miss Green; Mrs. Marr; Mrs. Edwards; and Mrs. Underwood. Mrs. J. K. Johnson, another of my teachers, had a ritual. If spelling and math tests were not mastered, you were required to march around the classroom, chanting "I-am-dumb. I didn't study my lesson." If students did this playfully; they were given a lick with a yard stick as they passed her. Also, Mrs. J. K. McNary, my sixth-grade teacher, was a dance instructor who later resigned and devoted her time to her dance classes. Her dance recitals were held at Memorial Auditorium annually and garnered great attendance from the Black community. While many of our elementary teachers had graduated from Normal School, they were good teachers who were very firm and maintained good discipline.

At Phyllis Wheatley Elementary there was health inspection every day, which took place after the Pledge of Allegiance. Teachers emphasized cleanliness, good health, dental and personal care. Dr. Emmerson, a local dentist, came to school to provide dental care for students. Teachers were thoughtful, took special interest in students, and consulted parents when there were problems. Special education students were in the regular classroom, but were not ridiculed.

Madison Junior High School and Jackson Junior High were the only schools for Black students in Grades 7, 8, and 9. Memorable teachers at Madison that I remember include Mrs. Elizabeth Ramsey saying, "I might be a little potato, but I am hard to peel." Eunice Wilson, wife of Atwood Wilson, the principal at Central High School, taught mathematics. She could look in our faces and tell if we did not comprehend the concept. Frances Munford taught English. When we became too talkative, she would say, "You can have the classroom," would turn around and walk out for about three minutes. Of course, we stayed after school to make up time lost. Ms. Woods taught syllabication by tapping on the desk. I got in trouble one time when I joined in the fun of tapping and wound up being reprimanded for too much tapping or "overly tapping." Mr. King taught music. He had a jazzy way of playing the piano which we enjoyed very much. Ms. Fishback, our gym teacher, had us marching like soldiers with a cadence count of "left, right, and left, right. Walk from the hips down, left-left." As she counted time, we marched like soldiers, never missing a step!

After graduating from Madison Jr. High School, my next years were spent at the old Central High School (CHS) at Eighth and Chestnut streets. Mr. Tisdale, a history teacher, gave out pennies for correct answers for recall questions. I still remember his sayings, "You are not acting like a civilized man," when we were not in order. Also, "Nothing to excess," and "Things done in moderation are quite alright." We were always reciting something related to parts of speech for Ms. Saunders. "A noun is the name of anything, a person, place, or thing. Instead of a noun, a pronoun stands: *he, she, it, or they.*" If it was your turn and you said "uh," you had to sit down and repeat it another day. Mrs. Kirkendall had us memorizing poetry, especially from the English and American poets. Mrs. Nanny B. Crumes was an outstanding music teacher, revered by students and staff alike. Our special chorus sang at Atherton High School and Halleck Hall before Louisville schools were desegregated. This was indeed a great honor. Additionally, we always had a concert at the end of the year where we wore formal attire.

I remember a protest from the students when the pipes burst and water flowed throughout the hallways in the old Central building. Students left school without permission, disgruntled about the old and dilapidated building. Of course, I could not leave, as I knew my parents would disapprove of my leaving without permission. I, along with a few other students, stayed in the room with Mr. Ramsey, my math teacher and Ormsby Street neighbor. Professor Atwood Wilson, principal, and Mrs. Maude Brown Porter, assistant principal, kept Central High School orderly along with Jesse Taylor, a respected and well-known African-American policeman who dropped by from time to time to assure and maintain security.

My homeroom teacher was Ms. Betty Johnson who guided the

students with "B" averages to skip a semester and graduate a semester earlier. I graduated from Central after two and a half years in 1951 by taking college preparatory courses. I took two English classes at the same time in anticipation of graduating earlier and was in the upper-quartile of my class. My older sister spent one year at Kentucky State College and later transferred to Nazareth where I commenced my higher education. Nazareth was recommended by Mrs. E. Ramsey, my former teacher and also neighbor. Louisville Municipal College for Blacks was closing and many of those students were coming to Nazareth as well. Ms. Ramsey told Mom that Nazareth was a good school, so my choice was made.

I had no idea what I wanted to do when I went to college and earned a Bachelor of Science Degree in General Education, graduating in 1955. I worked as a clerk in a doctor's office, ran an elevator, and worked at General Hospital (now University Hospital). When I decided that I wanted to teach, I returned to college for additional courses. I was a substitute teacher until I received my first permanent job in 1960 at Southwick Elementary, with all-Black students. I never did student teaching, but I had resource teachers and supervisors to help. I visited classrooms to see how outstanding teachers managed their classes and monitored their teaching techniques. Among them were Mrs. R. L. Carpenter (Music Supervisor); Ms. Trowell; and Mrs. Hughlyn Wilson who later became a JCPS District administrator.

When I began teaching, it was apparent that children did not conduct themselves according to our textbooks and ways that my generation was raised. The term "culturally deprived" was prevalent, though everyone has a culture that may be different from yours. Although some parents were rough around the edges, they were interested in their children. As a beginning teacher at Southwick Elementary School where Mr. Carl Barbour was principal, I recall taking 26 intermediate students to a symphony concert at Convention Center (now Louisville Gardens) using city transportation—not chartered buses as used now. A student in the Safety-Patrol assisted me. This was a "cool job" so their responsibilities were taken seriously. I remember the bus drivers commenting on the superb comportment of the students. How proud we were!

Over the years at Southwick Elementary, we wrapped the May Pole, visited the Cincinnati Zoo; explored a new car dealership; and ate lunch at Blue Boar Cafeteria where students were fascinated with the revolving doors. We were accompanied by Principal Herschel Martin who wanted to expand students' horizons outside of their community. When students participated in a United Nations Day Program, costumes were acquired from Metro Parks at no charge although they had to be returned by the end of the school day. My students were given an assignment to work on quietly while I returned the costumes. They were monitored by the principal and my neighboring teachers. The students remained in order and still on task when I returned. On another occasion when students were performing as a dance group and needed leotards, it was suggested that I call Ms. Byck, the owner of an upscale women's clothing store. I called. Ms. Byck sent leotards. Of course, the students wrote thank you notes in appreciation of her contribution.

The implementation of Focus/Impact teaching philosophy and techniques was a questionable time for me. I remember one of my first training sessions where John Whiting one of the directors of the project, called the class to order and would not let us speak. Every time someone said something, he said, "Shush." That went on for 30 minutes or more. A group of teachers began playing cards, but still, no talking. Teachers began whispering among themselves. Mrs. Elmore, who later became the first Black female member of the Jefferson County Board of Education, rang the fire bell to get everyone to leave the building, but all of the trainees did not leave. When the group finally reassembled and Mr. Whiting called us to order, he said, "If teachers cannot sit for 30 minutes without talking, why do you expect kids to do it?" I could agree with that, but I did not agree with the philosophy of ignoring sound academic principles. I continued teaching my way, teaching the way I thought I needed to teach. I taught spelling, recognized spelling errors, highlighted incorrect grammar when students were speaking or writing, and identified incorrect sentence construction, an error that teachers were to ignore in order to get students to communicate freely, for what was known as "free expression."

Several of my students stand out. I had one student who never spoke a word, but her achievement scores were at grade level and higher. Another student was accidently shot and continually suffered with medical related issues, but worked hard at being a good student. I taught the former Judge Janice Martin in fifth grade. Janice along with Donna Thompson and Linda Tandy, created a play and performed for one of my supervisors who thought the play was outstanding. I taught a student who was not a good reader but was good with money. He would buy candy at the Family Fair store and re-sell it at school for profit. Every now and then I see my former students. It makes me feel good when they recognize me even though I do not readily recognize some of them.

I was transferred to Portland Elementary in 1975 as part of Jefferson County and Louisville City School districts' staff integration plan under merger. It was possible that my principal at that time had limited contact with Blacks. The school was predominately white, and travelling through the Portland area of Louisville was a new experience for me. Blacks were reluctant or "scared" to go to Portland because Portland Caucasians had a reputation for being prejudiced and offensive toward them. White students had many of the same views toward Black students as white adults had toward Black adults. As I drove through the area, I was amazed to see people sitting on porches smoking cigarettes, half-dressed, and tattooed. Although there were some very nice homes in the Portland area and some residents had good paying jobs, there were also people in Portland who lived in poverty. I visited students' homes after school, sometimes stepping over broken glass on the front porch and trying unsuccessfully to see through the plastic covering on the broken widows spanning the front of the house. We were told that people in Portland "liked to fight." During those early years, it was not uncommon for students completing sixth grade and not continuing to junior high school. I also encountered a white parent who was embarrassed because her daughter was pregnant in elementary school.

Portland Elementary transitioned over time. Female teachers even transitioned from dresses to pants. Several African-American teachers and I worked well with Portland students. Parents began trusting us and were overall cooperative as fear and suspicion dissipated. We worked to improve student achievement, our students' test scores reflecting our efforts. When I began at Portland, each teacher taught every subject. Gradually, Jefferson County hired art, music, and physical education teachers, removing those subjects from the regular teachers' schedules. We produced a musical and invited people from Central Office to come. Portland later became a Fine Arts School, and our students and parents enjoyed the activities associated with our chosen curriculum.

Not all fourth graders at Portland could read well and many were not at grade level. Portland teachers worked hard on comprehension to attain target goals. My favorite subjects to teach were math and English, including punctuation. To reinforce punctuation, I used simple outlining, had students to write short stories or paragraphs, and emphasized knowing where to stop when reading. I taught sixth grade for a time, then moved back to fifth grade then fourth grade when I observed that fourth and fifth graders did not know nursery rhymes. I started "Memory Selections," beginning with four lines that students had to learn by heart and recite. They progressed to memorizing the "Prayer of St. Francis" and the "Gettysburg Address" by the end of the school year. I read to my students every day after lunch. I remember my students getting an attitude one day because I was hoarse so I allowed one of my students who was an excellent reader to read to the class. The students were disgruntled because, "They wanted their teacher to read to them." Later, students realized that they, too, could read to the class if they practiced what they were going to read.

Portland provided opportunities for parents to get involved to help their children. When "New Math" was introduced, we had a few parents come after school to learn the New Math, especially the concept of division. We had parent volunteers in and out of the school every day. Parents participated on field trips and always helped with our end-of-year activities. Sometimes it was difficult to get parents to cooperate with staff; however, most parents wanted their children to do well in school. I remember a Black parent at Portland who had a reputation of being difficult to work with. When we finally had a real conversation, he told me that "I came through Focus/Impact, but nobody made me learn what I needed and I was a good student." I then understood his insistence and persistence that his children be given every opportunity to learn what they needed to know.

The overall challenges to society's norms that we are experiencing today are reflected in children's challenges to school norms. Students see leaders of the country practicing new norms that are different, but accepted, and they think that they can emulate the same. Many students appear disenchanted, lack aspirations, and live for the day. They do not see that they have anything to offer. Parents see children out-of-control but maintain that they have done everything that they can do. They feel it is up to the school to instill acceptable norms and standards of society, refusing to own that they must set examples and expectations for students as well, by being good role models themselves.

As thoughtful educators, we must seek solutions based on the challenges we face today. We already try to find out about our students' homes, their environments, if they are hungry, if they have a different learning style, and whether or not they are poor or minority. But, do we think about looking at how we structure the academics? We do not have large numbers of great teachers, but we might make good teachers better and more effective by introducing more training, different training, and giving teachers a better understanding of from where their students are coming, which includes neighborhoods and environments. (I know firsthand what it says in the future teacher's textbook may not be the reality.) A new curriculum scheme "like having Grades 1 to 3 focusing on the basics, reading, writing, and math only, until students master those skills" may improve early academic attainment to get and keep students on track/grade level. The last hour of the day might introduce a variety of careers or provide a fun activity that students look forward to as well. Grades 4 to 6 could introduce students to society, citing civic responsibility, career opportunities, and scientific inquiry that they now might understand since they can read. Field trips with students exploring the community may serve as a source of knowledge and inspiration for them. We also might recognize that all students are not going to college and have no interest in college but need early preparation for vocational experiences that will equip them for well-paying jobs.

Education gave me the means to have a better life than my parents. I can look at things critically in life with a balanced perspective. I believe that you can learn something from somebody every day. Life is a journey where you add new experiences constantly. It is like a ball of yarn. You begin with a little piece and as you grow, the ball gets larger and larger. I understood that my students may have begun with a tiny piece, but through my patience, guidance, thoughtfulness, interest, and dedication, I strived to extend their ball of yarn.

June Owens received a Master's Degree from Indiana University in 1973. She retired in 1993, but continued working with the University of Kentucky on a program to assure that teachers were teaching about drug abuse and addiction. She was recognized by the Kentucky Department of Education and the Kentucky Education Foundation as a teacher delegate representing her school. She was married to the late Theodore E. Owens. Together they took several cruises and travelled to England, France, and Rome. On a different occasion, June travelled to Rome with the Cathedral of the Assumption Choir where she toured and sang for the Vatican. June has been a member of several organizations including the Epicurettes and Mannequins social clubs; the Retired Educators and Friends (REAF) exercise class at the Tenth and Chestnut Family YMCA; and the Scholarship Committee of Black Achievers at the Y. Also a member of Alpha Kappa Alpha Sorority, Inc., June has a daughter, Karen Root who is a digital media consultant in Stone Mountain, Georgia whose husband Geoffrey is a business intelligence developer for State Farm. June's son, Kirk Owens, a veteran as well as a community and political organizer, has been active in a number of community organizations including the Kentucky Alliance Against Racist and Political Repression and Citizens Against Police Abuse. He currently hosts two radio programs, "On the Edge" with K. A. Owens and the "Kentucky Alliance Radio Show."

Dr. Jewelene Richards-Brown

Elementary Teacher, Program Director, Head
Start Career Development and Volunteer
Coordinator, School Counselor, Adjunct Professor,
and Facilitator for Trainer of Trainers

Dissertation Title: *What Teachers Need to Know to
Help African-American Children Learn*

*Effective counselors must have knowledge, passion,
commitment, and ability to communicate, some of the
same characteristics needed by effective teachers. Great
teachers like Lyman Johnson enjoyed these characteristics.
He freely gave his energy and his investment was obvious.
He "rattled off" or "preached"
the minute the bell rang,
totally committed to sharing
his knowledge, never looking
at notes to teach.*

ALTHOUGH I LIVED IN THE
city of Louisville as an adult, I was
born and raised in Jeffersontown

Clinton Bennett Photographer

202

(J'town), Kentucky in the county, about 13 miles from Louisville. I am the oldest of six children. I attended Jeffersontown Colored Elementary School, a good-looking, well-kept two-story brick building with four classrooms for Grades 1 to 8. The building also had a lower level with an equipped kitchen, a lunchroom, maintenance room, and a small room used as a health room/part-time music room. Also, there was a large indoor play space.

Education was always important in my family. My father attended school at the elementary school level only, while my mother continued through the eleventh grade. Years later, Mother earned an associate degree from the community college. After getting her degree, she pursued a career in human services. Prior to that, she had been a domestic worker and my father was a laborer.

My siblings and I were expected to learn in school, and we received support from home. My mother was very active in the local PTA and also held a chairmanship in the Kentucky Negro Parent Teacher Association. Two of our teachers lived in the neighborhood and attended church with us in our small African-American community. Because we had two grades in each classroom, teachers had to have extraordinary management skills. Often students who were proficient in skills at their assigned levels were allowed to work at the next higher level because it was being taught in the same classroom.

I loved school. My third-grade teacher was older and had taught my father. I was in her class the last year she taught before retiring. She was replaced by an experienced teacher who was new to our school and our community. Her methods of teaching and classroom management were both captivating and interesting. She was different in a positive manner, nice but firm and accommodating. She covered material in ways that we were not accustomed to, talking about the subject or idea, expanding and relating the information to what was going on around us or what might be coming in our future. I enjoyed spelling and often participated successfully in spelling contests. I earned ribbons and awards, was pictured in the *Louisville Defender* newspaper as one of three top spellers in the area, and was a finalist in the KNEA Spelling Contest in fifth grade.

I encountered my first male teacher at Jackson Junior High School in ninth grade, the only year that I attended Jackson. I was slated to have a male teacher in Grades 7 and 8, but the teacher who was the principal retired and was replaced by a female. Mr. Martin, an experienced educator who had taught my mother, was my homeroom teacher and my social studies teacher. He was also my favorite teacher. He knew how to work with students at our developmental level and had no problem keeping our attention. I loved how he worked with us, interjecting something funny then going back to serious work.

The first time that I took a typing class was at Jackson. I really wanted to learn to type. I learned to type a little, but not as much as I had hoped I would. Physical Education (PE) was a class that I did not like. I had previously participated in recreation programs at our community park and at summer camps and enjoyed them. I think the organized PE class may have been too structured for me.

My next transition was to Central High School. It was in a brand new building located at Twelfth and Chestnut streets. It wasn't easy for me and the other students from Jeffersontown to get to Central. I walked about a half mile to catch a Blue Motor Coach Company bus which I rode to Fifth and Walnut streets. We then walked the rest of the way to CHS. For our return trip, we walked from school to Second and Liberty streets to catch the Blue Motor Coach bus back to J'town. We did not pay for riding the bus. By law, Jefferson County Schools had to provide a high school for its "colored" students. Jefferson County paid the Louisville Public Schools for us to attend and had an arrangement with the Blue Motor Coach bus company for our bus tokens. The other option was for us to attend Lincoln Institute with some of our other classmates. It was a boarding school and my mother felt Central was a better option for me.

My inspiration for becoming an elementary teacher and counselor came from as far back as my childhood and school experiences. When I was young, I would teach my dolls and play school. Later, my participation in various school and community activities enhanced my love for things academic and supported my career choice as an educator. During my high school years, I ushered for many school programs and events where I heard interesting speakers. I participated in many activities during high school: the citywide Youth Speaks Program; the

YWCA sponsored Y-Teens Program; was junior counselor and senior counselor at the YWCA Summer Camp Program; was homeroom Class President in the twelfth grade; and participated in the Alpha Kappa Alpha Sorority, Inc. sponsored Fashionetta and Debutante Ball. I also worked in the counselor's office during my study period. The counselor, Mrs. Betty Douglas Taylor, was also my English teacher and an excellent counselor as well as a great role model. After teaching a few years, I, too, became a school counselor.

I enrolled in Kentucky State College in 1955, on a $200 scholarship, and for three and a half years, in lieu of a meal ticket, I cooked for the Dean of Students and ate my meals there. This reduced the cost of my school expenses significantly. Becoming the Dean's cook was either an accident or providence. Mom and I had a plan to pay for my school expenses. Our plan was to use the $200 in the fall, giving Mom time to save money for the spring. We did not have a Plan B. However, upon arrival, we learned that only $100 could be used toward the fall semester. Mother took another job and paid the difference for that first semester. Mother also appealed to the Dean of Students for a work-assistance job for the spring semester. I received one, preparing meals for the Dean and her mom at the Dean's house. For three years, my mother continued to send me an allowance, and money from my summer jobs allowed us to meet my school expenses. We paid room and tuition, but did not purchase a meal ticket and that was O.K. I knew I had at least one great meal every day because I cooked it for the Dean!

My student-teaching experience was at the Rosenwald Laboratory School on campus, an old model Lab School. A significant portion of our time was spent creating hand-made teacher materials for use in class, such as flash cards, alphabet letters, cut pictures for bulletin boards, etc. My actual teaching experience was with the primary students. When I completed student teaching, I was nervous about teaching in a large, progressive district like Jefferson County. My feelings were relieved when I finally got a job in 1960 after working in Kansas City as the assistant Y-Teens director. During this era, Black teachers were only hired in schools where the school population was all- Black. New teachers were hired to replace a teacher who had left a position due to illness or had resigned, retired, or died. Neither of these had occurred in Jefferson County the year I graduated and was seeking a job.

I returned to Louisville in January 1960 to take a newly created class of students at Newburg Elementary School. This class was made up of students from the other three third-grade classes. At the end of that school year, my students had made progress but more was needed to meet the guidelines for the next level. I asked to keep that same group for the next full school year, 1960-61. My students made significant progress that year, so much so that I used their test scores in my research for my master's degree at Indiana University.

In 1965, the degree I earned was in education with a specialization in counseling and guidance. I then became certified as a school counselor in both Indiana and Kentucky. My various counseling experiences include a variety of assignments. I resigned from Jefferson County Public Schools in 1965 and began working as a Youth Motivation Counselor for the federally funded community-action program at the Market Street Neighborhood House. My counseling load was 13 high-risk students. This was a position where excuses did not work, but helping students have regular school attendance and school success was the priority. I quickly learned to employ nontraditional approaches to enhance student success. Examples of my approaches included making home visits; insuring that these students attended tutoring sessions with volunteer tutors on a scheduled basis; rewarding attendance and participation in a study club program sponsored by the Neighborhood House. This also included needs-based support for students with special issues. One 13-year-old student became pregnant. A retired principal and I worked together and negotiated with the Louisville Public Schools to accept her credits and allow her to return to school the next year if she met the requirements, after attending private classes with the retired principal. All of this happened. Another student was offered a job cleaning an adult night spot. I collaborated with the director of the YMCA to allow this student to work at the YMCA bowling alley. The Youth Motivation Project paid his salary.

The director of the Neighborhood House was a brilliant social worker with a passion for people. She was also a great teacher and mentor. I learned many grass- roots strategies for helping students succeed in school from this experience and from Mrs. Dorothy Nevaux. These benefitted me throughout the rest of my career. She taught me how to recruit volunteers and gave pointers on how to be creative in dealing with volatile students. For example, I recruited volunteers by providing them transportation to the tutoring site. I remember a student who was an outstanding artist but lacked basic skills and had no help from home. He was matched with a mentor who took his achievement personally and was undaunted in his attention to that student.

Working as an elementary school counselor and with the Head Start Program added variety to my skill set. As Career Development Coordinator with Heard Start, I focused on helping Head Start workers complete teacher certification programs. I also taught classes for Morehead State to assist in certification efforts. As Volunteer Coordinator, I collaborated with community organizations, sororities, fraternities, churches, businesses, and various industries to identify, recruit, and assign volunteers to work with Head Start students.

As a counselor at Wheatley, James Lowell, and Audubon Elementary schools, my role centered on helping students and families. I saw students who may have been at a disadvantage; however, because of the rapport I built with families, I could work more closely with those students to support their academic achievement. I was a proponent of parent participation on committees and in parent conferences where counselors and parents could actually talk and listen. I supported the idea of a Parenting Expo, bringing together community resources like the Bingham Child Guidance Clinic, the University of Louisville Learning Center, Family and Children's Agency, and other community agencies for parents to better understand services and options available for their children. Collaborating with other counselors, sharing ideas, and providing training through district professional development and my professional organization, the American Association of Counseling and Development, also contributed to my success as an effective counselor, working on behalf of children.

Counseling and counselors have changed since my retirement in

1994. Counselors no longer have to be certified as teachers but may enter counseling programs with a variety of undergraduate degrees. University training programs for counselors are content-oriented and special-education centered, not student-focused. School counselors are faced with meeting federal guidelines as their first priority rather than using their professional skills to support families and other school personnel in fostering success for students. Multi-disciplinary counseling programs where career counselors, social workers, health-care providers, and student personnel workers are trained together are not common today, although research shows that programs of this type are more effective for providing easily attainable wraparound services where parents move from asking "if" their children will obtain services to "when" will they receive services. The collaborative model does not eliminate services but allows all providers to work together to provide the best services for students and their families.

In my youth, many children had a village to help raise and support them. Today's youth need that same village concept in place. Youth and families cannot expect professional employees to be the sole contributors to children's academic, social, and emotional development. Teachers do make a major contribution, but families, friends, neighbors, the church, community agencies as well as volunteers are important in socializing and equalizing today's students. While schools are in a quandary over improving academic standards and reducing the gap in academic achievement, school leaders might consider things that worked in the past that can be tweaked to support today's challenges. We continue to discard the old because it is a "new day."

Before my official retirement, I spent one year as an administrative intern, directing the Minority Teacher Recruitment Project, a joint venture shared between the University of Louisville and JCPS. The need for African-American teachers continues to be a reality regardless of where one resides. JCPS was on the forefront in developing strategies to recruit and retain African-American teachers, but continues struggling to bring the percent of minority teachers in line with the percent of minority students, even though minority now translates to any non-white in contrast to minority meaning "Black or African-American" 20 years ago.

I believe that we should actively recruit potential teachers at the high school level, following the model used by business and industry. Teaching is a noble profession, and it needs the brightest and best African-American students to choose teaching as a career. I strongly support a model which introduces these students to teaching as a career while they are in high school and also allows them to have paid internships during summers before their college years. Districts with non-profit foundations could establish paid internships for high school students, allowing students to work in summer programs with actual students, doing professional development with teachers, and working in Central Office on tasks associated with the opening of school and New Teacher Induction. Interns would get a feel for the profession and firsthand knowledge for helping them decide about a college major. Scholarships and summer employment could also be added to the mix.

I have enjoyed my career experiences over the years, because working with students, parents, teachers, and community volunteers is a part of my calling. I have particularly enjoyed training parents on how to effectively communicate with their children; training fellow counselors as a trainer of trainers; recruiting and training community volunteers; and working with career development, especially helping individuals consider teaching as a career or completing certification requirements. Hopefully, through my varied experiences and collaborative efforts, larger numbers of students were positively impacted and became successful academically and in life.

Dr. Jewelene Richards-Brown is a member of First African Baptist Church in Lexington, Kentucky, where she currently resides. She received her doctorate from Spalding University in 1999. Jewelene has served as an adjunct instructor at Morehead State University, Sullivan University, and Simmons College of Kentucky. She has received a variety of awards and recognitions, including becoming one of 60 counselors selected and trained by the American Association for Counseling and Development as a Facilitator, Trainer of Trainers for their Family Communication Project. She is a former member of the American Association for Counseling and Development, and a member of Alpha Kappa Alpha Sorority, Inc. Jewelene has three grandchildren and two children, one of whom is an elementary teacher.

Richards-Brown Family Photo Collection

Counselor Richards works with students to collect
personal care and other items for Volunteers of America's
Homeless Shelter, a Student Council project.

Richards-Brown Family Photo Collection

Jewelene (second from left) receives Counselor of the Year Award.

0gati210avigation>

Gloria Talbott

Middle School Teacher, Deaf Educator, ECE Resource
Teacher, Administrative Specialist, ECE Placement
Specialist, and 504 Administrator

I AM PROBABLY AMONG A SMALL group of educators who is a third generation college graduate who became a teacher. Born in Louisville, Kentucky during the 1940s, I can count on one hand the number of Black teachers who taught me. I only attended school in Louisville for two days at James Bond Elementary School in the third grade, and that was my first introduction to segregated schools. Let me share some things about my family that will help clarify my childhood situation. Born in Madison Indiana, my father was a Tuskegee Airmen who

G. Talbott Family Photo Collection

graduated from Kentucky State College in 1941 and served in the Burma Theater during World War II. My mother graduated from Lewis Institute of Technology in Chicago, Illinois, with a Bachelor of Science degree in Nutrition and Home Economics. She was thought to be the first post-graduate student to attend Kentucky State.

I was three years old before my father saw me. My father made the military his career, so I lived my childhood in a military family. For my sister and me, being in a military family afforded us extensive travel and opportunities to make new friends in several states as well as on Guam and in Europe. I attended fifteen schools during my school career. I started first grade in Ohio; second and third grade in California and Guam, fourth through eighth grades in Washington, D.C., and all of my high school years in England, graduating from Lakenheath School near Cambridge, England. Three of my four years in high school were in boarding school, an experience that has impacted my life even today. I remember something about every grade and every teacher.

Ms. Reed was my kindergarten teacher; she was a Master's level teacher who turned her living room into a kindergarten class since the local school did not have room for the incoming Black children whose military parents had moved into a newly built area that catered to the incoming military personnel. Ms. Reed became a family friend as her husband was in the military, and she visited with us while she lived in Spain and we were in England. Ms. Petty, first-grade teacher, focused on reading, *Dick and Jane,* and I loved calendar time each month. Ohio did not have fluorinated water and I participated in a dental research project conducted by The Ohio State University. I graduated from The Ohio State University in the 1960s with my bachelor's degree. I experienced five different schools and five different teachers for Grades 2 and 3. I was taller than my fourth-grade teacher in Washington, D. C. and had to ride the bus and streetcar to attend fifth grade as the schools were segregated in D. C. The years I lived in Washington D. C. were the onset of many different experiences.

My father was an ROTC professor at Howard University, and my mother, after doing coursework for her master's degree became a cafeteria manager at Kelly Miller Jr. High School. Initially we lived in an apartment that was next to the Housing projects. I had never been in a school where all the students looked like me except for the two days at James Bond Elementary. My sister and I had a problem with the Black kids because we "talked white." I had never witnessed fights between students or the taunts about "I will beat you up after school or I will beat you up on the last day of school." I had never been in a situation where students were not like me economically and did not understand income disparities that created "haves and have nots." Academically I was far ahead of the students in my class, which was also the case of other military kids who attended the school. I remember being so bored.

With the Supreme Court Decision, Brown vs. Board of Education of Topeka Kansas in 1954, I attended the school in my neighborhood which integrated in the fall of 1954, allowing us to walk to school around the corner. I received the Daughter of American Revolution Award for Academics in the sixth grade. I lived in an integrated neighborhood and my friends were my classmates and neighborhood friends.

Traveling was an integral part of my education. Since our family lived in Indiana and in Kentucky, we visited them yearly as long as we were in the continental United States. My first memory of separate facilities for Blacks and whites was on a train trip to see cousins in Louisiana. At age five, I remember asking what *C-O-L-O-R-E-D* meant on the train when it left Saint Louis going south and magically disappeared when we reached St. Louis going back to Ohio. My cousins attended Catholic schools taught by white nuns in Louisiana, but they had to sit in the back of the bus when we went to visit an aunt. I remember the chain gangs in the South. When we traveled as a family, my father wore his military uniform and would ask at service stations, "Do you have accommodations for my family" before he would purchase gasoline. Most men had fought in WWII, and the military uniform seemed to affect how this Black family was treated, not always but many times. We always took food with us or used grocery stores to make food purchases when we traveled. We hopped from military base to military base when going cross country and stayed with friends. Hawaii was as racist as Mississippi when it came to accommodations for Blacks in the 1950s. Yes, I went to Hawaii twice in the 1950s.

Department of Defense (DOD) Schools had no-frills locations but had excellent instruction. Our teachers were master educators. They kept us ahead because they knew that we could be sent somewhere else and could miss weeks of school during the transfer. We did not have a television but went to the movies every time the feature changed. It only cost a quarter and popcorn was ten cents. I attended boarding school in London, England, and Lakenheath. Most of my classmates and all of my roommates were white. I still am in contact with my classmates. We had the same subjects as required by American high schools. We had required study hall in the dorm from 7 to 9 p.m. every evening except on Sunday. School did not start until nearly 10 a.m. as buses came from all over the London area with the day students. It took ten hours on Friday evening to ride a chartered bus home to our base in Suffolk County. I often traveled alone on day trips to London, and I traveled alone on the continent, in France, and in Germany. I was never afraid and never met any difficulty. I spent a month in France with a French family to perfect my French. When I flew back to London and a man asked me a question in English, I translated it into French before I answered him. Then realizing he was speaking English, I spoke English. I even knew how to navigate Paris by myself.

As we traveled, there were always things I wanted to see and do. The first time I went to California at age seven, I wanted to see the desert, drink water from a rushing stream, see a waterfall, and play in snow in June. I did all of them. I could hardly wait to see the Pacific Ocean and ended up crossing it on a ship for two weeks going from San Francisco to Guam. I wanted to go to Rome and throw coins in the Trevi Fountain, see the colosseum and the Sistine Chapel. Being a military dependent afforded me exposure to so many opportunities. I have been in 48 of the 50 states.

I wanted to be a medical doctor from fourth grade. We had a family friend who was a doctor. My mother did not encourage me to pursue a medical career. She said that I would eventually want to marry and have a family. Being a female doctor in the 1960s would have so many challenges. Since I did love the English language, I decided in the twelfth grade to teach. In later years my mother said that she wished she had never said that to me. It was just the time when most females were limited in career choices. I enrolled at the University of Washington in Seattle, Washington, as we were living on a base in the eastern part of Washington. I completed my degree at The Ohio State University in 1965 and moved to Louisville. I was offered a job at DuValle Junior High School teaching English and social studies for a salary of $4800 a year.

DuValle was a wonderful experience, different, but a real learning experience. I do understand how white middle class teachers can feel when they come into a school where the majority of the students do not look like them and many of the students come from impoverished circumstances. My students varied academically, some the best and brightest, others with academic and behavioral issues. I do not think that kids come to school to be "bad." The struggle between adult expectations and the uniqueness of the child affect reactions and responses. I had challenges, but as my mother told me when I started teaching, "You got what you got and you love them in spite of themselves." Kids often do not have a voice and cannot speak up for themselves, but I used my voice as a teacher. Parents should take that role, but they do not feel that they have a voice either.

Over the next 25 years, after leaving DuValle, my career took several turns. My Master's Degree in Speech Pathology and Audiology from the University of Louisville required almost 55 graduate hours. As I pursued that degree I taught Deaf Education for four years and completed Rank 1 in Supervision before merger. I kept my assignment at Cochran, Noe, and Manual. When school assignments became based on seniority and certification after the 1977 Teachers Strike, I chose Dunn Elementary and Stivers Elementary. Both of the schools were located in upper middle class neighbors with the Black students bussed to these schools. I witnessed the elitist attitudes and heard disparaging remarks in the teachers' lounge and from parents who volunteered at the school. I saw changes in policies that were based on their bussed students when really it benefitted all students in the schools. Fees were once the penalty for a late library book. Since it was thought that the bussed students did not have the money to pay the fee, the policy was changed that library privilege to take a book was withheld until the other book was returned, a better policy for all of the students, which I voiced in the teachers lunchroom when the subject of late library books surfaced.

I transitioned to ECE Regional Resource Teacher from 1979 to1981 and later became an administrative specialist: North Region

Speech Specialist; Regional Placement Specialist where I dealt with ECE students in the schools assigned to the North Region; and ECE Placement Specialist, which involved program placement for students across the District as well as the teachers and school administrators.

Following my retirement in 1995, I worked as the Section 504 Administrator under the Compliance and Investigations Office in the school district, totaling 50 years of service overall. My experiences taught me "never say never" to a student. You do not know that the one thing you do for a child may be life-changing. I truly like to teach. I am as anxious for my students in the formative years as well as for those pursuing degrees. As a teacher who never struggled with academics, it is pertinent that you develop strategies for your students. Teachers must be able to capture changes in their students and adopt methods to match those changes. The new teachers at DuValle did not have the luxury of knowing how it was always done, so we invented new ways of doing. For me I learned, "That's how we use to do it," did not exist. My job is to make it work for the student.

As a teacher, one has to teach the whole child so that the role of the teacher expands to impact social, emotional, mental, and physical aspects of students' lives. I did not understand that children come to school hungry. My teacher preparation did not include training to teach the entire gamut of students' needs. I only had an inkling of where to begin. As special education administrator and the inception of the Individual Education Plan (IEP), student-centered learning became the focus for some of the district's students. I have felt that all students need an IEP as it encompasses school life and transitions to life after school.

The importance of education has gone through generational changes, with dollars driving the choices. Unions created a false middle class, if class is determined by dollars earned. One could work in a factory and make more than a person with a college degree. The value of education took a hit and it affected the African-American population too. My parents passed down the belief that emphasized an education was a key to a decent life. Television opened a world of "I want" and "I got to have." "Things" became the measure of success. Education requires sacrifice of time, money, and energy. Students have opted out of education to satisfy their "Me" wants. Parents have to support education so that their child will have life-long options, not just the choices of their youth.

Money is not the only factor that decreases the value of an education. We do not value some students unless there is a rallying call. We have students and parents who are fragile, and we do not realize their predicament until a problem or issues surface. Socioeconomics should not keep one from being educated, but we are faced with a "them" and "us" scenario where those living in poverty are not respected except when they raise enough noise. Charter schools are not the answer. I see them as "cash cows" with the students being the product. They appeal to the uninformed and to those who feel that they have no voice and want some of the power. School districts are not political pawns.

Keeping good teachers in the profession and recruiting new teachers is a challenge. Today's teachers face declining respect for education in a quantity vs. quality market, with school administrators uncertain about their roles and responsibilities—providing quality education for all students including career and post-secondary instruction that supports making a living and meeting state-mandated test scores. We must make the profession more attractive to compete with Corporate America which includes paying what it takes to get quality. Our best pool may be the second-career people, 50 to 60 years old and first-generation college graduates. The adage, "If I cannot do anything else, I can always be a teacher needs to cease." Your degree may be a Bachelor of Science but what a teacher does is an "Art." The profession cannot afford to deal with such attitude as our children deserve so much more.

Gloria Talbott has been a child advocate throughout her career. As an administrator for Section 504 after her retirement, she continues her goal to do no harm in determining appropriate educational placement and services. She has taught for Murray State University, Jefferson Community College, the University of Louisville, and Spalding University. She has two daughters, one who works in Corporate America and one who really should be a teacher, but works in her chosen field of public administration. Gloria now proudly boasts five generations of women-college graduates in her family.

3

TEACHER JOURNEYS

Lessons and Insights

3

Lessons and Insights

Insights: Too Much, Too Little, but Never Too Late

Insight: The capacity to gain an accurate and deep intuitive understanding of a person, thing, situation, issue, or challenge. The ability to get to the "heart" of the matter.[6]

BE FIRM; BE FAIR; BE CONSISTENT; AND DON'T SMILE UNTIL Christmas. This was the extent of my professional insights when I walked into Shawnee Junior High School in August of 1971 to assume the responsibility of my own permanent classroom for the first time. I did not have the benefit of a student teaching experience as a participant in the Professional Commitment Program. I, along with 14 other students, had one three-hour introductory evening class with Ms. Helen Cunningham. She helped us understand how to use the teachers' manuals; how to set up our classroom using a seating chart; what needed to be placed on bulletin boards; how to introduce a lesson; what the different types of assessments were; how to check for understanding; methods teachers should use for rotating around the classroom to support students; and if teachers asked these questions, what would they expect students to say and what would the teachers say next, based on the students' responses.

We each designed, developed, and taught a lesson using our peers as students. We also had to submit our unit plans for the first two weeks of school. We used a Plan Book and wrote step-by-step what we would say; what we would do; questions we would ask the students; their responses; and our next strategy. We had the letters cut and materials for two generic bulletin boards and we had "dittos" (yesteryear's equivalent to a master copy) ready for Day 1 assignments based on the subjects and grades that we were expected to teach.

We were given a copy of a completed sheet from the "Bird Book" so that we would have an idea of how to keep records for attendance; and we were assured that we would be successful or we would not have been admitted into the program. On our final evening, our supervisor brought cake and punch to class for our celebration. She passed around a sheet so that we could schedule her first visit in our classroom, and she told us not to worry. We were to write down any major issues that we had during the first two weeks and we would discuss them at our next class meeting. Her parting words were, "You know your subjects and you've been in classrooms most of your lives. Own your classroom. Be prepared ahead of time. Get to know your students. Be firm; be fair; be consistent; and don't smile until Christmas. Call me if you need me."

I have always felt that I had an advantage over many of my classmates in the program because of the twelve years of outstanding teachers that I had encountered. They were my frame of reference for most things about classroom instruction. When something unexpected popped up, or I was in doubt, I sometimes assumed the mannerisms of Juanita Holt or Theresa Metcalf or James Mosby or Alene White or Elsie Sterling, some of my teachers at Jackson Junior High School. I had no real insights into teaching except my role models. Caring about my students was automatic. It never occurred to me that I was not supposed to care. My primary concerns were: Am I being effective? Are my kids learning what they need to learn? How do I make sure that they continue to build on what they have already learned? How do I help those slower achieving students move faster? These were the instructional issues that gave me pause and I had to contemplate.

Dealing with discipline was my greatest challenge because my K-12 classrooms as a student really did not have discipline issues other than some boy pulling a girl's pigtail or some girl sticking her leg out tripping a boy as he came down the aisle going to the teacher's desk. Fights, name-calling, and cursing in class were not a part of my school experience. Before school, after school, or in the neighborhood—yes, but not in school. Therefore, I had to create my own strategies and sometimes clean up my own mess. When I tried something that was not as effective as I wanted it to be, I had to change course. I learned early to own my mistakes, whether I was over the top or just skating under the radar. I also learned the importance of telling my students what I felt was ineffective and why; and to ask for their input before deciding on a new direction. Yes, I owned my classroom, but I had to build trust with my students. Listening to them and allowing them to give input into the rules and consequences helped build that trust. This was something totally new for me because I always trusted my teachers and felt they had my best interest at heart. The rules they set were the rules we lived by unquestionably. Times had changed, but caring and trust were still anchors for student-teacher relationships during my teaching years. They remain anchors in current times as well.

My first two years of teaching were a continuous learning process. I gained *Insights* into the hearts and minds of students and of teachers who were colleagues, classmates, and supervisors. More than 45 years later, I continue gaining *Insights* from others, and I have managed to develop a few additional ones of my own. However, I have maintained a core belief system about teaching, which includes "students first, subjects second, or, I teach kids, not social studies." And, for middle school students in Grade 7, it is doubly important: "be firm, be fair, and be consistent; let them know your expectations on Day 1; and don't smile until Christmas."

The following *Teacher Journeys* in this section offer varied *Insights* gained by African-American educators who share their stories here. One of those stories with shared *Insights* is told by Rosa Crumes (Lara) my high school Math Functions teacher at Central High School. Before her passing, Ms. Crumes asked me if I remembered what she use to say to my class. She said, "I always told my students that God gave them a brain and they were supposed to use it. Well, it is important that teachers help students recognize their gift, their brains. We as teachers must do our part to challenge students to use their brains. If they do not use it, they will lose it." I totally agree with Ms. Crumes' insight and hope that readers will find other *Insights* as thoughtful and as compelling.

Rita Bowman

Teacher, Speech Clinician, Resource Teacher,
Principal, and Early Childhood/
Pre-School Coordinator

I WAS EDUCATED IN THE '50S AND '60S and I never had a Black teacher. My mother was only 16 years old when I was born in Henderson, Kentucky, and I was raised by my great aunt and uncle who were Catholic. I attended segregated Catholic schools in Waverly, Kentucky, from kindergarten to Grade 5; an integrated Catholic school Grades 6 to 9; and an integrated public high school in Union County, graduating in 1970. Neither Mom nor Dad, as I called my great aunt and great uncle, graduated from high school. Dad completed tenth grade and Mom completed eleventh grade. I remember Dad often saying, "Opportunity is what separates us." He was a construction worker and many people thought he had a degree because he was so good; so good, in fact, that he and my uncle laid out the foundation for the first three buildings at Henderson Community College.

*Bowman Family
Photo Collection*

Mom was a homemaker who volunteered at school. She was the unofficial teacher assistant who volunteered at church and had a part-time job cleaning our church. She also washed altar clothes at another church. Our Catholic church was integrated but there were lines of demarcation. Whites sat on one side and Blacks sat on the other. There were no African-American priests or nuns. I had Ursuline Sisters in elementary school and Sisters of Charity as teachers in upper grades.

Dad and Mom, along with my four brothers (uncles), spoiled me rotten. We prayed together and ate together at the same table at the same time. They all valued education and felt that it was important to get as much education as you could because "nobody can take it away from you." They made me want to go to school to learn, and I remember all my teachers. One of my favorites was Sister Anna Elizabeth Maloney from Hyde Park, Massachusetts. She loved teaching and found a way to teach everybody. She was totally different from my second-grade teacher who did not like kids. Another favorite was Sister Jean Catherine in ninth grade. She and I both loved to read. She gave students a list of books if they were going to college. She told us, "You do not have to go every place, but you can take a book and travel."

My elementary school and junior high school were in the same building; the only change was walking across the hall. In ninth grade at my Catholic Jr. High, students stood up when the teacher entered the room. Sitting on the front row in tenth grade in public school, when the teacher entered the room, I stood up. Big mistake! However, Mr. Tommy Jenkins helped smooth it over. My favorite subjects were French and English and I loved biology because the teacher made learning it enjoyable, adding things that we never thought about, like including botany, and she broke it down to where we could relate to it. I liked my French teacher, Jeannie Edmonds, who looked French, but wasn't. She was passionate about French and did not mind if we talked in class, but we had to speak in French. I loved the way French sounded.

I always knew that I was going to college. My biological aunt Elizabeth who I am named after, went to Indiana University. In the tenth grade, I made up my mind that I was going to work for a scholarship. I had great grades, a 3.75/4.0 grade-point average, but "we Black," and many assumed that we would not do much of anything. I was No. 25 out of 225 students in my class, but I never received

any support from my high school counselor, even though I was a National Merit Semi-Finalist. I received information from various colleges because I was a Merit Scholar, but no one helped me. Boston College offered me a scholarship package, but my parents would not let me go—too far away from home. In the mix, Bellarmine College gave me a scholarship and "Honor Dollars" for their nursing program, so Louisville, Kentucky, became my destination.

I graduated from high school June 4, 1970, and graduated from Bellarmine in December 1973, three and a half years later. I tutored at the Ursuline Model School and tutored for Bellarmine as well. Along the way, I discovered that I wanted to do something with exceptional children. Sister Mary Ann told me that there were few African Americans in the speech and hearing sciences. I was able to do the science courses, including anatomy, with no problems. I took a couple of classes and I was hooked.

I completed student teaching at Southwick Elementary School under Anna K. Ransaw. It was different. I knocked on doors in the Southwick Housing Projects to talk to parents who missed meetings. I helped parents in Park Hill, teaching the parents so that the kids could learn. I had to work with parents on attendance. We could not give up on them when they have something that you need. In this case, we needed their children to get our services so that the children could progress. Southwick gave me my first experience with Black teachers. I never had a Black teacher in my entire K-12 experience or in undergraduate school at Bellarmine. My first Black teachers ever were Dr. Nettye Brazil and Dr. Joe McMillan at the University of Louisville during my master's program.

My first principal was Al Upton at Booker T. Washington Elementary School on Jackson and Breckenridge streets next to today's Meyzeek or the old Jackson Junior High School. I worked with children from the projects around the corner from the school. With the merger of the Louisville City and Jefferson County school districts, I was transferred to Minors Lane and Coral Ridge Elementary schools under A. B. Harmon and Harry Funk. During my teaching assignment at these schools in the South End of Jefferson County, I was run off the road and pushed into a ditch on my way to work. However, the staff was friendly and helpful, and I was accepted and treated well, much better than I was later treated in East End schools where parents wanted to see my degrees, stating, "How do we know that you are qualified?"

Over the years, I worked with good administrators and teachers at Portland, Sanders, King, St. Matthews, and Greathouse Elementary schools. At All Saints Academy, a West End Catholic school, I became principal, but I returned to Jefferson County Public Schools because of the racism that I experienced at All Saints. For me, to this day, comparing white students and Black students is like comparing apple and oranges. They are totally different entities. We might want to think about that as we think about challenges for today's children.

For 20 years, from 1989 to 2009, I held several positions within the JCPS District. I was Early Childhood resource teacher for a group of schools and travelled the county to aide teachers. As Placement Specialist I had to read the Bible to keep my sanity and to get direction for help with cooling off parents. I was an Exceptional Childhood Education resource teacher at VanHoose Education Center and coordinator of the Early Childhood Diagnostic Center. Throughout my career when I dealt with parents and children, I always remembered a situation that we had at home. Dad never gave a spanking. I had a brother who was six years older. One day we were watching TV but it was not on because "He might give us a spanking." Dad talked to us and made us feel so bad. My lesson from that experience was that I never reprimanded, but I reasoned with students and parents and made them think about what they were missing out on or what could happen if they missed this opportunity.

Schools changed over the years. Beginning with the Merger, there has been hostility toward Black children. Black students arriving on the bus were called "them" not children. Diversity was based on what you could see looking at the surface, not on what students knew or needed to learn. Furthermore, so often we have told parents that we are experts that now they do not bother to participate because, "The teachers are going to do what you want to do anyway." We should have been saying to parents, "You have been teachers up to now; tell us about your child."

I have seen four-year-olds who have been provided with their basic needs, over the top and ready to learn. They can do what all others do. As four-year-olds, their self-image is intact. I have seen them become angry as they move through the system because of "put-downs" rather than "build-ups" just because they are culturally different. Sure, they may be loud; then provide a mechanism for them to be loud, rather than taking the myopic view that everybody must fit into the same round hole.

I have seen the changes in ECE services, minimizing ECE classrooms by putting BD, LD, and other learning disabilities in the same classrooms. They are not the same. Having five LD students and three BD students in the same classroom does not work. Teachers must work with the children where they are. Multiple disabilities does not fit with LD. In preschool, half of the class may be ECE with the same support dynamic, one teacher and one aide. Students with Individualized Education Programs (IEP) vary by age since we must take them upon their third birthday. Like regular school, with testing and paperwork, accountability should not run the show, but it does.

The need to support academics is probably the most pressing challenge for schools. More collective planning with teachers designing units where another teacher can pick up and implement with opportunities to be creative may provide some consistency. We have gotten away from focusing on instructional leadership with mandates for more paperwork. Elementary school assistant principals need to focus their time on instructional support. If the academics are strong, the discipline problems will decline.

Expectations have changed—from boundaries that students did not cross and respect for teachers and students—to something that I do not have a word for. We have gone from the idea that school was going to offer something to help you really make a living, and if you were going to college, "I got you." We are at the point if a student is not going to college, there is no interest in helping. We seem to have forgotten that everybody is not going to college. Students never hear about Carl D. Perkins. Vocational Rehab counselors are unknown; they could be providing support, direction, and job skills for students in high school to be prepared for the better paying jobs that continuously go unfilled.

We face other challenges with getting and keeping good teachers, teachers who want to stay. One of the best teachers that I have ever seen was Ashley Byrd. She was so caught up in what she was teaching the students, never taking her focus off the kids and never missing a beat. The kids were engaged and everything came together for the kids. For good teachers, kids are all they see and they build around the needs of the kids. One of the best teachers that I had was my eleventh grade English teacher, Ms. Holt. She didn't just lecture. She combined reading, writing, and questioning. Students were important and she made English real and relevant and helped us understand that the best thing we could do for ourselves was reading. These teachers stayed because their focus was on us, the students first, and educating us was their priority.

Finally, we continue to struggle with educating poor, Black children who have limited resources, including lack of books at home, parents who have limited time to spend with their children and who have a language gap because of limited experiences and exposure. They have not experienced the zoo, a petting farm, or the country. They ride TARC, with no car to get them from place to place. They have never put their feet in sand, planted a garden, or picked a strawberry. Yet, they sit listening to someone reading to them about kids who are having these experiences, but have no frame of reference for the book's events, and yet are expected to make the same inferences and assumptions, as well as have the same interest and enthusiasm as those students with experiences that relate to the story. It does not work that way, and we as educators must recognize the disparity and seek different solutions. For me, if I could bring them up with similar experiences, they would go into kindergarten with everybody else—Ready!

Rita Bowman retired from JCPS in 2009. Since retirement she has devoted her time working in various ministries at her church, Greencastle Baptist Church. She is an ordained minister and a member of Delta Sigma Theta Sorority where she also serves as sorority chaplain. Rita is a widow with five children and eight grandchildren. Two of her children are also educators, one a preschool teacher and the other a middle school assistant principal.

Elizabeth Caples

Teacher, Musician, Playwright, Pianist,
and ExCEL Award Winner

ALTHOUGH MY PARENTS WERE from Tennessee, Mom from Memphis and Dad from Jackson, I grew up in Louisville, Kentucky, as an only child and lived in the West End and Newburg areas. Mom worked in the cafeteria at Virginia Avenue Elementary School and Dad worked at International Harvester. We lived in the Parkland area on Dumesnil,

Clinton Bennett Photographer

and I attended Virginia Avenue for my entire elementary grades. I had perfect attendance in several grades and I really liked school.

My favorite elementary teacher was Ms. Ruth Davis, my fifth-grade teacher. She had a nice personality and she liked kids. She was understanding, and it did not hurt that she was a member of the family. I attended DuValle Jr. High School in seventh grade and part of eighth grade. I was in the Student Council and participated in chorus under Dr. Mary Elisa Smith. When we moved to Nachand Lane, I transferred from the all-Black DuValle to predominately white Fern Creek in March of my eighth-grade year, going from city to county.

From Grades 8 to 12, I never again had a Black teacher, and I was usually the only Black student in each of my classes. At Fern Creek, I was treated well and was never called out of my name. I participated in the choir and the chorus as well as Future Homemakers of America. My counselor was Marion C. Moore for which Moore High School is named. Also, I was the first African American in the Concert Choir although a parent of another student had to intervene to make that happen.

I began developing my musical talents when I was seven years old, taking piano lessons from Thelma Hampton for whom Hampton Place was later named. I would often play at Fern Creek when the teacher was absent. I played the songs that we had rehearsed. When my teacher was there, she would tell me to "take my seat" and would never let me play even though at age sixteen, I began playing for Watson Memorial Baptist Church. Ms. Collins, my favorite high school teacher, acknowledged her students and was a great English teacher.

My mom had to talk to my high school counselor to assure that I was moved to the college-prep tract from the business tract. There was really no help for the twelve African-American students in my graduating class, the majority taking business classes and not college prep. I rode a school bus that picked me up in my neighborhood. During my junior and senior years, I attended the early session, 7 a.m. to 1 p.m., when Jefferson County Schools went to double sessions. I had perfect attendance. During my years at Fern Creek, there were no African-American majorettes, only one Black cheerleader, and one Black singer in the Concert Choir, me.

I graduated from Fern Creek High School in 1965, knowing that I was going to college with or without a scholarship. My mom had always told me that I would attend college and I did not want to disappoint her. Even though I had been overlooked for a music scholarship that had been given to a white student who sang but did not play an instrument, my parents were committed to my getting a degree. They paid my way through Kentucky State (K-State) College where I choose to go because I wanted to see and be with Black people again. I remember the first time that I went to the cafeteria at K-State, seeing Black people everywhere. I said to myself, "WOW, this is so unusual," and I loved it! I ran into old friends from elementary school and made new lifelong friends who looked like me.

There was never any doubt in my mind that I would not major in music. I was good at it. I played piano when I was at home and my mom was in the church choir. I made a little money playing the piano for various occasions and sometimes singing at special events. K-State had built new buildings for music and business. Music majors had to take classes in Strings, Woodwinds, Brass, and Percussions, demonstrating proficiency in one of those areas. I played the clarinet in the Marching Band, majored in piano and minored in organ. I practiced late at night, working on proficiency with the clarinet while working in the Music Library, checking out phonograph records and books as part of my work-study program. I also spent hours in the Listening Lab, listening to classical music.

For my senior recital, I had to memorize and play something from every period, without written music. Three weeks before the recital, I had nothing from the twentieth century and was at a loss. The piece that I finally chose had lots of sharps and an odd melody. As I sat before that grand piano in that formal setting playing *Le Petit Ane Blanc* by Jacques Ibert, I learned a lesson about style that has stayed with me throughout my career.

In 1969, I completed student teaching at Meyzeek Middle School under Genevieve Churchill. Afterwards, I taught at DuValle Jr. High as a substitute teacher for three months, holding a position for Gail Taylor before moving back to Meyzeek where I replaced my supervising teacher, Ms. Churchill. Three things stand out for me as a new teacher. First, you were on your own if you took the job, but, second, you asked for help if you needed it, and third, anybody/ everybody would help you.

I loved working with kids who lived in Smoketown. During the three years that I spent at Meyzeek, I received all kinds of gifts at Christmas, had students perform in concerts and at school functions on special occasions, and made sure that students were proud of themselves. The girls wore evening dresses for our spring concerts. They looked good and performed well. Students said, "We could tell that you cared about us." My students and I developed a bond. I had some students twice a day, for music and for English, a subject that I taught but was not certified to teach.

For the 1974-75 school year, I transferred to the old Male High School at Brook and Breckenridge streets for a different kind of assignment. I worked from 1 to 7 p.m. teaching Music in Period 5 and Period 6. After those classes, I worked in a special after-school program with students who had dropped out. I gave assessments, taught, and gave assignments on classwork that was needed to complete eligibility for graduation.

I was transferred to Moore High School the first year of merger and desegregation in 1975-76 and served as the music teacher for both the junior and senior high schools. I taught General Music and Choir I. While the teaching staff was integrated, Black students were again in the minority. I remained at Moore for six years until the middle school closed and I was transferred to Thomas Jefferson (T.J.) Middle where I taught for 19 years. I have to say that I never transferred on my own, but was always transferred because of something.

One of my favorite teacher stories is about a student that I taught in the seventh and eighth grades at T.J. When the student was in the twelfth grade, she nominated me for *Who's Who Among America's Teachers.* I had no idea that she would do such a thing. I do know that I have tried to be a great educator. For me, this meant going over and beyond day-to-day lessons and class work. I talked with students about other things. I needed to reach out to parents and I did. I had to go to homes, take students home after performances, buy things for students out of my own pocket, and showcase students so that they could see their own talents. I had student directors. When students performed, they were authentic like when we performed the Lion King. Students were in appropriate costumes, even if I had to chip in and absorb some of the cost.

My students are glad to see me, anytime, anywhere. They hug me and tell stories about songs that we sang and sometimes quote me, specifically telling me or others what I had said to them. Teachers really do not know the difference they are making today, but when you see your students years later and they run up to you and tell you your story, it makes you feel humble.

In 1994, I was selected as a WHAS ExCEL Award Winner. Mary Hardin was principal of T.J. at the time. The ExCEL Award honors teachers who have "excelled beyond expectations for their students and staff." ExCEL stands for Excellence in Classroom and Educational Leadership. This award also recognizes public school teachers who exemplify teaching excellence using innovation, excitement, and enthusiasm in their teaching methodology. These award winners also maintain meaningful personal relationships with students, parents, and the community. My principal had to endorse me, and I had to have letters of recommendation in order to complete the two-phase process that included conference observations and interviews. To know that my students and faculty thought so highly of me is one of the highlights of my career as well.

After my official retirement from JCPS, I continued working in the schools in various capacities, teaching, working with Extended School Services, and substitute teaching, so I have been in schools recently. My concern is that students today are a bit more hostile. They openly use profanity. They yell and generally show lack of respect for themselves, other students, and their teachers. For the most part, students do not seem to care about being successful and parent involvement does not appear to last past second grade. I have students say to me, "I don't care." I say to them, "You may not care, but I care."

It also disturbs me when I see how teachers respond to student behaviors. I kept an index card on every student. When I had to call home, I could tell parents what the student did or said and when, being specific. New teachers especially, should keep records on issues with kids. And, if you are a middle school teacher, you have to have a few tricks to keep the classes in line. Middle school teachers have to be a little bit crazy, sometimes a Jekyll and Hyde. They must be flexible and cannot stay mad about anything. They have to get the situation under control with one child, then turn and smile at the next child, with no carry over. However, teachers must be careful. Students see favoritism and prejudice. They notice when you tell some students that they are doing a good job and never tell others. If students are not doing a good job, tell them what they need to do to get better, then help them do it.

One other thing that I see is teachers teaching, but not pushing students. The work is too easy and kids are not expected to do much as they are not given enough work to do. Teachers tell students "good job" when it really isn't a good job, and sometimes parent involvement in homework doesn't help the student. When questioned about his homework, I heard a student tell a teacher, "My Mom said that she didn't know how to do that."

Our logo at T.J. Middle was "A Place To Be Somebody," and we worked to help students feel that they were somebody. It required a commitment to children and to teaching. Teachers had to stay current in the profession, love what they were doing, and care about the students that they worked with. New teachers had to give teaching a chance and stay around long enough to see and feel the results, understanding that they would not have a perfect classroom, but that they had to work continually toward improvement; and veteran teachers had to support them.

When I began studying music at K-State, I did not see myself as a teacher, but wanted to perform. As I reflect on my career, I know that if I had to choose today, I would choose teaching. My love has been giving the spotlight to my students and watching them perform and doing it well. I cannot think of a better legacy.

In addition to teaching, Liz Caples has performed in weddings, funerals, and on special occasions throughout the Louisville community. She has played for the Jefferson County Teachers Association King Dinner, been a last-minute substitute for concert pianists who have become ill, and has shared her expertise, giving private music lessons. She is a playwright whose play, "The Longest Struggle," has been performed several times. The grandmother of five (her daughter is deceased), Liz has one grandson, Gerron Hurt, who is a teacher as well as a Master Chef contestant. He also graduated from Louisville's Fern Creek High School and credits his grandmother as his inspiration. Liz has been the musician at Watson Memorial Baptist Church for 30-plus years and at the Ebenezer Missionary Baptist Church for10-plus years.

Rosa Crumes-Lara

High School Math Teacher and Fashion Model

It is with a sad heart that I share the passing of Ms. Rosa Maria Lara (Crumes) before the publication of this document. However, both Ms. Crumes and her daughter Maria, reviewed the text in Ms. Crumes' story and approved of its publication. I am so thankful that I had the opportunity to visit and talk with Ms. Crumes before her death and can commemorate her journey, career, and commitment as an educator on these pages. Thank you, Ms. Crumes.

FOR THE FIRST 18 YEARS OF MY LIFE, I never spoke English in my home. Born in Tampa, Florida, in 1931, I learned to speak Spanish before I learned to speak English. You see, my mother never spoke English nor did my father, sisters, or brothers speak English in our home since we were Cuban Americans. While I believe my mom may have been born in Tampa, my dad travelled back and forth between Cuba and Florida, eventually settling in Florida and marrying my mom. There were five children, an older brother and sister, my

Crumes-Lara Family Photo Collection

twin sister, my brother and myself. I was the bookworm who was quiet, studious, and soft-spoken, while my twin, the Drama Queen, was "Ms. Personality" and "Belle of the Ball."

I learned to speak English from the children in the neighborhood. We played with the American kids and learned from them. Cubans come in all different colors. My mom was dark. My dad was fair, very light-skinned. My older sister was brown; my younger brother, mulatto with red hair; my grandmother, who died when I was five years old, looked white and my grandfather was very dark. In those days, Cubans were considered more Black than white. I was light-skinned, but when I got older and did not plait my hair, Mom had to press (straighten) my hair as the Black children did. We then curled it by rolling it around strips of paper cut from a brown bag. Later, Mom would roll it around her finger and pin it down with a bobby-pin. My dad owned a Cuban-American barbershop, and my mom worked for a time at the cigar factory on a street behind our house. Tampa was a tobacco place. Mom spread the tobacco leaves out and smoothed them. One day when I was visiting with Mom, a white woman said, "Why don't you go for white?" I thought, "No, no. This is my mother and she is brown." I did not realize the extent of racism and prejudice that prevailed at the time.

We went to public schools—all Black schools with all Black teachers—we spoke English, but everyone knew we were Cuban. School for us was the 6-3-3 plan, with elementary school going to Grade 6. My first recollection of school is a one-room school house taught by an Episcopal priest and his wife, the Fenlensons. They picked us up and took us to Black downtown not white downtown. School was a house with the walls torn down to make it one big room where all grades were taught. I learned to speak proper English there and thought that I would stay there for elementary school, but my dad refused to pay the tuition, so we walked to the free public school where I was promoted from Grade 1 to Grade 3, spending only a couple of months in second grade. I remember my new elementary teacher looked like a tall model.

I loved school. We accepted segregation for what it was. I remember my history teacher who was short and wore high heels. I sat in my seat afraid to move. Well-dressed and prancing, she never sat down and we learned geography and history. Principal Bryant was tall and distinguished. I never had a problem in school. We had oil lamps, not electricity, until I was probably in ninth grade. We had no car; we walked everywhere we went and studied using the oil lamps. We did not see this as hard times. This is just what we did. We visited our aunt in the country, taking the bus. I loved going because it was something different. She cooked the best American food while Mom never learned to cook American and always cooked Cuban dishes.

I had to sit in the back of the bus that I caught daily to Middleton High School. I had interesting teachers who were smart, and I liked all subjects except English because Ms. Ruffin made us memorize everything. Ms. Wilson, well-dressed with long hair, taught biology. Everything not Cuban I learned at school, including patriotic things and songs. I loved physical education, baseball, and softball, playing both in the dirt at home. I began banging on an old player piano that Dad bought when I was in high school. Four houses down, Ms. Sweeley taught piano and talked Dad into allowing me to take free lessons from her. She taught me page-to-page after school until she decided that she could not teach me anything else. She paid for me to go to another teacher, a white man who was supposed to be outstanding.

Dad did not know my musical gifts. He died at age 96, but had always been detached from his children all of our lives. When he came home from work, he slammed the door and ate alone the Cuban foods that Mom had prepared. Dad did not buy canned food, only fresh food. We had to sneak in peanut butter. We had oatmeal and milk every day and grits at dinner.

Cuban parents believed that girls were to grow up and marry, nothing else. As young women, we were chaperoned everywhere we went other than school. We went downtown to movies and to the soda shop, my aunt accompanying us. When we were older, I was my sister's chaperone and I hated it. If we went downtown, somebody would yell out, "Here come the Cubans." I never had a boyfriend in high school and really did not want one. I wanted to go to college and told my principal, Mr. Stewart and his wife who taught me.

I knew that Dad would never pay for me to attend college, but I wanted to go and everyone knew that I was a good student. It so happened that a dean, Dr. Flood, at Tuskegee, came to town for some reason and met with my principal, Mr. Stewart, a friend of his. Mr. Stewart told Dr. Flood about me and convinced him to talk to Dad. They pleaded my case, telling Dad that he would not have to pay anything in the program that I would be in, the Five-Year Work Plan. Dad was a great businessman, charming in a way, but not with his family. He allowed me to accept the offer and agreed to get me to Tuskegee. I graduated from high school in the spring of 1949 and headed for Tuskegee in the late summer with a new wardrobe designed by my sister and constructed by my sister and my mom. I took the train from Florida to Alabama, with Dad along to make sure that everything was on the up and up. I got his final approval to stay at the college after he spent two days on campus, walking, looking, and checking.

It took two years of evening classes to complete my freshman year of college, working 8 to 4 and going to class in the evenings from 6 to 9 p.m. A young man from Tampa who also attended Tuskegee convinced me to work in the Registrar's Office where I was trained as a teletype operator. I typed a punch card for each student, proofreading as I went along. I maintained class rosters and grade reports for teachers and entered my data into huge machines that changed my punch card information into printed pages. These were the earlier computers. We were not paid in dollars, but were given vouchers.

I majored in math and science under the School of Education; went to classes in the Academic Building; and lived in the freshman dorm where no young men were allowed. I caught the train home alone at Christmas and had no fear of walking through the train station at Thomasville, Georgia, to change trains. I did not know that I was supposed to be afraid because I was not aware of the violence and crime in the area, even though things were segregated. I feel sorry for today's kids who live with violence and crime and the fear of living in some neighborhoods. During summers, I travelled to Tampa for two weeks and back to Tuskegee, always the fashion plate with designer clothes cut from patterns carved out of newspaper. My sister later became a well-known fashion designer and I modelled in shows across the country, displaying her creations.

I received a Bachelor of Science Degree from Tuskegee in 1954 and a scholarship to the University of Michigan that I could not accept because I had married during my senior year, and my husband, a Tuskegee graduate, was in the military stationed at Ft. Benning, Georgia. I have to tell this story about my wedding. My sister was married in 1953 with all of the pomp and circumstances financed by a rich Black family in Tampa. My boyfriend and I had attended her wedding. We later told my family that we planned to marry, but, we had no money, although his college was supported by his family since he was not on the Five-Year Work Plan, and he was graduating and joining the military. Mom and my older sister decided that I should have this fancy wedding; after all, I was in college. I was also a member of a sorority, Delta Sigma Theta, whose graduate alumni chapter had paid for me to join Delta since I really did not have extra money. My older sister and Mom carted up everything from my twin sister's lavish wedding— wedding gown, bridesmaid gowns, all the stuff, and brought it to Tuskegee where I was married, with my sorority giving me the wedding reception. I only had to buy a veil, and my husband paid for the flowers. My dad was there to give me away.

We moved to Louisville, Kentucky, in 1959 after my husband completed his master's degree, majoring in printing and English. Both of us had worked at Druitt High school in Tuscaloosa, Alabama, my husband as a teacher and me as the bookkeeper and later as a math teacher, teaching Pre-Algebra, Algebra I, and Algebra II. When we moved, we had two children, a daughter born with the assistance of a mid-wife in Tampa, and a son born in 1959 in Tuscaloosa. Druitt, an all-Black school, told its employees that it could not afford to pay our salaries. We liked Tuscaloosa, but we had to find employment. My husband took a job in Louisville as a printing teacher, and I applied for a teaching position the following year in 1960. I was assigned to Central High School.

I spent 12 great years at Central, from 1960 to 1972, with some of the best teachers in the school system: Mr. Woolridge, Mrs. Carroll, Mr. Whedbee, Mr. Tisdale, and Mr. and Mrs. Lauderdale to name a few. They were great teachers because they knew their content; knew how to get the content across to their students; and had high expectations for their students, teaching them concepts that they would need to know to go to college and be successful. They also tested their students to make sure that they knew what they was supposed to know. Teachers did not give grades; students earned grades. These teachers were also available to help students if students were struggling or needed additional direction, which they normally did not, because, for the most part, these students were smart. While teaching at Central, I earned a Master of Arts in Teaching with a major in math and history from University of Louisville. I also earned lifetime certification, which I still possess. I taught math, had great students, and enjoyed teaching and being a part of Central's faculty. My only regret was I never had the opportunity to speak Spanish. I was never invited to speak to the Spanish classes although the teacher knew that I was a native Spanish speaker.

My teaching skills evolved over time. I student taught at Tuskegee High School under Ms. Yates who had family in Louisville. I was young, sometimes just a few years older than my students, but I was the teacher and I looked and acted like a teacher. I dressed appropriately. I was tall and tried to be stately. I did not scream at students. I remember my teacher telling the class, "Are you hollering at your students? Are you a sergeant in the Army?" My voice was soft. I did not holler. I figured out what the students didn't know and I taught them the skills that they needed to do well in math. I helped some of my students to even like math. I remember telling my class, "If a monkey in the zoo can be trained, surely I can train you with a better brain." Schools change and Central was not immune to change. In 1972, I was talked into going to Iroquois High School. I worked at Iroquois from 1972 to 1987 when I retired, primarily because I was not feeling well.

I loved teaching. I loved my school and I loved my students. I could not function in the atmosphere in today's schools. What I see today is something different from teaching in my day. Children today are so busy talking that they cannot hear. The brain, a transmitter, keeps putting out talking so nothing goes in; meaning learning is a challenge because the brain is not taking anything in. Children's noise levels are the speaker structure, and they are the reality speakers not the teacher. Also, technology is putting children more into Disney World not life's reality or intention.

Discipline is inside self, not outside. Children are not aware the brain is the main controller of the body and what you do affects the body. Either allow the brain to do its work or destroy itself. The brain controls the inner discipline. Teachers cannot do it all and should not be expected to. They are not miracle workers and some things should be done at home. In a classroom, teachers cannot have everyone in charge. At home, everyone cannot be in charge. What creates problems for teachers is when the child, not the parent, is in charge at home and the child then expects to be in charge at school. Teachers should be in control, but, at the same time, the classroom is not a dictatorship. In today's school environment, children are seeking fun, fun, fun! They complain and do not want to work, work, work! The classroom should focus on work, and learning should be fun as teachers do what has to be done to correct what needs to be corrected. I believe that I would need to be part of the solution, not simply making noise. People cannot listen; therefore they cannot learn. I am out of place in today's schools. Too many people will not listen.

As I think about Black children, Black teachers, and Black people in general, I know that racism exists. I think about the white cameraman on a popular TV channel who shows a speck of a Black person. He is doing his job, keeping the Black family seen but not seen, invisible to whites in power. For years as a child, I made myself invisible to my dad who was a dictator parent. You feel even though you do not express. There are parents in today's schools who feel but are not allowed to express. There are Black teachers who are diminishing, feeling invisible, but not expressing and not encouraging others to be teachers. They are in situations where they have no voice, consequently, they sometimes tell students, "You do not want to be a teacher," and the students hear them, choosing to select other careers and not give teaching a second glance.

Life is not fair, but we are all born with brains. We may not always use that brain, but if we want things to change, we need to stimulate that brain to find solutions or be satisfied with being overlooked and invisible. Current teachers must promote the profession, and those of us who are retired and still maintain a fondness for the profession, must speak up and speak out to let all know that teaching is a worthy occupation, and we need those with good brains to join our ranks.

Ms. Rosa Lara (Crumes) taught Advanced Diploma students at Central for many years, assuring that their math skills were at the college level upon graduation. She has two children and four grandchildren. She has travelled the country modelling her sister's fashions that appeared in the Louisville Defender as well as Ebony Magazine. She said that one of the highlights of her career was attending a Fiftieth Reunion of one of her Central High School classes and seeing her students who remembered her and who were doing so well. She said, "I had teachers, lawyers, college professors, dentist, mechanics, secretaries, factory workers, small business owners, and millionaires—my students who remembered me," and I was one of those.

Crumes-Lara Family Photo Collection

Rosa Lara and her twin sister (Top row center) at the James Parish School in Miami Florida where Rosa first learned to speak English.

A. Frazier Curry

Teacher, Principal, and Central Office Administrator

EDUCATION IS REALLY IN MY DNA! I am a second-generation college graduate and the seventh family member to graduate from Kentucky State (K-State) College. Both my mom and dad were educators; in fact, we all were hired by Jefferson County Public Schools on the same day at the same time. Mom began teaching when she was 16-years-old and had an "emergency certificate," before completing her coursework in 1948. Dad graduated from K-State in 1936. My dad, Green Venton Curry, was born in Green County, Kentucky, and lived many years in Greensburg, Kentucky, on the Green River. My parents trained in what was then called the "Normal School." Dad majored in social studies but taught math most of his career. He could teach any subject. Although hired as a principal of his assigned school, Dad still taught.

Curry Family Photo Collection

I am an Eastern Kentucky transplant, born in Glasgow, Kentucky, and raised in Jenkins, Ky. I boast about my DNA, but I did not always recognize its existence. Having been in schoolrooms with Mom and Dad all of my life, when I graduated from K-State in 1964 with a degree in mathematics, I headed straight to industry, even though I had student taught at Manly Jr. High School and was fully certified to teach. I took a job as a trainee with the American Tobacco Company in Louisville.

I was familiar with Louisville because we lived here during the summers, sharing homes with families my dad knew while he waited tables to make ends meet. I hung out with kids in the city. I remember playing around and one kid saying, "We don't get to see you except in the summer." My reply was, "I go to school in the East." They did not know how far "East" actually was; that it was Jenkins, Kentucky in a K-12 school with 100 students total; or that my school housed Grades 4, 5, and 6 in the same room, with the high school occupying the second floor; or that I lived in a town where the Black community was separated from the white community, which was the norm in those days.

My "East" was also Mr. Wendell Lewis, a young high school science teacher from Chicago who also drove the school bus and coached various sports. He told us what life was really like and we considered him a peer. While our high school general science and biology classes were rigorous and our science lab was a science kit, we had Mr. Lewis as a sounding board and could talk about anything with him. I never considered myself smart. I was never a good writer, but I was extremely verbal. However, I had to do the assignments, including chemistry, a subject that intimidated me. As salutatorian of my 10-member senior class, I knew that I had achieved because my teachers believed that I was not going to fail. A quote that I remember that has guided me over the years is, "It's not where you come from, it's what you do with what you have."

In 1965, males were being drafted left and right. I did not want to go to war and needed a way to avoid it. Mom and Dad were looking for employment in Louisville because the school where they worked was closing due to integration. When they went to the Board to talk about jobs, I went with them. Being a math major with certification, I am sure, helped, even though I was only 21 years old. DuValle Jr. High was my first teaching assignment.

There were seventeen first-year teachers at DuValle during the 1965-66 school year. I taught seventh, eighth, and ninth graders who were only a few years younger than I. My beginning salary was $4,200, a $2,300 pay cut from what I was making at American Tobacco. My parents, however, received "raises," earning over $6,000 each because of their experience. The sad thing is that with all of their years of experience, my dad, as a principal and supervisor as well, and my mom each never made over $10,000 during their entire careers.

One of the reasons that I began exploring other avenues for moving ahead in the school system was pay. Having married after my first year of teaching and knowing what I could make in industry, I wanted and needed more money. I figured out that I liked working with children and I wanted to stay in education, but needed a different hook, so I began taking courses in business and in counseling. Two seasoned teachers, Joe Robinson and Dorothy Hubbard, had a knack for hanging out with new teachers and unofficially mentoring them. They were instrumental in my decision to flip to counseling. I received my Master's Degree in Counseling from the University of Louisville in 1970 and embarked on the next leg of my journey in a trailer, moving from school to school teaching Vocational Education and Career Guidance. This was a learning experience for me as well.

My dream job was for an assignment as counselor at Central High School. I did get there, but it took some time. My first real counseling job was at Atherton High School because Lucy Lark was retiring. Sonny Hubbs was principal. Two people had been assigned to the same Atherton counselor job, but I won the position in the end. I stayed and the other person was re-assigned. At the end of the year, however, I was transferred to Central High, and the other person replaced me at Atherton. It was great serving under Mr. Hackett and Joe McPherson and having the opportunity to take my tenth graders from their sophomore year to graduation in the spring of 1975. That class produced lawyers, judges, a Metro Louisville Board member, doctors, and numerous other professionals who are still impacting communities across the country.

How do you walk away from your dream job in a place that you love with people who care about you and your family? You do not. Court-ordered busing and desegregation in 1975 made that decision for me. I was the first Black administrator assigned to Jessie Stewart

High School. Told to report after lunch on the first day to avoid the turmoil and demonstrations taking place in the community and along Dixie Highway, I was thrust into a totally different environment and was happy to learn that we were moving away from the old counseling protocol with males reporting to one counselor and females reporting to the other to a process where each counselor took a class and followed it through to graduation. The assignment was difficult, to say the least, but faculty and students made adjustments over the three years that I was there. They learned that I was professional and cared about students. Trust and mutual respect grew and developed between us over time.

My journey over the next ten years involved both learning and doing. I received principal certification at University of Louisville and served as an administrator at Detrick, Mill Creek Vocational, and Ahrens. My job was to support and guide teachers. When I taught, I did try to be friends with my students, and I encouraged my teachers to be friends with their students. But, I also told my teachers, "I do not believe that children fail. Adults fail children. Everyone has the capacity to learn, but at different levels. As educators, we must find where students are and take them from there." My message to my staff was not always well-received by all, but our practice was to make sure that students got a second chance. Failure was not an option.

Young teachers do not always realize the impact that they have on their students. If they are new and trying to learn how to teach, they work on teaching skills, ignoring power and influence. They forget that the students are learning you while you are trying to learn to teach. Good teachers know that you learn to teach in order to teach kids, not for the sake of teaching content. Great educators understand that education is life and a continuum. Every day we are learning something and it keeps on going. For us to move and thrive, we must have different experiences. Great teachers provide those experiences to their students through exposure—book learning, academics, experiments, reading, analyzing, working with others, examining one's environment. Limited exposure among teachers and students produces tunnel vision for both.

Whenever I see or hear from my former students, or read the

arguments and sentiments in the newspaper, I shake my head. Education is in turmoil. The passion for education is gone. My teachers wanted to be there. Classrooms are now generic and sterile. Lots of talk circulates about students failing and student behavior, but no one is saying that teaching methods are not working. We have allowed non-educators to dictate what we do and when and how we do it. "Teachers must be on page __ by the end of the year." It makes no difference that Johnny cannot read page ___.

Furthermore, teacher education has not changed. We have more students who are visual learners than ever before. How many teacher education programs are using visuals to train teachers and emphasizing how to use visuals, including computers, television, YouTube, and other technology to help students learn to read, write, count and analyze? Programs that still emphasize all chairs in straight rows, information sharing through lecturing, and success based on regurgitation, do not understand that the learning process is more important than the answer and will not produce the types of teachers needed for students in today's classrooms.

As I think about students that I taught and encouraged years ago who became educators, about my own grandson who will be going to college in a few years, and about students that I encounter as I work with different organizations throughout the community, I do not know if I would encourage the old or the new to become teachers. Old seasoned educators were taught that we needed passion and patience and we were driven to make a difference in spite of the low salaries. So many young people feel that they cannot make a difference and that teaching is not financially rewarding. They see that teachers do not become millionaires and many are disrespected by students, parents, and their communities. They do not hear what we heard—the pride, commitment, and dedication to the value of education.

So, no, I am not sure that I can tell them to go to the university to become teachers. I can ask them, "Who helped that engineer or doctor to get the knowledge that he/she needed to get their degree?" I know that I am not going to say, "Go to school to be an elementary teacher." I also know that I could not teach in today's classrooms. My traditional training would not work. I would need to retrain and retool to take advantage of the available technology. I also know that one must be an automated actor in order to get today's students to listen. Education may be in turmoil, but there is still hope. We still have teachers in classrooms making a difference and students who are affected by their efforts. Hopefully, these students will cherish what their teachers do for them and some will choose teaching as a career to serve the next generation.

Frazier Curry retired from JCPS in 1995. He continues to work on the board of Elder Serve, the Kentucky State University Foundation Board, and the Advisory Board for U of L College of Education and Human Development. He is a former member of the U of L University Club Alumni Board. He has been married for fifty years and has one daughter and one grandson.

Carla Green Hillman

Teacher, School Technology Coordinator, Teacher
Educator, KTIP Resource Teacher, Alternative
Certification Resource
Teacher, Adjunct Professor, and ExCEL Award Winner

I AM A SECOND GENERATION ELEmentary educator, so I would like to begin my story by talking about my mom, Wadelle Green. She was born in Georgia and raised in Kansas City, Kansas. Her parents worked tirelessly to provide for her and her brother and to make sure Mom was able to go to college. Her dad labored at a meat-packing house and her mom did "day work." They were extremely proud of her because she was one of the first members of the family to graduate from college. Mom attended Pittsburg State University in Pittsburg,  *Hillman Family Photo Collection* Kansas, where she met and married my dad, Cecil Green. Although she received her degree in elementary education, she did not work outside of the home for a while. My parents lived with my grandparents for a short while in Pittsburg, Kansas, before moving to California so my dad could be near his brothers and sisters who had moved there. Some years later, my uncle, who was in the military, was transferred to Fort Knox, Kentucky. Dad, following his brother, came to Louisville, Kentucky. However, when my uncle was later transferred to Fort Wayne, Indiana, Mom and Dad remained in Louisville.

So now Mom, Dad, my two sisters, and I were the only family in Louisville. However, we travelled back and forth to Kansas City to visit grandparents, cousins, aunts, and uncles every summer. For a while we lived on Twenty-Third and West Jefferson streets in an apartment below the Lomax family. Sedalia Lomax, who later became the principal at Wilt Elementary, became one of Mom's very best friends. Dad worked for the Post Office at night and ran his own real estate company by day. When I was nine years old and my two sisters were six and three years old respectively, Mom began substitute teaching. Her first assignment was with a "tough class" at Joseph S. Cotter Elementary. When Mr. Long, the principal, dropped in to see how she was doing, he hired her on the spot to fill the vacancy. You see, Mom, who was a fantastic storyteller and had the usually rowdy students totally engaged in her reading. She was such a hard worker! We regularly watched as she prepared for her students, making, as she called them, "picture-book" lesson plans. We often helped her by doing jobs such as making copies (one page at a time) on a rudimentary "copy" machine. When a new school, Southwick Elementary, opened near Cotter, Mom was assigned there. At the beginning of the turbulent "busing era," she was transferred to Bates Elementary where she remained until her retirement.

My own elementary school years were interesting. Elementary schools in those days included Grades K-6. I attended James M. Bond (now Dan C. Byck) through fourth grade. I was a happy child who enjoyed school even though I was quiet by nature. Ms. Matthews, my second-grade teacher, was my favorite. She was always kind, considerate, and smiling. However, things changed when I was in fifth grade. We moved to Dumesnil Street in the West End of Louisville, and, therefore, I had to go to a new school. Although I was initially assigned to attend Virginia Avenue Elementary, my parents agreed to allow one of my sisters and me to go to Stephen Foster, a newly integrated school.

Attending this school was a scary and rather unhappy experience. I was seated in the rear of the classroom. I can remember that my fifth-grade teacher yelled at students, something that I had never experienced. It was evident that the white teachers did not want Black students in their classrooms, nor did the white students. I was so nervous that I did not do well academically. I had always been a good student, but struggled somewhat while I was there. When I went to junior high school, Mom took my sister out of Foster, sending her back to Virginia Avenue.

At DuValle, I knew that I was behind because we were tracked by academic levels in those days, and I was not in 7101 (the Excel Level)! Nevertheless, I caught up by the eighth grade and continued to be placed in the top classes. DuValle had wonderful teachers who encouraged me and I thrived. For example, Ms. LaRue, I remember, was firm and stern, but the students respected her, and she made students feel good about themselves. We had plays at DuValle and I was chosen for a role. I also had the opportunity to participate in a variety of other activities and I had many friends. The school itself was filled with beautiful bulletin boards, and I can recall that there were extremely high expectations for all students and zero-tolerance for inappropriate or bad behavior.

Another fond memory is the field trips we took. On one occasion, when returning home from Mammoth Cave, our bus broke down. We were a group of hungry children, stuck on a bus in walking distance of a restaurant with plenty of food that we had money to purchase. The problem was that we could buy the food, but we could not eat it *in* the restaurant; we had to bring it back to the bus. We decided not to buy the food. This was my first memory of discrimination. However, Mom had told me about many of her experiences. For example, while she traveled on a train, the Japanese prisoners were allowed to eat in the dining car but Black passengers could not.

I loved attending Central High School and was blessed to have teachers like Lyman Johnson who made history come alive with his stories. Although I was still the shy, quiet person, I was hardworking and wanted to go to college. In fact, there never was a time that I felt that I would not go to college. I also knew that I wanted to be a nurse. Rather than have us work during the summer months, Mom encouraged us to volunteer. So I was a candy striper at Jewish Hospital. I also volunteered at the Market Street Neighborhood House where I had an opportunity to work with and read to students.

During my senior year in high school, I researched many colleges and was accepted at several. However, Ms. Perry, our counselor, gave me information about a scholarship or "full ride" to Gustavus Adolphus College in St. Peter, Minnesota. So my parents and I drove there to check it out. I loved the campus and the nursing program there, so I accepted. However, my goals changed during the summer of my high school graduation. I was assigned to volunteer in the radiology department at Jewish, which was my first time as a candy striper working directly with patients. A pregnant patient was scheduled for an EKG that showed her unborn baby had died. I was devastated. I had read everything about nursing and knew that nurses had to put their own feelings aside for the sake of their patients. However, after this REAL experience, I quickly realized that I could not feel the way I felt and be a good nurse. So I began contemplating seriously, my choice to be a nurse. Before I even arrived at Gustavus, I switched majors! I changed to elementary education, a choice that I still deeply value!

Being that far from home in a freshman class of only a few African-American students, with a white roommate, and with nothing to do on campus on the weekend was a big adjustment. However, as students got to know me, several of them invited me to spend weekends with them. One place where I spent many weekends was Keister, Minnesota, farm country with people who were always kind. They asked me where I was from, and they thought my hair was fascinating, but they were never rude or disrespectful. While visiting in Minnesota, one little boy saw me and exclaimed, "Mama, look at the people with the brown faces." At the end of my freshman year, I wanted to come home, not because of any academic struggle—no—Ms. Lauderdale had prepared me so well, but because I was just homesick! I applied and was accepted to Spalding University. However, my mother strongly suggested that I needed to stick with my decision and stay at Gustavus. So that's exactly what I did, and I was very glad. Some of my fellow classmates who left Gustavus after that first year never did finish college.

As an education major, I was taught well. I did my student teaching in St. Louis Park, a suburb of Minneapolis/St. Paul, Minnesota. I cannot overemphasize the level of excellence in instruction in our teacher training program. Our teachers were tough on everyone. Our supervising teacher, a former nun who had left the convent to marry, was tough and no-nonsense. We were taught to do it all—planning, instruction, evaluation, re-teaching as well as understanding teachable moments, creating bulletin boards, and classroom-management methods—they left nothing out. One of my cooperating teachers and I had similar personalities and I learned to emulate her methods. She was calm, patient, loving and did not embarrass children. She was smart, knowing how to reach all children and making sure there were no gaps. I've thought of her example many times during my career and imitated her expertise!

Minnesota was icy and cold; however, school rarely was closed because of snow or bad weather. During the summers, I came home and worked at Southern Bell as a directory assistance operator. Upon graduation, I was offered an extremely lucrative position, having worked in the office there several times during the summer. Although I did ponder the offer momentarily, I turned it down. No amount of money could change my mind. I had developed a passion for the profession and I wanted to teach. I accepted my first assignment at John F. Kennedy Elementary in the fall of 1970 and quickly understood that I had much more to learn, and I had to learn it quickly.

I was not ready for kids stealing their mother's food stamps and selling them for marijuana. I also was not ready for the management issues that my students believed my quiet demeanor implied—a teacher who was a pushover. I was not. I developed an "I mean business persona and voice" and dug in. I fell in love with my students, all Black, many poor and needy with academic talents differing across the board.

In addition, I dealt with a tough administrator, Principal Lena Waders. We had staff meeting every Tuesday. Ms. Waders' expectations were clear, from no eating or drinking in the meeting, to what she expected to see when she came into our classrooms, to how she expected us to deal with students and parents. When I lost my key the last day of school, it was the middle of the next school year before I received a new key. Someone walked me to my room and opened the door each morning. I learned to cherish that key!

When I was sent to Dixie Elementary in 1975, I was confident, caring, diplomatic, and kind. Kennedy had taught me that I could teach any place in the world and deal with parents, students, administration, and fellow teachers. Herschel Martin was an excellent principal fit for Dixie Elementary. He kept things normal in an extremely volatile time, even though he sometimes bowed to unreasonable demands of parents. Leaving Kennedy was tough—I did not want to go. My husband drove me to school each morning. My car was spat upon and things were thrown at us. Bomb threats escalated at Valley High School first, then at Dixie Elementary. Parents did not want their children in my room. Consequently, I had fewer students in my first-grade class than the other first-grade teachers. However, it didn't take long for the parents to get to know me. After the first year, parents were asking to have students placed in my room. They figured out that I was a good teacher, that I provided quality instruction, and that my students were happy. Furthermore, students in my class worked hard and could read well. The most important thing is that my students knew that I cared about them. When I had a "kid problem," I always managed to spend a couple of minutes with just that child to build that one-on-one relationship. It worked.

In 1978, I applied for a transfer from Dixie because I had moved to the Westport Road area. I was able to teach at Bashford Manor for two years before it closed due to "white-flight." At that time, I was assigned to Chenoweth Elementary where I happily stayed until I retired from teaching full-time in 2003.

Although the majority of parents at Dixie Elementary were disgruntled during the first year of busing, some were kind, supportive, and embarrassed that parents acted the way they did about having their children in my class. For example, one student's mom and dad went out of their way to be nice. While walking through the hall at Chenoweth just before my retirement, I ran into these dear people. The mom and I recognized one another right away! She was excited to see me at Chenoweth and she let me know that one of her daughter's children was going to school there.

Similarly, over the years, I have run into my students as well as their parents who have shared stories about their lives and my influence as their teacher. Although it is gratifying, even if no one told me, I know quality work and how I strived to achieve it. All teachers know the level of quality that they put forth. Therefore, I self-evaluated my performance, and I always taught those that I mentored to do the same thing.

Many times, I was offered the opportunity to do administrative work or have other positions outside of the classroom. However, I turned them down because I had such a passion for teaching! Nevertheless, I did enjoy helping younger teachers hone their craft! I had enumerable student teachers, participated in and taught professional development sessions for early childhood teachers, worked as a Kentucky Teacher Internship Program (K-TIP) resource teacher and Teacher Educator for many new teachers. Furthermore, I did many teacher-related things at my schools, including being team leader and school technology coordinator, and worked with Alternative Certification teacher candidates. Helping shape and mold new teachers so that they do a good job teaching and touching the lives of their children makes a difference for me, giving me pride in the profession and my contribution to it.

In today's schools, children have a great need for quality instruction. Teachers are expected to do some of the things that used to be the parents' responsibility, taking up time that we once could use for teaching. Young teachers find it difficult to get the job done when they are confronted with so many unfamiliar issues and challenges such as classroom management of student behavior at the top of the list and lack of parent involvement and support next in line.

As we think about change for better education, we must consider smaller class sizes and a creative program designed to meet the individual needs of each child. We should also consider a "center like" plan where needs other than education can be met. Resources for clothes, food, supplies, and snacks should be provided, and children should not be ashamed to utilize the resources but made to feel happy and accepted. We also must consider ways of getting parents re-engaged.

There is no doubt about it; teaching is hard work! Great teachers fall in love with teaching, teach from the heart, have a passion for the profession, love people, stay current with instructional strategies, stay up-to-date on methods, and want to be involved with school life. I don't always see that in today's teachers, and I do not know how to bottle and sell a great teacher concoction.

In my role as a mentor, at times I do see teachers not as vested in educating students as they should be. The state of our current society has deeply affected them. After struggling with students all day, they often have no time or energy to go the extra mile for them. Some even have to take off to a second job to make ends meet! On the other hand, I see great teachers doing everything that they can to help and support their students. At times, while teachers are giving their all for their students, the needs of their own dear children are not being met by their teachers. This is heartbreaking and discouraging, and it happened to me. As a result, I was even more determined that parents would never say that I was not doing everything that I could to help their child. I hope that future teachers, mothers on one side of the table and teachers on the other, will always treat their students the way they want their own children to be treated.

Carla Hillman received the ExCEL Award in September 1999. She retired after 33 years of service and continued as an Adjunct Professor and Teacher Educator for the University of Louisville. She was a resource teacher for various teacher-recruitment and development programs in JCPS. She also worked with the Alternative Certification Program in several capacities: Resource Teacher, Teacher Educator and Instructor, and District Instructional Leader until 2018. She has two children and two grandchildren.

Beverly Johnson

Elementary Teacher, Middle School Teacher, and
Middle School Counselor

MY NAME IS BEVERLY JOHNSON! NO, not the model or the principal! I'm Beverly Butler Johnson, the third child of Ann and Calvin Butler's four children to become an educator. My oldest brother, Dr. Anthony Butler, led the way by graduating Male High School and Morehead University. He received his master's at the University of Maryland and Doctorate in Psychology at Howard University. He worked as a school psychologist in the Maryland School System. My sister, Sherrie Lyons, and brother, Calvin Butler, and I attended Male High as well, but

B. Johnson Family
Photo Collection

our college of choice was Western Kentucky University. Sherrie and I graduated Western Kentucky University with degrees in education and went on to teach in the Louisville Public Schools, which eventually became Jefferson County Public Schools (JCPS). We both received our master's degrees and became school counselors. Calvin started at Western Kentucky University but graduated University of Louisville with a degree in education and he also taught school for JCPS.

Our mom, a hairdresser, who also worked nights at the Starks Building, and our dad, who worked two full-time jobs at International Harvester and the U.S. Post Office, were determined that we had opportunities that they could only imagine. The regular weekdays' routine for the children in our house was going to school, completing homework, attending Boy Scouts/Girl Scouts meetings, taking piano lessons, and doing daily chores. Even though we had chores such as taking out the garbage, washing dishes, and running to the grocery from time to time, our real responsibilities were concentrating on school work. Cleaning the house on Saturday morning, playing outside on Saturday evening with our cousins, preparing for church on Saturday night and attending Sunday School, morning church services and eating Sunday dinner as a family were the activities for the weekends.

My family attended Brown Memorial CME Church under the leadership of Reverend C.L. Finch. Reverend Finch, who when I was a child I thought as "Black Jesus," was loved and respected by his congregation. Many influential people and especially powerful women attended Brown. Ms. Evelyn Waldrop, the City Director of Public Works and Services for the City of Louisville, was my Sunday School teacher. Mrs. Maude Brown Porter, the assistant principal of Central High School and the International President of Alpha Kappa Alpha Sorority, Inc., made sure I sat beside her every Sunday until I was old enough to join the children's choir. Both Mrs. Katherine Lowery and Ms. Lucille Martin were educators who made sure that every child at the church could properly recite an assigned poem or part in the many children's plays and programs at Brown Memorial. The members of our church, teachers, scout leaders, neighbors, along with our parents gave us the inspiration to strive for higher education and the desire to become productive members of our community.

Our parents made sure we lived in a community that was safe and surrounded with good people who had similar expectations. That community was in the Parkland area of the West End of Louisville, Kentucky. The business section of Parkland was located at Twenty-Eighth Street. In the heart of Twenty-Eighth Street was A&P Grocery, as well as clothing stores, a bank, a five-and-dime store, and any other store one could ever need. On one corner of Twenty-Eighth Street was the public library, which we frequently visited. If anyone needed gas or cars repaired, two full-service gas stations were on adjacent corners. All were in walking distance from our house. We lived on a tree-lined street where our pediatrician, elementary principal, Girl Scout leader, ministers, teachers, and friends also lived. Everyone knew everyone and took pride in the upkeep of their property and didn't hesitate to discipline any of the children in the neighborhood.

Virginia Avenue Elementary School was the school for African-American children. Parkland was the elementary school for the children of our white neighbors. We did have one white family, the Bradens, who enrolled their children at Virginia Avenue. Mr. and Mrs. Braden were civil-rights workers and their son, Jimmy, was in class with me for at least three years. Teachers at Virginia Avenue were perfect examples for anyone who had an inkling to become a teacher. I fondly remember Mrs. Katherine Parks, my teacher for Grades 1-3 who was our "Miss Loretta Young," the TV star from back in the day who always started her show walking down the stairs in a beautiful sparkling evening gown. When Mrs. Parks entered the classroom, she had that same effect. She was not wearing an evening gown, but she was a beautiful black woman with a sense of style and glamour that got our attention. Most of the female students wanted to look like our beautiful Mrs. Parks and all the young males had crushes on her!

Mrs. Josephine Trowell, my teacher for Grades 4, 5, and 6, was a "no-nonsense" strong woman. Mrs. Trowell kept the same students for a three-year period, which was not the norm. Most of the students in Mrs. Trowell's class went on to an institution of higher learning once they graduated high school. Mrs. Lillian Carpenter, our music teacher with the blue hair, directed our school's own production of Tchaikovsky's play, *The Nutcracker*, with the participation of all the students and staff at the school. It was a major production with a set, props, costumes, music, dance, and our introduction to the composer, Tchaikovsky! Mrs. Carpenter took our school chorus, in which my sister and I were members, to a state competition, and she also introduced us to the "Making Music" concerts.

After elementary school I attended Parkland Junior High School, when most of the other students in Mrs. Trowell's class attended

DuValle Junior High. Parkland was predominantly white, while DuValle was predominantly Black. I do not remember the names of many of the teachers, but I do remember the principal of Parkland, Owen Clifford. Mr. Clifford, a tall, burly man, walked the halls during school, rounding up any student who dared to be in the halls unattended. Mr. Clifford was in total control of his school until the teachers went on strike. With the teachers on strike, Mr. Clifford looked like a "lost man." Many benefits evolved from my attending Parkland, but the main one was being academically and socially prepared for Male High School.

I remember many of my teachers at Male High School: Ms. Schaeffer, Ms. Striepe, Ms. Opper, and Mr. Walsh to name a few. The teachers had high expectations for the students. Homework was assigned daily, and test and pop quizzes were given on a regular basis. A student had to be prepared because the teachers expected sensible answers to questions. Algebra was not my favorite subject, but my Algebra teacher's teaching method proved to be very beneficial to those of us who were a bit intimidated by the subject.

Students could not walk into social studies class and not be prepared. The social studies teacher would make sure she called on every student in the class, especially any student who dared to not make eye contact with her. In the beginning, I was not always prepared, but I quickly learned that taking notes, rereading and reviewing the assigned chapter daily would help in my preparation. Two Black teachers were employed at Male, but I had neither. I was asked to work in the office as a student office aide. I had good times, developed lifelong friendships, and established an allegiance to "Our Dear Old High School," Louisville Male High. My allegiance to Male was so strong that all three of our children attended Male.

I always knew I was going to college and I was going to be a teacher. With Mrs. Parks and Mrs. Trowell as role models, I never thought of doing anything else. I filled out the college application and the student loan form without any help from the counselor or my parents. My father gave me two college choices, Western Kentucky University (WKU) or Morehead. Western was the more attractive of the two choices and Sherrie was already there. When I arrived on Western's campus I was referred to as "Little Sherrie," and her friends helped me with everything.

The second semester of my freshman year, I became a member of Alpha Kappa Alpha Sorority, Inc., the first African-American sorority on Western's campus. Between the sorority and teacher preparation, there was not a dull moment. I became president of the chapter of my sorority my sophomore year and travelled to various places for activities pertaining to Alpha Kappa Alpha Sorority, Inc. On campus, we initiated the first Miss Black Western Pageant and "Pledges on Parade," which was our version of a step show. We were also the first African-American group to build a float for the homecoming parade. We rendered service projects in the community and on campus. The members of the sorority were a guiding force in my success at WKU. Most of the sorority members were education majors, and we were able to share books, notes, experiences, the expectations of a professor, and professors we should avoid if possible. I am presently active in the graduate chapter of my sorority.

While at Western, I was instructed by all-white teachers as I prepared for elementary certification. As an elementary education major we were required to observe at the University's Observatory School on campus. That school was composed of the children of the staff and professors. It was an ideal teaching situation but very unlike the schools and students that I would eventually encounter. I felt well-prepared and met the high expectations that the instructional team presented. However, I did not have any close relationships with any of the professors on campus.

My dad died the day after Thanksgiving my senior year while I was preparing to student teach the next semester. My parents did not share how ill my father was; in fact, I did not know he was fighting cancer. They referred to his illness as "a spot on his lungs"! I remember when he was in the hospital, the nurse asked, "Didn't you know he had cancer and was going to expire?" My dad's passing was devastating; he was the first person in my immediate family to die. Going back to school was difficult. I took a few weeks off from school but somehow managed to make up all the work with the help of sorority members and professors. I was able to start student teaching the next semester at the local neighborhood school with Black and white children. The socio-economic difference between these children and those at the campus school were magnified. It was a new experience for me, but I enjoyed working with students who did not have very much but were quite eager to learn. My student teaching experience was quite different and not nearly as demanding as today's requirements for aspiring teachers.

Graduating in 1972 after four years at WKU, I was hired as a teacher at Dolfinger Elementary School in the Portland area of Louisville, the oldest elementary school in the Old Louisville School System. I remember wearing a white dress for the interview and the principal, Mr. Hydes, saying, "Oh, you won't dress like that coming here." I didn't wear that dress, but I did my best to emulate Mrs. Parks and Mrs. Trowell, looking professional with a bit of glamour and the no-nonsense attitude of "All of you are going to learn something this year and love it"! My first class was a fourth-grade group of Black and white students, and the teacher across the hall, Jaye Sparber, was my guiding star. She helped me with those little details that were not taught in education classes or learned during the student teaching experience.

My teaching career began at a time when hippies were taking over under the guise of the Focus/Impact Program. The teachers wore ragged jeans and sandals every day, and the students could call you by your first name. My students addressed me as Miss Butler and they were called "Ms. Butler's kids." I enjoyed teaching "my kids," who became my family. I talked to their parents who relied on me to help their children. That is what a teacher did. It was hard to believe that I was paid for something I enjoyed doing. Dolfinger had a higher percentage of low-income white students than Black, but it did not qualify for student loan forgiveness under the federal government's guidelines; therefore, at the end of my second year, I asked for a transfer to a school where my student loan would be repaid while I taught there.

I was assigned to Benjamin Franklin Elementary on Frankfort Avenue, a Title I school, with students from the neighborhood as well as students from the housing projects that were located about ten miles from the school. To my delight, Mrs. Parks, my former "glamourous" teacher from Virginia Avenue, was principal of Franklin. I taught fifth grade and was well-prepared to teach the intermediate grade students. The school was small with a nice community of students and teachers. I worked in the after-school programs for students, and if Mrs. Parks had to attend a meeting, she left me in charge. I married my husband, Mario, during my four years at Franklin and we bought our first home in the southeast area of Louisville on Michael Edward Drive. Imagine my shock in 1978, when school had been in session for about three months and I had already "fallen in love" with my class, I was transferred to another school, Watterson Elementary School. I cried, and the students cried! I did not want to leave, and my students did not want me to go.

At Watterson, it was a struggle to adjust to the administration of the school. The principal of Watterson was disturbed that she lost the teacher whose place I was taking. At our first meeting she informed me that I would not stay long at "her" school. I thought, "What a welcome"! It took a while for the students and me to make the adjustment to our new situation, but we did, and completed the year on a high note. Before the school year ended I was pregnant with the first of our three children, and my students were very excited with the thought of their teacher having a baby! I was on maternity leave when the next school year began, and some of my former students from Watterson came to visit me and my first-born son, Drae! When my maternity leave was almost over, I met with the principal to discuss my return to Watterson. At that meeting the principal informed me that I would have a second-and third-grade split and would be responsible for the safety patrol. Great teachers worked at the school, people with whom I am still in contact, but I was not a good fit for that environment.

Positive Motivator Coordinator was the title for my next position with JCPS. My task was to work with students who exhibited social, academic, or behavior concerns. Carrithers and Newburg Middle were the two schools assigned to me. The atmosphere at Newburg Middle reminded me of DuValle Junior High School, very soulful. The students who attended Newburg were mostly from the Newburg community and surrounding areas. Carrithers' students were from the Jeffersontown area and students that were bused in from the West End of Louisville. One of my students in this program went on to play for the NFL and another one became a social worker. Overall, students at both schools needed someone to help guide and motivate them. I participated in this program for only one year.

After working at Carrithers and Newburg I fell in love with middle school. I started at Barret Middle School in 1980 as a math teacher. I had great relationships with the administrators, Mr. Butler and Mr. Walker, and they had high expectations for the staff. They encouraged me to be "that" outstanding teacher. While a teacher at Barret, I gave birth to our two daughters, Brandy and Brittany. When Barret became a Traditional School and Mr. Matlock became the principal, he interviewed all teachers to make sure that he had the right mix. The Exceptional Childhood Education Program was removed from the school. He wanted the school to be the No.1 middle school and he instilled that in the faculty and students. Students who attended Barret were pushed to be tops academically and athletically. I was very fortunate to have our three children to become students at this school. Barret students had the opportunity to have Reneice Reese, Kate McGruder, Brenda Russell, Billie Shulhafer, James Thompson, George Karem, Vanessa Moss, Patty Hart, and many other excellent teachers. With good teachers and top administrators, we did our best to prepare our students for the next level, high school.

Barret was a fun place for both the students and the teachers. If I go down memory lane, I remember the spirit rallies that initially were to motivate the students to participate in the school's fund-raiser. Eventually, the spirit rallies were used to hype students to do their best on the state tests. The lock-ins, where we spent the entire night at school entertaining the students with a variety of activities until eight o'clock the next morning, were a great incentive for students to support the fund-raiser of the school. The class trips to Chicago, New York, St. Louis, Indianapolis, and Toronto offered the students and staff opportunities to experience a variety of cultural institutions. Barret students had the opportunity to participate in a variety of social, athletic, and cultural activities that served as an enhancement to brighten their social, academic, and athletic awareness. I see some of my former Barret students on Facebook, often reminiscing about their good times at Barret. Recently, I came across a letter from a student expressing his appreciation for what I did for him as his teacher. This is how teachers are rewarded!

In 1988 I became a counselor at Barret. Being the counselor at Barret was "My Dream Job!" It almost felt like my first year of teaching, when my thoughts were, "I'm getting paid to do something I love doing!" With all three of our children attending Barret, I had the opportunity to experience Barret as a parent, teacher, and administrator. It was not always fun and games; I did have a few teachers who expressed a concern about my helping African-American students more than white students. Those few teachers who voiced this concern were the very ones who referred the African-American students for counseling. On the other hand, there were also a few parents who expected Barret to work magic with students who were deficient in behavior and academics. We didn't work magic, but we did put time and effort into helping each child meet some type of success. Sometimes we were successful and sometimes we were not. I enjoyed working with all students. My desire was to help any student who needed nurturing, counseling, and guidance. After 34 years of full-time employment, twenty-six of those years at Barret, I retired. My own children would tell me I smelled like Barret. It was a perfect time for me to leave because our daughter, Brandy, was getting married.

Over the last few years, I have substituted as a counselor at schools all over the District. When I compare today's schools to schools of my generation, I think about the role that testing plays in today's schools. If our teachers, when I was a student, were trying to prepare us for any test, we did not know it. We were just there listening and learning. Our classroom atmosphere was not that you had to outdo someone else or another class. Teachers automatically did what they needed to do because they wanted their students to learn. Today our schools, administrators, teachers, and students are under a tremendous amount of pressure to produce scores not productive individuals. Along with the pressure, they are publicly shamed once the scores are published for all to see. There must be a better way! Children today want to learn and enjoy school. Those students who may not have had parents skilled in parenting could provide challenges for educators. Some of these children may have lived lives that make them a bit fearless. If in their short lives they have not been taught to be respectful to adults, once they enter school, it may be hard for them to make that adjustment. I am sure that some students are as respectful and look up to teachers just as we did. They would not dare say anything out of order to an adult or teacher. Some of our students are living in situations that may promote bad behavior where respect is not taught or recognized.

A big difference exists between adult/parents and children/parents. Adult/Parents of my day kept children centered and disciplined. The adult made decisions, set the rules, established expectations, and told the children what was acceptable and not acceptable. Children/Parents allow children to be in charge. Children today have choices of what they are going to eat, what they are going to wear, and when they will go to sleep. Most parents are mimicking their parents. In many cases that's great! In some situations, help is needed!

When you look at the overall picture of education in America today, children have many more concerns than we did growing up. They should not have to bear the burden of wondering if some lunatic is coming into the school building and shooting for absolutely no apparent reason. They should not be burdened with the inequities in the quality of schools and education that exist across the country. Good teachers are in all schools, but location, neighborhood, the number of experienced teachers, the level of expectations for all students, parental involvement, and the available resources, monetary and human resources, impact equity. When a child walks into a classroom, there should not be any doubt that the teacher is caring, energized, knowledgeable, fearless, determined, and focused on the ultimate goal of every student succeeding in that class!

I take pride in being an educator and have had students tell me, "I want to be like you, Ms. Johnson." I tell them how fulfilling this profession is, the challenges that they will face, the knowledge that they will need to acquire, and the love that they will need to maintain. Joy for me is when I see "a light" come on the faces of children when they understand why learning vowels and consonant sounds will help them learn to read or that learning to count lends itself to adding, subtracting, multiplying, and dividing. Finally, joy for me is when children don't want to miss a day of school because they know the teacher and the other students will miss them. When that former student utters the words," Thank you, Ms. Johnson," then I know that the "light" came on!

Beverly Johnson spent 34 years as an educator, 26 of those years at Barret Traditional Middle School. She has been quoted saying, "When you say the school you attend, you say it with pride! I attend Barret Traditional Middle School!" Her own children told her she "smelled like Barret." She has received several awards and recognitions, including Project 1 Woman of the Year; Black Achiever Adult Achiever; Service Award for Alpha Kappa Alpha Sorority, Inc.; Educator of the Year at Brown Memorial CME Church; and Brotherhood and Sisterhood Educators' Award for JCPS. In addition, she has been a member of AKA Sorority for over 49 years. She currently attends Brown Memorial CME Church where she is a steward, member of the usher board, and chairperson for many church activities. She enjoys spending time with her three adult children and her six grandchildren. She has been married to Mario Johnson for more than 40 years and they enjoy travelling and vacationing with the entire family.

Dr. Eugene Kelly

Teacher, Principal, School Psychologist
and Adjunct Professor

Dissertation Title: *A Temperament X Treatment
Interaction Study of Affective Interventions: A Match of
Behavioral Styles between At-Risk Students and Their
Instructors*

I WAS RAISED SURROUNDED BY A litany of strong women in Asheville, North Carolina, the oldest male among five brothers and sisters. My grandmother and great-grandmother were the primary influencers for my older sister and me. They made the rules, set the examples, and provided the care, direction, and support. I had one uncle who was my only male family role model. He worked and respected the females in our family.

Clinton Bennett Photographer

Although I didn't live with my mother, we all lived in the same neighborhood within walking distance of one another.

In Grades K-5, I attended Lucy S. Herring Elementary School with all-Black students and all-Black teachers. Joe Roach was my elementary school principal. I had a great time in elementary school because I followed my sister, and everyone knew my grandparents and because I was a "Mama's Boy," following the rules, making good grades, and staying out of trouble. Besides, the neighborhood was full of teachers. I learned to read because Granny read the Bible every night and I wanted to read with her. Ms. White, one of my favorite teachers, took me under her wing and gave me jobs to do to make a little extra money, and Ms. Bowman was always kind to me, knowing my family situation, an absentee father and Grands working for minimum wages as housekeepers.

Herring was a large elementary school that sat at the bottom of Mountain Street where students walked daily to school. We were slated to attend French Broad Jr. High, a Black school in Grades 6 through 8. However, in 1961, due to desegregation, we were given the option of attending David Miller Jr. High, the white middle school, which was an entirely new environment for me. There was a gym, a swimming pool, P.E. classes, showers in the school, and no Black teachers. While I cannot recall any major problems, I do not remember any favorite teachers. We changed classes and were protective of one another; and in many classes, I was the only Black student.

There was a Black high school and a white high school that everyone from all over the city could opt to attend. Some of my friends chose to attend the Black high school while I chose the formerly white school, Lee H. Edwards High which was now integrated, both teachers and students. One of my high school teachers, Ms. Burton, lived down the street in our still segregated community and knew my family. I took a heavy academic load and was made fun of by other Black students because I was considered "high-falutin." I was in the Spanish Club and my high school counselor actually worked with me, helping me to select medical technology as a career and looking at trade school options. Out of the blue one day, a woman working in the counselor's area, maybe a social worker, said to me, "I got this school and I think you need to apply." I applied, got accepted and was also given a scholarship. Now, I was bound for college, the first in my family to attend.

The first time I saw Berea College in Berea, Kentucky, was when I arrived on the bus. It was much smaller than my high school that enrolled 2500 students, including 400 seniors of which 44 were African Americans. There were only fifty African Americans in my freshman class at Berea and one white girl from my high school that I initially met at Berea. I stayed on campus and worked like everyone else at Berea since the Day Law had been rescinded and the campus was fully integrated. I didn't take remedial classes because, to my surprise, I passed all of the placement tests. My first job was in food service and I later became a teacher assistant. I had so many majors that I can't remember them all, but I finally became a psychology major. I went home during the summers and worked with my uncle at the VA Hospital for incidentals and travel money. Berea took care of tuition and room and board for all of its students as long as the student got there. I graduated in 1972 with a Bachelor of Arts Degree in Psychology and later applied to the Teacher Corps to be trained as an elementary teacher.

I truly did not believe that I was smart enough to be a teacher or that I would be accepted into the Corps, but after a month at home, I headed for Louisville, enrolled in University of Louisville's two-year Master's program and began preparation to teach elementary grades at Wheatley Elementary School as a primary teacher in the Teacher Corps under Principal Wiley Daniels. In this program, participants were students and teachers who attended classes and were placed with veteran teachers who critiqued, mentored, and evaluated their progress. U of L College of Education faculty also observed and evaluated participants.

Wheatley Elementary had outstanding teachers, including several males on staff. This was unusual because males at the elementary level were generally scarce. My first assignment was K-1 with all-Black students and an all-Black faculty who scrutinized my every move because they wanted their students to have the highest quality of education, even though this was a training site. This placement was enriching since I was able to apply some of that developmental psychology with those 5- and 6-year-old students. Myrtle Forbes was my mentor and teacher supervisor. In reflection, I remembered how nurturing and supportive she was in making my year and our students' year enjoyable but productive. They had to learn how to read and I had to teach them how to read well. During my second year, I taught fourth grade, and was more comfortable with that age group. I continued at Wheatley teaching fourth grade an additional year after earning my master's degree before being transferred to Cochrane (Jeffersontown) Elementary during the 1975-76 school year of merger, where I taught language arts to fifth and sixth graders under the Stoddard Program.

I was a non-traditional teacher who worked hard at developing my skills and knowledge. (This proved to be a valuable lesson when I later became a teacher of teachers in a non-traditional program at Spalding University.) I knew that I did not have the traditional training and experiences of most teachers. On the other hand, I had John Miles and Rothel Farris, seasoned male teachers, as role models whom I could emulate. I often wonder if I would have been successful and effective as a teacher without the level of support that Teacher Corps at Wheatley Elementary provided.

I continued taking classes, earning a certification in Counseling and a Specialist Degree in Counseling Psychology. I left Cochrane in 1979 to accept an assignment in Jefferson County Public Schools as a School Psychometrist. The Exceptional Childhood Education (ECE) Department of JCPS was under corrective action for not giving IQ tests to students provided ECE services. Stationed at Hikes Annex, I was one of two African Americans involved with testing. Since our jobs were mandated by legislation, our primary duties revolved around intellectual assessment. At times it seemed as if we were working in a factory since we had time clocks and cards that had to be punched for monitoring our arrival, lunch break, and departure, in spite of the fact that we were certified professionals. I liked testing and the counseling psychology area and became certified as a school psychologist in 1981, the only African-American male holding this position in JCPS at that time.

In 1991, after acquiring certification as principal and Director of Pupil Personnel, I received a Doctorate in Educational Psychology from the University of Kentucky. My education attainment and my unusual field of study (school psychology) were door openers for me and allowed me to support teachers and help children in a different way. As a result, I became principal of Slaughter Elementary School after serving as interim principal for approximately one year.

When I began considering becoming a principal in earnest, I was a little apprehensive, somewhat indecisive and uncomfortable with the interview process. Dr. Dick Kirkpatrick in the Human Resources Department spent extra time actually working with me on interviewing skills. I still give myself a "C" although I am an "A" student in most areas. The Kentucky Education Reform Act (KERA), passed in 1990 and brought crazy times and changes to the principal-selection process. Dr. Kirkpatrick sent me to schools on principal interviews. I was selected as the permanent principal at Slaughter Elementary at the beginning of the 1991-92 school year.

My tenure at Slaughter began on good footing. The majority of the students were white and the white parents were ready for change. Slaughter had not had a male principal and was one of only a few elementary schools in the District with a Black principal and Black counselor. ECE students at Slaughter were needy. We had student-assignment issues because teachers were so resistant to change. Twenty years after busing and desegregation, issues of "those students in my school" still existed among the staff who resisted opening the school to ESL students, "another minority." Site-Based Decision Making (SBDM) Councils gave teachers power that they were unaccustomed to holding and created situations and solutions that were not always in the best interest of the school or its students.

Slaughter had the normal problems of elementary schools with a diverse student body. We addressed issues of reading and math disparities, and teachers worked to improve student achievement overall. Some years our test scores were up and other years they were down. Part of the challenge was that the District started us on one program for improvement, but rather than seeing it through, the program was dropped and we went to the next best thing. Slaughter had kids with reading problems back then as they do now. I am a believer that all kids do not learn the same way and cannot show what they learn in the same way, so standardized testing may not be the best measure of what was learned and retained. Slaughter teachers tried to work with students in different ways to get them to show what they learned or understood aside from the standard test.

During my tenth year as principal, I developed a medical condition that left me without a speaking voice. After surgery at Vanderbilt and recovery, I resigned my position as principal at Slaughter, choosing to return from medical leave as a school psychologist.

As I think about teachers and teaching, one teacher comes to mind as mesmerizing—Irma Ash, an ECE teacher whose presence and stature were magnetic with kids. How she interacted, molded, and got students to cooperate by her presence alone was so unusual. I also think about the other great teachers that I have encountered. They were introspective, open to new and different ways of doing things, flexible; they saw people as people and did not take themselves too seriously.

As a school psychologist, I have dealt with student-related issues that were uncomfortable and sometimes discriminatory. For example, I have had instances where the data indicated that we were not meeting the needs of all EBD students even though we were under a mandate to do so. I have seen instances where minorities and non-minorities had the same characteristics but were provided different placements and different services; non-minorities were placed in Learning Disabled or Other Health Impaired programs while minority students were placed in ED, Emotionally Disturbed programs. I have had to speak up and speak out, sometimes demanding that we rethink placement. When looking at the data today, the numbers tell the story. Today, there is a continuation of practices of the old status quo. Why?

Today's teachers are faced with issues, challenges, insecurities, and uncertainties that they were not trained to handle. There is an opioid problem with parents that is reflected in the behaviors of their children who do not sit and cannot pay attention; therefore, retention is an issue. Yet classrooms have the same seats in rows with the teacher's desk up front for the teacher to use the same old lecture. *"If you cannot get info in, they cannot give it back to you." "If kids didn't learn it, you didn't teach it!"* Yet, teachers still use the same old paper-and-pencil test with the same cut- off scores, and kids still fill in the bubbles rather than showing or telling what they know. Students can tell in their own words what they have been taught; teachers will know they have gotten it and can even teach it to someone else.

When I think of teacher stories, I think about Cochrane Elementary where we had inclusionary ECE classes. I had a student that I would consider educable. During handwriting class, she copied so well, so precise, but she could not read anything that she copied. Also, it was encouraging to see students out in the street who remembered. They say, I remember when. . . " They tell you a story but you do not remember them; or kids waving at you—they know you, but you have no idea who they are. And educators don't forget the students who are telling their children, "That was my principal," or "That was my teacher."

When I think about the education of poor and or Black children, I revert to the purpose of education that I think is off-track. The purpose of education goes beyond helping people get good jobs. The purpose is to aid in developing good citizens and good people with purpose and function who can navigate democracy and understand what a free democratic society is about. We have moved from a democracy for white males to rights for all. Politics of the day make you wonder, but the problems of our democracy are people-driven and the solutions must be people-driven not political. Poor and Black children become adults and must be educated to have voices that can be heard as they evaluate truth from fiction. Today's teachers play a key role. The grandiose statement that "everyone can learn" must be put into practice with teachers committed to having high expectations and being willing to nurture and care for all children, passing knowledge and skills, inspiring hope and teaching students, regardless of color or socioeconomic status, to read, analyze, and evaluate information, to ask questions and seek "truth." Our democracy depends on an educated populous that depends on dedicated teachers willing to stay the course.

Eugene Kelly retired in 2005. He has been an adjunct professor at Jefferson Community and Technical College (JCTC) where he taught History of Education and Introduction to Psychology. He also taught at Spalding University in the Psychology and Education Departments for seventeen years. Dr. Kelly also assisted with the Alternative

Certification programs at University of Louisville and Spalding for several years, mentoring and supporting future teachers. Throughout his career he has been an advocate for public education and has worked diligently to support that mission through volunteerism and service in the following organizations: Kentucky Association of Black School Educators (KABSE), National Alliance of Black School Educators (NABSE), Kentucky Association of Elementary School Principals (KAESP), Association of Black Psychologists (ABPsi), Kentucky Association of School Psychologists (KAPS), Kentucky Association of School Administrators (KASA), National Association of School Psychologist (NASP), and Phi Delta Kappa (PDK).

Theodore "Boone" Martin

High School Physics and Math Teacher, Department Chair, and Track Coach

I LOST MY DAD DURING WORLD WAR II and my mom worked three jobs at one time to keep our family going. I was the oldest of the three children, with two younger sisters. Mom graduated from Louisville Central High School and worked for a company downtown. My sister, Orwille, who later became a teacher and school counselor, often told the story of going downtown and asking to speak with her mom, only to be told that "no colored people work here."

Martin Family Photo Collection

I attended Frederick Douglass Elementary School, named Pearl Street Elementary before I attended, and Omer Carmichael after I attended. When I walked through the neighborhood, I could watch people shoeing horses, see clothes waving in the wind on clotheslines, and watch gardens growing in backyards. My principal was Mr. Brown who always knew what he saw and would tell students, "Don't tell me anything. I saw you," before he used his strap on your butt while he held your hand and you danced around the floor. On one of his hand-holding sessions with me, I remember thinking that this old man was in shape because he would not let go regardless of how I hopped and skipped around as a third grader. When he finished, I went to the closet and washed my face before going to class. When I opened the door to the classroom and walked in, ready to give the teacher an explanation, she said, "We already know." The class had heard the whole thing since it was next door to the office.

My mother was instrumental in giving us a head start before we went to school. She taught us our ABC's and my sisters and I learned to read early. Mom used a reading series for teaching us and we learned to enjoy reading. My third-grade teacher, Ms. Jones, would give treats for whoever read the most. She would take us downtown, walking down Walnut Street to find different leaves to take back to school. We would sprinkle water on our leaves, place them on a sheet of paper, set something heavy on them and let the leaves dry against the paper, forming a silhouette. We would name the parts of the leaf from the silhouette. Students loved doing the different things that were outside of the book, but we knew that we had to learn what was in the book to get to do the other activities.

I remember every teacher that I had in elementary school and can honestly say that all were my favorites. There was something unique about each of them. They were all different with different personalities, and they each helped me in their own way to mature as a child. They also used different teaching methods. In sixth grade, there was a war between Ms. Tucker and an older student who acted as if he did not want to pay attention and learn. I watched that interaction and decided to change my seat and move up front so I would not miss anything. I was an "A" student and wanted to remain an "A" student. I loved math and always completed my homework. I could solve problems with fractions, whole numbers, exponents, negative numbers, base numbers, and multipliers—it did not matter. I would roll up my sleeves and get busy solving the problem.

Jackson Junior High School was my home for Grades 7, 8, and 9. Again, I cannot name a favorite teacher because they, too, were all different. Ms. Stringer, who was my cousin and taught English, had me step outside her classroom before the first day started. Her message was, "Because we are related, don't let that go to your head. I am expecting more—better behavior, best homework, and top presentations from you." Mr. Clark taught science and was a funeral director. He set the bar on Day One. On one occasion, a student behind me kept jabbing me in the rear with his pencil. I told him to stop. He did it again. I told him to stop. On the third jab, when the teacher's back was to the class, I picked him up by the collar just as Mr. Clark turned around. He did not ask for an explanation, but invited us both to the front of the room, stating, "You performed at my desk, now it's my time to perform." He used a wooden paddle drilled with holes. He told us that, "Now that I am warmed up, we are going another round," which meant another lick. He also told us that if we found our way into this situation again, our punishment would double at each round. I asked if I could move my seat to the back of the room to make sure that no one was sitting behind me.

Our teachers were personal. We were their daughters, their sons, even though they disciplined us. We learned early on to respect them. We got the message that we were expected to act as if we had some sense in school and that there were consequences if we didn't, because the teacher "would have to go to work again," and leave a message on your behind. Sometimes they would use a different strategy if the boys were going after each other. Mr. Price, our gym teacher and coach, made me and another student put on these heavy boxing gloves and slug it out until we couldn't lift our arms to throw a punch. He did not have to call our parents, and we never fought again.

I loved sports and played football, basketball, and baseball in junior high school. Boys didn't have real uniforms and girls wore bloomers. However, both boys and girls were competitive. Our teachers were muscular and fit. Everybody, teachers and students, walked in those days. Students walked quickly and softly down the halls, getting to their classes on time. Ms. Madry, Ms. Bullock, and Ms. Metcalf taught me math which remained among my favorite subjects. Also, we did more than pencil and paper drawings for art; we made mannequins for putting on an art show. Bob Douglas, the University of Louisville artist, and I also made puppets for our puppet show. There were always things to do at school to keep us busy and engaged, and our teachers were there to help, direct, and support.

I graduated from Central High School June 4, 1953, a member of the first class graduating from the newly built school building at Twelfth and Chestnut streets. In Grades 10 and 11, I had attended the old school at Eighth and Chestnut streets. My first day as a twelfth grader at Central High School is one I will never forget. I went across the street to "Pages" to buy a tall milkshake and a chili dog with my friends. Then somebody hollered, "Here she comes!" I just sat there because I didn't know what they were talking about. Suddenly, my friends started running back to school. When I finally got up to leave, Maude Brown Porter, the assistant principal at Central High School, had me follow her to the office, where my friends were waiting. She called us in one-by-one. When she called my name, I entered her office. As I entered, I noticed one wall contained a one-way window that was located perpendicular and adjacent to the entrance and exit doors. All the doors were electrically operated by her. It helped her to control and patrol the hallways, like today's security guards. She explained to me what I did wrong and the consequence that was to follow. When she "hit" me with her wooden paddle, I knew I wouldn't be back again. It is amazing how fast one learns.

I loved art, science, and math, which included plain and solid geometry taught by Mr. Addison Ramsey. I made "As" in every class except Advanced English Literature taught by Robert Stanley Lawery. High school sports were a natural for me because I always stayed fit. Football was the sport that I settled upon and I made the team as a sophomore. My team members sometimes struggled with math, and we had to pass all classes in order to play. One thing that I did as a team member was to go around and help the football players with math. I was their unofficial tutor. We would kill each other on the field in the summer during practice, but work like dogs to help each other stay on the team.

Although teams from other Black schools came to Louisville to play Central, many of our games were away, because we were not allowed to play the white schools in Louisville, and we were the only Black school. We played teams in Ohio, Mississippi, Georgia,

Tennessee, Florida, and Missouri, riding the yellow school bus across the back roads because there were no expressways. The rides were long, with 33 football players crammed on a bus with Coach Kean, Mr. Perry, Mr. White, Mr. Adams, and "Dribble Dry" Johnson. The only other Kentucky team that we played was Lexington Dunbar. I always went to the back of the bus so that I could go to sleep and be fresh for the game. Another twist in those days was if you were an "End" in football, you played basketball too. If you were a running back, you automatically ran track. In the summer, everybody played baseball.

Central High School was an important part of Louisville's Black community. The school and the teachers were well-respected. The Thanksgiving Day Football games were always packed at Male High School's field. Although two Black teams were playing, officials for the games were always white. The football teams were always happy to leave the "Rock Crib", which was our practice field at the Old Central, to play elsewhere in real grass and mud.

I am a member of Central's Football Hall of Fame; however, how I got there is unusual. I learned to play football by sitting at Chickasaw Park and watching the players who all came to the park to help each other. All of the guys knew each other, including their talents and their weaknesses. When it was time to try out for Central's football team, an announcement was placed in the *Louisville Defender*. I wanted to be a first-string Quarterback, but I was never selected. Assistant football coach Dan White went to Coach Kean and vouched for me. I was the seventh-string quarterback when the season began. We played a team in Ohio and Quarterbacks 1 and 2 were injured. Our gear was not regulated. We had cardboard pads and no face masks. It was not unusual for players to have broken noses, missing teeth, and black eyes. We played Tennessee and Q3, Q4, and Q5 were injured. Tennessee's players looked like professionals. Our next game began with Q6 who had a problem handling the ball and whispered the plays to the team. They could not hear him. When they asked Coach White who else they could put in, I, Q7, volunteered and finished the season. I received three awards for football and Central was State Football Champion along with Male High School—two Louisville schools, two state champions.

Black schools did not play white schools in 1953 although we may have used the same track or field to play our games or run our track meets. Male and Central football teams wanted to play each other to settle the score, but school officials said no. The teams back-doored an arrangement where they would play a deciding game. Central players would walk to Male for the event. When Central's players neared Male's track, they were met with squad cars, flashing lights, coaches, and city officials who refused to allow them to play. So, 1953 yearbooks and records show Male High School and Central High School as State Football Champions.

With my senior year ending, I had choices to make. My grades were fine, but money was an issue for me to continue to college. Also, my sister, whom I sometimes had to throw over my shoulder to take to school, announced that she wanted to go to college. That left only one avenue for me—the military. When my class decorated Central's gym in its new building, bought material, made canopies to drape across the ceiling, built a wishing well, and used our class dues to host a picnic, I knew that I was headed for the Marines. I cannot reveal much about that experience, except that when I was tested, the administrators did not believe my scores. I had three MOS's and I was blindfolded when I was moved from base to base. I stayed four years, was honorably discharged, and used the GI Bill to go to college at Central State College in Wilberforce, Ohio, the same college that my sister attended.

I taught five years in Gary, Indiana, before coming to Louisville. At Central State, I majored in physics, chemistry, and mathematics because I did not want to be pigeonholed. I was told that those three majors would be extremely difficult. School officials really did not understand "difficult" nor were they aware of the amount of preparation that I had from Central and during active duty military. I also took a class in Russian because it was something different. I did not know how different until a man on the street called me by name and asked me about the class.

My student teaching was at an integrated school in Xenia, Ohio. While I was waiting for my Cooperating Teacher, I saw kids on the track, practicing the wrong way, pitching the baton. When I questioned them, they did not know who their "leg man" was or how to come out of the blocks. I watched them run and taught them how to "explode out of the blocks." Their coach called me because the students told him about how I helped. I was offered a job teaching and coaching and quoted a salary. However, Gary, Indiana's recruiter gave me a better deal—money because I was a Veteran; money for the subjects that I would teach; and additional money for coaching. I began teaching in Gary, Indiana, in 1962.

My first day to report to segregated Pulaski Junior High in Gary, I crawled out of the window because the snow was so packed that I could not get out of the door and I did not have a radio to learn if schools were opened or closed. Schools were closed that day. I was assigned to teach chemistry, physics, and math, matching my college majors. On the first day with students, I had an encounter with a student who threw chairs across the floor, dropped his books, and got in my face. I hit him so quickly that I didn't realize it until I saw his nose bleeding and heard girls running and screaming. I was saved because the student had a history. He had hit a teacher with a pop bottle and had run his car through a crowd of students and was back in school after three days because his mom worked for an important government official. My principal said, "Next time, please use the telephone."

Student discipline, an issue continuously on the minds of today's teachers, was commonplace at my school. Bad behavior was handled through a Discipline Team that I chaired for several years. If a student acted out in class, the teacher called a specific telephone number for someone on the discipline team and also called the principal. Students were usually not sent home, expelled, or suspended for ordinary discipline issues. As chair of the Discipline Team, I talked to the parents and told them the issue to get their permission to paddle. Every team member had to hit the kid on the butt with a paddle. It was not uncommon for parents to ask, "Can you give some for me?" Three was the common number that parents wanted on their behalf. The kid had to hold onto the table with both hands. The coaches and I administered the discipline. The principal was the overseer, assuring that the process was done correctly. The principal signed and dated the Discipline Sheet, verifying that correct procedures had been followed.

The Discipline Team was a deterrent, but it did not solve all of the discipline issues in the school, especially since schools were heavily laden with gangs who wanted to be in control and who challenged new teachers. There were five gangs who played sports in their respective high schools. I cannot remember all that happened, but I gave a kid, a gang member, a lick for some reason and the kid cried. He said I was the hardest hitter in the school. After that, I had no problems with discipline in my classes. That student took charge of discipline. He saw to it that the class was quiet and students were on task. I gave the student a Thank-You card with a $10 bill.

I taught Trig, Advanced Math, and Pre-Calculus classes in junior high school. I always asked my students if they had any difficulty or if they needed help. I learned from being an inquisitive student that students like to learn things that they do not know. When the teacher has the right attitude, students have the right attitude and like to be pushed. Children turned in homework, completed assignments, and were hard workers, helping each other as I helped them.

My interview for a teaching position in Louisville, Kentucky, began (to the best of my recollection) sometimes in July, 1967. The school principal, Dr. James Coleman, called me after learning from my brother-in-law that I was interested in returning to Louisville because my mother and mother-in-law were extremely ill. He asked if I would be interested in teaching math at Russell Junior High School. My answer was . . . YES! This would allow me to stay on course, teach mathematics, and reset my priorities, in addition to staying off the road driving back and forth from Gary to Louisville. I was happy to accept a position.

I received a letter from the Louisville Public Schools acknowledging my assignment to Russell Junior High School at Eighteenth and Madison streets as a mathematics teacher and I was to report immediately. However, three weeks later, I received another letter that stated a change in assignment. Instead of Russell, I was assigned to DuPont Manual High School as a mathematics teacher. It took a little time for me and Russell's principal, Dr. James Coleman, to regroup, but we did and I went to the new assignment at Manual. I am not sure to this day why I was assigned to the new school. There was only one other Black teacher on faculty, Mr. Rowan, and he had formerly taught at Central.

What a shock! I was assigned by Principal Ries to an old, standing portable that stood next to a parking lot behind the school. When I opened the door, my eyes blurred and watered from the dust and dirt within the room. It was a disturbing sight, a classroom not fit to house students that anyone cared about, and I cared about my students. I was assigned to teach a new program called a "Class of Twenty," and my 20 were going to be in a decent environment. I went to work cleaning and was joined by several of my students and their parents who volunteered to dust, sweep, mop, and paint the metal parts of rusted chair and table legs. The students had a steady hand and painted evenly. The room was a 100% transformation and we were tired and sweaty. However, that task brought us together as a team and the team felt proud of its accomplishment. My task was not over. When I entered the school office, Principal Ries gave me Holy H___. I listened, knowing that I had another list of things that we needed from him. My list included white paint for the outside walls and two entrance ramps. He hollered, "WHAT!!!!" Nevertheless, over the weekend the outside portable walls were spray-painted white. The ramps were painted black.

Working at Manual was not easy. I felt unwanted and definitely undervalued because of the racist nature of the school faculty. White teachers asked my white distance runners, "Why are you running for that N_____?" However, team members refused to quit or be divided. They challenged their white teachers about racism and hate. Racist attitudes and discrimination were not unique to Manual. Other African-American teachers throughout the Louisville district were faced with everyday occurrences prompted by school administrators, other teachers and parents as well as some students. Although the Louisville City Schools were hiring more African-American teachers, discriminatory practices were still in place. This was evident in our school assignments, the rooms we were assigned to, the students we were assigned to teach, the subjects that we were allowed to teach, and the support that we received from our colleagues and school administration. I often wonder what would have happened if teachers had come together to address these issues and attack the establishment whose practices and policies were impacting our youngsters, both African-American and white, and preventing them from experiencing maximized learning opportunities.

I was at DuPont Manual for two years. I had seniors in high school who did not know their "Times Tables," multiplication facts; students who could not do any algebraic functions; students who never heard of trigonometry; and high school students whose basic math skills did not come close to the skill level of the students that I taught in Gary at the junior high level. Our work was cut out for us. I say, "us" because again, my classes functioned as teams. We worked in small groups. I used flash cards daily. I rewarded students who pushed themselves, for example, the person who took less time to finish the task correctly. I helped my students to become competitive, and I incorporated simple step-by-step activities to individualize math learning with models where each student had to find the answers for given word problems.

The learning environment that I created made students love learning and eager to try new approaches. I also kept a large sign in my room, black letters on a white background that said, "MATH POWER," a spin-off from the Black Power movement around the country. My principal was not happy with my sign. Also, during that time the Class of Twenty wrote a chapter for a book to be published by the Kentucky Department of Education. The chapter was about making polyhedrons. A polyhedron is a geometric figure that is solid in three dimensions with flat polygonal faces, straight edges, and sharp corners or vertices. The information that the chapter contained was acceptable, but the pictures with Black and white children working together would not be included. I protested, but nothing changed.

In 1969, I began teaching in a new program, Focus/Impact, developed by Superintendent Newman Walker and coordinated by John Whiting, and I transferred to DuValle Junior High School. All kinds of stories have been written about how students could call teachers by their first names, the relaxed atmosphere in schools, and the free choice that students had over their learning. I do not remember if my mind was always there, but I do remember being designated to develop a summer program with a small team of teachers. We developed our own curriculum, designed our textbook, looked for materials to include, reviewed other textbooks, and voted to determine the publishing company to use.

We worked relentlessly in Nancy Price's basement to develop our manuscript, each person taking a section and presenting to the faculty.

Nearing the end, we needed money to pay for supplies and were under the impression that the Board was supporting our efforts. The Board would not give us money to pay for the materials we needed, did not compensate us for our time, and took our product, claiming it as their production, never giving recognition to the team that actually developed the curriculum. Again, I protested and resigned from the project. I was reassigned to Shawnee High School with 87 Black teachers and remained there until I was assigned to Durrett in 1975, because of Merger and Desegregation.

Durrett, along with Thomas Jefferson High School, closed at the end of the 1975-76 school year and I was transferred back to DuPont Manual. The new principal, Joe Liedtke, was familiar with me and my work and I returned to somewhat of a different environment at Manual. There were still portable classrooms, but I was in the building. I served as math teacher and track coach again. I did not have the smartest children, the No. 5's, but I had the No. 4's. I always smile when I remember how the teacher who taught the No. 5's would show up at my door during lunch time, asking if the answers in the back of the book that we both used were correct because that was not the answer she got. She was Department Chair and deemed the smartest teacher. I explained how I got the correct answers just as my students explained to her students how to get the correct answers. Part of the problem was that she began on page 425 and jumped around. I began with the Index in the front of the book and went page-by-page. By the way, my No. 4's math test scores were comparable to No. 5's math test scores.

I am a strong believer that academic success in any subject begins with children learning the basics, because those are your building blocks, your foundation. Learning those basics begins before students enter formal schooling. I also believe the following:

- Pop Tests or quick assessments are important in determining which children are ready for the next level.
- Repetition is important for memorizing concepts and understanding processes and procedures.
- "One and Done" is not an appropriate teaching strategy for learning math or any subject.

- Students should practice applying/using concepts in multiple environments. For example, reading comprehension can be practiced in an English class as well as with math, science, and social studies.
- Teachers must understand that students are different just like teachers are different, and "different" does not mean that one is better than the other.
- Individualization includes teachers putting their chairs next to their students' and watching them work, asking questions about their procedures that redirect, clarify, or guide their students' thinking.
- Reading is fundamental, regardless of subject.
- Students need hands-on prompts or models to help them internalize concepts.
- Failure is not an option for students. A child who really tries should not ever walk out of a classroom with an "F."
- Limited academic achievement for students is a reflection on the teacher's ability to teach. "Teachers do not teach if students do not learn."
- Teachers should consider changing their teaching styles rather than expecting students to change their learning styles.

Many of the academic challenges facing teachers today are not new. Mathematics has always been a challenging subject for most children and shortage of math teachers has been an issue across the country, including Jefferson County, for decades. Just like all of my teachers were my favorite teachers, perhaps we can help today's teachers become favorites to each of their students. I felt that every student in my class was my child. I tried to make every child feel comfortable, happy, and loved. I gave each child my attention when I sat next to that child and listened, then guided. I remember telling my students, "I do not do your homework or classwork; however, I will sit with you to get you off on the right track to get it done." My students never doubted that I cared about them. They welcomed me to sit next to them.

Ted Martin retired in 2000 after nearly twenty-five years at DuPont Manual. He watched the transformation of Manual from a

Comprehensive High School to a Magnet School with added facilities, specialty programs, and recognition as a Blue Ribbon School. Upon retirement, Ted continued to work with Jefferson County High School, teaching math and science. He and his wife, Carrie, attended Grades 1-3 in elementary school together, then junior high and high school, both graduating from Central. They were married nearly sixty years before her death shortly after this story was written. They have four sons, two in Louisville, one in Florida, and another in Michigan. Carrie was extremely proud of their seven grandchildren who all excel and were introduced to learning at home using flash cards, prompts, memorization, and repetition.

Dr. Bernard Minnis

Teacher, Principal, State Director of Special Vocational
Programs, Assistant Superintendent,
and Adjunct Professor

THE "MINNIS" NAME IS RECOGNIZED
throughout the community for its family
of educators and for involvement with
Adventism. My great grandfather, Madison
Beaumont Minnis, a slave, escaped to the
North with the Underground Railroad and
returned to Kentucky after the Civil War.
Over time, he became the first African
American to be head of maintenance in
City Hall. The mayor closed City Hall on
the day of his funeral in 1884. My great
grandmother, Elizabeth, became connected
to Adventism in 1889 after he died. She co-

Photo by Geoff Oliver-Bugbee
Courtesy of Bellarmine University

founded the first Seventh Day Adventist
church, which was chartered in her home in Louisville, either on
Madison Street or Magazine Street where she also taught music.

Three of Madison's daughters, my great aunts, Ella, Emma, and

Elizabeth, were teachers and principals. Great Aunt Ella was one of the first Black teachers in Louisville, and she later became principal of the Seventh Day Adventist Church School, opened in 1903. Great Aunt Emma was a teacher, college professor, and perhaps the first African-American female principal in Kentucky. She did not teach at the church school for whom the current Seventh Day Adventist School, the Emma L. Minnis Junior Academy, located in Louisville, Kentucky at Nineteenth and Magazine streets, is named. Aunt Elizabeth, a teacher, was principal at the Colored School for the Blind. My brother and cousins attended the earlier Church School, but I did not. My brother, Albert, Jr., was a coach and teacher at Lincoln Institute and was the first Black teacher and coach at Southern High School in Louisville. He also taught at Ballard High School in Jefferson County.

My dad, Albert, Sr., taught engineering at Lincoln Institute, a private school in Simpsonville, Kentucky. A graduate of Oakwood College in Huntsville, Alabama, Dad also attended college in New Jersey. Mom was a high school graduate with some college. We lived on campus at Lincoln Institute because Dad was also responsible for helping to maintain the campus. He was in charge of general maintenance and electricity. Lincoln Institute opened in 1912 in Simpsonville in Shelby County as a boarding school for African-American children.

I attended Montclair Elementary School, an all-Black rural school about five miles from Lincoln. We rode the bus to school but had to walk to get to the bus stop. I did not like getting up to go to school, which was a four-room building with four teachers. Classes were divided by Grades, 1-2, 3-4, 5-6, and 7-8. Ms. Miles taught me in Grades 1-2. A kind person and good teacher, she began with the basics and made sure that we could read and comprehend. Spelling was important and understanding numbers was emphasized. Ms. Mason taught Grades 5-6, and Mr. Miles, also principal, taught Grades 7-8. He was tough and demanded no nonsense.

When I attended Lincoln Institute for high school, I was in class with Black students who rode in on buses from other counties around Kentucky as well as some students from other states who lived in campus housing and in private homes on campus. The curriculum was difficult. Dr. Whitney Young, Sr., who was president, liked mixed courses, so math, science, and engineering courses were combined. My favorite class was English, taught by Ms. Williams. I sang in the concert choir and loved to draw, although I never took an art course since my Aunt Ella taught me how to draw and to paint. My grandfather was an artist as well. He worked with his hands. He built three houses in Louisville's West End. He also taught church Adventism principles. I played basketball in Grades 9-11 but did not play as a senior. During the summers, I met Black, white, and mixed groups of students from across the state who came to Lincoln for summer religious conferences, living in the dorms and staying weeks at a time.

My father did not "mess" around. He told me that I would go to college. Upon my high school graduation in 1960, both my brother and I were at Kentucky State College while Dad continued working at Lincoln Institute. I was an industrial arts major, following in my dad's footsteps. Industrial arts for us was mechanical drawing, drafting, electrical engineering, and architectural type courses. I also loved my drama class with Dr. Fletcher, a very attractive woman who taught us how to perform in public. I did not pledge a fraternity but travelled with the choir.

I had a teaching contract before I finished student teaching at Central High School under Mr. Bill Aiken who taught electricity. On a tour to Paducah, Kentucky, with Kentucky State's Classical Choir, I was introduced to Newman Walker, superintendent of the Paducah School System at that time. Dr. Walker asked me to come to Paducah to teach and offered me a contract that I accepted. In 1964, I graduated, married Ethel Eaves, who worked in a store and had not completed her college degree. We moved to Paducah where I taught shop and art classes that first year. I was also assistant basketball coach. We returned to Louisville after that first year because districts in the Paducah area were letting Black teachers go. My first job with the Louisville Independent System was at Jackson (Meyzeek) Jr. High teaching metal shop. My great aunt, Ella, taught next door at Booker T. Washington Elementary School. Milburn T. Maupin was my principal.

When I married Ethel, I promised her father that I would help her return to school to get her degree. I kept that promise. Ethel was from Louisville and her parents valued education. Ethel's mother was also a teacher. Ethel and her family were friends with Albert Meyzeek, the man for whom Meyzeek Jr. High School is named. Mr. Meyzeek lived on their block at Seventeenth and Chestnut streets. Ethel often told the story of how Meyzeek would read to her when she was a young child and how she read to him when he was older and his sight was failing. I kept my promise to Ethel's father. Ethel completed Kentucky State College and was certified in Elementary Education. She taught in the various cities where we lived, including Louisville where she spent the majority of her career as well. She liked the "little people," preferring the early elementary grades.

During the first 20 years of my career, I worked in several educational programs in addition to teaching. I was a job developer for potential dropouts at Shawnee Jr. High School; I supervised vocational programs for the disadvantaged for the Kentucky Department of Education (KDE); and I directed special vocational and cooperative work programs for KDE as well. I provided in-service for teachers, and as Associate Superintendent for Human and Community Relations for Jefferson County Public Schools, I supervised 100 positions focused on human relations, multicultural education, student services, and community relations associated with court-ordered desegregation for JCPS. In addition, I was principal of DuValle Middle School and director of Public Relations and Community Relations for Charlestown (South Carolina) Public Schools.

During the second half of my career, I was deputy associate superintendent for the Office of Instruction at KDE. I dealt with accreditation, program audits, teacher and administrator certification, compensatory education, adult and continuing education, school improvement, instructional support, curriculum services, and student services. This was the last position that I held before returning to JCPS to serve as director of Vocational Programs, Adult Alternative Programs, and the Louisville Educational Partnership; director of School-to-Career Initiatives; assistant superintendent for Equity and Poverty Issues; and assistant superintendent for Diversity, Equity, and Poverty Programs. I completed a Doctorate in Educational Administration at the University of Kentucky and participated in additional training for managing educational change and assessing teacher preparation programs. I also participated in IBM's Educational Executive Training, Leadership Louisville Seminars, and Bingham Fellows.

Over my career, I have contributed to efforts for transitioning the Louisville and Jefferson County systems through merger and desegregation, working with the community, both anti-busing leaders and busing proponents. I also lead and supported JCPS through the challenges of striving for equity. While we made strides, we are yet to meet our goals. Yes, we made progress and things got better, but with busing and desegregation over 40 years old, we now have second generation issues of inequities in suspensions, special education referral and placement, and academic achievement, identified as both racial and socioeconomic disparities. Although the JCPS District and the Board are focused on maintaining equity, extinguishing racism and alleviating poverty are truly beyond their control.

The various positions that I have held reflect my dedication to helping children gain equitable access to public education. My focus is influenced by my family of educators that transcends five generations. The Martin Luther King, Jr., Freedom Award for "promoting justice, peace, freedom, nonviolence, racial equity, and civic activism," is one of my most cherished awards since Ethel and I participated in the march on Frankfort back in the 60s with Dr. King.

Yes, we have work to do, but we have a new group of emerging leaders like my doctoral students at Bellarmine University who are poised to help guide us through the next phase of challenges associated with diversity, poverty, and equity. I am excited about the outlook for our future transformation.

Dr. Minnis was married to Ethel for more than fifty years before her death. They have three children, two of whom are educators, constituting the fifth generation of educators in the Minnis family. Dr. Minnis is a member of a number of professional and civic organizations, including the National Alliance of Black School Educators, the Louisville Branch of the NAACP, Youth Alive, Inc., Black Achievers, the National Conference of Christians and Jews, and the Metropolitan Housing Coalition. Bernard has served on several boards, including the Cathedral Heritage Foundation Board, the Community Action

Agency Board of Directors, the Cabbage Patch Settlement House Board of Directors, the Louisville-Jefferson County Human Relations Commission, the Chestnut Street YMCA Board of Directors, the Lincoln Foundation Board of Directors, and the Boy Scouts of America Board of Directors. He and his current wife, Woody Jayne, enjoy travelling and remodeling their current home. They also continue working with the Emma L. Minnis, Jr. Academy. Bernard's master's degree is from Western Kentucky University and his Doctorate is from the University of Kentucky.

Warren Shelton

Teacher, Coach, Team Leader, Counselor, Assistant
Principal, Principal, and Association President

*We are here to provide services for students. They are
not here to provide jobs for us. (Dawson Orman, JCPS
administrator and mentor)*

MY MOM WAS ONE OF THREE REGIS-
tered nurses employed in my birthplace, Hot
Springs, Arkansas. However, my dad, a college
graduate with a Bachelor's Degree in Business
from Philander Smith College, could not get a
job in his professional field, so, he supported
our family by working part-time at a hotel, in
a bath house, and on the railroad.

Hot Springs, Arkansas, is where President
Bill Clinton grew up and is a reflection of most
southern cities of that time—segregated—but

Shelton Family Photo Collection

our school configuration was unusual. There
were uptown and downtown schools for both African Americans and
whites about a mile and a half apart. Our elementary schools held
Grades 1-4 in one building and Grades 5-6 in another. Junior high/
high schools housed Grades 7-12.

I feel that I had good teachers, but the elementary standout was Ms. Jackson in fourth grade. She was friendly, but she held us accountable; she stressed the basics and had a reward system that allowed us to "play" when we had done well or completed what we were supposed to do. My favorite elementary memory is a contest for learning—a math competition and a competition for conjugating verbs. We took pride in competing even though it was among friends. Fifth and sixth grades being housed in different buildings was a different experience. There were three teachers in the school and the principal also taught sixth grade.

When I graduated from high school, there were 40 students in my class. There was no ability grouping and teachers taught multiple subjects and multi-levels. Teachers supported one another. My choir teacher sent me to band because it needed an extra trombone player. I knew nothing about the trombone and was so small that I had to catch the slide with my toe and kick it back up, but I stayed in band. The band director I remember because he was patient and willing to teach each of us even though we knew nothing about music or the instruments. My all-time favorite high school teachers were Ms. Logan and Mr. Brown who were tough. Mr. Brown taught ninth-grade science, biology, and chemistry. He told us repeatedly that the Author "A", He "B", but to do "C," which means you do everything assigned to get your "C." If a student misspelled a word on a paper, he tore it up.

Our teachers helped us understand and appreciate the value of education. Another incident that I remember is meeting a girl from Little Rock at summer camp sponsored by my church. This girl had experienced integration and talked about the importance of education as well. I guess I took it to heart because I became a National Merit Semi-Finalist. I became college bound because two of my friends were checking out colleges and I joined them. Kentucky State (K-State) was the final choice because my friend's grandparents lived in Louisville, and college entrance meant I would not be drafted since war in Viet Nam was hot and heavy.

While I had scholarship money to attend college in Arkansas, I turned it down. My parents and I paid $980 for tuition, room and board, and out-of-state fees to attend K-State in 1963. My major was biology, and I had gotten in my head that I would do research or go to medical school. Education (teaching) was not in my plans. I worked

on campus during my sophomore, junior, and senior years and went home only at Christmas. To stay on campus, students were required to be enrolled in 12 hours. I had completed my required classes by the second semester of my senior year so I took classes in business math, organic chemistry, and education to meet the residency requirement. To my surprise, I enjoyed the education classes.

I graduated in 1967 with a Bachelor of Science Degree in Biology. By the way, my two friends also graduated, each of us having pledged a different fraternity. A different friend worked for Seagram's Distillery and was helping me get a job in Louisville since I had chemistry coursework. I stayed with a minister who was fairly well-known and connected around the city. By chance, he told me about the superintendent of the Catholic system needing a French teacher. I applied and was appointed with the agreement that I complete my master's degree. I did not do student teaching.

I was the first African-American teacher at Flaget High School, teaching French for two years. The assignment with all males, Grades 9-12, was difficult and demanding for a new teacher in his first integrated setting. I was also the tennis coach. At the end of my second year, 1968-69, I was hired by Louisville's city school system that supplied science teachers for Flaget, to teach science at Russell Jr. High School. That next year, with the implementation of Focus-Impact, I was transferred to Shawnee Jr. High School to desegregate the staff. Dawson Orman was principal.

I could not have asked for a better mentor than Dawson Orman. I do not know why he chose me, but I will always be grateful. I was new. I was young. I had experience in parochial schools. All I know is that he took me to meetings that he had to attend. We worked on designing the new Brown School. He talked to me about my next steps after my Professional Commitment (Masters in Education) to complete my science certification. Ultimately, I took counseling classes at Spalding, added another certification, worked half a year on drop-out prevention as director of the Frederick Douglas Project and became the first African-American junior high counselor in the South End upon being assigned to Gottschalk/Iroquois Jr. High School in 1973 and remaining there through the Merger of the school systems.

I remember the first day of busing in the 1975-76 school year and kids screaming as they got off the bus. The dynamics of schools changed. Iroquois Housing Project was assigned to Southern, making Southern exempt because it was felt that Southern would be too volatile if students were bused there from the West End. Iroquois was paired with Parkland. The principal was Paul Willinger. That year was an adjustment for all, more so for the Black students from Parkland than the white students who were at Iroquois Jr. We had previously received Black students from Hazelwood and Rutherford.

Following my three years at Iroquois, I served as Moore High School counselor for nine years then assistant principal for three years before moving to principal at Johnson Middle for two years. My last assignment was principal of Moore High School where I served 11 years. The best teacher that I ever had was Daisy Wright who taught English at Moore. She could teach anybody. She was a motivator. Students knew that she cared about them and was willing to help them. I had another teacher there, Ms. Murphy, who did not believe in paid Extended School Services (ESS) but believed in staying after school without pay to help kids. She never refused a kid being put in her class and you never knew if she was upset because she never showed it with students or with faculty. Her only request was, "Don't ask me to take students after school who do not pay attention in regular class."

One of my success stories is about one of my ECE students who actually persevered and became an ECE teacher. She did not have it easy, but she had support from great teachers. My favorite Moore story is about a young man who was out of English class and sent to the office when we had visitors in the building. I asked him why he was causing a disturbance. He gave no answer. Real answer—students were taking turns reading out loud. The student would rather be put out of class than to let the other students know that he could not read. That was a wake-up call for me and my faculty. I had great teachers who were creative and dedicated to seeing students succeed. Teaching was not just a job but a career.

Although I retired as principal in 2001, I stayed active as an educator, working to support teachers and students. I've worked with a group of fraternity brothers, Omega Psi Phi, who serve as mentors in several high schools. I supported "Shoot for Peace" to raise money for the West End Boys School, and I have worked with "Black Lives Matter," listening to Black students talk about themselves and their generation. One student's comment resonates. "We cannot throw them away, but why should they be in classrooms keeping others from learning. What about Black-on-Black crime and lumping us all together. Is that fair?"

If I could turn back time. I would try to be a better French teacher at Flaget; I would have been tougher on more teachers instead of at times making allowances for some; but I would have continued to enjoy the kids. I loved being a counselor because of individual actions with students, and I loved being principal because of the influence over the entire school. I remember Dr. Dick Kirkpatrick in the Personnel Department boasting, "Your most important job is your next hire," and I believed him. I tried to get counselors who focused on "people work" from 7:40 to 2:20, and before and after those times on "paperwork." I see counselors as underutilized today when they could head off problems. Other people without skills are trying to do jobs that counselors should be dealing with, the entire child. Instead they are extras, scheduling ECE meetings, counting test booklets, etc., rather than dealing directly with student achievement, student mental health, and college- and career-related guidance.

Schools changed over my career. To begin with, parent involvement changed from parents being interested in what their children were doing, what classes they were taking, and what activities they were in; from being supporters of teachers to being adversaries. Then, it seemed that we went from holding students accountable for academics and behavior to making excuses for students. Next, the people who went into education changed. Teaching became a job. In addition, teacher training and teacher assignments were not realistic. Training did not fit the students and the schools of the day, and new teachers were not matched with the culture of the schools where they were placed. Furthermore, teachers no longer had control of their classrooms. They were not taught classroom-management skills and could not manage students. Lastly, there were teachers who just could not teach. They needed to make career decisions.

Today's schools have more resources but not individuals who care as much. Educators were once looked up to in our communities and by the students. We (Blacks) were told that we had to be better to be considered good. In a conversation with a Grade 5 African-American male, the student lamented, "I have a teacher who acted surprised when I gave the correct answer. I felt good for knowing, but I felt bad because she didn't think I would know."

Teachers who let students put their heads down and do nothing do not care about kids or they think those kids are too dumb to care about. They do not have high expectations for their students, and consequently, the students do not develop high expectations for themselves. This is too often true for Black males and poor children whose ability to be successful is questioned. When the counselor says to a student, "You are doing well. Keep doing it and pick a great vocational school to go to," to whom do you think she/he is speaking?

I believe that I could teach today. I use some of the same strategies with the kids that I mentor—being firm, fair, and consistent. However, for persons considering teaching as a career, I think the first question that they should ask themselves is, "Do I like kids?" Then they should do some volunteer work where they can work with young people. I told my own son that I did not know if he would have the patience to work with kids like him. Next, they should ask which is more important, kids or making money. We can make the profession more attractive and let everyone know the opportunities available in the profession, but if a person does not like kids and does not understand their importance to our future, they must keep going and find another career! I can teach a person everything he/she needs to know about teaching, but I cannot teach a person to love the kids that they will teach.

Warren Shelton served as president of the Counselor's Association and the Assistant Principal's Association. He is Executive Director of the Jefferson County Association of School Administrators. His civic activities include mentoring, Board of Directors of Chestnut Street YMCA, serving on the JCPS Policy Committee, participating in voter registration and with activities sponsored by his fraternity, Omega Psi Phi, as well as various projects with his church. He is the recipient of the Milburn T. Maupin Award for his work as an outstanding administrator in JCPS. Warren is married to Nancy Cole Shelton. They have one child and three grandchildren.

Dr. Deanna Shobe Tinsley

Teacher, Principal, Director of Student Assignment,
Assistant Superintendent, and Community Volunteer

Dissertation Title: *Management Styles Found in
Participatory and Non-Participatory Management
Elementary Schools*

I AM THE OLDEST OF FOUR CHILDREN born in Rushville, Indiana, 30 miles from Indianapolis, to parents who were surrounded by educators most of their lives. My dad, Judge Benjamin Shobe, the first African American to serve as a judge since Reconstruction, considered Louisville his home, although he was born in Bowling Green, Kentucky. My grandparents, his mom and dad, were educators. My grandfather, Walter, was a high school principal and Dean of Men at Kentucky State College where Dad earned his

Carol A. Shobe Photographer

bachelor's degree. My grandmother, Anna, a Latin teacher, taught my dad for a time.

Mom's people lived in small towns and Indiana and had basic

education. She had three elementary principals in her family. Mom and Dad met in Ann Arbor, Michigan, where Mom worked and Dad attended the University of Michigan Law School with tuition and fees paid by the Commonwealth of Kentucky because state law prohibited African Americans from attending graduate or professional schools in Kentucky at that time. Later, Dad was one of the attorneys who won the case that opened the doors for Blacks to attend graduate and professional schools in Kentucky, *Lyman T. Johnson v. University of Kentucky.*

My grandparents retired in Louisville after working in the Lynch area where there was a great community of Black educators that we encountered when we visited. For as long as I remember, I have been surrounded by educators in my neighborhood and friends of my parents. The teachers were ladylike, old-fashioned, and smart. They drove nice cars, had nice homes, and were well-spoken, well-dressed, well-traveled, and admired.

I attended James Bond Elementary School at Twenty-Third and Cedar streets; it is today's Dan C. Byck Elementary. Mr. Diggs was principal and my mom was president of the PTA. Ms. Wilhite, my first-grade teacher, taught us enhanced reading because we already knew the basics. My elementary teachers looked professional, encouraged the arts, and emphasized music at every grade. We had to learn and sing the scale and we performed in a variety of musicals every year. I also remember one of my teachers, Miss B. J. Daniels, who could fold construction paper, take scissors and cut letters without any pattern. We were fascinated seeing those letters take shape.

My teachers had foresight. In the fourth, fifth and sixth grades, they were getting us ready because they knew we might be the class going into integrated schools. They pushed us, and we worked harder. Not only did they stress reading, math, and science, but they talked about behavior, speaking correctly, and acting appropriately, stressing that we had to be the best. They prepared us for success in the new environment. I attended Western Junior High School in Grade 7, along with students from several other Black elementary schools. We were met by all-white teachers.

I had a great music class. In sewing class, using an old sewing machine with a foot trundle, I made clothes that I wore to school. The art class was boring, and I never learned anything. I liked algebra and made all *A's*, but it did not transfer to high school where I struggled in math but loved English. I had white friends and felt no prejudice. The only real problem that I remember was a teacher deciding that she was going to wash a Black student's hair. All the Black girls freaked out.

While I could have gone to any high school, I chose Central High School while my sister and brother later chose to attend Shawnee. Dan White, Dad's first cousin, taught at Central. His wife, Decora, taught at Coleridge Taylor Elementary. They both encouraged me to attend Central where I had the opportunity to again work with amazing Black teachers like Daisy Rhodes, Thelma Lauderdale, and Lyman Johnson, teachers who were knowledgeable, strong and organized, and encouraging. Ms. Betty Taylor, our counselor, had sessions about college with people from colleges talking to the group. I have to say here that we were tracked academically. I did not know that there were students who did not graduate and students that were treated differently based of their track.

In addition, Central teachers and staff were supportive of the Civil Rights Movement. Mr. Wilson, our principal, would announce, "Those of you going to march, leave now," meaning go over to Quinn Chapel AME Church to organize and get ready. We were never penalized grade-wise. Frank Stanley, Jr. who was associated with the *Louisville Defender Newspaper*, would meet us there to administer the Non-Violent Oath before we picked up our placards and headed out to Fourth Street, singing our protest songs.

I attended West Virginia State College (WVSC) in 1962 where Decora White was an alumna. I had visited with my friend at WVSC and liked the campus. WVSC was one of the original groups of Black land grant colleges. I was impressed with the professors who had degrees from University of Chicago, University of Michigan, Ohio State, Meharry, Howard, and several others. Also, a friend of the family, Dr. Grace James, attended WVSC and had family living in Charleston.

Education and social work were the two majors that were prominent on campus and I planned to be an elementary teacher. Author Alex Haley's aunt, a teacher at WVSC, was in charge of student teaching. I was introduced to the concept of "DNA" by Dr. Oden. I remember being in the top English class and being assigned a paper, "The History of West Virginia as reflected in selected names from the Charleston, West Virginia Directory." I had always been a good English student, but I was lost. I did not know how to do the paper and got an "Incomplete," but I bugged the professor until I understood and got a passing grade. There were lots of rules at WVSC that students had to follow if they wanted to graduate. For example, all students had to pass swimming class and several students were afraid of water. I was fine because I had learned to swim over the years living in Louisville.

I attended WVSC for three years and three summers and was ready to graduate in 1965 after student teaching at West Sattes Elementary School in Grades 2 and 5. My experience there was nothing like student teaching today. First, I had to drive across town to get to my assignment. That was OK because my father bought me a car to get back and forth. The problem was, the car had a stick-shift and I just could not drive it. I was saved by my best friend, Max Tinsley, James Bond's grandson whom I later married, and was attending WVSC. Max drove me to student teaching every morning. Student teaching was not the intense experience that it is today. We were directed what not to wear—anything red; wear your dresses this way; walk this way; sit like this; stand over there—superficial "stuff." We had learned stuff, but student teaching was not structured like it is today. I taught my class music or tried to teach music. Everybody had music when I grew up. I was not very successful teaching music.

My first teaching assignment in Louisville was at Brandeis Elementary School, Grade 5 in a portable. I had to learn the "Blue Book" or "Bird Book" as it was called because this was your daily attendance that had to be errorless. The secretary oversaw the book and would give it back to you if it were incorrect. Other teachers helped us new teachers. Mrs. Bea McHenry helped me a great deal. A family friend, another elementary teacher from Indianapolis, Mrs. Mickey Patterson, brought me a boatload of materials, a fifth-grade log and lesson plans. I needed a guide, some direction to keep them on track, and her materials helped a great deal that first year.

My students lived in the neighborhood and walked to school. I loved my fifth graders. I don't remember how many students were in my class, and there were no class-size limits, but my kids did what they were supposed to do. I had to divide them into groups because some needed more help than others. My bright group did things on their own while I worked with the others. I taught at Brandeis Elementary for one year before going to the University of Louisville to work in the Upward Bound Program with Dr. Eleanor Love. I was there for two years, working and completing my master's degree that was partially paid for by the university. I returned to teaching at Henry Clay Elementary 1968 to 1970, teaching Grades 2 and 5.

From 1970 to 1973, I taught at Whitney Young Elementary under Principal Ann Downs. Our school was open-concept, built with very few walls. This was another different teaching experience. My room was a corner room next to the rest rooms. At one time, the roof had a leak, and carpets had to be removed. It was a mess, but teachers continued to teach, and we expected our students to behave, more so because noise in that open area traveled. In those days, we looked for innovative teaching strategies, and our teachers received training or professional development to implement the strategies. My next assignment focused on helping teachers implement strategies to improve reading comprehension—the Follow-Through Program (FTP).

I was trained locally for this initiative and visited the sponsor school, the University of Kansas, with two others from the Louisville system, Alma Davis and Joyce Moore. Follow-Through was based on behavior analysis. We used physical rewards in what was called a "token economy." Students worked with programmed learning materials. Students were rewarded as they progressed through the program and their skills improved. Kids learned to read, and their scores improved. For the1974-75 and 1975-76 school years, I was a Staff Development Trainer for FTP, serving Whitney Young and Breckenridge Elementary schools, with offices at the Brown Education Center. The program and the position were phased out with the merger of the city and county school districts. Program supervisors did not fit the county's organizational structure that included County supervisors. I was assigned to Hikes Annex and worked with Professional Development and In-service programs.

Being an elementary school principal was the favorite assignment of my career. I had contact with children, worked with teachers for the benefit of the school, and had a degree of autonomy to make instructional decisions. I spent eighteen years as principal, six at Atkinson and twelve at Norton Elementary, the first African-American principal at both locations. J. B. Atkinson was an old building that I walked around every day. In my first year, Josephine Trowell, principal at Middletown Elementary, mentored me. The lesson that I learned was, as principal you are totally held responsible for outcomes, and you must think about how your decisions affect others. Principals are very influential. They need to be "people persons not people pleasers."

I also learned that people in the Portland area needed respect because of gangs in the neighborhood and lots of poor people with poor-people issues. I have never seen harder working teachers, but the school had low test scores. We had to develop a plan to improve those scores. It took time, but we worked at it. I got to know the community and they had time to get to know me. The Portland Community Center was an asset and I was able to hire some of the residents from the neighborhood.

Norton and Atkinson Elementary schools were as different as night and day, one urban and the other suburban. At Norton, I had parents walking the building, kids running out the back door at dismissal because they never saw safety or security as an issue, and teachers who had not been observed and did not want to be watched. There was a different level of parental involvement and expectations. Parents were quick to tell me, "Norton is different from what you have been accustomed to." I actually loved both schools because of their differences.

I cannot tell you how many funerals, how much hand-holding, and how much craziness I experienced as a principal. I wasn't always liked, but I believe I was respected. As principal, test scores must go up, but human conditions are the contradictions. Sometimes it is the teacher standing in the middle of the hall in her bathrobe, shoes, and pajamas asking for a soft drink as other teachers and students are watching; or the teacher whose husband is dying and no one knows it; or the sweet teacher who was the curser, who, as it turns out, was having a diabetic episode.

Being principal is a fabulous job if you like it and you can affect change. When you can no longer affect change, it is probably time for a career change. When the Kentucky Education Reform Act came into effect, we had to adjust to changes in reading requirements; in creative writing, with no need to spell correctly; and in cooperative learning lessons. Testing was measuring one thing, but the learning curve was difficult for some teachers. One of the things that I shared with my teachers was test requirements change teaching and some individual creativity may be lost or enhanced. One team of teachers organized the "Star Burst Express Primary School." The excitement in trying something new gave us new energy.

When I felt that I had done all that I knew how to do as a principal at Norton, I decided that it was time to move. I tell teachers the same thing—change schools, change grades, change how you do things, change bulletin boards. I moved to Central Office as Director of Elementary Student Assignment and later as Assistant Superintendent of Elementary Schools before my retirement in 2005.

Over my career, I have seen up-close, kids in poverty. We have covered basic needs—food, clothing, material needs, and nutritional needs—but do we show them that we like them and care about them? If we do, we must teach them to read by Grade 4. If the kids like us, they act better. They care about you, the way you care about them. Our children are capable. They may need extra time, one-on-one instruction, or different methods, but teachers should have that mindset about all kids, including poor kids and Black kids. Also, we have enough money and knowledge to figure out how to extend learning time and bring the light back into the eyes of some of our students. Something happens to them and they can turn off. Sometimes a special teacher can light them up. I love it when teachers make the classroom environment happy and colorful, with plenty of bright, pretty bulletin boards, when they take the time to talk to children, read with them, and give them a smile. We do not know what that child has experienced that day, at home, in the neighborhood, or walking down the hall.

High expectations work. They make children believe they can achieve. I've seen that setting expectations, encouraging kids, and holding them accountable, helps children grow. We have to find the culture and the pride that connect students to academic achievement.

I have been in schools all my life and never stopped being an educator and encouraging others to think about teaching, even though it may not be as prestigious as some other professions and not as lucrative for beginning teachers. I believe teaching is a proud profession and a calling; teachers also have chances to do other things in the education profession. If you want to be a principal, you must be energetic, thick-skinned, and willing to work with adults. If you want to work in Central Office, there are interesting positions; while you can provide support to schools in these positions, it's in the school where the actual change occurs.

It was a pleasure to work in and learn about the various schools, cultures, and communities in Jefferson County. Throughout the years, I've had opportunities to see how children from varying backgrounds can learn from each other and learn about each other. As a member of a team designed to support elementary schools, working with Executive Director of Student Assignment, Pat Todd, I felt we had an important mission—to racially integrate our schools, to provide children with diverse learning experiences, and to help close the achievement gap between groups of children. While the implementation of the original plan has been greatly modified, I continue to believe in the mission. My hope is that when all children enter a school, they receive the blessings of a caring, welcoming, environment where they will be met with high expectations and support.

Dr. Tinsley, a cancer survivor and member of Delta Sigma Theta Sorority, has tutored at Park Hill Community Center for several years. She has been a member of the LINKS, Incorporated, for more than 30 years and has worked in a variety of civic activities with that organization and with her sorority. Her awards and recognitions include Jefferson County Association of School Administrators, Milburn T. Maupin School Administrators Award, and the Gheens Institute for Innovation, Creativity, and Entrepreneurship Award. A member of St. Stephen Baptist Church, Dr. Tinsley is a world traveler, most recently traveling to South Africa, Spain, and Dubai. She was also inducted into the Central High School Distinguished Alumni Hall of Fame. She has been married to Max Tinsley for more than fifty years. They have two children and three grandchildren.

Marva Wigginton

Elementary Teacher, Resource Teacher, Reading
Specialist, Math Specialist, Chapter 1 Specialist, and
Head Start Child Development Unit Manager

LIVING IN VIRGINIA, ONE OF THE states that so adamantly opposed integration of any kind, I never knew about the *Brown v. Board of Education* case in 1954 and went to segregated schools, elementary through high school, until graduation in 1962. I started school in first grade and I already knew how to read. My mother and grandmother read stories to me and taught me now to read when I was four or five years old. Born in Dendron, Virginia to parents of age fifteen who were farmers and had attended high school, I was almost seven

Wigginton Family Photo Collection

years before I attended school with my sister, two years older than I. My first grade teacher, Georgia Harris, lived in the area and was one of the six teachers in the white, clapboard, segregated school with potbellied stoves and lift top desk where we kept our school materials. She rode the bus to school with us, sitting beside students, helping them learn to read and count as we travelled. We had to walk a mile and a half to get to the bus pick-up. Dendron is a small town in Surry County, Virginia about eighteen miles from Williamsburg. It wasn't until I was in high school that the bus was re-routed and students didn't have to walk over a mile to get it.

I liked school and remember something about almost every grade. In first grade, I learned the May-Pole Dance for May Day which was a big event every year. We did lots of arts and crafts, collecting cigar boxes and creating different things. My second-grade teacher took each student home with her for one night to get to know them better and to meet her family. Ms. Sarah Warren was low-keyed, soft spoken and laid back. The work was easy. Our third-grade teacher, Ms. Irene Holland, was strong, strict and worked us hard. Fourth grade was more difficult with Ms. Williams. As fifth graders we went to D.C., walked through the White House without a pass, and attended the Jamestown Festival to see a re-enactment of an encounter between Captain John Smith and Pocahontas. Ms. Banks, in sixth grade, called me by my middle name, "Sally." A boy in my class teased me and said, "You have an old woman's name." I was named after my grandmother and Joe Louis's first wife. We also had a ceremony and received certificates when we completed sixth grade.

All of my teachers were very good teachers. We had homework every night and every teacher expected all of us to do well. They worked with all students even though some would have qualified for Exceptional Childhood Education (ECE), however we were all in the same class. Until we went to high school, most of our books were hand-me-downs from the white school. Everybody in our community knew everybody. We did not pass the white school on the way to our school which had Grades 1 through 6 on one side and Grades 7 through 12 on the other. I always did what my teachers said and made good grades, no *C*'s, *D*'s or *F*'s. My family encouraged and supported education and wanted us to do well. My aunt and uncle, who did not have children, gave us gifts. My Aunt Molly in New York worked for white families and sent us clothes. Another aunt with no children sent things. And of course, we never went hungry with the large garden that Mother maintained and the fruit from the cherry, apple, plum, peach, and pear trees that we picked, and Mother canned.

High school was different and exciting. We changed classes—math, science, chemistry, social studies, literature, and English. I worked in the Library and was a cheerleader. The librarian, Ms. Bertha Taylor, taught French and was the cheerleader sponsor. She went to our homes to talk to our parents face-to-face to get permission for us to cheer. She also picked us up and took us to games. We did not have a senior prom. Instead, we saved our money for a 3-day senior trip to New York City, the first time for many of us.

When I graduated from high school, my aunt and uncle came to Virginia and took me back to Kentucky where I had never been. My aunt, with a Ph.D. earned at Stanford, met and married my uncle when she taught at Hampton University and he attended there on the GI Bill. She was a professor in the Sociology Department at Kentucky State (K-State) College. My uncle was an administrator at the Louisville Red Cross Hospital. I wanted to be a nurse and had written them a letter, seeking their guidance.

I began summer school at Kentucky State College the summer after I graduated high school and interviewed with the Dean for admission. My aunt and uncle had a home on Cecil Avenue where my uncle stayed while my aunt and I stayed on campus. He visited some weekends and arranged for me to visit at the hospital to see what nurses actually did. I changed my mind and my career choice. I did not want to be a nurse because I did not want to work at night. My second choice was education. I could become a teacher. At the same time that I was deciding on a major, I was interested in Alpha Kappa Alpha (AKA) Sorority. I did not know much about sororities, but my aunt was active in the graduate chapter and encouraged me to write a letter of interest. I was initiated in December 1963 and involved in projects and activities on campus.

My first teaching assignment was baptism by fire at Carmichael Elementary School in first grade, following student teaching at Elkhorn Elementary, a white school in Frankfort where I was the first Black teacher. I had teacher training at the Rosenwald School on campus before finishing Kentucky State College in November 1965 and I graduated May 1966. My first-grade class had mostly Black boys and a few white boys with three girls in the mix. Many of the boys were troublemakers and bad actors who had not gone to kindergarten and would crawl under the desk. I bought materials, sat on the floor at home and made learning folders and games, and used patterns that the other first-grade teacher gave me. This was the most difficult class and the most rewarding. When parents brought children to school, I gave parents things to work on at home with their children. Parents would have been upset if they knew that when children came to school on Monday, they told me everything that had happened at home over the weekend.

By the end of the year, we could see academic progress. Students could read, count, add and subtract, say the Pledge of Allegiance, recite poetry from memory. They were ready for second grade. I taught first grade at Carmichael for five years, the most challenging and the most rewarding assignment of my career, partially because I learned so much as a new teacher and, on the other hand, because my students showed so much academic improvement that I knew that my teaching had made a difference. I will never forget my last year at Carmichael at the end of the year when students performed and told what they had learned. My first graders were now fifth graders and I was a proud teacher. I sometimes see those students who recognize me, but I do not recognize them. They remind me of what I did with them.

When Carmichael Elementary became a Focus/Impact School, I transferred to Shawnee Elementary School and moved to teaching second grade. Focus/Impact was a different concept that all principals did not support and it was sometimes difficult for teachers to support their principals and support the new program. . My focus, however was on my students, helping them read and teaching them the concepts and skills that would make them successful in third grade.

I had completed my Master's degree and certification as a Reading Specialists. I knew a lot more about teaching and working with parents and I could help other teachers like more experienced teachers helped me. Because of my Reading Endorsement, I had the opportunity to move to Title I, focusing on reading in the Diagnostic Prescriptive Individualized Reading Program (DPI). For the next several years, including through merger of Louisville and Jefferson County schools, reading, was my instructional focus at Camp Taylor and Gilmore

Lane Elementary Schools until I took a position in North Region as the Language Arts/Social Studies Resource Teacher. I implemented pull-out programs as well as modeled in classrooms with teachers to support reading and math instruction, providing in-service to teachers to help them attain additional instructional strategies.

As my career unfolded, I spent three years as Resource Teacher for Educational Assessment, the job I liked least; three years as Math Specialist; six years as Chapter 1 Specialists for Elementary Programs; and seven years as Head Start Child Development Unit Manager. I witnessed changes in schools, teachers, curriculum, and leadership. I worked with outstanding leaders like Rosemary Chambers who worked long hours, evenings and weekends, and who visited outstanding programs across the country to identify systems that JCPS could implement to improve our students' readiness and achievement. I watched parent participation in schools decline at the same time the number of students from single-parent homes increased and working parents became less helpful for their children. I also saw the increase in discipline problems among students and the growing uncertainty of how to deal with those problems among teachers.

Throughout my journey, I learned and adapted to do my job well. I remember when I began working with Head Start, I did not know all of the services available for parents or the amount of red tape and documentation required for every aspect of the program from assuring that students were up-to-date with their shots to following up and documenting any instances where parents refused services or refused to comply with program requirements.

Over the years, I encountered outstanding teachers. One that comes to mind is a teacher who began as an assistant before she was certified. She was totally absorbed in her classroom, using everything that she learned to help her students. She tried new things, used different approaches for different students, and used a motivation strategy that I completely agree with—Model, outline expectations, give accolades and praise, telling students specifically what they do well so they know what they are being praised for and giving them specific direction on what they can improve upon. She went beyond what was expected, using her time and professional resources around her and asking the question, "What can I do to make this better?" She created exciting activities that related to real life for students, telling them "why" they were doing those activities and challenging them to be creative and outsmart her.

Over time, I have wondered about changes in schools, students and teachers. Students are more prepared because of pre-school and Head Start programs. They have more knowledge and exposure to technology. They are involved and exposed to travel, educational programs, and summer experiences in person or through technology, yet statistics say they are not making academic progress or achieving proficiency, and they lose what they know over the summer.

I see teachers and I sometimes question their professionalism when I see how they are dressed and their demeanor. I wonder about their respect for students, even though I believe they care. Their tone and how they talk to students do not reflect caring. For my generation, professionalism was demonstrated by teachers being role models and how they treated parents and students.

Furthermore, I am not sure that schools recognize their atmosphere contributes to students being able to compete. School atmosphere or culture begins with the front office, in the halls, with the bulletin boards, as well as with the behavior of everyone in the building. Schools focus on lack of resources, money, and teacher training as reasons why students do poorly—only one part of the full picture. They ignore how students feel about their school and how they believe their school feels about them as contributors to academic growth.

More so, all teachers may not be trained to teach students from different abilities, backgrounds, and ethnicities. Poor/Black children are being short-changed because teachers do not know how to teach all children. Boys learn differently from girls. They are more actively engaged and involved. If a teacher does not know how to talk to and motivate students, that teacher cannot teach. Several proposed remedies including the all Black boys' academies fail to see the bigger picture. Students must learn to work together and isolation may widen the academic and socioeconomic gap.

Only certain parents, the "Somebody Parents" are heard in some schools. Parents, all parents, should be pushing to assure that their children have what they need. They must be involved in motivating their children to learn more and in holding schools and teachers accountable for inspiring and exposing students to available opportunities and giving them the skills to pursue those opportunities. Many of the "Nobody Parents" are turned off by our schools because of their treatment and history as students. We must motivate those parents to motivate their children. They see other children going on field trips, making honor roll, participating in international travel, getting scholarships, and they want this for their children as well, but they do not know how to make it happen. Our churches, fraternities, sororities, and community organizations must help us help our parents learn more and do more.

Finally, the education profession is the greatest profession of all because it touches so many lives that grow over time. It is hard work, exciting and engaging. It builds higher-level thinking skills in students and gives them fundamentals upon which to build their lives. Teaching is harder today because it has so much competition, not only from other professions, but to keep students interested and engaged, and because of the lack of value placed on education. Students say, "If education is so important, why are teacher salaries so low?" and I cannot argue the point. However, I can say that you will not find a more rewarding profession than teaching.

Marva spent 11 years after her retirement from Jefferson County Public Schools reviewing Head Start Programs across the United States, including the U.S. Virgin Islands, St. Thomas and St. Croix, excluding Kentucky because she was a Kentucky resident. She has been an active member of Alpha Kappa Alpha Sorority, Inc. for 53 years and has volunteered and mentored high school students who were preparing to go to college. She encouraged them to complete the necessary forms to get into college and to apply for available scholarships. Marva has received awards and recognitions including the 15th District PTA Award. A member of The Church of Our Merciful Saviour, she is married to Guy Wigginton, an educator who also retired from JCPS. They have two children and one grandchild.

Daisy Roberts Wright

Middle School and High School English Teacher,
and Mentor-Teacher

BORN IN CLARKSVILLE, TENNESSEE, a small town about 45 miles from Nashville, I am among my father's last group of five children. The oldest of this group, my brother, began college the same year I entered first grade. For years, mom had been a stay-at-home mom while Dad taught elementary students in a county segregated school. Even though my dad did not pass away until 1959 when I was 11 years old, my mom had been the head of our household since Dad suffered his second stroke, which left him partially paralyzed in 1953.

Wright Family Photo Collection

Women's liberation was nothing new to my family. When mom went to work after Dad died, my three sisters and I were latch-key kids and my oldest sister was in charge.

Of the five siblings, I was next to the baby of the group. We all attended the same Black elementary school in Grades 1 through 6, and the same segregated high school, Burt High, that closed in 1970 when area schools integrated. Named in honor of the first Black doctor in Clarksville, Burt is currently used as an education center. Burt's alumni, dating back to the class of 1921, have become active in planning and participating in reunions every two years, generating funds to provide scholarships for their descendants who live all over the country.

Education was important to my family and Burt High School played an important role in the community and with my family as well. My older sister was valedictorian in 1963. My younger sister was salutatorian in 1968. I was salutatorian in 1966. Doing well in high school was not automatic for me, my siblings, or the students of my time. You worked and earned your grades, and you valued the knowledge that you acquired. Also, your teachers expected you to do well and prepared you from Day 1 in elementary school. My first-grade teacher, Ms. McReynolds was very strict. Ms. Quarles, who taught me in Grade 2, was colorful and an excellent teacher, one you would never forget. She was also one of my dad's elementary students. I liked all my teachers and lived only two houses from my cousin who taught Grade 5 in the elementary school. Teachers were fixtures in our community. They attended the same churches and shopped at the same corner grocery stores. They were real people in a community where everybody knew everybody—kids, parents, and teachers. Teachers could correct students, no questions asked.

Our elementary school, Cobb Elementary, was small with one teacher per grade to serve the city's Black community. However, our high school served the city and the county, including a Kentucky county. The state line ran through the center of Todd County. On one side of the street was Tennessee. On the other side was Kentucky. Black students from Guthrie, Kentucky attended our Black high school. They were students primarily from county farming areas and were not allowed to attend the segregated white high school in their Kentucky home county.

English was my favorite subject in high school and Ms. Flowers, who taught freshman English, was my favorite teacher. Several of my extracurricular activities were English-related. I was a columnist for our high school newspaper as well as editor of our yearbook. I was an officer of the Thespian Society, our drama club. Mr. Williams was our sponsor and my favorite teacher when I was a senior. I was a member of the National Honor Society and vice-president of the Senior Class.

Earning the honor of valedictorian or salutatorian also earned scholarships, which were actually work-study arrangements at Austin Peay State College that admitted its first Black students during the late 1950s or early 1960s. A minister of one our Black churches, Rev. Daniels, was one of the first Black students to attend. When I enrolled with a $20 registration fee and $12.50 book fee, few Blacks from the community attended Austin Peay which became a university in the late 60s. I lived at home and walked the mile and a half to the campus each day, approximately the same distance that I had walked to high school every day, except I walked in a different direction.

As a college student, I worked in the English Department doing research, making copies of instructional materials, and grading papers for various professors. I performed similar tasks in the Psychology Department; and I worked in the Public Works Department at Ft. Campbell, carpooling with others who worked at the army base. Those workers never charged me a dime to ride with them. Austin Peay grew rapidly as Black students from Hopkinsville, Nashville, Chattanooga, and Memphis began attending. More local Black students also enrolled. Eventually, the college bought additional property nearby and expanded its campus.

Mom, our family's major bread winner, put in double duty to help the five of us acquire an education. She worked as a domestic in private homes and worked as a cook in a catering business that she did not own. Because of her support, my brother went to Tennessee State College and became a minister, even though he almost gave Mom a heart attack when he told her he wanted to be a professional athlete. My eldest sister married. My sister next to me became an elementary teacher like my dad. My younger sister attended nursing school, and I followed my dream of becoming an English teacher.

Maintaining a 3.6 grade-point average while working on campus, I kept my scholarship for the four years until I graduated. As an education major, I took courses for my English major and one course for teaching English in the high school. I spent a semester student teaching in Grade 7 and Grade 8 classes at Greenwood Junior High School, an integrated school. While my cooperating teacher, Ms. Pelligo, was helpful, her students were in higher level courses and were all-white except for one student. The experience did not provide any major challenges.

Teaching in Louisville came about because of my husband's job. My husband, Howard, graduated from Austin Peay and was a member of the Louisville Colonels professional basketball team whose home base was Louisville at that time. The Colonel's management team arranged interviews for me with the Jefferson County school system. I was offered a position at Stuart High School beginning the Fall 1972-73 school year. With time on my hands, I decided to begin substitute teaching. On the recommendation of a friend, I applied and was hired as a permanent substitute for Spring 1972. I began that January at Shawnee Junior High School. I will never forget the greeting from one of my classes, "We ran the lady out and we're going to run you out." My response, "I don't think so!" At the end of that school year, Mr. Harris, principal at Shawnee, offered me a permanent position teaching full-time there. I resigned from the upcoming position at Stuart and accepted the position at Shawnee Junior High where I taught three years prior to merger which began the 1975-76 school year.

In the 1970s, life looked so bright for minorities. We had moved past segregation and wanted to take part in the American dream. The students at Shawnee needed help to do so. I saw students struggling with poor language skills who could not code and decode. It never occurred to me that students would/could not read. Kids could speak well, but they wrote in all consonants, and again—they could not read! I felt that English was the bridge. Students would not be successful if they did not understand the language. Reading and language were important for students' success and I needed to be at Shawnee where people needed my help. My team designed and implemented a schoolwide reading course for improving reading skills for all students. Our entire Shawnee Junior High School faculty and staff participated in professional development to learn to teach reading. Ironically, 40 years later, middle schools are still dealing with the same problem—students cannot read!

I spent 30 years at Moore High School. Transferred to Moore because of desegregation, I drove 30 minutes each way to Moore and never requested a transfer to a different school. Why? Because the students at Moore needed me. Kids needed to see teachers with Black faces, especially those kids who were bused to Moore from Black neighborhoods. When I began at Moore, I taught high school classes on the junior high school side of the building. The school had 1800 students Grades 7-12 and I taught fewer than ten Blacks. On one occasion, a student said, "Ms. Wright, will you give me a note to see my counselor? I am the only one in here. I will be the only Black. I won't have any friends." I told the student, "You stay here. I'll be your friend." The student stayed and made a "C" in the Honors course. Years later, she came back to visit me.

Unexpectedly, I discovered there were both Black and white students at Moore who could not read and contributed to the dilemma that Black students had to take a course in African Geography. If you cannot read English, how are you going to read African names? The remedy—the teacher turned out the lights, turned on a film, and the kids learned nothing except how to become racists and many still could not read.

I had three student deaths during my tenure at Moore. One of my students in Senior English that I had known since his freshman year, was a cut-up in the halls. When a fellow teacher saw his name on her class list, she said, "This has to change. I will not be his teacher." I said that I would take him and added him to my class list. I had no problems with the student. He performed well for me and was always on his best behavior. One week after school ended, he was found shot in the head at McNeely Lake—drug deal gone wrong. When I attended his memorial services, I told his mother how much respect I had for her son and how much I had enjoyed being his teacher.

Another student, a white female whom I will refer to as *Carlie*, loved Black boys and loved Ms. Wright. She would come by my room after school just to talk. During her senior year, she became pregnant at the end of the school year. That fall, the young woman and her boyfriend came by to visit. Her parents had put her out, but she later went back home. Her boyfriend came by one afternoon to tell me that the young lady had her baby but was back in the hospital. She passed away from an infection related to childbirth. I was crushed! Her funeral was very difficult because her life had held so much promise.

Ironically, I met the third student who passed away as a teen through Carlie. During one of those after-school visits, she brought another kid whom she had known since middle school. He was a tall, handsome, very well-mannered Black male. When Andy was 15-years-old, his family had moved to North Carolina to keep the dad's job with one of the tobacco companies. They left Andy alone in the family home. A year later the family home went into foreclosure, and Andy became homeless. He stopped by Moore one day before classes started, probably because he had nowhere else to go. He was living in his car! As he assisted me and other teachers in setting up our classrooms, he shared the difficulties of being alone in the city. When he left, the other teachers and I agreed, "Andy needs a home!" The next morning before school began, we got the news: Andy had wrecked his car that night. He did not survive—more potential lost!

Staying at the same school for 30 years, you get to know families and you know when it is time to retire. When you have a 16-year-old student who tells you, "My mom said you were her teacher," or the kid who says, "Mom said she read *Beowulf* when she was in your class," you have to ask yourself if you have become stagnant. You may still have your moments like working with average juniors and homeless children, helping them improve their work ethic; or knowing that a student requested your Honors English class, telling the counselor, "Put me in her class. I will work as hard as I can." You also know that you are not as young; not as enthusiastic; and it is more difficult for you to create a level of excitement within your students so that they want to come to class and are excited about learning. When you notice what energy first-year teachers bring; that kids are no longer begging to read *Romeo and Juliet*; and your eyes do not light up in anticipation of teaching it—the time has come to move over.

I loved teaching! I enjoyed the classroom. I met students where they were and took them a couple of steps further. I created lessons that built on each other. I tried to do different activities like learning games with candy prizes; giving student stickers; and creating word walls. My objective for my students was to create a love for English, a love for school, and a love for learning by making it fun. I am a firm believer that in every learner there is a kid, too, and to make students successful, you really must touch them.

Today's young teachers have their work cut out for them in their efforts to touch their students. In my generation, we had confidence in schools, built on respect and mutual trust that teachers had the best interests of students in mind. We believed that teachers cared about their students and would do what was needed to help students personally and academically. Our teachers wanted us to have equal access to resources and prepared us to have equal access to opportunities. Lack of trust among students, parents, and teachers exists today. Trust was eroded when we moved from neighborhood schools. We want Black kids to have the same advantages of other students, but we may not be preparing them at the same level of excellence or holding high expectations for all students.

In my day as a student, we spent time thinking and reading to experience the world. We used our minds to memorize poems and songs. We played games to train our minds. We made our own entertainment. We had to transfer what we heard on the radio to a vision that we could close our eyes and see. I could visualize a basketball game from listening to the commentator on the radio. Living in today's modern world, students say they don't need to know how to read, spell, or memorize. They say that they can, "just look at the pictures or find the information on their phones."

Today's teachers have a tough act to follow as academic expectations continue to increase and resources to fulfill those expectations dwindle. Kids come to the table at different points and learning curves are in wide variation. Teachers may have kids in kindergarten who cannot hold a pencil; do not know their ABCs; cannot count to ten even when using their fingers; and may not know their real names. These are the same kids who may be in education environments where instructional resources are limited, and teacher expectations vary according to where students live; what their parents do for a living; and how the kid looks.

Teacher attitudes are major issues and challenges for students. Whenever any teacher holds low expectations for any child, they hamper the education process. When they fail to engage Jonnie because he is a reluctant learner, they do disservice to the profession and to the student. How does a teacher really know who can learn and who cannot? They do not know and cannot tell!

Teaching is not an easy job and individuals who choose teaching and do it well, should be applauded. Teachers should be given their due respect. They are more than glorified babysitters and they need help and support from parents and from the students they teach. Parents have a hand in educating their children because learning should begin at home. Some students are doomed before they start because their parents are not engaged in parenting. Parents of old expected their kids to learn. If those parents believed that their children were not putting forth the effort, they might say, "If that is all you can do, I might as well break your plate. Why should I feed you?"

Teachers learn over time. Most do not begin their careers as great educators, but I believe they all want to be good teachers. As good teachers, their ideal should be to inspire their students, but they may not do it consistently. Over time as their skills develop, they are able to inspire kids 90 percent of the time. They can reach all kinds of students. They are calm during chaos and make students want to learn. Great teachers are optimistic. They truly believe every kid can learn something and they communicate that belief to their students— yes you can, if you want to! Great teachers are creative, communicative, concerned, and competent. They are able to discern differences in the needs of students and adjust instruction to meet those various needs.

We must have outstanding teachers in today's schools. Expectations are key to student performance and teacher success. If teachers have realistic expectations, our kids will try to live up to them. No child wants to be a failure and no good teacher wants their students to fail. Be certain, if teachers expect nothing, they will get nothing. However, our students deserve teachers *who can open their minds to a taste of everything.*

Daisy Wright is considered an outstanding teacher by her principals, students, and fellow teachers. For many years, she served as mentor-teacher for first-year teachers. She also worked with teacher-education majors preparing for the PRAXIS examinations, the state required examination for teacher certification. She is adamant in her beliefs about the value of education and the need for outstanding teachers for today's students. Daisy is married to Howard Wright, a former professional ABA basketball player and retired educator as well.

4

TEACHER JOURNEYS

Legacies and Legends

Legacies and
Legends

Legacy: Something handed down by a predecessor.
Legend: Someone extremely well known, popular or
famous especially in a particular field or area of expertise.[7]

TEACHER JOURNEYS IS HUMBLED TO SHARE A FEW STORIES of outstanding educators recognized in the Louisville community by the naming of schools in their honor. Minor Daniels, Lucie DuValle, Lyman T. Johnson, Milburn T. Maupin, and Albert Meyzeek are included as **Legacies,** honoring their work, achievements, and vision. As an elementary student, I travelled to far-away countries and learned to dream by reading books at the Western Branch Library whose existence is attributed to Albert Meyzeek. I also attended the Jackson Junior High School that later became Meyzeek Middle School. Milburn Maupin was my principal at Jackson Jr. High School. Lyman T. Johnson taught my mother, my sister, and he was my teacher. His influence has been paramount throughout my life and the lives of several of my family members. In addition, as I completed requirements for a bachelor's degree to qualify for a Professional Commitment, I worked as a long-term substitute teacher at DuValle Junior High School, Ms. Lucie's namesake. Finally, I had the distinct pleasure of working with Minor Daniels during my tenure in Human Resources at the Jefferson County Public Schools. On one occasion when I wanted to buy new equipment at the end of the budget year, I did not have enough money left in my budget. Minor learned of my predicament and gave me all of the available money in his budget to buy the equipment.

Each of the individuals noted in this section is deceased. However, their students, colleagues, relatives, spouses, and children helped make their *Journeys* come alive. Our **Legacies**' contributions as outstanding educators remain cornerstones in the Louisville community today. In addition to the Legacies, two other individuals are well known **Legends** for their contributions to the educational landscape.

While Rev. Dr. Clyde Liggin and Dr. Sam Robinson do not have schools named in their honor, they are recognized throughout the community as staunch soldiers who encouraged, created, and supported educational opportunities for African-American children. Dr. Liggin touched thousands of students while serving as principal of Virginia Avenue Elementary School and Coleridge-Taylor Elementary and as a minister in the community. The school culture, curricular offerings, and teacher-student expectations that Principal Liggin expounded continue today as models for elementary schools seeking ideas for positively impacting diverse learners.

Dr. Robinson, the only living member of this prestigious entourage, made his mark while principal and during his reign with the Lincoln Foundation. The Foundation sponsors the Whitney M. Young Scholars Programs that assist talented, socio-economically disadvantaged youth in their academic pursuits. Dr. Robinson's vision and persistence were instrumental in expanding and maintaining the financial stability of the Foundation's educational enrichment programs that continue to impact students across the region.

I have grown to know Dr. Liggin through his family, through several teachers under his principalship, and through students under his tutelage. However, I have known Dr. Robinson from the beginning of my career as an educator. As some may recall, it was Dr. Robinson whom I called when I began pondering writing this book. His wisdom, foresight, and reach into the educational arena is recognized and appreciated by a nationwide audience. So, thank you all, **Legacies and Legends,** for your enduring gifts to the profession and to the community.

Lucie N. DuValle

Principal and Prophet (1868-1928)

First Woman Principal in the Louisville City School
System and Namesake for DuValle Junior High School,
Opened in 1956

In 1956 a new junior high school was opened in West Louisville due to the overcrowded conditions of the area that was once considered "Little Africa." The area had been rebuilt with new housing "Projects" that accommodated various family sizes. The new school erected at 3500 Bohne Avenue was dedicated November 13, 1956, after the completed construction of the Joseph S. Cotter Elementary School included in the junior high school-elementary school complex. Earlier in 1954 when the

Courtesy of Jefferson County Public Schools Archives

school complex was being conceptualized, proponents suggested various candidates for "naming rights" for the schools. Among those candidates was Lucie DuValle. Her strongest proponent was Marguerite Parks who collected and developed the various artifacts presented to the Louisville Board of Education supporting naming the junior high school after Ms. DuValle. The following excerpts are part of the artifacts presented to the BOE. [8] Ms. Parks wrote:

December 1, 1938, marked the tenth anniversary of the death of an outstanding educational prophet in Kentucky. The name "prophet" may be applied to one who foretells future events. The prophet is an advanced thinker, seeing beforehand the things that are to happen and making corresponding changes in the present. Such a one was Lucie N. DuValle of Louisville, Kentucky. The story of her noteworthy achievements as a pioneer in the case of public school education on the elementary level reveals Lucie N. DuValle to be not only a great teacher, but one of the brightest and best of the early morning stars of prophecy.

A great historian tells us, "Happy are the people whose annals are short." Perhaps this is true of individuals as well. Reviewing her life one might say Lucie DuValle was born, reared and died in Louisville, Kentucky. She lived and breathed for the thousands of Louisville school children who came under her tutelage. Her mother used to tell her that the only home she really needed was a tent to sleep in pitched just as near the California School (now Phyllis Wheatley) as she could get it. Her mother also recalled that at four years of age, she attempted to read the newspapers and always treasured her books above all other possessions.

Lucie DuValle was the eldest daughter of a widowed mother who had three other daughters. The early struggle of the family to gain economic independence was said to have given Lucie a strong economic sense which was an asset throughout her life. She was educated in the common schools of Louisville. While quite a young woman, still in her teens, Lucie became a teacher in the graded schools of Louisville. She rose steadily from the ranks until she was appointed principal of what is currently Phyllis Wheatley Elementary School. Lucie's success as a principal spanned over 40 years. In all of those years she was never known to be absent or tardy. She was said to be "a living witness and inspiration to her students for punctuality and regularity."[9]

Ms. Parks said that, "Lucy was described as a charming personality—gracious, intelligent, lovable," and quoted one of her former students who said, "She gave you encouragement to go forward. I remember well the night I graduated. A beautiful token bore her name and it read, *Acquit yourself like a man.*"[10]

Miss DuValle was considered a devout Christian who loved her church, the Episcopal Church of her childhood which she attended and supported regularly every Sunday until the week of her death. Ms. Parks comments indicated that Ms. DuValle's death was unexpected and a surprise to many. She indicated that Ms. DuValle's heart attack came suddenly while she was at home on Saturday, December 1, 1928. Ms. DuValle had been at her post of duty at her school the day before, and only the immediate family knew she was not her usual self and was not feeling well. Ms. Parks also noted that Ms. DuValle's career as principal of Phyllis Wheatley School was outstanding because of the distinctive innovations made by her in the elementary school of that day. Ms. Parks also attributed the modern curriculum changes, school citizenship, and extra-curricular activities to Miss DuValle's thinking and organization that she implemented 30 years before although her courses and innovations were called by different names.

As part of Ms. Parks' artifacts, the secretary of the Kentucky Negro Education Association (KNEA), Mr. Atwood S. Wilson, principal of Central High School and former pupil of Ms. DuValle, recalled some of the activities which were in operation during his elementary school days. Mr Wilson indicated that:

> There was a daily inspection for cleanliness of the pupils, the provision of soap and water, and the serving of school lunches to undernourished or indigent children. Good citizenship was instituted by participation of students as traffic directors and class officers. There were assembly programs featuring reading and discussion of such stories as *Pilgrim's Progress* and *Black Beauty*. At dismissal time, a bell for boys and a bell for girls was rung five minutes apart, facilitating less congestion in passing. This arrangement also tended to minimize problems of loitering boys and girls on the streets.[11]

Ms. Parks also indicated that during Ms. DuValle's tenure, the school was the actual center of community life. Miss DuValle organized the first "Parents Meetings" before we had the PTA. Mother Clubs and neighborhood groups provided extra equipment needed at the school due to the principal's advanced ideas. One notable instance identified is the provision of a piano for the kindergarten class. This school attracted city wide attention after a visit from The *Courier Journal Newspaper* whose reporters wrote about the school including the following comments:[12]

> Six years ago (1898) there began among these children—existion for a large part in discomfort and destitute of training that would fit them for better living—a movement for manual training. They did not call it that. It had no place in the recognized curriculum of the school, no paid instructor or outside aid from affluent friends, but the need was great and the invention matched the need. Twenty-five volunteer teachers were giving their time to this industrial work during out of school hours. Classes in sewing, millinery and carpentry were in progress and the children came gladly in large numbers. Miss Lucie DuValle, principal of the school, dark of face, with a trim figure clad in black skirt and the neatest of white shirt waists and collars, animated in expression, shrewd and capable and quick to respond to every demand upon her attention, speaks with intense enthusiasm of the industrial work. She said that, *"we realize what it means to the children, for manual training is the salvation of the Negro. Some parents have a foolish idea of encouraging their children to go into professional life to be nothing if not doctors or teachers or preachers. Manual training will teach the girl or the boy the value of other work and dignity of labor, that right labor instead of degrading dignifies workers."*

The Courier Journal story also referred to a magazine portrait of Booker T. Washington hung on the wall and quoted Miss DuValle as saying:

He has done a great work for the people who need the practical education. When he visited this school several years ago, he did a great deal for a boy of the school. I had much trouble keeping this boy in school; he could do so little with books. He listened to Mr. Washington's speech and he got a new idea. Later he came to me and said, 'I am going to make something of myself. I can and will be somebody.' He got a fresh start and has progressed satisfactorily since that time.[13]

Ms. Parks' comments in support of naming the new junior high school after Lucie DuValle were numerous and praiseworthy. Her final thoughts included:

This article sets forth the advanced ideas of the first woman principal in the city of Louisville. To her we are indebted for instituting 30 years ago a modern program of education sanctioned now by all leading school authorities.

The activities especially prominent and unique at her school to which we have called attention are four. They would now be called (1) a program for health; (2) a program of school citizenship; (3) a program of parent education; (4) a program of industrial training as an extra-curricular activity. In addition to classes in sewing and carpentry, a class in shoe repairing was first organized at this school, the late William H. Hunter being the instructor. Afterwards, he took charge of a class in shoe repairing at Booker T. Washington School. If we would teach race pride to the colored youth of Kentucky, we may find in Lucie N. DuValle a worthy example. To her we may point with pride as (1) one who chose a vocation for which she was well-fitted; (2) who prepared herself for the vocation continuously; (3) who throughout fifty years of service in that vocation exhibited the fundamental qualities necessary for success. She gave to her work all she had—an abundance of energy, enthusiasm, and faith.

This career story would not be complete if we did not mention the unselfish devotion of the mother and the splendid cooperation of the sisters who made Lucie DuValle's life possible, three of whom have joined her in the great beyond. The remaining representative of this distinguished family, Mrs. Helen DuValle Rogers, now resides at the old family residence in Louisville, Kentucky.

It would be most fitting if the Louisville Board of Education named a colored school of the city in memory of this beloved teacher and principal who gave 53 years of service and devotion to the youth of Louisville. [14]

Courtesy of Jefferson County Public Schools Archives

Lucie DuValle's Sate Teaching License/Certification

Courtesy of Jefferson County Public Schools Archives

Lucie and Helen's thank you letter to the
Louisville Board of Education.[15]

Author's Note:

DuValle Jr. High School closed in 1986 and reopened as DuValle Education Center under the leadership of Ms. Georgia Eugene, a veteran community organizer and proponent of equal education opportunity for poor and minority children. The new center focused on Early Childhood Education, housing Head-start, and Pre-Kindergarten classes for area residents. Currently, the DuValle building houses Carter Traditional Elementary School as well as early childhood programs, a Neighborhood Place Center, and a variety of community and adult education programs.

Professor Albert E. Meyzeek

(1862-1963)

Teacher, Principal, Community Civil-Rights Activist,
"Dean of Negro Educators," and Namesake for Meyzeek
Middle School (Formerly Jackson Junior High School)
Renamed in 1963

Born in Toledo, Ohio, November 5, 1862, Albert Meyzeek, for whom Jackson Jr. High School (Louisville, Kentucky) was renamed, became one of the most outspoken African-American leaders in Kentucky at the turn of the century. During his permanent residence at 1701 West Chestnut Street until his death in 1963, Meyzeek witnessed the teetering evolution in the treatment of Blacks, their bid for access to quality public education, as well as the awakening desegregation of public facilities and housing. Meyzeek's Grandfather Lott was

*Courtesy of Jefferson County
Public Schools Archives*

a Pennsylvanian who became an Indiana farmer and is credited with organizing the Ohio River portion of the Underground Railroad with the help of Harriet Beecher Stowe's brother, Henry Ward Beecher, a Presbyterian minister. Lott's farm is thought to be one of the hiding places for runaway slaves who navigated the freezing Ohio River or who escaped, hiding along the highway or through the cavernous terrain of the underground route.[16]

Chatham, Canada, which has historically been identified as the terminal station of the Underground Railroad, was the home of Meyzeek's father. Mr. Meyzeek often related the story of how his grandmother Mary Lott brought her children, including Albert's father, from Madison, Indiana, to Chatham, Canada, by means of the Underground Railroad when they were forced to flee because of their suspected relationship to runaway slaves. Albert was regaled with inspirational stories of heroism and fortitude by his father. They were supported by recounts of stories in the book, *Uncle Tom's Cabin*.

Fighting for justice and equality was said to come natural to Albert Meyzeek because of his father's and his grandfather's infectious spirits. The only "colored" student to graduate in his class at the integrated Terre Haute Classical High School, Albert was also valedictorian. Although law was his first career choice, he pursued an education degree at the Indiana State Normal School, was awarded a bachelor's degree from Indiana University and also earned a master's degree from Wilberforce (Ohio) University. Upon passing a competitive exam for principals, Albert moved to Louisville to become principal of Booker T. Washington Elementary School, his first administrative assignment in Louisville.[17]

A History of Louisville Central High School,[18] written by Thelma Weathers, notes that Albert was principal of Central from 1895 to 1896, serving as Interim for John Maxwell who resumed his duties from 1896 to 1900. During Meyzeek's temporary appointment at Central High, he was pushed to the forefront as a civil-rights activist. The story for which Meyzeek is noted began with his concern over the lack of adequate reading and reference materials at school for his Central High students. As an alternative, Meyzeek took his students to the Polytechnic Society Library where they were allowed to use the facility on several occasions. It is rumored that Society officials thought Meyzeek and his students were "white." However, after several visits,

Meyzeek and his students were denied entry. This incident sparked his determination to have a library facility with adequate materials and resources where Blacks could go freely, feeling comfortable, safe, and welcomed.

Meyzeek's outrage is said to have led to his meeting with Louisville's Free Public Library Board and ultimately to the establishment of the first "colored" library branch in the United States, the Western Branch Colored Library, established with funds from Andrew Carnegie, a wealthy industrialist whose funding later established the Andrew Carnegie Foundation. Records show that the library opened in 1905 in a temporary location until its final reopening at tenth and Chestnut streets in the Carnegie Building in 1908.

In 1914, the opening of the Eastern Colored Branch Library on the corner of Hancock and Lampton streets was also attributed to the persistence of Albert Meyzeek and his colleague, Rev. C. C. Bates who continuously lobbied for a public library facility to service "colored residents in Louisville's East End." Thus, Louisville became the only city in the United States with two libraries servicing the "colored" communities.[19]

Albert Meyzeek's career spanned more than fifty years as an educator and civil- rights activist. During his career he was charged with training elementary teachers at a Normal School established at Booker T. Washington where "75 percent of the teachers were trained under his supervision" during the 12 years of its existence. He also served as principal of Jackson Junior High School from the time it was built until 1943. He was instrumental in the establishment of a colored branch of the YMCA in the area near Ninth and Chestnut streets as well as instrumental in starting the movement to improve housing conditions in the East End. Because of the publicity around unsafe and unhealthy housing and his organization of a housing club, social workers took note of the movement, sparking the beginning of Urban League work in Louisville.

Outspoken and consistent in his beliefs about injustices rendered to African Americans, Meyzeek openly denounced discrimination of all types, but especially the education of Black children. He was verbal in his description of the differences between "colored" and white school facilities, books, classroom resources, teacher salaries, and employment opportunities. Many believe that his outspoken, determined, and straight-forward persona that openly championed controversial issues prevented Meyzeek from rising to the permanent position of principal of Central High School, at that time the most coveted position of school principalships.

He was "admired by the general public for his forthright attitude on all public questions affecting the race, beloved by his teachers and students, for strict integrity and high ideals. . ." Upon his death in 1963, Jackson Jr. High School was renamed in his honor and is currently Meyzeek Middle School, with a focus on science, technology, engineering and mathematics. Meyzeek, considered "the last of the old fighting guard," was often called "Old War Horse."[20]

Courtesy of Jefferson County Public Schools Archives. Author Unknown.

Sketch of Professor A. E. Meyzeek

Courtesy of Jefferson County Public Schools Archives

Meyzeek's invitation to the Mayor of Louisville for the opening of Jackson Jr. High School.

Dr. Lyman T. Johnson

(1906-1997)

Teacher, Principal, Civic Leader, Social Activist,
Jefferson County Public Schools Board Member, and
Namesake for Johnson Traditional Middle
School (Formerly Parkland
Middle School) Renamed in 1981

I REMEMBER THE FIRST DAY OF MY senior year at Central High School, walking into the building with my schedule in hand, excited and scared that this was my final year in high school. For the two previous years I walked through the Chestnut Street door looking slick in my back-to-school outfit purchased at the Eighth and Broadway Sears Roebuck. I don't remember being scared, however. I was early as usual because I caught the 7 A.M. Broadway bus rather than the 7:20 bus. It only took about ten minutes to get to Twelfth and Broadway and less than five minutes to walk to Chestnut Street. As I strolled past the office, Mr. Johnson was coming out of the door.

Box 11, Series II, Photo Collection
University of Louisville
Photographic Archives

Although I had not been in his class, he was a familiar character since I had spoken to and interviewed him on several occasions in my capacity as a reporter for the *Central Current,* our school newspaper, and I was a member of the student council and various other school clubs that Mr. Johnson sponsored. Mr. Johnson had also been instrumental in my being selected to attend Girls' State, a summer leadership and citizenship program at the University of Kentucky sponsored by the American Legion. Selected female students across Kentucky stayed on campus, debated issues, held political rallies, and voted for their candidates to assume party leadership. There were fewer than ten Black girls in the group of nearly 200. Mr. Johnson tutored me to make sure that I was ready for the experience, that is, I wouldn't embarrass myself or Central High School.

"Ms. Gilbert, (he never called students by their first name), you are in my fifth period class. Good. I will see you this afternoon." He turned left, walked through the door and up the steps. I turned right, walked down the hall toward the back steps to the cafeteria, my main thought being, "Finally, I get Mr. Johnson," meaning, I get to be in Lyman T. Johnson's class at last!

Mr. Lyman T. Johnson was known to me and my sister forever. He taught my mom at Central and she related stories and quotes from Mr. Johnson on many occasions. Mama followed current events religiously, reading the newspaper and watching television news daily. When I was in junior high school, she followed the integration efforts organized by Mr. Johnson, pointing him out during the sit-ins and demonstrations on Fourth Street. She told us things that he had taught her in high school like the "crabs in the barrel syndrome"—when one crab starts climbing up the walls of the barrel and is about to get out of the bucket, then a couple of the other crabs jump up and pull him back down. This was a metaphor of how Black people kept other Black people back when they saw one who was trying to move ahead. Mr. Johnson taught us a different version of the same lesson—when you see people trying to improve their circumstance, don't hold them back, but give them the extra shove that they need to reach the top. This is something that I have tried to practice my entire life.

Mr. Johnson was 91 years old when he died in Louisville, Kentucky, in 1997. He was memorialized as an educator and community activist. A native of Columbia, Tennessee, Mr. Johnson was the son of a college graduate who was an educator and whose parents were slaves. He attended the segregated school where his father was principal, completing his high school education at Knoxville Academy in Knoxville, Tennessee, before attending Virginia Union University for his bachelor's degree and the University of Michigan for his master's degree. He taught at Central High for 33 years, 1933 to1966. My senior year was his last full school year as teacher at Central before he became an assistant principal at Parkland Junior High School. While at Central, Mr. Johnson had perfect attendance his entire tenure. In his biography, *The Rest of the Dream: The Black Odyssey of Lyman Johnson,*[21] Mr. Johnson talks about how he began his career as an educator. He says:

> When I came along, there weren't many professions open to Negroes. Teaching and preaching were about the only ones I could choose from. Since my father and uncle were teachers, that's the profession I finally chose. But I got out of school during the depths of the Depression when there were no teaching jobs open. Then in September of 1933, I got lucky. I was living in Louisville with my sister and brother-in-law, doing odd jobs for my room and board, when a fellow who was supposed to teach at Central Colored High School unexpectedly resigned. It was two weeks before school opened. The Depression was getting worse. Jobs were so scarce that within two days thirty-one people had applied for that job. I was one of them. When the principal looked down the list of applicants, he said, 'Well, if everything else checks out, I'm going to give the job to that fellow who has two and a half years of study beyond the college degree, and he has it in the field we're looking for.' I was that fellow. My last year at Michigan I had taken a special program in education

to get a teacher's certificate. Then I had done my six weeks of practice teaching in Louisville at Madison Junior High School. So I was fully qualified. I got the job, and that first year I taught two classes in history and three in math. (p. 71)

My year as a student under Mr. Johnson was remarkable. He was smart. All of the students in my Government and Economics class were excited to get to class to see what was next as he splattered history throughout our curriculum. He didn't use a book; he told stories. We did have a textbook and had to read portions, analyze, synthesize, and make inferences. We had to think! When we were questioned, we had to stand and deliver. When your answer was challenged, you had to methodically respond to the challenge. We took tests on a half sheet of notebook paper, sometimes using only a fourth of sheet. We debated, sometimes championing positions to which we were diametrically opposed. Mr. Johnson told us that "you have to know both sides of the issue before you can debate it." He was never braggadocios, even when we asked him questions about his experiences. We all knew that he had sued to have the University of Kentucky integrated in 1949, and he won. We did not know anything about his efforts to equalize Negro teachers' salaries. He told us about the NAACP, the National Association for the Advancement of Colored People, and taught us about how the organization worked in a historical context. He was adamant about students registering to vote and getting their parents and relatives out to vote. He said, "What good is it to register to vote if you are too lazy to go to the polls, or too ignorant to know who you are voting for, or what you are voting against."

After I graduated from high school, I did not see Mr. Johnson often, but I sometimes heard him on television talking about community issues and challenges, the draft for the Vietnamese War, and economic issues affecting Louisville's Black community. My exposure to Lyman Johnson and the summer that I spent at Girls' State influenced my decision to attend the University of Kentucky (U of K) when I graduated from Central. I remember Mr. Johnson whispering in my ear, "It won't be easy, but you can do it." While I did not stay at U of K for the four years, I did graduate with a Bachelor's Degree in Political Science from University of Louisville. When I decided that I wanted to teach, Mr. Johnson was assistant principal at Parkland Jr. High School. I became a permanent substitute at Parkland. When I was working on my doctoral dissertation, I called Mr. Johnson when there were discrepancies in historical data about Louisville. When I graduated with my doctorate, Mr. Johnson sent me a message, saying that he was proud of me. I was proud that he was proud.

Lyman T. Johnson is an icon. When I looked at the database to get updated information about Mr. Johnson, more than 5,000 references to him appeared. This is a tribute to his lifetime achievement and distinguished career. He has four honorary doctoral degrees, including one from the University of Kentucky. He is remembered for his leadership in integrating public accommodations, including parks, restaurants, theaters, and libraries. He was also instrumental in desegregating Louisville's and Jefferson County's schools, advocating for merger, and serving as plaintiff in the lawsuit that was finally settled in 1975. He served on the Jefferson County Board of Education from 1978 to 1982. Parkland Jr. High School, where Mr. Johnson served as assistant principal, was later renamed for him, Johnson Traditional Middle School, as a tribute to his contribution to the Louisville community and the nation as a whole. While his wife, Juanita, preceded him in death, upon his death, Mr. Johnson did not have a final resting place because his daughter, Florence, and his son, Lyman Jr., honored his wishes that his body be donated to the University of Louisville School of Medicine, although he was a World War II Navy veteran and could have been buried with honors in a veteran's cemetery.

The University of Louisville, University Archives, houses the collected papers of Lyman T. Johnson, and there is a marker in front of his home at 2340 Muhammad Ali Boulevard (formerly Walnut Street) as a reminder of this exceptional individual. For me, what I will always remember are the lessons of life that he taught his students as he stood on the top of a table as "master" and sent a student to the "auction block" starting the bid on "light-skinned" "house niggers" higher than the bid for "darkies" who would only be field hands; or having five students to stand and another student tying limbs together to reduce those five bodies to three bodies to reflect the "Three-fifths clause" in the Constitution. Mr. Johnson taught us that "Black Lives Matter" decades before the quote became popular. He preached "integrity," knowing who you are and what you stand for. For 40 years or more, I have told my students to "know who you are and what you stand for—lines in the concrete and lines in the sand," another lesson Mr. Johnson taught my mother who taught it to me, only to have it re-emphasized again by Mr. Johnson. His colorful language and examples were honest and real and are reflected in his quote, "I've always tried to teach my students straight history—not colored or white or black or brown or yellow,"—and he did.

Thank you, Mr. Johnson, for your gift to your students and to the community.

Dr. Rita Gilbert Greer
Central High School Class of 1966

Curtesy of Jefferson County Public Schools Archives
Picture of Lyman T. Johnson at the beginning of his
teaching career in Louisville Public Schools.[22]

Milburn T. Maupin

(1926-1990)

Teacher, Principal, Assistant Principal, Assistant
Superintendent, Interim Superintendent, Deputy
Superintendent, Alderman, and Namesake for Milburn
T. Maupin Elementary School (Formerly Parkland
Elementary School) Renamed in 1985,
New School Dedicated in 1998

My dad thought all kids could learn, given the appropriate stimulus and support. He also felt that children needed more than reading, writing and arithmetic, but art and music as enrichment helped develop the whole child. He preached "Excellence without excuses," meaning give it your all, whatever you do.

Dr. Madeline Maupin Hicks,
Daughter

Courtesy of the Louisville
Defender Newspaper

DAD, IN THIS CASE, IS MILBURN T. Maupin, was a Louisville native and career educator who was Deputy Superintendent of Jefferson County Schools when he retired in 1978. Serving as Interim Superintendent of Louisville Public Schools in 1975 prior to merger of the two systems, Milburn, also a WWII veteran, was a product of the Louisville Public Schools and Oakwood Academy in Huntsville, Alabama. The son of Mary and Miller Maupin, Milburn attributed his good fortune to being born in Louisville to outstanding parents. A faded copy of galley proofs of an article "Milburn Maupin's Louisville, Kentucky" found in Dad's papers but from an unknown source, quotes Dad at age fifty. I smiled at the first time reading the article and nodded my head as the facts stated were true. [23]

> Fifty years ago (on March 23, 1926) I had the good luck to be born in Louisville, KY. My good fortune moreover, includes being born to two of the best parents anyone could have. My father, Miller Reuben Maupin, is unquestionably the finest man I have ever known. A "gentleman" in the most literal definition of the term, he, to my knowledge, has never had an enemy in this world. . . Daddy was and is a voracious reader. My first recollection of him is his reading books such as the Bible and *Les Miserable*. But his great love was for figures, problems, and puzzles. . . . . Mother, the former Mary Tacoma Taylor, was the driving force in the home. Her zeal was contagious. It was she who taught all seven of her children to read before entering school.

In the article, Milburn lamented about being the oldest child and the chief recipient of his mother's never-ending admonition because his brothers and sisters would be judged in school by the record that he made. He stated that, "Her tremendous ambition for me led to relentless checking on homework, assignments, frequent visits to whatever school I attended and provision of every kind of lesson she could think of including violin and piano." He also related memories of his childhood stating that, "I was rarely permitted to play with other children in the neighborhood and on those infrequent occasions it was for only one hour."He sang the praises of Virginia Avenue Elementary School principal, C.A. Liggin, whose "total impact on our neighborhood is incalculable," in spite of the fact that he lived at 3508 Greenwood Avenue, a neighborhood adjacent to "Little Africa."

Milburn earned a Bachelor of Arts in Economics and Political Science from Municipal College, the "Colored" branch of the University of Louisville (U of L), and a Master of Science in Education Administration from Indiana University. He completed additional coursework at U of L, the University of Kentucky, and the American Management Association in New York City. His career as an educator began as a social studies teacher in 1949 at Jackson Jr. High School where he later became principal. He also taught at DuValle Jr. High and Central High School. A 1955 Ford Foundation Fellow who observed curriculum practices in selected eastern and Midwestern schools, during his teaching career, Milburn also assisted with textbook selection, writing curriculum guides, as well as authoring resource books about the Louisville schools and guides for health. His works were *Your Louisville Public Schools* and *Keeping Louisville's People Healthy and Happy*.

Assistant principal at Jackson Jr. High School for one year was Milburn's first administrative position. From 1959 to 1965, he served as principal of Jackson Jr. High and Booker T. Washington Elementary schools. His daughter, Dr. Madeline Hicks, related that her mother and grandmother who were teachers at Booker T., both had to transfer when her dad became principal. Mom went to Southwick Elementary school and Grams went to Roosevelt-Perry Elementary. Madeline also stated that:

> Both of my parents were strong believers that with God, all things are possible. By faith in him, our provision would be fulfilled. I remember Mom and Dad discussing at the dinner table whether or not he should apply for principal positions. Mom told him to apply. Dad was reluctant to put himself out there because of an incident that had happened in 1956. When *Brown vs. Board of Education* required schools

to integrate, Superintendent Carmichael put a plan in place for the Louisville Public Schools. Carmichael also made some disparaging remarks about Black teachers during an interview stating: 'Black teachers had to be inferior because they came from inferior training.' Dad challenged Carmichael and led a meeting at DuValle where Black teachers expressed their anger and disappointment. Dad was afraid that he would lose his job, but he spoke out. To apply for principal positions, applicants had to take a national exam. I do not know if it was for everyone or just Black applicants. Dad took the test and was told that he made the second highest score in the District. They would not tell him who made the highest score, but he was hired as principal.

Beginning the 1965-66 school year, Milburn Maupin was the first African-American administrator hired in Central Office at the Louisville Public Schools. As Director of Community Programs, Milburn continued a legacy of "firsts" including the first African-American Director of Title I, the first African-American Assistant Superintendent, and the first African-American head of a mainline department, Human Resource. He also implemented a number of "firsts" including the first full-day Head Start Program; the first elementary guidance program in Kentucky; the first Community School program involving the utilization of school buildings for community and educational related purposes after school hours; and the first Prospective Principal Training Program.

While serving as a career educator, Milburn engaged in a wide variety of civic, social, and professional responsibilities. He served on the Board of Directors for the Kentucky Center for the Arts, the Louisville Orchestra, the American Red Cross, the Natural History Museum, and Norton-Kosair Children's Hospital. He was a member of the Prichard Committee on Academic Excellence, the Old Kentucky Home Council, Boy Scouts of America, the Kentucky Commission on Children and Youth, the Kentucky Education Association Commission on Professional Negotiations, and the Louisville Education Association where he was the first Black association president as well. He also served on the Jefferson County Education Consortium, the Kentucky Humanities Council, the Kentucky Corrections Commission, and the Louisville and Jefferson County Human Relations Commission. In addition, he served on the Louisville Board of Aldermen for the First Ward, the first African-American Alderman in that district representing a predominately white constituency.

Among his many awards and recognitions, Milburn received the Equality Award from the Louisville Urban League. He was recognized as Man of the Year by the Theta Omega Chapter of Omega Psi Phi Fraternity; presented the 1974 Honor Roll of Local Black Achievers Award by the *Louisville Defender*; given the Outstanding Service Award by the Louisville Education Association for his educational and community leadership; presented the Outstanding Service Award by the College of Arts and Sciences at the University of Louisville; and named as the Mayor's Distinguished Citizen for his work with the activities and programs in the Louisville community. Most noteworthy of these honors was the renaming of the former Parkland Elementary School in 1985 to the 'Milburn T. Maupin Elementary School.'

Upon his death, the Jefferson County Association of School Administrators saluted Milburn for his dedication and contributions as an educator. *Torch Topics,* the Association's official newsletter reprinted Geneva Hawkins' tribute to Milburn that she had delivered on behalf of the association. As President of JCASA and a longtime friend of Mr. Maupin, Ms. Hawkins stated that Milburn was a man that you could not forget in part because of his outstanding organizational skills. She also referred to emotional stress, strain,conflict, confusion and controversy brought about by the 1975 court ordered merger and desegregation that created "unresolved problems, unmet needs and administrative infighting at all levels," and how JCASA was able to respond. Ms. Hawkins stated:

> Like a phoenix, the JCASA, under the leadership
> of Milburn T. Maupin, rose from disorganization
> and disorientation to bond loosely organized, often

antagonistic administrator groups into one clear voice—a beacon to safe harbor. . . Milburn lived for something. He did good and left behind him a monument of virtue that the storm of life can never destroy. He wrote his name in kindness, love, and mercy on the hearts of thousands he came in contact with . . . and he will never be forgotten. His name, his deeds, will be as legible on the hearts he leaves behind as the stars on the brow of the evening. Good deeds will shine as the stars of heaven.[24]

In addition, Mr. Maupin's youngest daughter, Jackie, shared these loving and heartwarming memories about her dad.

There are many stories and articles written about my dad, Milburn Maupin, and his many accomplishments as an educator and community servant. However, I want to talk about Dad from my perspective, that of his baby daughter. My father and I had a special bond. After all, he was the one who taught me to ride a bike, fly a kite, and drive a car. He always made me feel like I could do anything if I tried hard enough and didn't give up. And I knew that he was always there to catch me if I fell.

It was my father who I convinced that I really must have a Pekinese dog. He got it for me and I named it Powderpuff. I also told him that I really needed one of the first talking dolls named "Chatty Kathy." He got it for me, but there was a price—good grades on my report card. His lesson for me—you have to work hard and earn rewards, not getting into any trouble.

Dad always loved to garden, growing green beans, tomatoes and greens. Even though I was afraid of bugs in the ground, I would spend hours with him gardening. I remember once telling him that I saw a beautiful worm. That worm turned out to be a snake. When Dad told me, I ran as fast as I could to get away, although I knew he would never let that snake hurt me. He is the one who cooked Sunday dinners and made the best strawberry shortcake. The family knew when he cooked, you had better be on time to the dinner table. Dad always believed in being on time and never showing up late, even if it was only for Sunday dinner.

My father told me that if I studied and got good grades that I could become anything I wanted to be when I grew up. I studied, got those good grades, and became the first in our family to work in finance. Although I miss him every day, I know that I am truly lucky to have had such a great dad.

Jackie Maupin Clay,
Youngest Daughter of Milburn T. Maupin

On a final note, Dr. Hicks, the eldest daughter of Milburn Maupin, offered these personal reflections:

As a product of a segregated Louisville, Kentucky, my father was well-aware that white society and many Blacks, indoctrinated with socio/political/cultural negativism, taught, directly or indirectly by a racist society, that African Americans were inferior.

It was dad's mission to foster just the opposite ideology in the hearts and minds of every student and individual with whom he had any influence. He believed that in this society, African Americans had to work harder, do more, and be better than their white counterparts, if they would have a chance to succeed. He believed that the beginning of their chance to excel began with understanding their cultural past and with their believing in themselves as equal to, or better than, their white counterparts. He wanted them to be better prepared for the journey than those above them would anticipate. He wanted students to have the tools and internal fortitude to make that happen. He believed that exposure to the arts and the expansion of their worldview, the world beyond their neighborhoods, were keys to that possibility. He did not believe in lowering expectations for their educational performance. Instead, he stressed that they could compete well in life, on the world stage, if they were given the proper nurturing and educational preparation that was focused on their individual needs and talents.

Dad believed that God would be with us individually and as a people if we trusted Him and his provision for each of us. He did not believe that with, "true grit" alone, apart from Him, that we would accomplish our life goals. He knew that his own talents in music (as a composer, pianist, and talent, playing horns in the orchestra), his ability as an orator, writer, educator, and school administrator, were accomplishments by virtue of God's work and gifts to and through him.

He encouraged my sister and me to think outside the cultural norms of our time to explore our career paths. I pursued a career in dentistry, a field that was male-dominated when I started in dental school as the first African-American female student to "ever" attend the University Of Louisville School Of Dentistry. My sister pursued and excelled in the world of finance as an investment banker. It was dad's life goal to expand the thinking and the number of students who would win at life by virtue of the gift of a great, well-balanced education and the belief that they were created by God to WIN!

Dr. Madeline Maupin Hicks,
Eldest Daughter of Milburn T. Maupin

Curtesy of Jefferson County Public Schools Archives
Dedication Program for the original Milburn
T. Maupin Elementary School

MAUPIN

ELEMENTARY SCHOOL

DEDICATED 1998

JEFFERSON COUNTY
PUBLIC SCHOOLS

BOARD OF EDUCATION
JOSEPH L. HARDESTY, CHAIRMAN
CAROL ANN HADDAD, VICE-CHAIRMAN
SAM CORBETT
ANN V. ELMORE
JOYCE McCLAIN
BEVERLY MOORE
DOTTIE PRIDDY

EPHEN W. DAESCHNER, Ph.D., SUPERINTENDEN

FRANK J. COLLESANO, Ed.D.
CUTIVE DIRECTOR, FACILITIES/TRANSPORTAT

JOHN R. LEE, DIRECTOR, FACILITY PLANNING

McCULLOCH SMITH ARCHITECTS
SLESSER ENGINEERING
BIAGI CHANCE CUMMINS LONDON

Curtesy of Jefferson County Public Schools Archives

Dedication Plaque in newly erected Maupin Elementary School

Minor Ulysses Daniels

(1942-2008)

Teacher, District Administrator, Community Activist,
and Namesake for the Minor Daniels Academy
(Formerly Breckenridge Metropolitan Alternative
School) Opened in 2015

*The following story of Minor Daniels is composed and
contributed by his wife, Jessie who indicated that,
"Minor is and always will be my hero."
Jessie Daniels, widow.*

MINOR ULYSSES DANIELS WAS A "gentle giant" of six feet, four inches who was always considered an impressive figure when entering a room, being noticed in a crowd, or speaking to or in a group. He was an educated African-American male who was respected and considered a role model for children, youth, and adults in schools and the community at large. He had a quiet and thoughtful demeanor and was well-liked

*Curtesy of Jefferson County
Public Schools Archives*

and respected by neighborhood residents, friends, classmates, and co-workers. Minor was always helpful and appeared to be a "natural-born" leader.

Born in Louisville, Kentucky on March 21, 1942, as the ninth of ten children of Mr. William Henry and Mrs. Evabelle (Overstreet) Daniels, Minor grew up in the Russell Neighborhood in western Louisville. He attended elementary and middle schools in the Russell and Portland neighborhoods, respectively. In Russell, he attended James Bond Elementary School, which was renamed Dan C. Byck Elementary School; and, for one year, he attended Madison Junior High School (which became Russell Jr. High and currently houses elderly and disabled residents). Minor completed his middle school education at Western Middle School in the Portland neighborhood.

During his childhood and youth, Minor joined R. E. Jones Methodist Episcopal Church and remained a member until R. E. Jones was closed in the late 1980s. He was a member of Boy Scout Troop No. 82 and walked the 50-mile Lincoln Trail to earn the Lincoln Trail Medal of Honor. He completed all Scouting requirements to achieve the status of Eagle Scout.

Knowing early in life that he needed to become responsible for himself and to help others, Minor, as a middle school student, became a paperboy for the *Louisville Defender* newspaper. In high school, he became a typesetter for the newspaper and a party server for the newspaper's owner, Mr. Frank L. Stanley, Sr. He delivered newspapers to residents of the Russell neighborhood and served food at Mr. Stanley's Derby parties.

As a teenager, Minor became a charter member of the JBB Delphi Club, a socially conscious organization for high-achieving, Black males. The club held wholesome picnics, parties, and dances that promoted positive attitudes and behavior among its members, friends, and community participants.

Attending Louisville Male High School to obtain his high school diploma, Minor was a member of Male's ROTC and basketball team. Often capturing the spotlight for rebounding, he was highlighted in the *Courier-Journal* newspaper as a major asset to Male's team. Minor earned his high school diploma from Louisville Male High School in 1961.

Knowing that he wanted to attend college and needed funds to do so, Minor worked, for a short while, at the Phillip Morris Tobacco Company, stocking boxes of cigarettes, and at the Pepsi-Cola Bottling Company, stacking crates of Pepsi-Cola onto Pepsi-Cola trucks. Earning money from the two jobs and receiving family encouragement and a bit of financial support, Minor began to pursue his college education. In 1961, with familial help in securing a work-study program at Kentucky State College (now Kentucky State University), Minor enrolled in Kentucky State, where he completed his freshman and sophomore years from 1961 to 1963.

As a result of his industriousness and his mother's outstanding work in the Methodist Church, Minor received a Bishop Keller Scholarship from the Methodists to support his attendance at Philander Smith College—a small, Historically Black College in Little Rock, Arkansas. Philander Smith is supported by the Methodists, other philanthropists, and the United Negro College Fund (UNCF) or "College Fund," a fund which is now supported by Jefferson County Public Schools employees through payroll deduction, a process that Minor was instrumental in establishing.

Applying and being accepted at Philander Smith in the spring of 1963, Minor transferred from Kentucky State College to complete his college education at Philander Smith College. Adding his Bishop Keller Scholarship to Philander Smith's work-study program, Minor enrolled in Philander Smith in the fall of 1963 and earned a Bachelor of Science in Secondary Education, with Lifetime Kentucky Teacher Certification, from Philander Smith in the summer of 1965.

As a student at Philander Smith College, Minor was a leader of freshman-orientation activities, a junior instructor of sociology, a counselor in the men's dormitory, chairman of the Young Men's Christian Association, a basketball player, and a Philander Smith "Man of the Year." Becoming a member of the national Alpha Phi Omega Service Fraternity, Minor helped Philander plan and develop programs and policies that supported the school's legacy of excellence, while providing flexibility for students to express themselves in wholesome ways. Minor joined Philander Smith's Beta Tau Chapter of Kappa Alpha Psi, a social fraternity that engages college-level men in appropriate fun activities and community service. In fact, Minor was a life member of Kappa Alpha Psi for more than 45 years.

Furthermore, to help Minor earn income in support of his education, Philander Smith's dean of students helped him to become a forest ranger with the U.S. Department of Interior. Assuming his park-ranger duties in Jackson Hole, Wyoming, Minor provided park services in the Grand Tetons National Park, which included security services for First Lady Claudia Alta Taylor "Lady Bird" Johnson.

After graduating from Philander Smith in 1965, Minor returned to Louisville to obtain a job, further his education, and establish a career. He obtained a job at the *Louisville Defender* newspaper, the business for which he worked in middle and high school. During his brief, two-month stay at the *Defender*, Minor obtained printer paper from Henderson, Kentucky, for printing the newspaper and completed other tasks as assigned.

In 1965, Minor obtained the position of Community Organizer with Louisville and Jefferson County's Community Action Commission (CAC)—the city and county's federally funded War on Poverty Program. In this position, he was housed at St. George Community Center at Twenty-six and Oak streets in western Louisville to coordinate community organizing activities with the now-defunct West End Community Council. As a community organizer, he met with West End community residents to discuss their needs and the services of CAC and the West End Community Council.

After becoming employed with CAC, in 1965, Minor and I, his college sweetheart, Jessie Mae Sanders, married in my hometown of Marianna, Arkansas. Ensuring that accommodations and furnishings were available for us to be comfortably housed, Minor rented and furnished an apartment at 1131 South Brook Street, then a diverse, southeast inner-city neighborhood. Demonstrating his maturity as a young responsible husband, Minor had everything in place for us to begin our life together—a marriage that lasted for 42 wonderful years, until his death.

Being proactive in his work at CAC, Minor was promoted to Area Program Coordinator, and approximately a year later was promoted to Director of Community Organization and Neighborhood Operations, a position he held until 1969. As Director of Community Organization and Neighborhood Operations, Minor assisted in establishing the city's and county's "Neighborhood Stations" (now named "Neighborhood Places") to help low-income residents meet their needs, including financial assistance, food, housing, educational support, and jobs. Also, as director, he helped to establish program activities at middle schools and community centers to engage families in fun learning activities after school hours. For example, Minor was instrumental in developing a cooperative liaison among CAC, Dr. James Coleman (principal at Russell Middle School at that time), and the Louisville Independent School District to implement the Learn More, Earn More Program designed to helped low-income residents improve their educational skills in support of employment. Parents learned to use the then technologically new IBM typewriters, with some of the program graduates obtaining clerical positions with CAC and other community agencies and organizations. Family activities included parents and their children participating in fun activities together, in martial arts, arts and crafts, and other social events.

As a professional with CAC from 1965 to 1969—a time when urban planning and community-development initiatives were moving forward in Louisville and Jefferson County—Minor enrolled in the University of Louisville's Urban Studies Center. Along with other urban professionals, he helped to establish the University's Master's Degree in Community Development. As a part of the program, Minor and other Center students studied "New Town" developments in England and Europe. The study trip helped Minor and the students to learn how government and citizens worked together to develop new towns in war-torn areas and in areas where more land was needed to support population growth. Minor earned a Master's Degree in Community Development from the University of Louisville in 1971. Further, to assist in understanding urban crises, Minor completed two programs of Advanced Studies in Urban Problems—one at Columbia University in New York City and another at Temple University in Philadelphia, Pennsylvania.

In 1969, Minor accepted a teaching position at Meyzeek Middle School in the Louisville Independent School District, and, in that same year, was promoted to the Central Office position of Director of Employee Staff Development. He also held other administrative positions, including Coordinator of Athletics; Coordinator of Safety; and Director of Career Opportunities Program (COP), which helped Vietnam-era veterans and other community residents earn a college degree.

Always striving to improve himself, in 1973 Minor earned a Master of Science in Education, with emphasis on urban education, from Indiana University. Continuing to expand his knowledge, he enrolled in doctoral programs at the University of Louisville and Union College in Jackson County, Kentucky, from 1973 to 1975. Although he did not earn a doctorate degree, he did earn a Professional Certificate in School Administration and Supervision from the University of Louisville. Also, in 1972-1973, Harvard University invited Minor to earn a doctorate degree in education. However, because of already established commitments, Minor expressed his gratitude for the opportunity but respectfully declined the invitation.

In 1975, after the Louisville Independent School District merged with the Jefferson County Public School District, Minor held several administrative positions. He was Coordinator of Athletics; Coordinator of Safety; Director of Employee Relations and Services; Director of Risk Management; and Executive Director of Business Affairs, which included fringe benefits, employee assistance, investigations, and serving as the District's "Top Cop." In this position, Minor worked with District staff and youth to solve problems that negatively affected teaching and learning. He often met with District court staff to discuss the disposition of JCPS staff and with juvenile court staff to discuss the disposition of youth.

Participating in President Clinton's "Improving America's Schools" conferences, particularly one in Washington, D.C., that focused in part on school safety issues, Minor was interviewed by former U.S. Secretary of Education Richard Riley. Paraphrasing Minor's expressions in the radio-broadcast discussion of youth, school, and community problems—absenteeism, suspensions, truancy, and school and community violence—Minor explained that the problems of inner-city youth are not just the problems of the inner city, but the community as a whole. He said that problems exist among both urban and suburban children and youth; therefore, the problems cannot be compartmentalized to a specific area, be it poor or upper-income. Minor said that the causes of problems must be identified and addressed in both urban and suburban communities. He felt that both the "powers-that-be" and the media focus primarily on poor, urban areas, while ignoring the problems of suburban youth. Consideration of the problems of all youth must occur before "things get totally out-of-hand." Secretary Riley respected Minor's thoughts and the interview was broadcast throughout the North and southeastern United States.

Not only did Minor work in and for the JCPS District, but he also worked in and for the Louisville-Jefferson County community and the nation at-large, as a part of his district-compensated duties or for compensation during vacation and weekends. Always willing to help, Minor accepted consultancies for the following organizations: the Episcopal Diocese of Kentucky; the U.S. Department of Education's COP; Stanford University's Urban-Rural Education Program in the southeastern United States; U.S. Office of Education's Program Development for Minorities; and the U.S. Department of Justice Community Development Division of Community Services. Minor also served on the U.S. Office of Economic Opportunity and War on Poverty program-planning committees; and the U.S. Department of Agriculture Committee for the Development of the National Food Stamp Program.

Being a pillar of the Louisville community, Minor served on many boards, task forces, committees, and councils. His memberships included the now-defunct, West End Community Council; Metro-United Way Governmental Relations Committee; the Louisville Urban League Education, Labor, and Training committees; the Governor's Task Force on Human Services; the U.S Navy Commendation Council; chairman of the Russell Neighborhood and Revitalization Board; the Louisville-Jefferson County Human Relations Commission; the Neighborhood House; the Louisville Community Development Bank and Real-Estate Board; and the Louisville Metro Urban Renewal Commission.

In his many endeavors, Minor always tried to help children, youth, and adults improve their quality of life. Examples of his connection with children and youth include his rearing of five brothers- and sisters-in-law, and the mentoring of a teenager in the Park-Hill Public Housing Development. An example of his connection with adults is the sharing of his personal funds to help a low-income person pay a utility bill, and meeting with community residents to discuss their needs and solutions to meet their needs. Minor accepted speaking engagements in classes and at churches in Louisville and Southern Indiana.

Working tirelessly in all of his efforts, Minor received more than 30 civic honors, awards and citations, a few of which include a *Louisville Defender* newspaper Award of Appreciation presented to him posthumously; a posthumous honor by Shawnee High School Career Academy during its Martin Luther King Day celebration; a Public Risk and Insurance Management Award; a Safety and Loss Prevention in the Workplace Award; Philander Smith College Outstanding Man of the Year Award; the Public Risk Management Association's Public Entity Risk Manager of the Year in 1991; the JCPS Stand-Up Award; and former Louisville Mayor Jerry Abramson's Proclamation of May 20, 1998, as Minor Daniels' Day in Louisville, Kentucky.

After 33 plus years of educational services to the JCPS District, Minor retired from the District in 2003. Two years after his retirement, he returned to work as a substitute administrator, assisting with staff investigations and serving as an assistant principal at JCPS middle and high schools. In 2008, Minor was assigned as an assistant principal at Shawnee High School Career Academy, whose reputation was a school with all-encompassing problems of low-performing students from low-income families. Minor built trust and respect with Shawnee's students and was planning to participate in professional development sessions to return to Shawnee in the 2008-09 school year. However, his return did not happen; he experienced a stroke on June 17, 2008, and died 19 days later on July 6, 2008.

In honor of Minor's work with the JCPS District's UNCF or College Fund, the District renamed its UNCF or College Fund Scholarship the "JCPS Minor Daniels Scholarship." The College Fund Scholarships help students to continue implementing Minor's motto, "Learn to Struggle and Struggle to Learn," a phrase he adopted from one of his employers and role models, Mr. Stanley, the owner of the *Louisville Defender* newspaper.

Having knowledge of urban problems, an educational background, experiences working with children and youth with various kinds of urban problems, as well as the myriad of civic and community activities with which Minor was engaged throughout his career, Minor was honored by the Jefferson County Public Schools that named its merged alternative schools, the Minor Daniels Academy in 2015, recognizing Minor as an African-American educator who was known and respected by children, youth, and adults throughout the community. I am blessed to have been beside Minor as he made his career journey.

Jessie Daniels
Widow of Minor Daniels, Retired Employee
Jefferson County (KY) Public Schools[25]

Rev. Dr. Clyde Absalom Liggin

(1902-1980)

Teacher, Principal, and AME Minister

Reverend Carl Liggin is the eldest son of Dr. Clyde Liggin. A 1946 graduate of Louisville Central High School, Carl is the author of several books about his family, including an anthology about his dad. He continuously extends his gratitude to those who remember and honor his father, a source of his pride and homage.

Liggin Family Photo Collection

MY DAD, CLYDE ABSALOM LIGGIN, WAS A LEGEND IN HIS time. I would like to begin my father's story by sharing a letter that he wrote to me about his life. I am not going to share the entire content, but will share some of the sparks related to his career as an educator, one of the two professions that he loved and felt blessed to be able to fulfill as a calling rather than a job. Dad wrote:

Dear Carl,

I was born on April 6, 1902, the eldest son of Ester Absalom Liggin and Rosa Charlotte Liggin, on the Hugh Hanna Farm, Gibson County, Lyles Station, Indiana.

In 1908 I was enrolled by my parents in the Lyles Elementary School, District 21, in the primer class with Miss Ann Nash, teacher. I continued to attend this school until 1912. Other teachers during that period were: Mr. Mervin Kaufman and Miss Oreatha Green. The principals were Mr. W. H. Langford and Miss Bertha Carter.

(My early religious training was received at the Wayman Chapel A.M.E. Church of Lyles Station, IN; built on Absalom Liggin's, my great grandfather's farm.)

In 1912, my father, Ester A. Liggin, took the family consisting of mother, Rosa Liggin and brother, (George) Everett Liggin, and himself to Terre Haute, IN because of the superior educational opportunities offered at Terre Haute, home of Indiana State University.

(My religious training was continued at the Spruce Street A.M.E. Church of Terre Haute.)

Here (after attending public schools) I matriculated in Indiana State University, then called Indiana State Normal School. This was in the year 1920, month of October. The major portion of my college and university training was to be received in this nationally outstanding university in education where I received the A.B. Degree in 1924 and M.A. Degree in 1935. Post graduate work was done at Boston University in 1949. I received the D.D. Degree from Wilberforce University in 1952.

(On the advice of Professor A.E. Meyzeek, a native of Canada who was a graduate of Indiana University

*in Terre Haute, I came to Louisville from Terre Haute
to seek employment in the Normal School.)*

*My career as an educator started in 1924 as
instructor in education, Louisville City Normal School.
From 1925 to 1931 I was hired to teach Social Studies,
Biology and English at Central High School, Louisville,
KY. 1931-1934 I was Social Studies instructor at
Madison Jr. High School. From 1934 to 1958, I was
principal at the Virginia Avenue School known now
as Jessie R. Carter Elementary School, Louisville, KY.
1958-1969 I was principal of the S. Coleridge Taylor
Elementary School of Louisville.*

*In 1969, I retired from S. Coleridge Taylor School
with a brilliant farewell luncheon at Howard Johnson's
Cafeteria, Brook and Jefferson Streets, Louisville, KY,
Friday, 12 Noon, June 6, 1969. The faculty committee
in charge of affair was Geraldine Louise McCall, Anna
McCormack and LaVera Roland. . . .*[26]

Your Father

Dad's official ministerial career began in 1941 when he was
admitted as a licentiate in the African Methodist Episcopal (A.M.E.)
Church West Kentucky Conference. Over the years, I have heard many
stories about my father, Clyde Liggin, both about his contributions
to the development of the A.M.E. church and what went on in his
schools when he was principal. From my point of view and that of my
sibling, we knew that Dad was a historian and a strong supporter of
Black achievement, perpetuated by positive thinking. His ministerial
philosophy and his educational philosophy complimented each other
to the point that sometimes you did not know where one stopped and
the other began, like being a Sunday School teacher at Quinn Chapel
(KY) and marshalling 13 high school males as a scout master, leading
them from Scouts to Eagle Scouts.

There are many stories that I can tell, but the one that always
makes me laugh is the story about Dad graduating from high school

and not being interested in going to college. My grandfather, who grew up in the country, had a variety of jobs, including laying track for the railroad and working in iron works. Dad worked in the summer on easy "fluff" jobs when he was in high school. When he decided that he was not going to college, my grandparents never lectured, screamed, or questioned his decision to go to work instead of college. Instead Granddaddy put him to work that summer shoveling coal into furnaces at the ironworks. Dad decided to enroll in college—for the October enrollment date rather than the August-September date.

It should also be noted that we had educators throughout our family. Mom attended Normal School. She and Dad met and married in 1925. Mom taught kindergarten, but not in public schools. Her mom, my grandmother, taught at Newburg Elementary School and at Lincoln Elementary School. Papa always wanted to keep an eye on his own children and was adamant about my going to Virginia Avenue. However, when I was in third grade, I was in Grandma's class at Lincoln, the only elementary year that I was not at Virginia Avenue. My uncle, James Edmundson, who was married to Mom's sister, taught at Madison. My Aunt Florence Edmunds taught at Jackson Jr. High School, and James and Sedalia Lomax are relatives who were educators as well.

Papa was a "Possibility Thinker," believing it can be done! The halls and walls at Virginia Avenue were covered with pictures of individuals that were noted to have done it, and stood as beacons of success for poor Black boys and girls to learn about and emulate. They were walls of hope that students, such as Muhammed Ali who attended Virginia Avenue, could look up to and believe, "I am the Greatest." Claudia Smiley Guerin wrote for me "In Memory of Rev. Dr. Clyde Absalom Liggin." It pays tribute to Papa and provides a glimpse of how his students saw him at the first school that he led for 24 years, as well as the environment and experiences that were so instrumental in positively shaping so many students for such a long period of time.

In Memory of Rev. Dr. Clyde Absalom Liggin
By
Claudia Smiley Geurin[27]

Sitting at the southwest corner, at the intersection of Thirty-six Street and Virginia Avenue, is an institution that created the prototype of what I have become today. I can hardly believe that it was in September 1951, nearly 64 years next month, at the age of five that I entered the first grade at Virginia Avenue School.

I did not attend kindergarten because my birthday came in December and after the September 11 cut-off date. I shall never forget the disappointment I felt the year before when my father took me to register on the cut-off date and I was denied admission. I was four at the time, but I remember that day so well. Thanks to my mother teaching me at home, I had no problems with first-grade curriculum.

My first-grade teacher was Mrs. Mae Etta Wilson, a short, small-framed woman who knew my timidity and was sensitive to it. I loved the first grade and took part in my first Christmas pageant, where I played an angel pantomiming to the carol, "It Came upon a Midnight Clear." Mrs. Wilson's class was across the hall from Mrs. Black who was a fifth-grade teacher. My long-range goal was to be in her class when I got to the fifth grade. In those days, elementary school in the Old Louisville Public School System included the sixth grade.

Our principal was Mr. Clyde A. Liggin who was also a minister. Just to look at Mr. Liggin gave you the perception that he was a man who was dignified, professional, and a man of great wisdom. When he spoke, all of the students had his attention whether we were in the auditorium or whether he was making an announcement on the public address system. He had a deep "down in the barrel-like" sound baritone voice.

Every time Mr. Liggin would come to our classroom, every student was on their best behavior. No one wanted to end up in his office to be reprimanded. He had our respect! One day Mr. Liggin came to my fifth grade class. Mrs. Cleopatra Gregory was the teacher who was excited that he had dropped in to greet the students. He awarded me with a nickel because I answered a question correctly that he had asked our class. Oh, boy, how proud I was not only to get the prize, but I was also the first one whose hand went up quickly! I have never forgotten that scene!

Negro History Week was celebrated every February. For one week, we learned and sang Negro spirituals and read poems and excerpts of books by Negro writers such as Paul Lawrence Dunbar and Langston Hughes. We learned that Jesse Carter was the first principal of our school. Today it is called the Jesse Carter Traditional Elementary School. We learned more in that week than students learn today who have a month of awareness of African-American history. During that week, Mr Liggin made sure that all of the students in our school sang the Negro National Anthem, "Lift Every Voice and Sing," by James Weldon Johnson, and that we could recite all three verses of the song. I have never forgotten those words. Wherever I go, whether to a community function or church worship, and it is sung, I still know the words.

My husband also attended Virginia Avenue, and he and I are always sharing our memories end experiences with our son about the school. I am proud to have been a product of the old Virginia Avenue School which was only four blocks from my house and where I got my foundation and the best elementary education in the entire United Sates of America and where I learned so much!

CSG August 2016

I was reminded of one of Papa's sayings when he spoke to his students, "We lead and let those who can, follow." Papa was a true leader when it came to educating his students and when ministering to his flock. Thanks to all who testify to the lasting impressions that he made upon untold numbers of people that he impacted. Ethel Ingram King, author of *From Parkland to the River's Edge* also paid tribute to Papa stating:

> The Rev. Clyde A. Liggin was my principal in kindergarten and through grades one, two, and three at Parkland Elementary School. Parkland was the three-room white-frame building that opened at Thirty-six Street and Southern Avenue (across the railroad tracks.) . . .The Rev. Liggin was also my principal in grades four, five, and six at Virginia Avenue Colored

School in Parkland or "Little Africa" where I was born and reared. . . I highly esteem the late Rev. Clyde A. Liggin. May his name be forever blessed![28]

And my family is truly blessed that Papa left such a legacy.—Carl C. Liggin, Son

Author's Note:

Clyde Absalom Liggin died in 1980. Although he had retired as a school administrator, he continued his work with the A.M.E. Church in Charlotte, N.C., where he resided at the time of his passing. Dr. Liggin received numerous awards and recognitions during his lifetime; however, the students at Virginia Avenue remember him for the culture and environment that he established at the school. "Colored" was dropped from the school name by Dr. Liggin who also organized the first violin classes, school band, drama and glee club, and school newspaper, as well as establishing an African-American history curriculum. Liggin also helped Parkland community gain a branch of Louisville Free Public Library for its African-American citizenry. Although Dr. Liggin was its longest reigning principal, Virginia Avenue School was renamed in 1970 in honor of its first principal, Ms. Jessie Carter. The school is currently part of the DuValle Education Complex and is listed as Carter Traditional School under the Jefferson County (KY) Public Schools.

Dr. Samuel Robinson

Teacher, School Administrator, Principal,
Foundation Director, and Community Leader

Dissertation Title: *Educational Needs of Predominantly
African-American High School Students in Louisville,
Kentucky*

THE MIDDLE CHILD OF NINE SIB-
lings, all of us went to college; eight graduated from college, and four of us hold doctorate degrees. Not bad for children whose
parents did not finish high school! I was
born in Memphis, Tennessee, in 1935, a
time when education was valued by African
Americans, but the reality of pursuing educational opportunities was limited. My
mother was a domestic who did day work
cleaning homes and my father was a truck
driver. They married when they were in
high school and began a family shortly afterwards. We lived in a semi-rural commu-
nity where some factories were located, but we saw lots of gardens and

*Bernard Minnis, Artist.
Curtesy of the Lincoln Foundation*

374

animals as we drove down the road. In our low-income neighborhood, it was unusual for children to go to college. The norm was go to school, quit school before graduating, go to work, help the family pay the bills; then get married and have children who go to school, quit school, and go to work, repeating the cycle.

My parents were inspired by my grandfather, an educator who made sure that my aunts were educated, but not his sons. My aunts were teachers. My parents wanted more for their children than they had. While many of my neighbors thought more about children working to add to the family income to get by day-to-day, my parents believed in working to achieve a higher goal, working to help the family increase its income so that the children could go to college. I had my first job when I was five years old, selling newspapers. Over the years, I worked as a delivery boy, a cook, and a bell hop, and I also worked in a drug store. My family had someone in college from 1940, the year I began working, until 1970 when my youngest sister graduated from Spelman College.

Having three sisters and one brother ahead of me and all attending the same school that I attended, Douglass High School, the Robinson family had a reputation that preceded me. Our school was large with different sections for elementary, junior high, and high school. Students passed from room to room for grade to grade. We had a limited curriculum that included music, art, and some vocational courses. All of the students lived in the community and some of them participated in sports. I did not. I was academically oriented and was known to be ranked first in my class in first through third grade, when a student from Mississippi challenged me for my spot and won. He became first and I became number two. We were antagonistic toward one another for several years before becoming best friends.

Although more than 65 years have passed, I can still name all of my teachers. My first-grade teacher, Ms. Virginia Johnson, was loving, but caring and firm. I remember her making me redo some math and writing assignments. She visited my home and reported on my progress to my parents. I always wanted to be an outstanding speller and she helped me focus. I always wanted to be involved in something. Because of my small stature, football and basketball did not appeal to me, but participating in the Spelling Bee, learning music, singing in the church choir and the choir at school, and playing tennis were a fit for me. I thought I wanted to play the piano until my piano teacher used a ruler to hit my hand when I played a wrong note.

My favorite teacher in junior high school was Ms. Simms, an English teacher. My biology teacher, Mr. Gray, was my favorite high school teacher. He bought scientific equipment so his students could participate in the science fair. He inspired me to major in biology and to aspire to become a doctor. In retrospect, all of my teachers were influential. If students were talented in a particular area, they sent those students to the next level to learn more and to excel regardless of grade. My teachers helped my family that struggled financially with children in college and children at home. They sometimes bought us clothes, gave us lunch money, bought tickets for us to attend cultural events like orchestra performances and tickets to attend the opera. They understood that we were academically talented, but we had limited cultural exposure which was also extremely important. My teachers helped provide that exposure. My brother became an accomplished pianist because of that exposure.

There were 38 students in my graduating class. My Mississippi-born best friend graduated in first place and I in second. We both attended Tennessee State College where my four siblings had attended before me. Again, the Robinson reputation preceded me. I had jobs on campus to assist with costs and I had a scholarship. My brother and sisters were noted for their hard work and academic excellence. They set a high bar that I had to live up to, and I did. I was known on campus as a social activist, engaged in all sorts of campus activities in addition to participating with my fraternity, Phi Beta Sigma, and being a member of three honor societies. I earned a Bachelor of Science in Biology, graduating with honors in three years at age 20. I completed student teaching at Pearl High School in Nashville teaching chemistry. I was certified to teach, but my dreams of becoming a doctor differed because of cost. I stayed an additional year to earn a Master's Degree in Educational Guidance, graduating with honors as well.

My first and only teaching job in Tennessee was at various schools as a substitute. My promising teaching career was interrupted by my being drafted into the Army where I served from 1958 to 1960, assigned as a psychological research assistant. After my discharge, I had the opportunity to stay in Memphis and teach, but I wanted to spread my wings. I heard about Lincoln Institute's recruiting African-American teachers and sent my application. I was interviewed by phone, sight unseen for them, and I had never been in Kentucky. My wife; my daughter who had been born in Ft. Benning Georgia; and I knew two people in Louisville, Joe McPherson and his wife Sarah who had attended Tennessee State.

I taught at Lincoln Institute from 1960 until it closed in 1966. My first job there was teaching biology and algebra. My wife was also employed at Lincoln, teaching social studies, and we lived in Simpsonville. I had the blessing of being mentored by Dr. Whitney M. Young, Sr., who was president of the Institute. During my second year, I was promoted to teacher/assistant principal. We moved to Louisville, and I was provided a station wagon for transportation. Included in my role was transporting Louisville-based teachers to campus. I picked up teachers each morning and delivered them home at the close of the day. Although an unusual arrangement, it worked for the Institute and for the teachers. This was our early rendition of "car-pooling." Eventually, I worked my way up to becoming Dean of Education and administrative assistant to the president.

When Lincoln Institute closed its doors, at the encouragement of Dr. Young I stayed on as campus coordinator for the new school, Lincoln School for the Gifted to open in 1967. At the same time, I began taking additional courses in school administration. We were back living on campus, and my wife was one of the few African-American teachers employed in Shelby County. For three years, I shepherded Black and white gifted, disadvantaged students from all across Kentucky who lived together on campus. The integrated school was very controversial in a time when civil-rights issues were dominant, when students could wear long hair, and when both Black and white students could say things about race in an open environment. Class size dwindled to 10 or 15 students and the Gifted School closed in 1970.

What had transpired at Lincoln drew the attention of educators across Kentucky, including Superintendent Newman Walker with the Louisville Public Schools. Dr. Walker was intrigued by what we managed to accomplish with disadvantaged children and offered me a position in Louisville as assistant principal at Shawnee High School under George Sauer, for the 1970-71 school year. I was promoted to principal, serving from 1971 to 1973. I worked with John Whiting who directed the Shawnee Complex Grades 7 and 8 in the junior high school and Grades 9 through 12 in the high school.

Shawnee High School had an enrollment of more than 1,000 students and employed some outstanding teachers, including Ann Elmore, English teacher who later became a member of the school board; Jeff Brill; Dorothy Franklin; and Melvin Turner who later became instrumental in developing programs for supporting African-American students at the University of Louisville. I did not like dealing with student discipline, but I loved working with teachers to improve instruction. While principal, I helped develop a collaboration with Indiana University (IU) that allowed teachers to work on their master's degrees. Advanced courses were taught at Shawnee in the afternoon by IU faculty. I took several courses with teachers and was later encouraged to complete my doctoral studies because of the number and breath of courses that I had accumulated over the years.

My wife and I took another leap of faith in 1973 when I took a leave of absence from Shawnee to enter the doctoral program at Indiana University. I completed 24 hours of coursework, a dissertation, and a dissertation defense in one year and one summer, graduating with a Doctorate in Curriculum and Urban Education in August 1974, the second doctorate earned among me and my siblings.

I did not return to the Louisville Public Schools upon completing my doctorate. Instead, I was asked to assume the helm as Executive Director of the Lincoln Foundation, the first African American to head a foundation in Louisville, Kentucky. I have always felt that Dr. Whitney Young, Sr. was directly responsible for this opportunity afforded me since he had watched my dedication to the education of Black youth develop over my career. In 1974, the Foundation had limited scholarships and a limited endowment fund. My job was to fund raise and develop unique programs to further the education of African-American youth.

When Dr. Young died in 1975, I was feeling my way, but extending the reach of the Foundation throughout the community by increasing my association with the business, civic, and cultural communities. Integration of the public schools began, and I had a voice in desegregation efforts as co-chair of the council that helped map the desegregation plan for merger. I also had to reach out and go where people were to be heard. My solution was getting involved with the Arts, something that I loved. I met people at Arts functions, the Louisville Orchestra, and the Louisville Ballet. I accepted invitations to serve on executive boards, which gave me exposure to other individuals and they had an opportunity to meet me and hear about our work at the Foundation. I collaborated with the Urban League and the Council for Christians and Jews. Our emphasis in working to support disadvantaged youth was appealing and our efforts to collaborate were fruitful. Additional collaborations with Bellarmine College, Spalding College, and the University of Louisville were successful and provided those universities with an additional pool of smart African-American recruits.

Just as my parents had taught me and my siblings to expand our horizons, I used the same concept to grow the Lincoln Foundation. I became president of the Foundation in 1991. While I was motivated to start programs out of my mission and desire to make a difference, I am a strong believer that you must broaden the horizons of students to help them understand the broader world. This inclusive world view impacted the design of programs within the Foundation and has continued through the leadership of Larry McDonald, the Foundation president upon my retirement in 2000 after 26 years. The Whitney M. Young Scholars Program, a flagship program that the Foundation continues to promote, is one example of the results of financial commitment and support from community business partners, philanthropists, government agencies, social and civic organizations, churches, Greek organizations, and everyday citizens. Project Build, the Nia Day Camp, Neighborhood Pre-School Program, and the We Love the Arts Program are also recognized throughout the community. Continued growth in the Foundation's endowment also has resulted in the purchase of the Foundation's own headquarters here in Louisville.

My wife Hugh Ella and I have been married more than 60 years and have worked together on our shared vision. While I was busy with the various roles that I held, she was steadfast in raising our two daughters while teaching as well, finally retiring in 1986 from a position as a social studies teacher at Iroquois High School in JCPS. We both have continued to get involved in educational issues, and we see a variety of challenges on the horizon. We firmly believe that we need to give teachers support to do their jobs. This includes teachers receiving adequate pay for their professional responsibility, and working on strategies to effectively communicate among teachers, parents, the school, and the community. Students need a voice in education programming. They also need tutorial assistance to stay on track and excel. Scholarships are paramount for poor and disadvantaged students just as broadening horizons are commiserate with reducing violence and pessimism that are causing problems with this same population.

We must recognize contributions of educators who have retired. Vibrant retirees are ignored and sometimes not respected for the knowledge and skills that they could contribute. Parents must be given the tools to help their children learn to read. Furthermore, we are not making the best use of resources in our community, magnificent structures across the community where activities related to school could be conducted with effective planning and coordination and applicable funding. Finally, we see a lack of feeling of community as an impediment. So many African-American educators moved out of the inner-city and did not return. We run in to go to church on Sunday and run back out until the next Sunday, but many do not make that connection to the community.

There are good teachers and there are great teachers. Great teachers have all of the content knowledge that good teachers have, in addition to compassion and awareness. They have a willingness to make a difference and insights into what they are attempting to do as well as the expected outcome. They also have the resources and time to make a difference. When I think of great educators, I think about Dr. Whitney Young, Sr.; Dr. Mary McCloud Bethune and her story in founding Bethune-Cookman College; and Lyman T. Johnson taking a stand and being forthright. One must come from a standpoint of a reverence for God for giving you inspiration to make a difference.

The education of poor and Black children, though identified as challenging, must be among the priorities of our community and our school district. As plans are developed, educators must consider giving more education related to personal culture—local, national, and international; helping students broaden their understanding of compassion; extending mentoring programs—one-on-one mentoring using community resources; and stressing power in numbers—collaborate with big churches, small churches, fraternities, sororities, social organizations—all play a role.

I think mentally, I could teach in today's schools because of my experience and insights, but I do not have the energy and youthfulness that is important as well. My advice to today's teachers would be to become more aware of the importance of political activism; to develop a deeper understanding of your own culture and of the culture of the children that you are teaching; to better prepare yourself with content knowledge and knowledge of how to teach; and to challenge teacher-training institutions to be more responsive to the needs of teachers teaching in urban environments.

Teacher recruitment is important and necessary to sustain the profession. If someone is thinking about becoming a teacher, volunteer for opportunities to expand knowledge of culture and environments of different groups of people; identify a mentor for guidance; and get as much education as possible to prepare yourself. Completing a master's degree is no longer required in Kentucky and other states, but the additional knowledge gained in advanced studies and internships is invaluable. Opportunities to receive exposure to outstanding African-American teachers and mentors and to work informally with African-American children before teacher training are also great recruitment tools. Strengthening African-American educator groups to become more involved with recruitment is also important to the profession.

My nearly 60 years of experience, my competitiveness, and my tenacity have fueled my initiative to create, motivate, and make a difference. I am thankful for the opportunities that I have had to build on a fulfilling career, to contribute to my community, to enjoy the support of a loving family, and to help children.

Dr. Sam Robinson served on a number of Boards and participated in a variety of civic activities throughout the community, including serving for 12 years on the Kentucky State Board of Education, serving on the Board of the Muhammed Ali Center, and serving on the African American Heritage Center Board. He is also a co-founder of the Louisville Chapter of One Hundred Black Men. Upon his retirement, he served as Executive in Residence at Bellarmine University and Director of the Urban Montessori School. He also received a Presidential Appointment from President Carter as Civilian Aide to the Secretary of the Army for the Commonwealth of Kentucky where he advised on what civilians do related to Army installations in Kentucky. Dr. Robinson and his wife have two daughters and six grandchildren. He is a charter member of Westwood Presbyterian Church where he served as Elder, Sunday School teacher, and member of the choir. He holds Honorary Doctorates from Bellarmine University and Northern Kentucky University. Although he has received a number of awards and recognitions over his career, one of his most treasured accolades is a foundation named in his honor and sponsored by his fraternity, Phi Beta Sigma.

5

TEACHER JOURNEYS

21st Century Teachers and Teaching: Who Wants to Teach?

Part 5—
21st Century Teachers and Teaching: Who Wants to Teach?

JOURNEYS—WOW! EACH OF THE STORIES SHARED OVER THE previous pages created various emotions and reactions every time I read them. Sometimes I fought back the tears. Other times memories flashed in my mind of a similar experience that I had encountered. For example, as I saw children hunched and huddled braving the winter cold to walk miles transversing rugged terrain to get to school, to get to their teachers, I remember standing on the corner of Fifteenth and Walnut streets trying to get to my school, my teachers. Holding on to Olivia's hand, I stood behind Mama in her thin plaid dress, short pea coat, white men's socks, and slides. She was barelegged and cold, so much so that the silent snot easing from her nose almost froze on her face as the bitter corner crosswinds in the early morning bore down upon us. Clutched in her hand were the pennies that she had counted out of the glass Ball Mason Jar kept hidden under the head of her sagging brass bed. Those pennies Mama would give to Olivia to pay our bus fare as we boarded the city bus that would take us to the backside of James Bond Elementary, our school that Mama insisted we continue to attend because she wanted us to finish the year with the teachers that we loved, revered, and talked about so often.

The *Teacher Journeys* of the twentieth century educators shared here provide glimpses of another legacy that had begun to slowly deteriorate—the respect for teachers, the value of the teaching profession, and interest in teaching as a career—a heart-wrenching epitaph that we continue dealing with today. Part 5, **21ˢᵗ Century Teachers and Teaching, Who Wants to Teach?** provides an opportunity for me to address this issue by reflecting on the lessons learned from other educators; to share some of the interesting data and research that I have reviewed; and to pontificate about the journey ahead of us as professionals or possible future professionals while we continue grappling with the question, "Who wants to teach?"

Choices and Opportunities

Employment opportunities have flourished for minorities, increasing competition for smart African-American students to even think about teaching as a career choice and making it more difficult for school districts across the country to maintain qualified teaching personnel. In recent years, more African Americans began choosing professional careers as accountants, physical therapists, computer specialists, engineers, pharmacists, lawyers, and vocational and educational counselors. Jobs as managers and workers in industry and manufacturing also have come into play, and many actually pay more than beginning teacher salaries. These employment opportunities continue to pluck education majors from the teacher pipeline.

At the close of the twentieth century, large urban districts across the country were immersed in government-sponsored programs focused on teacher recruitment of minorities and teachers for shortage areas. Grants for creative teacher-recruitment efforts were numerous and were enhanced with district dollars and collaborations with other school districts across the nation. Members of the Council of Great City Schools met regularly to share ideas and possible solutions for increasing the number of minority teachers and teachers needed in identified shortage areas. Alternative certification programs, designed to attract career changers and college graduates who had not found their employment niche in their chosen fields, were abundant across the country as well. However, today, programs designed to attract minority teachers who had been primarily African-American are waning as the term "minority" now includes other races/ethnicities. Also, government dollars for minority teacher recruitment programs have evaporated.

Precedents, like the use of Singleton, one of the policies used across the nation for staffing schools that set guidelines for the percent of minority teachers in a school based on the percent of minority teachers at the school level minus exempt teachers like special education and kindergarten teachers, are no longer in effect in many districts. Teacher hiring and teacher transfers were based on the Singleton ratio requiring schools to be within the school district's guidelines for minority representation among staff. Guidelines were challenged in the courts and lost ground. Also, children of migrants from a variety of countries have changed the student complexion of public schools.

Currently, school districts across the country are suffering from "bleed-out" as teacher pipelines in large urban districts have narrowed and closed in many cases. Across the nation, many colleges of education report decreases in enrollments; several HBCUs that at one time had produced large numbers of Black teachers, are shuttered; and students, regardless of race/ethnicity, are not banging on the doors of school districts' Human Resource (HR) personnel screaming, "Let me in!" In fact, the opposite is occurring. Students are running from the teaching profession and HR personnel are chasing them, in what appears almost a lost cause.

School districts are flashing the same Help-Wanted signs on Web sites, in educational journals, in newspapers and social media advertisements, on bulletin boards at colleges of education, through mailings to former teachers, and even in church bulletins. The same song has been sung for several years now—we need teachers! Ironically, as academic standards are becoming more stringent and students' academic expectations are increasing, **teachers**, the personnel who are to share their academic prowess and help students gain the knowledge and skills that national standards demand are so important, are diminishing.

At the beginning of the twenty-first century, teacher shortages were "spot" shortages, that is, in specific fields and generally in larger, urban school districts. Shortages of elementary teachers were not a major concern. Today, however, shortages appear at every level and in every academic field/subject, with some shortage areas greater than others. A closer look at today's schools may be helpful in understanding teacher supply and demand issues that will be discussed later.

HELP WANTED TEACHERS
Elementary School, Middle School, and High School[29]

SCOPE OF RESPONSIBILITIES
Plans, organizes and delivers the program of instruction based on approved curriculum; monitors, evaluates, and communicates student progress; maintains records and makes reports; enforces Board policies, regulations, and rules; supervises students, and secures and maintains school property and materials.
PERFORMANCE RESPONSIBILITIES AND EVALUATION CRITERIA
Meets and instructs assigned classes in the locations and at the times designated.
Creates and maintains a classroom environment that is conducive to learning and appropriate to the maturity and interests of students.
Guides the learning process toward the achievement of curriculum goals and establishes objectives for all lessons, units, projects, and the like in order to communicate these objectives to students
Employs instructional methods and materials that are appropriate for meeting stated objectives, prepares for classes, and maintains written evidence of preparation.
Assists the administration in implementing Board policies, administrative regulations and school rules governing student life and conduct, develops reasonable rules of classroom behavior and procedure, and maintains order in the classroom in a fair and just manner.
Assesses the accomplishments of students on a regular basis and provides progress reports and counseling to parents as required concerning academic and behavioral progress of all assigned students.
Participates in parent/teacher conferences as necessary to assist the parent's participation and support of a child's education.
Maintains accurate, complete and correct records as required by law, district policy, and administrative regulation.
Continues personal professional growth and upgrading of skills appropriate to teaching assignments.
Attends staff meetings, serves on staff committees, and accepts a share of responsibility for extracurricular activities.
Duties may include performance of health services, for which training will be provided.
Performs other duties as assigned by the principal or school center head.
MINIMUM QUALIFICATIONS
Kentucky certification appropriate to the grade level and curricular assignment Experience and preparation required by the Board

Today's Schools and Today's Students

The National Center for Education Statistics (NCES) maintains the nation's official records and counts of students, schools, and teachers. Beginning the 2015-16 school year, more than 98,300 public schools have been in operation in the United States including nearly 7,000 public charter schools. Approximately 35,000 private schools that also offered instruction within the K-12 arena also exist. NCES reported that at least 51 million students were onboard to receive instruction in Grades K-12 America's public schools in the Fall of 2018. Approximately 15 million of this group were slated for classes in secondary settings, Grades 9-12, while the remaining 35.6 million attended classes for Grades K-8.

NCES also forewarns an increase in public elementary and secondary enrollment over the next ten years. The report indicates that at least one million additional students will be in public schools by 2027. Of the approximately 52 million students, minority students—Blacks, Hispanics, Asians, Pacific Islanders and Indian/Alaska Native students—will constitute a higher percentage than white students. NCES projections also indicate that the percentage of white students and Black students will continue to decline as the percentage of students who are Hispanic, Asian, and Two or More Races will continue to increase. It should be noted that changes in government policies regarding immigration may impact these projections.[30]

Another widely read report, *The Condition of Education,* provides additional characteristics for today's twenty-first century students, indicating that 10 percent of children under age eighteen lived in households without a parent who had completed high school; 27 percent lived in mother-only households; 8 percent lived in father-only households; and 19 percent lived in poverty (2015-2016). It is anticipated that significant changes will occur beginning 2020-2021. *COE* (2019) also indicated that when considering the concentration of public school students eligible for free or reduced-priced lunch:

Higher percentages of Hispanic (45 percent), Black (45 percent), American Indian/Alaska Native (37 percent), and Pacific Islander (25 percent) students attend high-poverty schools than of White students (8 percent) in school year 2015-16. The percentages of students of Two or More Races (18 percent) and Asian students (15 percent) in high poverty schools were higher than the percentages for White students but lower than the nation average (24 percent).[31]

The belief that the education level of parents influences their decisions to enroll their children in preschool programs, is growing. Parents with graduate or professional degrees are believed to be more inclined to enroll their 3- to 5-year olds in preschool programs. COE (2019) projects that the difference of 24 percent fewer parents—30 percent parents with less than high school credentials compared to 54 percent parents with graduate credentials—enrolled their children in preschool and may exacerbate. In addition, at least 6.7 million students or 13 percent of all public school students ages 3 to 21 received special education services at the close of the previous decade. There were nearly five million students who were English Language Learners (ELLs) as well. Students graduating from high school with a regular high school diploma within four years of starting Grade 9 tallied nearly 85 percent. Finally, the national **average** for per-pupil spending continues at less than $13,000.[32] It should be noted that government support for school choice and charter schools is a wild card that may impact per-pupil spending in the future.

Today's Teachers

The U.S. Department of Education has been collecting data on educators since 1987.

A new "National Teacher and Principal Survey" was implemented on a two-year cycle beginning in 2017.

Fall 2018 federal projections from NCES indicated
that the teaching force is growing. It estimated that
traditional public schools in America employed 3.2
million full-time-equivalent teachers while charter
schools employed an additional 6 percent or 218,500
teachers. 2020 may see numbers closer to 3.4 million
teachers employed between public and charter
schools.[33]

Today's teachers are approximately 23 percent male, with women
continuing to dominate the profession at approximately 77 percent.
Nearly 9 in 10 teachers at the elementary level are women, while
approximately 66 percent of high school teachers are female. The
average age of teachers fluctuated during the last several years from
41 to 43 years old. These numbers and percentages are expected to
seesaw as larger pools of teachers reach retirement age and as increased
numbers of teachers enter the profession as their second career.
Furthermore, the teaching force is projected to maintain its white
majority currently at approximately 80.1 percent white, 8.8 percent
Hispanic, 6.7 percent Black, 2.2 percent Asian, 1.4 percent with Two
or More Races, 0.4 percent American Indian/Alaska Native, and 0.2
percent Native Hawaiian/Pacific Islander.[34]

Today's teaching force is a stark contrast to today's student
enrollment. Public elementary and secondary students are
approximately 51 percent nonwhite compared to their teachers who
are approximately 20 percent nonwhite. Teachers as a whole are less
racially and ethnically diverse than their students—as well as less
diverse than the nation as a whole. School districts across the nation
continue to monitor the data to determine how closely their teaching
forces match-up to the national trends that have some negative
connotations. Trends identified in a study by the Pew Research Center
provide food for thought as colleges of education and school districts
grapple with their own data of how student academic achievement and
the factors surrounding the school's teaching force impact each other.
Diversity issues that are highlighted include the following:

- The majority teachers are nonwhite at schools with more nonwhite students, while the reverse is true for schools with more white students;
- In schools where at least 90 percent of students are white, nearly all teachers are white;
- A higher percentage of teachers are nonwhite in schools with higher percentages of students eligible for free or reduced-price lunch;
- Nonwhites represent at least one-third of teachers in schools where at least three-quarters of students are eligible for free or reduced-price lunch;
- Approximately one-tenth of teachers are nonwhite in schools where a quarter or fewer of students are low-income;
- While the number of Black teachers has increased since the late '80s, the percent of Black teachers is declining. The number and percent of Black teachers and Black teacher candidates are lumped under "minority" to meet district diversity goals; and
- Hispanic teachers are overtaking Blacks in many large urban districts. They are currently the second-largest racial or ethnic group among U.S. public school teachers. Approximately 338,000 Hispanic teachers are currently employed, compared to 256,000 Black teachers.[35] Recruitment efforts to increase the number of Hispanic teachers are given as much consideration as efforts to recruit Blacks.

Data also indicate that teachers in general continue to value learning. More teachers held advanced degrees in 2015-16 than they did in 2000. Roughly 55 percent of elementary school teachers and 59 percent of secondary school teachers held a post-baccalaureate degree in 2015, whereas 45 and 50 percent respectively held post-baccalaureate degrees in 1999-2000. Most states do not require teachers to hold master's degrees and Kentucky has recently joined that group. However, increased salary incentives are still among the bargaining power of teachers who continue to pursue advanced degrees. The idea that teachers with graduate degrees make better instructors continues to be a widely accepted perception.[36]

In addition, teacher salaries have been a point of contention for many years. In 2020 the median teacher salary is over $60,000. However, the average starting teacher salary for teachers in many states is below $40,000 although there is a wide variation from state to state. Sixty-three percent of public school districts still offer a starting salary below $40,000. Teachers who belong to unions or education associations are more likely to be satisfied with their salaries than those who are not.[37]

On another note, today's teachers have additional concerns about the profession in general and about their day-to-day issues and challenges. Various reports have enumerated teacher concerns and classroom challenges. Several reports indicate that teachers feel they are trading an increased focus on individual student performance while de-emphasizing social interaction and teamwork skills. Teachers report that they continue to wear multiple hats and often step in to help students in areas and in situations where they may lack training. Because they are multitasking and do not receive actual "breaks," many teachers maintain that they are often forced to neglect their own bodies. The top challenges teachers currently agree upon are the following:[38]

1. Lack of teamwork, empathy, and support between students;
2. Teachers working too many roles at the same time;
3. No time to deal with bodily functions;
4. Teachers being made accountable for more than they should;
5. Not enough time to plan;
6. Excessive paperwork for data collection;
7. Keeping up with expectations of school administrators;
8. Being required to utilize a prescribed curriculum to all types of students;
9. Teacher salaries not commensurate with teacher expectations; and
10. Lack of autonomy.

Teachers feel that accountability for students' success is primarily on their shoulders, and parents as well as students do not own up to their part of the responsibility. Time to plan, prepare, and execute the numerous tasks assigned to them is limited. They are prohibited from executing other tasks that they feel important—like preparing quality content—because of time issues. They suggest that responsibilities to compile large amounts of data for school statistics is also time-consuming and overshadows their primary responsibility—working on students' academic challenges.

Another challenge that teachers identified is growing expectations to offer constant support to students. Providing personalized and outside-of-class help and assistance as well as keeping lines of communications open with parents is another time-consuming challenge. Finally, teachers feel that they are being driven to a one-size-fits-all curriculum approach, being directed to apply a fixed curriculum to students with different needs. Their creativity is being stifled at the same time their instructional expertise is being overlooked when they are not able to tailor content to individual students' needs.[39]

Student Discipline: Teachers' No. 1 Problem

Today's public school teachers are challenged with a wide variety of discipline issues that have gained national prominence from a "big picture" perspective. These issues have related nemesis at the state and local levels. The nation is aware of the devastation caused by mass shootings at schools; they have created continuous anxiety among school administrators, teachers, parents, and students over school safety. Policies and practices are regularly reviewed and modified to address this large-scale devastation at school and district levels, as well as related mental health issues.

For the everyday classroom teacher, however, discipline takes a different shape that relates school and classroom climate to learning time for students. Teachers readily recognize that school disorder and violence have a negative effect on all students. A fundamental belief among past educators and current educators is that a safe and positive classroom climate is essential for student success. However, students' disruptive behavior, tardiness, verbal abuse to other students, bullying, unwelcomed physical contact, cursing, and open defiance are related classroom problems that have been on the rise for the past two decades. Teachers report that they face classroom discipline issues of some kind with their students *every day*. Student-discipline challenges have spurred both new and seasoned teachers to continually seek and learn strategies for helping sustain positive classroom climates which enhance student safety and academic achievement. Furthermore, it cannot be overly emphasized that the discipline challenges that today's teachers face, were not the primary challenges of twentieth century educators, especially when schools were segregated and parents as well as students respected the authority of teachers.

Discipline Reform

Research on school-discipline reform is fraught with questions about the impact of discipline-reform efforts that the national government, state governments, and local school districts are advocating. Spurred by disproportionately higher suspension rates among racial minorities and students with disabilities, critical eyes have been examining suspension data. Reform efforts have introduced teachers to programs like Restorative Justice Practices, strategies for non-punitive discipline like those found in Positive Behavior Intervention and Supports, and simple strategies for conflict resolution.

Creative effort among teachers for managing classrooms is not new. The nuance is the degree to which some teachers must deal with discipline every period of every day and the wide-spread canvas where problems occur. Bullying, outward displays of disobedience toward teachers, use of e-cigarettes, and vaping occur in predominantly white schools in middle-class neighborhoods as well as in schools located in minority communities next to housing projects. Classroom discipline issues are not because classroom teachers are "weak," but may be enhanced by an overall school climate that is unwelcoming to certain groups or selected groups of students. On the other hand, research claims that discipline issues may be related to a host of factors beyond the school's control, including the degree to which their students are living in poverty, fatherlessness among the group, and current and past trauma experienced by the students.[40]

Petrilli (2017) also suggests that data indicate poor children of color are more likely to misbehave at school than are their peers because they are more likely to be fatherless and to have experienced trauma.[41] While this may be true, it should not preclude teachers from having high expectations for **all** of their students. (I was poor, fatherless, and experienced trauma. However, my teachers expected me to behave and to learn, and they gave me the tools to do so.)

Finally, today's teachers are also dealing with research that indicates discipline issues are related to achievement-gap issues. This ball is being batted around, yet there is no solid hit. The idea of something called the "Domino Effect" posits that "**exposure** to disruptive peers during elementary school worsens student achievement and later life outcomes, including high school achievement, college enrollment and earnings."[42] If research proves this theory to be true, the impact on elementary schools and elementary teachers will be overwhelming and the impact on teacher recruitment efforts will be devastating.

Yes, today's teachers are in a quandary over discipline challenges. One of our old school strategies when dealing with discipline was, "The best discipline plan begins with a sound instructional plan that captures the interest and needs of each individual student in that classroom." Perhaps shoring up instruction might be a place to begin shoring up discipline.

Student Achievement and the Achievement Gap

Student academic achievement and achievement-gap issues are prevalent topics in school districts across the nation as racial related and/or economic related. Gap issues and discussions of equitable attainment of academic success form the bases of arguments supporting private schools and charter schools to give students "school choice." A call for tax-payer scholarships to help expand education options is a clear counter punch to the support for public schools, with charter school supporters making the argument that charter schools will better support those populations who have been left behind. To this end, the achievement gap phenomenon requires clarification.

Common Core State Standards Initiative, a cousin to the No Child Left Behind Act and Race to the Top initiatives, were implemented around 2010. With a collaborative team of developers, teachers, school administrators, and school chiefs, Common Core was thought to provide a clear and consistent framework for educators. Researched and evidence-based, Common Core was a set of high-quality academic standards in English, language arts/literacy, and mathematics. The Standards were created to ensure that "all students graduate from high school with the skills and knowledge necessary to succeed in college, in careers, and in life." Since its implementation, greater rigor in coursework that high school students take has been reported. More high school students have been exposed to upper-level mathematics and science courses are among the claims of successful implementation.

Additionally, one of the academic assessments used across the country, the National Assessment of Education Progress (NAEP), assesses changes in the educational achievement of fourth- and eighth-grade students in mathematics and reading every other year and several other subjects less frequently; for example, U.S. History is assessed every four years. NAEP scores have gone up, for all students, but reported gains in mathematics in Grades 4 and 8 have been greater for Blacks than for white students.[43]

In reviewing Common Core and NAEP data, several researchers indicate that the red flags raised nearly 40 years ago with the publication of *A Nation at Risk,* continue to blow in the winds today. The achievement gaps between white students and Black and Hispanic students, have not been eradicated. Several postulate that improvement in the performance of white students exacerbates the gap between whites and Blacks and whites and Hispanics. Demographic changes are also seen as culprits in closing the gap. It is speculated that by 2050, at least 50 percent of U.S. students will be Hispanic.[44]

Furthermore, a school's composition, percent of black students compared to percent of white students and other minorities; individual student characteristics, including mother's and father's highest level of education; and the percent of students eligible for free and/or reduced-priced lunch are seen as plausible factors related to achievement. The composition of the teaching staff, new teachers vs. experienced teachers and white teachers vs. Black teachers, is also among the arguments relating to contributors to students' academic progress. Class composition and teaching methodology, including the extent to which teachers use different standards and different methods for different students, are all believed to impact achievement. The question whether test scores indicate that students actually "know more" and if we are still *A Nation at Risk* has also been raised.[45]

While many parents and the general public may not understand the ramifications of this question, educators, new and seasoned, should and must continue to ponder the serious state of America's education and the plight of all of our children. Our competition is no longer next door, but worldwide. Our children must be able to compete on universal stages not just Main Street's Actor's Theater. Broader visions of equity, accountability, creativity, and commitment are essential for addressing achievement gap issues and challenges.

Technology Integration in 21st Century Schools

At the end of the twentieth century, educators were just beginning to learn and use computers as an educational tool and had no idea of their forthcoming impact. The first Apple personal computer, Apple I, was built in a garage and went on display in 1976. (I bought my first Apple computer in 1985.) A math class in California was the first classroom to receive an Apple computer. Now, almost a half century later, educators across the nation, both new and seasoned, agree that the greatest impact on education today, both in teaching and learning, is technology. The U.S. Department of Education and most education gurus, K12 and postsecondary, believe that technology has ushered in fundamental structural changes that are significant for improving student achievement and student productivity. Digital learning tools, such as computers and hand-held devices, when used to support both teaching and learning, expands course offerings; enhances learning experiences and learning materials; supports learning 24 hours a day, 7 days a week; builds twenty-first century skills; increases student engagement and motivation; and accelerates learning. Technology also transforms teaching by ushering in a new model of connected teaching. This model links teachers to their students and professional content, resources, and systems to help them improve their own instruction and personalized learning.

The impact of technology education is unparalleled. The use of technology is touted as a means for enhancing student achievement or proficiency. Teachers have migrated from the use of chalkboards to interactive whiteboards; from hand-held textbooks to virtual text; and from technology serving to enhance teaching to sometimes serving to replace teachers. Full-time online virtual schools are available in several states, providing instruction and offering full credits toward high school graduation, with students never being required to take a seat in a bricks-and-mortar facility with a teacher at the head of the class. In addition, colleges and universities in many states now offer bachelor, masters, and doctoral degrees on-line, taking advantage of technological advances and innovation. Virtual classrooms for instructing future educators are also becoming more popular among teacher education institutions that continue to struggle with declining enrollments, reductions in staff, and budgetary issues.[46]

Experts in the field of technology are predicting major shifts in the integration of classroom technology over the next decade in the twenty-first century. Computers, smartphones, iPads and virtual reality are teacher-student friendly and are expected to be mainstays in K12 classrooms. At the close of the last decade, more than 30 million primary and secondary students used Google education apps, such as Docs and Gmail. Of the K-12 public schools in the U.S., 58 percent used Google, 22 percent used Microsoft Windows, and 19 percent used MacOS and iOS. Technology trends felt to create and improve education have been identified and widely disseminated. Five trends in technology expected to create new paths for learning as well as to improve education in the future are being explored and evaluated as this decade gets underway.[47] These future technology trends or experimental approaches include:

- Creating new Learning Management Systems (LMS) allowing technology to be used as a platform to create and track online learning initiatives. These systems will allow teachers to upload materials that can be accessed by students remotely and allow teachers to monitor student progress remotely;

- Expanding gamification which uses algorithms in educational games which create personalized and engaging learning experiences for students;

- Amplifying coding initiatives and robotics programs which are being embraced more widely in schools at every level. These developing concepts require teachers to be trained in adapting curriculum to teach these new technical skills;

- Initiating additional opportunities for students to participate in scenarios using Augmented Reality (AR), which adds a layer of digital reality over the current environment, and Virtual Reality (VR), which allows the user to be immersed in a totally fabricated world. These technological innovations are projected to enhance students' experiences to both excite and invite them to take deeper dives into learning. Issues of privacy, security, and cost, which includes teacher training, are factors which will impact the speed that reality environments are adapted as teaching tools; and

- Accelerating the use of smart classrooms that continue to grow in popularity at all levels. Smart classrooms include smart tables, biometric devices, voice recognition technology, and natural language processing using sensors and artificial intelligence. These classrooms are deemed to create individualized and personalized learning experiences that accelerate academic proficiency. (These innovations will also demand that students be able to read and comprehend to an even greater extent than they are expected to currently or we will leave a larger proportion of our students behind.)

In conclusion, there is general agreement that changes in education due to technology are inevitable and will be expansive. An overwhelming majority of the nation's teachers believe that in fewer than ten years, printed textbooks will be replaced by digital learning content. More and more public schools are issuing students laptops in lieu of books and also providing students with Chromebooks and Chrome Tablets. More schools are creating Makerspace for multimedia labs and STEM or STEAM (Science, Technology, Engineering, Arts, and Mathematics) labs that change the learning environment, enriching student engagement and innovation while enhancing available instructional strategies for teachers.[48]

In technologically enhanced environments, teachers are expected to be able to multi-task—tailoring instruction to specific groups of students, providing more challenging problem sets to accelerated learners, while simultaneously reviewing concepts with those who require reinforcement. The implication here is that how teachers are trained must reflect the new trends and expectations that technology adds to the mix. Colleges and universities who train teachers must be onboard with a vision of where schools are and where they are going. They must reconstitute teacher education curriculum to be in concert with what teachers need to know; what they are expected to do with that knowledge; and the tools that they will be expected to use.[49]

Use of technological advancements also will allow colleges and universities to further enhance the effectiveness of teacher education programs by providing students with teaching experiences using up to date curriculum; with ease of exposure to multiple, diverse instructional strategies; with instructional techniques for how to teach reading and improve comprehension across grade levels and content areas; with methods for individualized instruction based on students' needs; and with exposure and practice using various discipline strategies to enhance student engagement and create classroom learning climates where students thrive rather than survive. Without appropriate and progressive teacher education programs, more nails will be driven into the coffin of the teaching profession and into the stability of public education.

The information provided in this section has not been all-inclusive, but was designed to give touch-points on education in our nation today as we steadily move through the first quarter of this century. Reflections upon education at the end of the twentieth century and where we are today reveal major changes that have occurred over what seems like a short period of time. Changes expected to occur between now and 2050—thirty years from now—are staggering. Thoughtful readers may be questioning whether the writer is attempting to invite individuals to consider teaching as a career or to run them away as quickly as possible. The intent here is to provide readers with an honest assessment or "real-deal" picture of what the research and the data say about the current education arena. Current and past educators, practicing and retired, must continue being knowledgeable and diligent about our profession as well. If, on the other hand, this data can be used to help individuals make thoughtful decisions about career choices and provide honest answers to fundamental questions about becoming a teacher, then that is another plus!

Staffing the Nation's Schools with Qualified Teachers

As we entered the twenty-first century, American education and educators were bombarded with issues, challenges, and changes that created a new set of problems and questions around who we are educating, what we are teaching, and who is doing the educating. Ironically, some of these same questions were pondered by twentieth century educators as they navigated their educational journeys. "Who are the teachers; what should they teach; and to whom should they teach, what?" are questions continuously floating through the educational circuit. Information previously provided has explored how our schools are evolving; how our students are changing; and what the educational outlook is for the next several decades. With all that has been discussed and explained, the final data point that is essential for understanding twenty-first century schools is the notion of educator supply and demand. This is particularly important as efforts to attract and sustain a viable teaching force is foremost on every school district's agenda across the nation, whether urban, rural, or suburban.

Data from a variety of sources are available to guide education policy makers and educators as they continue to try to make sense of today's education environment. Be clear; today's schools are not the schools of the twentieth century, nor are today's students. Just as the standards and needs of twentieth century education and educators evolved, so will the needs of twenty-first century education and educators. Educators continue to grapple with what we should be doing with students, for students, and to students to encourage, educate, and empower them to become productive citizens in our society. Regardless of the issues, challenges, and changes that we anticipate are part of the future education landscape, *for now*, the certainty is that **teachers** will continue to play a major role in educating youth. The questions that require answers are how many teachers will be available; what skills will they have; and where will we find them?

Understanding how we sustain an educator workforce that is capable, ready, and willing to meet the needs of twenty-first century students who trod the halls of America's public schools is critical. An overview of teacher demand and supply trends provides some insights.

Teacher Demand and Supply

Teacher shortages have been widespread since 2015. The Great Recession is linked to teacher-supply issues in that massive teacher layoffs in several school districts created unemployment scenarios that brought attention to teacher plights at the time. Many school districts were surprised when teachers were unavailable in later years as districts resumed hiring. Unable to meet hiring needs with fully certified personnel, "a number of states greatly expanded emergency permits to allow hiring of untrained teachers."[50]

Demands for teachers in the fields of mathematics, science, special education, and bilingual education were among the greatest need. A common definition for teacher shortage, "the inability to staff vacancies at current wages with individuals qualified to teach in the fields needed," is accepted by most HR professionals who staff the nation's public schools.[51] The year 2020 is predicted to mark a milestone with an estimated 300,000 new teachers having opportunities to staff the nation's schools. Continuing demand for teachers is expected to escalate with growths in student enrollment estimated to increase by three million students by 2030. Reinstatement of various education programs closed as budgets were trimmed during the recession and teacher attrition are expected to contribute to teacher demand and the forecasted crisis.

The supply of teachers in the first two decades of the twenty-first century dropped considerably. Over a five-year period between 2009 and 2014, students enrolled in teacher preparation programs declined by approximately 240,000 participants. This 35 percent reduction in teacher education majors at the same time K-12 enrollments were increasing, wreaked havoc on school districts' ability to sustain fully certified teaching forces. Teacher attrition, measured by qualified teachers who leave the classroom, and low numbers of re-entrants, teachers who quit teaching then return at a later date, added to the perfect storm, pushing teacher supply to record low levels.

Teacher attrition is characterized as the single factor that will most impact projected teacher shortages commonly known as supply levels. Teacher educators and school district HR personnel agree that knowing who, why, and where of attrition is essential for future teacher retention. Teachers in high-poverty, high-minority schools are believed to have higher rates of attrition. To this end, teachers of color are positioned to have high rates of attrition because they are the largest population of teachers in high-poverty, high-minority schools. Urban school districts and schools in the South have higher attrition rates than suburban and rural schools in other parts of the country.[52]

Furthermore, why teachers choose to leave the profession has been associated with school-climate factors like the level and kind of administrative support, the collegiality among faculty, professional-development opportunities, and voice or input in decision making. These same factors are identified as contributors to job satisfaction.

Teacher demand and supply do not share equal footing across regions, across states, within school districts, or across subjects. School resources and working conditions, in addition to union, association, or district policies on school selection and transfer practices, often dictate what vacancies will ultimately occur in schools that are less desirable and have higher poverty indexes. Less qualified teachers who are not fully certified more easily find homes as "warm bodies" in those schools. The number of institutions in a given area or region preparing teachers also impacts the availability of qualified professional staff.

Specific content area majors or fields and the number of degreed graduates are reflective in the teacher demand-supply scenario. For the past several years, Physics and seven different areas in special education remain the fields with the highest teacher shortages across the nation. Colleges and universities report shortages of students entering these fields, and school districts report similar shortages in finding qualified candidates for jobs in the same fields. Social studies education and physical education remain the only two fields where school districts report "some surplus" of qualified candidates, but there have been no fields with "considerable surplus" in the past five years.[53]

Physical Therapy, Intermediate Education, and Kindergarten/ Primary Education have the most graduates per degree-offering institutions while Classical Languages (Greek/Latin), Chinese, German, Japanese, and ESL/ELL English Language Learners are projected to have the fewest number of degree graduates as the new decade emerges. Also, suburban districts with student populations of 10,001 to 20,000 continue to attract and employ teachers prepared by traditional teacher-education programs. Those districts also have the smallest percentage (2 percent) of emergency hires. At the same time, urban and rural districts that currently employ fewer than 5 percent emergency hires also employ 78 and 82 percent respectively of their hires graduating from traditional preparation programs. Large urban districts with more than 20,000 students will continue to lead in the employment of teachers prepared by non-traditional or alternative methods, approximately 17 percent. That number is expected to increase as teacher shortages loom in the future. [54]

The shortage of minority teachers in our nation's schools remains an area of concern, spanning the last two decades of the twentieth century to the present. While the nation's student population continues to become more racially/ethnically diverse, the population of K-12 classroom teachers has become more white and stilted, as was mentioned earlier. The demand for teachers in general is progressing steadily while the supply continues in a downward spiral fueled by the absence of minority candidates.

Who Wants to Teach?

As *Teacher Journeys* flash through my mind and I revisit the experiences told by the twentieth century educators, I cannot get an answer to the question, "Who wants to teach?" Because so many years of my career have been focused on general teacher recruitment and retention, and the identification and development of Black teacher candidates, I am dumbstruck by the declining numbers and lack of interest in teaching as a career. When I realized that my own grandchildren have had only two Black teachers in their entire K-12 careers—the same two for both of them even though they are five years apart—I remember shaking my head. Now, I am still befuddled.

I am not sure if I have learned or re-learned too much data. (Remember, I had a stroke in the middle of writing this book.) I do know that I am more aware of the overall educational landscape and I have a different vision. When I told a colleague that I am more than frightened about the outlook for the teaching profession, that I am "scared," I fought back the tears. This was the morning after I had spent time with eight focus groups of average to very bright students, juniors and seniors ages 15 to 19, from six different schools and areas of town. I asked the questions, "What do you want to be when you grow up?" "What are your career goals?" Approximately 124 students, 52 percent African-American, 44 percent white; 2 percent Hispanic, and 2 percent of Two or more (combined) races, formed the group that also consisted of 59 males and 65 females, with grade-point averages from 2.7 to 3.8. They had no problem responding to my questions. Within this entire group, only four students said they wanted to be teachers.

This scenario is not uncommon. When I speak to colleagues across the country, they are not surprised. While, like my daughter, many of their children are teachers, their grandchildren "barf" at the idea of becoming teachers. When colleagues ask children in their Sunday School groups about their career aspirations, my colleagues get the same type of response that I received from my focus groups. Students want to be doctors, physical therapists, and health-care providers; business owners and entrepreneurs; financial analysts and stock brokers; veterinarians; lawyers; engineers; and of course, professional athletes.

If I were trying to recruit individuals to think about teaching as a career (remember I said I was not going to do that) then my dilemma would be wanting to make a sound argument about why students, both minority and nonminority, should at least give teaching a thought when they are making decisions about career choices in light of the data presented here or the reasons that students themselves give when rejecting the idea of teaching as a career. Listed below are some of the comments students made about teaching and teachers:

- I like my teachers, but I do not have their patience.
- Teachers do not make enough money for the job they are expected to do. They put in all of their time and get paid so little.
- They have all of these papers and assignments to grade, and they can't do things with their own children. My mom never could come to my Open House when I was in elementary school because she had to be at her school's Open House on the same evening.
- I don't want to be a teacher because I have had too many bad ones. I keep thinking what if I turned out to be one of those.
- I never even thought about teaching. It just never crossed my mind.
- The children that are coming to school are getting worse. We thought we were bad, but I do not know what to say about these students. This year's freshman class had more fights than my entire class, freshman through senior year. I don't see how teachers continue to deal with those kinds of students. I could not.
- Teachers have to spend too much of their own money to buy things for class. That isn't fair, but my teachers do it anyway.
- There are kids that disrupt class and teachers try to keep them in line. I don't know why they can't just put them out of class. They are disrupting my education, but the teachers let them stay in class anyway. They always talk about it is important to help every student. Some students don't want help.
- Teachers say that they are trying not to suspend students because students won't learn anything sitting at home. Well,

with them in class, I am having trouble learning anything sitting in school.
- We are a smart group, but we are missing something. School is not like what my mama and grandmamma talk about. They loved school and they loved their teachers. I like school and I like my teachers, but I do not want to be like them.

There is no denying that these statements are representative of how many students feel. Their responses paint a bleak picture for the future of teacher recruitment. The need for recruiting is supported by the declining numbers of students entering teacher-education programs as well as the increasing numbers of qualified teachers leaving the field, and these responses are not providing much hope.

However, there were four students who indicated that teaching was among their career choices. Their comments helped me put a knot in the thread by which I am hanging. (My mama said, "When you are hanging by a thread and start slipping, put a knot in it, and hang on.") So, here are responses from those who said, "I think I want to be a teacher."

- I never had a favorite teacher. I liked them all. I watched them work with children and I helped them sometimes. I saw how teachers molded students, even the bad ones. Lord knows we have enough bad ones who need our help now.
- Teaching is me. I am smart, and, yes, I can be an engineer. But I would rather use my talents working with kids. I can help some other kid become an engineer. There is nothing more important than educating a young mind and I think I can do a great job as a teacher.
- When you have teachers who care about their students, students do better. My teachers cared about me, so I guess I want to give back and care about some other kids. Teachers who care do a better job of teaching. I care about kids. My students will do great.
- I know that I will be taking a chance being a teacher, but I'm O.K. with that. I won't make as much money as my sister

who will be a doctor, but teachers are doctors too. They help children heal. There are a lot of kids who have been through stuff. They need teachers to help them heal.

When I read these students' positive comments, my immediate response was how do I bottle and bond their thoughts to stock convenient stores with a new "wisdom drink"; or, is there a new "M-E for T-E" (ME for TE-aching) vaccine that can be developed to transfer this type of thinking into the masses and block the negativity surrounding teaching as a profession. It is ironic that many of the issues that students who do not want to be teachers listed, were identified by educators who shared their journeys as well. However, twentieth century educators saw many of these same behaviors as positive, inspiring, and compelling—moving them toward careers as educators rather than away from education.

Finally, I asked the students what were the characteristics of good teachers. I was amazed that their list encompassed so many of the characteristics that were spoken about in *Journeys*. The list below details what today's students say good teachers do. Note the similarities in "Insights" from twentieth century educators with the insights of these students. The depth of their responses was unexpected. Sometimes, as seniors, we so often see kids on their phones and IPads, and shake our heads confirming our beliefs that they are not paying attention. We forget how observant, resourceful, and intuitive they actually can be. The following responses are examples.

What Good Teachers Do According to 21ˢᵗ Century Students	Characteristics of Good Teachers Identified by 20ᵗʰ Century Educators
• Know their subject, what they are teaching and do not have to read it out of the book.	• Continuous learners; know their content.
• Tell students that they expect respect and are willing to give respect.	• Evaluate their own teaching.
• Have different ways of teaching the same thing so that if you don't get it the first time, you might get it the second time around.	• Give respect to earn respect. • Instructionally sound; use a variety of techniques; use multiple teaching styles.
• Look like teachers and not like one of the students.	• Build relationships with students, parents, and staff; team players.
• Work with other teachers so if we are doing something in U.S. History, we can be reading something in our English class that goes with it.	• Independent thinkers; visionary. • Flexible • Create an inviting learning environment.
• Have flexibility. Sometimes teachers need to stop and listen to the students, especially when something is going on and kids are upset. Teachers who don't listen don't care.	• Excited about teaching and learning. • Make learning fun. • Encourage students. • Have a positive outlook.
• Do different things in class instead of the same old thing. When you come to class you do not know what to expect. That makes you want to come to class.	• Assess student work and give feedback quickly. • Care about their students and show it.
• Allow students to use computers and their devices to help with classwork.	• Have high expectations for all students and tell students what they expect.
• Don't make the work easy. We might gripe, but we work hard in those classes.	• Use technology to support instruction.
• Don't give grades. They make all of us earn our grades.	
• They always say, "Come on. You can do this."	

Students see good teachers in action and have real insights into the characteristics of good teachers. Yet, unlike twentieth century educators, they are not inspired. So I am back to square one, "Who wants to be a teacher?"

Good Teachers: Lessons from 20th Century Educators

Teacher Journeys explained a great deal about the teaching profession then and the teaching profession now. Regardless of their origins, family, fortunes, or paths to become educators, the storytellers were in concert about the value of education, the importance of the profession, and characteristics of good teachers. Their insights were based on their experiences as well as their values which were deep-rooted in love for the profession and caring about children.

Teaching is a profession not designed for everybody and anybody. The idea that anybody can teach is fostered by those who do not respect teachers or teaching and is preposterous. Good teachers must be effective teachers—able to inspire students to learn! If students do not learn, the question remains, did you teach them? Good teachers realize that teaching and learning go hand-in-hand. One does not happen without the other. If students did not learn it, I did not teach it.

Good teachers are kind, caring, and good-natured, having a fundamental belief system. They value education and the benefits that education brings. They see teaching as a profession more so than a job. Good teachers want to be respected, and they give respect to their students, parents, and fellow teachers. Good teachers are lifelong learners. Whether the state requires a master's degree for continuing certification or dismisses the requirement, good teachers stay abreast of changes in their field, in both content and in instructional strategies and practices.

Good teachers like children and care about their future. They understand that "a mind is a terrible thing to waste" and strive to open students' minds, even when they are being challenged by the wrath of poverty, ignorance, disillusionment, or imposed educational policies and practices.

Good teachers stand up for fair and equal treatment of all students. They are visionaries in that they see positive futures for their students and they work to make their visions a reality. Good teachers understand that children are different and that they learn differently; therefore, they must adapt teaching styles to the learning styles of their students. They understand that children come from different learning environments, and they value what each child brings to the table. They also find creative ways to use and grow the contributions that each child makes. They do not make excuses for their students or for themselves. No one has shortcomings. Everyone has contributions.

Good teachers realize that students may have needs that keep the brain from focusing on the ABCs or *Harry Potter,* and they find ways to assist students in taking care of those needs rather than using those needs as an excuse for not working toward academic excellence. Regardless of what subject or grade that they teach, good teachers recognize children must know how to read and comprehend, and it is their job to assist students in improving reading and comprehension skills.

Good teachers teach students more than what is in the books. They teach students about life. They are organized and relish being prepared. They believe that they have a gift and they must give back, as part of their calling. They give children hope that they can go anywhere they want to go, do anything they want to do, and be anything they want to be, if they are educated. They respect the creativity, integrity, capacity, and intelligence of every child that they teach.

Good teachers want to teach and spread the idea that education is a value that cannot be matched. They still believe that education is something that nobody can take away from them and that knowledge is power. They are concerned, committed, and convinced that their responsibility is to ensure that every child has a love for learning. Good teachers teach children first and subjects second. Good teachers still believe that education is the wing that makes dreams fly.

Now, I ask the question again, "Who wants to be a teacher?" Even though we have dire needs, the profession must maintain lines in the concrete when it comes to certain issues. We are at a precipice where we must recruit those who want to be good teachers and who are willing to strive to be great teachers. The profession should be strong in its belief that everybody cannot teach and not be willing to give everybody and anybody a "try" simply because we are experiencing a teacher shortage. Who we place in our classrooms in front of our most valuable possession, our children, should be of the highest quality with intelligence, ingenuity, and integrity. These should be our lines in the concrete.

This applies to all teachers, including minorities. Minority teachers are important as role models for all students, both minority and non-minority, and they bring racial/ethnic diversity to a teaching force that is diametrically opposite to the student population. Minority teachers are pursued because of the belief that they may have common life experiences, similar cultural backgrounds, and exposure to viewpoints that minority students have, which may be in contrast to those of the majority. Minority teachers on staff are sounding boards for administrators and colleagues proposing policies and procedures that may sometimes seem biased.

In addition, minority teachers are believed to be able to relate more effectively with minority students, many of whom are from low socioeconomic backgrounds. That may have been so in 1975, but not today. Today's minority teachers are as bourgeoisie as white teachers, sharing the same middle-class values and attitudes. They do not necessarily live in predominately minority neighborhoods as they did in the '50s and '60s, and their trip "downtown" is generally on Sunday morning to their old home church.

This is not said disrespectfully. The point here is that we must invite minorities to join the profession the same as we invite everyone else to join the profession. As we look for teacher candidates the same sense of purpose, persistence, and perseverance as any other good teacher must apply to minorities as well. The fact that they are minority is an added bonus on one hand, and no assumption should be made that because they **are** minority, that they are not high-quality candidates.

You see, I know good teachers who are minority. I have worked with them; I have taught them, and they have taught me. The preceding litany about what good teachers do, feel, act, and believe is not from a book, but from experiences. The kid who lived in one room in Reed Alley and shared a kitchen and toilet with two other families had a first-grade teacher who wrote 2+2+2+2= on the blackboard and told her to change the problem from addition to multiplication and explain it to the class. She had a second-grade teacher who hugged her and cried with her because she was leaving her class, but the teacher assured her that she would do well because she knew she was ready. She had a third-grade teacher who gave her books to read that allowed her to travel to places across the world and to Mars. That same teacher in fourth grade brought her back into the classroom after she had run out crying and embarrassed when one of her male classmates announced that she was wearing a bra. That teacher had the class to give her a standing ovation when she returned because she was the first to enter maturity and gave her a star on the "Moving On Up" Board.

She had a fifth-grade teacher who taught her to be competitive but not "cut-throat." Her sixth-grade teacher modeled grace and kindness and taught her the importance of giving back and helping others even when you think you have nothing to give. Her teachers in Grades 7 through 9 taught her to question when she saw inequities and to be willing to put in the work to make changes. When the other junior high schools had a school newspaper and a junior honor society and her school didn't, she became editor of the school newspaper and wrote the bylaws for their National Junior Honor Society Charter. Those teachers took her on field trips all over the city to reward her, and students like her, for achieving academic excellence and to "expand her horizons."

Her high school teachers continued the legacy begun in first grade—having high expectations for her; telling her that she could achieve whatever she wanted to achieve; being available when she needed extra help or coaching; and reinforcing what her mother told her way back when: "Where you live does not define who you are or who you can be."

Yes, I know good teachers and I know great teachers. Good teachers are those who are learning and practicing all of those things that they need to know to become great teachers. In the beginning, it's "good." When you are touching every child that you teach, it is "great."

So, who wants to be a teacher?

There have been no rose-colored glasses used here. What twenty-first century teaching and teachers look like, feel like, smell like, and taste like have been thoughtfully presented over these pages. My hope is that readers will share our stories, some of the data, and information presented here with others—some high school students that they know; parents and friends of college enrollees perhaps at their church; their neighbors who are contemplating switching careers; support staff who work in schools with their children; friends who are stay-at-home moms who are now empty nesters and are thinking about re-entering the job market; their friends in their social clubs; their colleagues at work; their own children and grandchildren, as well as others that I cannot name at the moment—all who may need reminders about the important role teachers played in their lives and the value of the education profession. After careful self-scrutiny, some readers may be willing to give teaching as a career an honest assessment, but only if you pass the first check-off list—I like kids; I like working with kids; I am smart; I am committed to making a difference in children's lives. If you cannot check each of these boxes, do not bother to go back or reread these pages. However, reread a couple of the wonderful *Teacher Journeys* that are overflowing with Inspiration, Initiative, and Insights. Then, the next time you see one of your teachers, give them a hug and say, "Thank you."

However, if you did check each of the boxes, you know the issues, challenges, changes, concerns, expectations, and nuances surrounding the profession, and you know yourself—that you are willing to engage in the hard work, dedication, and sometimes sacrifice that it takes to be a good teacher moving to greatness—then let's begin thinking about your journey as a teacher in the twenty-first century.

Now, What's Next?

You passed the tests, and now you say, "Yes." So, what's next? I struggled with trying to determine how to answer this question because I know that one size does not fit all and may not fit many. When I began the journey of writing this book, recruiting teachers was a primary goal. (But remember, I'm not trying to do that anymore.) I thought about trying to appeal to multiple audiences with different needs and perspectives. I anticipated that when the book was published, my former students would buy copies to give to their friends and children. I knew that the educators who shared their *Teacher Journeys* wanted multiple copies for their children and family as well. I hoped that high school teachers who are engaged in career exploration courses would assign this book as optional reading for their students who were considering service professions. I also wanted teacher education professors who taught introductory education classes to include this book as part of their supplemental readings. So, you see, depending on where you are in the chain and what your needs are, what's next includes a gamut of choices, steps, and opportunities.

Different ages, different stages of career development, and different financial circumstances all provide fodder for answering the question, "What's next?" Some readers may be about to graduate from high school and are contemplating choosing a college as well as a career. Others may already be attending college but were undecided about a career up until now. Still, some may be steeped in a major, but realize teaching is where they want to be. Career changers and those anticipating a second career under whatever circumstance are within the "I want to be a teacher and I said yes to the test" orbit.

However, I cannot bring you as readers this far and not offer something. Many of the shared *Journeys* gave advice and were directional to some extent, which is welcoming. Hence, I want to share my final personal story about someone who didn't consider teaching as a first career choice in spite of the fact that she had been surrounded by teachers her entire life. That person would be my daughter Paulette.

Paulette (Lette), an only child, sat in the middle of the floor of the storage closet that had been converted to a classroom and assigned to me as a social studies teacher at Shawnee Junior High School, my first teaching assignment as part of the Professional Commitment that I had made to the University of Louisville and Louisville Public Schools. She watched her dad and me spread the yellow semi-gloss paint on the scarred white-gray walls that had not been painted in years because the small room had been used to store books. This was 11-month-old Lette's first encounter with school.

For the next nine years of her life, Shawnee Junior High would become Paulette's second home. Teachers in the building before Merger saw her either stationed on my hip or toddling down the hallway during the summers when I spent unpaid days getting ready for the next school year or organizing professional development for me and my colleagues. By the time she was five years old, Lette knew Shawnee's building and the teachers knew Lette. It was not unusual for a teacher to "borrow" her to help place books in the lower bookshelves beneath the windows or to stack supplies on the lower shelves of classroom closets. As she grew older, teachers at Shawnee after Merger knew that she was a helping hand. They were always glad to see her and borrow her as well.

Teachers were everywhere in Paulette's life—from my sister, Olivia, her aunt who was a math teacher, to my friends and colleague who were educators as well. Lette's only teacher-free- zone was at our family gatherings. Olivia was the first college graduate in our family, followed by a doctor, a nurse, a chemist, and other professionals, but no teachers other than me, her mom. With Merger in 1975, Paulette attended kindergarten at a church about a block from our house on Glendora Avenue and later attended a Catholic school down the street from Shawnee. Her assigned school was across town and junior high school start time was earlier than the elementary school's starting time which was problematic for our family.

At the end of her school day when Lette got out of elementary school, I was waiting in the parking lot to pick her up and take her back to Shawnee with me while I worked on something—lesson plans, a school project, an event after school, a parent conference, professional development—something. I also took her with me to U of L where she sat outside of my classroom door as I completed final classes for my master's degree. At break time, Lette ate snacks with me and my fellow students, all teachers who talked to her about school and invariably at some point, asked her what she wanted to be when she grew up. My professors knew Lette and marveled at her behavior. A couple of them eventually told me to sit her in the back of the room, probably to keep me from craning my neck to look around the open door to make sure she was still in place.

During her junior high and high school days, teachers were peppered throughout our suburban community. She played with their children, met them at sporting and social events; and loved her teachers at Kammerer Middle School and Ballard High School. Because of her demeanor with children; the ease with which she spoke and worked with youth and adults; her exposure to teachers her entire life; and her positivity about school and teachers, Paulette's choices of Engineering and Accounting as college majors, were a complete surprise to me when it was so evident that she would make a great teacher. However, when she made her career-choice announcement, it took prayer, tongue biting, and my husband's hand on my shoulder to keep my mouth closed.

For Lette's first two years at the University of Kentucky (U of K), she was a typical freshman/sophomore—taking general education requirements, partying, changing hair styles every other month, and trying to grow up in an environment that was not mama- and daddy-dominated. Her grades were O.K. but not great and she still managed to spend spring break with me in whatever state I was recruiting. Each year, we visited five colleges at least, looking for teachers for JCPS. Paulette actually manned the recruitment booth at two colleges in Virginia when I became ill with some kind of virus. She could talk about teaching and the type of teachers that JCPS was looking for as well as any professional recruiter.

When Lette began her junior year at U of K, something happened. Bombarded with engineering and business-related coursework that required more computer-time than people-time, Paulette became unhappy. I could tell it in her voice over the phone and in her eyes when we made our every-other-Sunday visit. Finally, on a sunny Spring day in April, the direct line on my office phone rang in the middle of the day. It was Paulette. She said, "Mama, I've been thinking. I want to go over to Taylor Hall and talk to the people there about changing my major." Although I knew what was in Taylor Hall, I asked the question, "Changing your major to what?" Her reply, "Teaching."

I still remember placing my hand across the receiver and saying aloud, "Thank you, Jesus," as tears slid down my cheeks while I tried to keep my voice calm and neutral because I did not want to scare her away. I said, "That sounds like a great idea. Call me tonight and let me know what they tell you." She agreed to call later. I hung up the phone, ran to my office door, and shouted to my secretary and clerks, "I think we got her! Paulette wants to be a teacher!" At this point in time, we were approaching, "What's next?"

I spoke to Paulette that evening after she made an appointment with an advisor in the Education Department. I was in "Dr. Greer" mode rather than "Mama" mode. Believe it or not, my first question to her was, "Why do you want to be a teacher?" She talked and I listened and prodded. Finally satisfied with her responses, my next questions were, "**Who** do you want to teach, for example, regular program or special education?" **What level**—elementary, middle, or high school?" and "What is your strong suit, that is, **what subjects**?" Lette still had some uncertainties, but she was making progress. The one thing that she knew for sure was that she did not want to teach high school kids. I told her to **research** the programs since she had an interest in elementary and middle school education.

The following week when Lette was scheduled to meet with an advisor, I sent my husband, Coach Greer, to be my eyes and ears and to be a support for her. I wasn't sure that she wouldn't be overwhelmed because of the additional coursework since she was switching majors. Lette digested the curriculum changes and adapted to her new program. She later graduated with a Bachelor's Degree in Elementary Education and was certified in Kentucky for Grades K-4, 5, and 6 Self-Contained. Two master degrees, twenty-five years, three states, and four school districts later, Paulette is supervisor of High School Instructional Support Services in her district with duties that include teacher recruitment, onboarding, support for teachers of special needs students, and curriculum/instructional design.

So, what's next? Individuals who want to teach should already have a clear picture of why they want to teach. However, the same questions that Lette had to explore are still questions for consideration—"Who do you want to teach? What level? What subject(s)? Research into program requirements; program structure; financial support in terms of special scholarships, grants and loans for teachers; pass rates for program completion tests; and employment opportunities for various area of certification should be part of data gathering and decision making before anyone moves forward with making a final decision. In addition, one might benefit from having a good mentor, a role that can be helpful to career development.

I am partial because I have had great mentors along the way. Anyone contemplating teaching already knows that every day is an uphill climb and today's teachers were never promised a rose garden. However, there are educators, current and retired, and others who want to help those who are seeking to become teachers. Find a mentor, someone who is knowledgeable, who is trustworthy and who will be honest, having your best interest at heart is important—a former teacher, a church member, a sorority sister, or a fraternity brother—is a good place to begin looking. Furthermore, for those not already engaged in a teacher-training program, exploring the various teacher-training programs at those colleges or universities available to you is a must. Teacher education programs are different. Use available technology to investigate, compare, contrast, and analyze. Visit college campuses and education department headquarters. Go unannounced to get a "feel" without the pomp and circumstance of a scheduled visit.

Be assured that there are multiple pathways, both traditional and nontraditional, to becoming a teacher. Finding the road to begin a twenty-first century teacher journey will be unique for some because of particular circumstances, and most assuredly will contain bumps and perhaps some detours. However, let me again say, "Thank you," for your answer to my question, "Who wants to be a teacher?" Smile, and get ready for the ride of your life. Remember, you were never promised a rose garden, just some of the roses from the gardens that you plant.

Take care.
RGG

EPILOGUE

P.S. A note from one of my middle school students:
*Ms. Greer, remember to stay out of trees because
squirrels love nuts. We love you.*

AS I RUMMAGED THROUGH PAPERS IN MY OLD FILE CABINET,
I ran across a yearbook from the 1979-80 school year at Shawnee
Middle School, the school where I taught for nine years, the bulk of
my K-12 teaching experience. The quote above is one of the many
quotes from my students whom I loved dearly and pray that they are
doing well, staying healthy, and leading productive, meaningful lives.
I know that many of them are happy and successful because I see
them, hear from them, and in some cases hear from their children
and grandchildren.

In thinking about those years, I remembered that sometimes I had
to be as crazy as my middle school students to get my point across. On
one of those occasions, I remember giving an entire class "Fs" because
my students boycotted my class and did not do it *right*. They had to
reorganize the boycott, remake the signs with appropriate paper;
make sure all words were spelled correctly; be able to articulate how
their civil rights were being violated as well as the remedy sought;
and walk the halls in protest again, this time orderly and organized.
I gave them two class periods to organize, plan, and prepare while I
sat outside the door in the hallway. My principal thought I had gone
bonkers. My students said that was the lesson that they would always
remember.

Also stuck down in that yearbook was a folded piece of paper in my
handwriting that said, "Teachers at Shawnee Middle School." Shawnee
Middle closed at the end of spring semester, 1980, and Shawnee's

teachers were scattered across the Jefferson County district. As I complete this journey, I hope that you enjoy my final reflections about another set of great teachers that I encountered over my career and salute them as well.

Teachers at Shawnee Middle School
1979-1980

T   Team players; timely and talented.

E   Energetic; engaging professionals with students and parents.

A   Anchors for their students—they actively engage and encourage all students to dream beyond their circumstances of the day.

C   Caring, compassionate, competent community of professionals who embrace creativity and respect cultural differences.

H   Have high expectations for all students; helpers not hinderers. Healers—they dispense with negativity and build self-confidence in their students.

E   Elevate and empower all students by imparting knowledge, building skills and motivating students to strive for excellence.

R   Relationship builders who see past race and poverty.

S   Skill-builders who understand today's issues and work to assure that students are ready for tomorrow's challenges.

These are characteristics of great teachers yesterday, of great teachers today, and of great teachers tomorrow. They all believed that education is possible for all students; every student should be encouraged to achieve; and the needs, interests, and talents of our students should impact our teaching. They also practiced their beliefs.

Thanks again.
RGG

APPENDIX 1
RITA'S TEACHERS

Ms. Harrison

Ms. Eades

Ms. Hughlyn Wilson

Ms. Carrye Evans

Mr. John Miles, Jr.

Ms. Penelope Fisher

Ms. Juanita O. Holt

Mr. James Mosby

Ms. Hale

Mr. Sam Gilliam

Mr. Harris

Ms. McCarley

Ms. Alene White

Ms. Lucy Bond Tinsley

Ms. Hall

Mr. Marion Martin

Ms. Theresa Metcalf

Ms. Lillian Henderson

Ms. Elsie Sterling

Ms. Crowder

Mr. William Price

Ms. Harriette Porter

Mr. Harold Brown

Mr. Ellis Whedbee

Ms. F. Louise Matthews

Mr. William Tisdale

Mr. John Whiting

Ms. Faye Anderson
Ms. Daisy Rhodes
Ms. Rosa Crumes
Ms. Thelma Tilford
Mr. Gano Caywood
Ms. Thelma Lauderdale
Mr. Lyman T. Johnson
Mr. Victor K. Perry
Ms. Hortense B. Perry

Thank You.

APPENDIX 2
INTERVIEW CONTACT SUMMARY

Interviewee*	Date of Primary Contact**	Interview Location
Anderson, Leroy	February 2019	Personal Home
Bowman, Rita	May 2018	Author's Home
Byrd, Gladys Louise	May 2018	Goldsmith Lane Library
Cahoon, Verna	May 2018	Personal Home
Caples, Elizabeth	July 2018	Personal Home
Coleman, Robert	May 2018	University of Louisville
Crumes-Lara, Rosa	August 2018	Personal Home
Curry, A. Frazier	May 2018	University of Louisville
Daniels, Jessie (for Minor)	November 2018	Phone
Donaldson, William	May 2018	Personal Home
Farris, Rothel	July 2018	Personal Home
Fuqua-Jackson, Shirley	July 2018	Fern Creek Library
Greer, Ernesteen	September 2018	Phone/Author's Home
Hamilton, Bernadette	July 2018	University of Louisville
Hillman, Carla Green	June 2018	Newburg Library
House-Cork, Gwen	September 2018	Personal Home
Howard-Hobbs, LeDita	May 2018	Personal Home
Johnson, Lonnie	July 2018	Newburg Library
Johnson, Beverly	July 2018	Personal Home
Kelly, Eugene	May 2018	Middletown Library
Liggin, Carl (for Clyde)	October 2018	Personal Home
Lyons, Sherri	July 2018	Personal Home
Marshall, Bonnie Nelson	September 2018	Phone
Martin, Ted "Boone"	February 2019	Personal Home

Interviewee*	Date of Primary Contact**	Interview Location
Maupin-Hicks Madeline (for Milburn)	November 2018	University of Louisville
Minnis, Bernard	September 2018	Personal Home
Newton, Edward	February 2019	Chestnut Street YMCA
Owens, Faye	May 2018	University of Louisville
Owens, June	October n2018	Phone
Pointer, Patricia	June 2018	Phone
Richardson-Brown, Jewelene	October 2018	Phone
Robinson, Samuel	February 2019	Phone
Shelton, Warren	May 2018	Middletown Library
Stewart, Loretta	May 2018	Personal Home
Talbott, Emma	September 2018	Phone
Talbott, Gloria	May 2018	Personal Home
Taylor, Gail	May 2018	Author's Home
Tinsley, Deanna	July 2018	Author's Home
Wigginton, Jr. Guy	February 2019	University of Louisville
Wigginton, Marva	July 2018	University of Louisville
Withers, Daniel	September 2018	Phone
Wright, Daisy R.	April 2019	Phone

*Stories for Lucie DuValle, Albert Meyzeek, and Lyman T. Johnson were compiled by author from public records, documented histories, personal recollections and data found in the Jefferson County Public Schools Archives Department and the Louisville Western Branch Library Collections.

**Dates represent only one of several dates of conversations between author and interviewee. Additional contacts in person and by mail include review and update of transcripts and final approval to use reported journey.

BIBLIOGRAPHY

African-American Schools in Louisville and Jefferson County. Notable Kentucky African American Database. http://ncaa.uky.edu/nkaa/items/show/2631.

Aldeman, Chad. *Educator Supply and Demand Reports: Lessons for States.* Bellwether Education Partners. Bellwethereducation.org. February 2018.

Allegretto, Sylvia and Lawrence Mishel. *The Teacher pay penalty has hit a new high: Trends in the Teacher Wage and Compensation Gaps Through 2017.* Economic Policy Institute: Center on Wage and Employment Dynamics, September 2018.

Allegretto, Sylvia and Lawrence Mishel. *The Teacher weekly wage penalty hits 21.4 percent in 2018, a record high: Trends in the Teacher Wage and Compensation Penalties through 2018.* Economic Policy Institute: Center on Wage and Employment Dynamics, April 2019.

American Association of Colleges for Teacher Education. *The Changing Teacher Preparation Profession.* Washington, DC: Author, 2013.

American Association for Employment in Education. *Educator Supply and Demand Report 2017-18.* Sycamore, IL: Author, 2018.

American Association for Employment in Education. *Educator Supply and Demand Report 2018-2019.* Sycamore, IL: Author, 2019.

The American College Dictionary, Barnhart and Stein, Editors. New York, NY: Random House, Inc. 1964.

The American Heritage College Dictionary, Fourth Edition. New York, NY: Houghton Mifflin Company, 2004.

The American Heritage College Thesaurus, First Edition. New York, NY: Houghton Mifflin Company, 2004.

The American Heritage Dictionary New Second College Edition. New York, NY: Dell Publishing Co., Inc., 1983.

Aubespin, Mervin, Kenneth Clay, and J. Blaine Hudson. *Two Centuries of Black Louisville: A Photographic History.* Louisville. KY: Butler Books, 2011.

Bengfort, Jacquelyn. "Q and A: Rachel Gorton on How K-12 Schools Envision the Future of Education." *EdTech Magazine*, 2018. https://edtechmagazine.com/k12/article/2018/11/qa-rachel-gorton-how-k-12-schools-envision-future-education.

Bohrnstedt, G., S. Kitmitto, B. Ogut, D. Sherman, and D. Chan. *School Composition and the Black—White Achievement Gap.* (NCES 2015-018). U.S. Department of Education, Washington, DC: National Center for Education Statistics, 2015. http://nces.ed.gov/pubsearch. Retrieved March 2018.

Carver-Thomas, Desiree. *Diversifying the Teaching Profession: How to Recruit and Retain Teachers of Color.* Palo Alto: CA: Learning Policy Institute, 2018.

Choy, Susan, Sharon Bobbitt, Robin Henke, Elliott Medrich, Laura Horn, and Joanne Lieberman. *America's Teachers: Profile of a Profession.* (NCES 93-025). Washington, DC: U.S. Department of Education Office of Educational Research and Improvement, May 1993.

Digest of Education Statistics, 2017. https://nces.gov/programs/digest/. Retrieved March 2018.

D'Orio, Wayne. *Is School Discipline Moving Too Fast?* https://www.theatlantic.com/education/archive/2018/01/15-school-discipline-reform-moving-too-fast/550196/. Retrieved January 2019.

Doyle, Ruby Wilkins. *Recalling the Record: A Documentary History of the African-American Experience with the Louisville Public School System of Kentucky (1870-1975)*. Chapel Hill, NC: Professional Press, 2005.

Dussault, Adrien. *2018's Top Eight Classroom Challenges, According to Teachers*. Classcraft Blog. https://www.classcraft. com/blog/features/8-teachers-challenges-2018/. Retrieved April 2019.

Education Statistics: Facts about American Schools. *Education Week*. https://www.edweek.org/ew/issues/education-statistics/index. html.4.16.2019.

Espinoza, Danny, Ryan Saunders, Tara Kini, & Linda Darling-Hammond. *Taking the long view: State efforts to solve teacher shortages by strengthening the profession*. Palo Alto: CA: Learning Policy Institute, 2018.

Feistritzer, C. Emily. *Profile of Teachers in the U.S. 2011*. Washington, DC: National Center for Education Information, 2011.

Garcia, Emma and Elaine Weise. *The teacher shortage is real, large and growing, and worse than we thought*. The first report in "The Perfect Storm in the Teacher Labor Market" series. Washington, DC: Economic Policy Institute, March 2019.

Gasman, M., A. Samoyoa. & A. Ginsberg. "Minority Serving Institutions: Incubators for Teachers of Color." *The Teacher Educator* 52, no. 2 (2017) 84-98.

Geiger, Abigail. *America's public school teachers are far less racially and ethnically diverse than their students*. Pew Research Center. https://www.pewresearch.org/fact tank/2018/08/27/american s-public-school-teachers-ethically-diverse-than-their-students/. FactTank News in the Numbers, 2018. Retrieved April 2019.

Greer, Rita G. *The Attitudes of Academically Talented High School Students toward Teaching as a Career*. Louisville, KY: University of Louisville Doctoral Dissertation, 1989.

Greer, Rita and William Husk. *Recruiting Minorities into Teaching.* Bloomington, IN: Phi Delta Kappa Educational Foundation, 1989.

Guest, Edgar Albert. *Myself.* Original publication date of poem unknown. Poem reviewed on line in the public domain, April 2019.

Hall, Wade. *The Rest of the Dream: The Black Odyssey of Lyman Johnson.* Lexington, KY: University Press of Kentucky, 1988.

Hammer, C. and E. Gerald. *Selected Characteristics of Public and Private School Teachers: 1987-1988.* NCES 90-087. Washington, DC: National Center for Education Statistics, U.S. Department of Education, July 1990.

Houghton Mifflin Company. *Roget's II New Thesaurus.* Boston, MA: Houghton Mifflin Co., 1980

Ingersoll, R. "Teacher Turnover and Teacher Shortages: An Organizational Analysis." *American Education Research Journal* 38, no. 3 (2001): 499-534.

Ingersoll, R. & H. May. *Recruitment, Retention and the Minority Teacher Shortage.* Philadelphia, PA: Consortium for Policy Research in Education, University of Pennsylvania. CPRE Research Report # RR-69, 2011.

Ingersoll, Richard, Henry May & Greg Collins. *Minority Teacher Recruitment, Employment and Retention: 1987 to 2013.* Palo Alto, CA: Learning Policy Institute, 2017.

Jefferson County Association of School Administrators. *The Ole Landmark.* Louisville, KY: Vol.8, Issue 2, Spring 2005.

Jefferson County Association of School Administrators. *Torch Topics.* "Tribute to Milburn T. Maupin." Louisville, KY: Vol. XIII, No. 4, March 1990.

K'Meyer, Tracy E. *From Brown to Meredith: The Long Struggle for School Desegregation in Louisville, Kentucky, 1954-2007.* Chapel Hill, NC: University of North Carolina Press, 2013.

Katz, Michael. *Class Bureaucracy and School: The Illusion of Educational Change in America.* New York: Praeger, 1971.

Keigher, Ashley. *Teacher Attrition and Mobility: Results from the 2008-2009 Teacher Follow-Up Survey (NCES 2010-353).* Washington, DC: National Center for Education Statistics, Institute Education Science, 2010. Retrieved Aug. 2017. http://nces.ed.gov/pubsearch.

The Kentucky Negro Education Association Journal. January-February, 1939. Louisville, KY: KNEA. Retrieved from Louisville (KY) Western Branch Library, Special Collections.

Kleber, John E., Mary Kinsman, Thomas Clark, Clyde Crews, and George H. Yater. *The Encyclopedia of Louisville.* Lexington, KY: University Press of Kentucky, 2001.

Liggin, Carl. *Liggin Family Memoir.* Louisville, KY: Unpublished documentation of Liggin family history, 2016.

Loewenberg, David. *What Do Teachers Really Think About School Discipline Reform?* https://www.ewa.org/blog-educated-reporter/what-do-teachers-really-think-about-school-discipline-reform. Retrieved January 2019.

Loewus, Liana. *The Nation's Teaching Force is Still Mostly White and Female: What the Numbers Tell Us about U.S. Teachers.* https://www.edweek.org/ew/articles/2017/08/15/the-nations-teaching-force-is-still-mostly.html?print=1. Retrieved April 2019.

Logan, John R. *Separate and Unequal: The Neighborhood Gap for Blacks, Hispanics, and Asians in Metropolitan America.* Providence, RI: Brown University Russell Sage Foundation American Communities Project, 2010.

Long, Cindy. *Experts Discuss How to Find and Keep Teachers of Color.* http://neatoday.org/2017/06/02/experts-discuss-teacher-diversity/. Retrieved July 2017.

Mansfield, Edward D. *American Education Principles and Elements Dedicated to the Teachers of the United States.* New York: A.S. Barnes and Co., 1857. https://archive.org/stream/americaneducatioOOmansiala?ref=ol#page/10/mode/2up. Retrieved: March 2018.

McFarland, J., B. Hussar, J. Zhang, X. Wang, K. Wang, S. Hein, M. Diliberti, E. Forrest Cataldi, F. Bullock Mann, and A. Barmer. *The Condition of Education 2019* (NCES 2019-144). U.S. Department of Education. Washington, DC: National Center for Education Statistics. https://nces.ed.gov/pubsearch/pubsinfo.asp?pubid=2019144. Retrieved June 2019.

National Center for Education Statistics (NCES). *2015-2016 National Teacher and Principal Survey (NTPS).* Washington, DC: U.S. Department of Education. Retrieved April 2019.

National Center for Education Statistics (NCES). *Documentation for the 2011-2012 School and Staffing Survey.* Washington, DC: U.S. Department of Education. Retrieved March 2019.

National Education Association (NEA). "Average Teacher Salaries Down 4.5 percent, NEA Report Finds." www.nea.org//home/74876.htm. Retrieved June 2019.

The Nation's Report Card: Data Tools, State Profiles, Kentucky Overview. https://wwwnationsreportcard.gov/profiles/stateprofile/overview/Ky?cti=PgTab_OT=chart=1&sub=MAT$sj=KY&fs=Grade&st=MN&year=2017. Retrieved April 2019.

The Negro History Bulletin. "The Record of Albert Ernest Meyzeek." Washington, DC: The Association of Study of Negro Life and History, Inc., 1946.

Notable Kentucky African American Database. Lexington, KY: University of Kentucky, on-line resource.

Petrilli, Michael. *Are Discipline Disparities Due to the Behavior of Students or the Responses of Adults?* https://www.educationnext.

org/how-to-think-about-discipline-disparities-suspensions/. Retrieved April 2019.

Podolsky, Anne, Tara Kini, Joseph Bishop, & Linda Darling Hammond. *Solving the Teacher Shortage: How to Attract and Retain Excellent Educators.* (Research Brief) Palo Alto, CA: Learning Policy Institute, 2016.

Random House Webster's Unabridged Dictionary of the English Language, Second Edition. New York, NY: Random House, 2001.

Snyder, Thomas, Cristobal de Brey & Sally Dillow. *Digest of Education Statistics 2017 53rd Edition* (NCES 2018-070). Washington, DC: National Center for Education Statistics, Institute of Education Science, 2019. https://nces.ed.gov/programs/digest. Retrieved June 2019.

Steinberg, Matthew and Johanna Lacoe. *What do We Know about School Discipline Reform? Assessing the Alternatives to Suspension and Expulsion.* https://educationnext.org/what-do-we-know-abou t-discipline-reform-suspensions-expulsions/. Retrieved April 2019.

Sutcher, Leib, L. Darling-Hammond, & D. Carver-Thomas. *A Coming Crisis in Teaching? Teacher Supply, Demand, and Shortages in the United States.* Palo Alto, CA: Learning Policy Institute, 2016.

Thompson, Ashley. *America's Teacher Shortage Is a Bigger Problem than Thought.* https://Learningenglish.voanews.com/a/study-america-s-teacher-shortage-is-a-bigger-problem-than-thought/4859004.html. Retrieved April 2019.

U.S. Department of Education. *Use of Technology in Teaching and Learning.* https://www.ed.gov/oii-news/use-technology-teaching-and-learning. Retrieved April 2019.

U.S. Department of Education, National Center for Education Statistics. *Digest of Education Statistics, 2016.* Washington, DC: NCES 2017-094. https://nces.ed.gov/fastfacts/display.asp?id=28. Retrieved March 2019.

U.S. Department of Education, National Center for Education Statistics. *Fast Facts: Teacher Trends: Teacher Attrition and Mobility, Results from the 2012-2013 Teacher Follow-Up Survey.* Washington, DC: NCES 2014-077. https://nces.edu.gov/fastsfacts/display.asp?id=28. Retrieved March 2019.

Walker, Tim. *Snapshot of the Teaching Profession: What's Changed Over a Decade?* http://neatoday.org/2016/05/19/snapshot-of-the-teaching-profession/. Retrieved April 2019.

Walker, Tim. "Who is the Average U.S. Teacher?" http://neatoday.org/2018/06/08/who-is-the-average-u-s-teacher/. Retrieved April 2019.

Weathers, Thelma C. *A History of Central High School 1882-1982. Louisville, KY: Central High School, 1981.*

Weeden, Henry C. *Weeden's History of the Colored People of Louisville.* Louisville, KY: H. C. Weeded, Publishers, 1897. Louisville (KY) Western Branch Library, Special Collections.

Werra, Erin. "The Yin and Yang of Augmented Reality." *Augmented Reality in Classrooms\Advancing K-12.* http://www.skyward.com/discover/blog/skyward-blogs/skyward-executive. Blog: January-2018/ the-Yin -&- Yang-of-augmented-reality/.

Will, Madeline. "Teachers around the World Say They're Satisfied with Their Jobs." *Education Week,* June 19, 2019. https://mobile.edweek.org/c.jsp?cid=25919901&bcid=25919901.

Zimmerman, Eli. "The Current State of Education Technology and Where it is Going." *EdTech Magazine.* https://edtechmagazine.com/k12/article/2018/12/current-state-education-technology-and-where-it-going-infographic. Retrieved April 2019.

AUTHOR'S CREDENTIALS: RITA G. GREER, ED. D.

DR. RITA GREER, A NATIVE OF Louisville, Kentucky, is a graduate of Central High School and the University of Louisville, from which she received three degrees, including a Doctorate of Education. A professional educator for nearly fifty years, Dr. Greer divided her time between the K-12 education arena and university teaching. Initiating her career as an educator with the Louisville Public Schools in 1971, she taught middle and high school for thirteen years before matriculating to Central Office as an administrative intern with Jefferson County Public Schools (JCPS). Later she served as Human Resources specialist, Data Management Coordinator, and Human Resources director. During her tenure with JCPS, Dr. Greer was either teaching; directing the recruitment or hiring of teachers for elementary and special schools; training teachers for elementary, middle, and high school positions; or developing programs to recruit and nurture teachers and administrators for employment in JCPS. After her retirement in 2004, Dr. Greer continued serving as Special Projects Consultant for the District.

Among her various accomplishments, Dr. Greer is also credited with the development and implementation of several teacher recruitment and training initiatives for supporting teacher certification and providing quality teachers for JCPS. Initiatives to her credit include the Minority Teacher Recruitment Project (MTRP), the longest continuous school district/university teacher recruitment collaborative program in existence in the country, begun in 1985. In addition, she co-designed the Alternative Certification in Elementary and Secondary Program (ACES), the only certification program in Kentucky that allowed a school district (JCPS) to certify teachers. Furthermore, Dr. Greer was instrumental in designing and developing a number of specifically focused recruitment and training programs, including the Para-Educator Teacher Training Program (PETT); the Montessori Teacher Training Program; the Exceptional Childhood Education Teacher Training Program with Bellarmine University; Career Opportunities in Special Education (COSE) with the University of Louisville; the Extended Alt-Cert Program with Indiana University Southeast and Western Kentucky University; the Stillman College Student Teacher Training Program; the Barbadian Teacher Recruitment Initiative; and the Professional Educator Teacher Training Program. Through her recruitment efforts, leadership, and program development, thousands of educators, including minority teachers and those in high-needs areas, have joined the profession. Many have subsequently migrated to various administrative and leadership positions in JCPS and throughout the Commonwealth.

In 2010, Dr. Greer joined Spalding University's faculty as Director of the Leadership Education Doctoral Degree (EDD) Program and Advanced Graduate Education Programs. At Spalding, she shepherded the EDD Program as well as the Masters and Rank Programs for certifying counselors, teacher-leaders, and principals. She also served as co-chair for the 15,000 Degrees Initiative, a project under the Community Foundation of Louisville designed to encourage and support degree attainment within Metro Louisville's African-American community. She officially retired in 2014, but continues her professional commitment as an education consultant and adjunct professor.

Dr. Greer currently serves on several boards, including the University of Louisville College of Education and Human Development Advisory Board. She and James, her high school sweetheart/husband of more than fifty-two years, have one daughter who is a public school educator, and two grandchildren.

ENDNOTES

1   "Teacher" definition is a combination of definitions from The American College Dictionary, The American Heritage College Dictionary, explanations and definitions derived from *Journeys*, and author's interpretation.

2   Definition of "Inspiration" is derived from various dictionaries in addition to The American Heritage College Thesaurus, and author interpretations.

3   "What's Love Got to do With It?" was written by the author and reprinted from the Ole Landmark, Vol. 8, Issue 2, Spring 2005. This quarterly magazine was distributed to selected employees of the Jefferson County (Kentucky) Public Schools in collaboration with the Jefferson County Association of School Administrators as an update and inspirational memoire to encourage and support African-American leadership and the pursuit of minority teacher efficacy, retention, and sustainability.

4   "Myself" was among the many poems written by Edgar Albert Guest. The excerpt included here is from the last stanza of the poem. The original date of publication is undetermined. The poem is in the public domain.

5   The definition of "Initiative" is a compilation of definitions from various dictionaries and the author's interpretation.

6   The definition of "Insight" is a composite definition from various dictionaries and the author's interpretation.

7   Ibid.

8   "In Memory of Lucie DuValle" annotated from the *Kentucky Negro Education Association Journal*, January-February, 1939, pages 9-11. Additional information from "An Early Educator: Ms. Lucy N. DuValle." Doyle, Ruby. *Recalling the Record*, pp. 112-113.

9   Ibid. Park's remarks were compiled from a variety of edited notes found in Jefferson County Public Schools Archives file for Lucie DuValle and DuValle Jr. High School. Artifacts include copies of the dedication program for DuValle, curriculum offerings for the school,

short biographies for principals of Cotter Elementary and DuValle Jr. High and excerpts from the *Kentucky Negro Education Association Journal.*

10 Ibid.

11 Ibid. *I Memory of Lucie DuValle.*

12 Notes copied from SACS Interim Review 1982-1983, "A Brief History of Lucie DuValle Middle School," retrieved from JCPS Archives for DuValle School.

13 Ibid. Kentucky Negro Education Journal.

14 Ibid.

15 Picture of handwritten letter retrieved from Ms. DuValle's original Personnel File in JCPS Archives.

16 "A Fearless Champion of the Negro Cause: A. E. Meyzeek." Doyle, Ruby. *Recalling the Record* p. 513-515.

17 Additional story elements from The Negro History Bulletin. "The Record of Albert Ernest Meyzeek." The Association of Study of Negro Life and History, Inc. Washington, DC, Vol. X 1946-1947, p. 186-189, retrieved from the Louisville Western Branch Library, Special Collections and Western Branch Library Mural Brochure.

18 Weathers, Thelma C. *A History of Central High School 1882-1922, p. vii.*

19 Elements of Meyzeek's early history from Louisville Western Branch Library Storyboard and the *Encyclopedia of Louisville.*

20 "Albert Ernest Meyzeek Biographical Portrait." http://www.lfps.org/western/htms/meyzeek.htm. Retrieved November 14, 2018. Reference to Horton's "Old War Horse of Kentucky" in Notable Kentucky African American Database included.

21 Hall, Wade. *The Rest of the Dream: The Black Odyssey of Lyman Johnson.* Lexington, KY: University Press of Kentucky, 1988, p. 71.

22 Copy of picture of Lyman T. Johnson retrieved from his official Personnel File in JCPS Archives. Permission for use courtesy of Jefferson County Public Schools.

23 Unknown source. Milburn Maupin's Louisville, Kentucky was a faded galley proof found among Mr. Maupin's personal papers and memoirs provided by daughter, Dr. Madeline Maupin Hicks. We were unsuccessful in determining if the article was published or who wrote the article. Dr. Hicks verified the accuracy of the information and approved its inclusion.

24 Ms. Hawkins remarks reprinted in the Jefferson County Association of School Administrator's *Torch Topics,* Vol. XIII, No. 4, March 1990.

25 Minor Daniels' story was composed by his wife, Jessie, from personal papers and from the original request to consider re-naming the combined Jefferson County (KY) alternative schools in Minor's honor.

26 Dr. Clyde Liggin's original letter to his son was printed in the unpublished *Liggin Family Memoir*. The excerpt included here is with permission of Carl Liggin, his son, to whom the letter is written.

27 Geurin, Claudia. Letter In Memory of Dr. Clyde Absalom Liggin was given to Carl Liggin for inclusion in the *Liggin Family Memoir*. Reproduction and inclusion of the letter are with the permission of the author, Claudia Smiley Geurin and Carl Liggin.

28 Excerpt is copied from the Liggin Family Memoir and is reproduced with the permission of Carl Liggin.

29 Adapted from the 2020 Jefferson County (KY) Public Schools Teacher Job Descriptions for elementary, middle and high school teachers. Used with permission.

30 National Center for Education Statistics (NCES). 2015-2016 National Teacher and Principal Survey (NTPS). Washington, DC: U.S. Department of Education.

31 McFarland, J.B., Hussar, J. Zhang, X. Wand, K. Wang, S. Hein, M. Diliberti, E. Forrest Cataldi, F. Bullock Man, and A. Barmer. The Condition of Education 2019 (NCES 2019-144). U.S. Department of Education. Washington, DC: National Center for Education Statistics. Retrieved June 2019.

32 Ibid.

33 Statistics and perspectives from multiple sources including the National Center for Education Statistics (2019); Walker, Tim. *Who is the Average Teacher*; and Walker, Tim. *Snapshot of the Teaching Profession: What's Changed Over a Decade?*

34 Geiger, Abigail. *America's public school teachers are far less racially and ethnically diverse than their students.* Pew Research Center. https://www.pewresearch.org/fact-tank/2018/08/27/americans-public-school-teachers-ethnically-diverse-than-their-students/. FactTank News in the Numbers, 2018. Retrieved April 2019

35 Ibid.

36 U.S. Department of Education. *Fast Facts.* "Certification Requirements by State." www2.ed.gov. National Center for Education Statistics (2018). Characteristics of Public School Teachers. Retrieved 6.20.2019

37 Review of data from the National Education Association (NEA). Average Teacher Salaries Down 4.5 percent, NEA Report Finds. www.nea.org//home/74876.htm. Retrieved June 2019.

38 Dussault, Adrien. *2018's Top Eight Classroom Challenges, According to Teachers*. Classcraft Blog. https://www.classcraft.com/blog/features/8-teachers-challenges-2018/. Retrieved April 2019.

39 *Ibid.*

40 Petrilli, Michael. Are Discipline Disparities Due to the Behavior or Students or the Responses of Adults? https://www.educationnext.org/how-to-think-about-discipline-disparities-suspencions/. Retrieved April 2019.

41 Ibid

42 Steinberg, Matthew and Johanna Lacoe. What do We Know about School Discipline Reforms? Assessing the Alternatives to Suspension and Expulsion. https://edcationnext.org/what-do-we-know-about-discipline-reform-suspensions-expulsions/. Retrieved April 2019.

43 Bohrnstedt, George. "Gains and Gaps: Education Performance After A Nation at Risk." *Three Decades of Education Reform: Are We Still a Nation at Risk?* American Institute for Research. https://www.air.org/resources/-three-decades-education-reform-are-we-still-nation-risk#Bornstedt. Retrieved April 2019.

44 Ibid.

45 Bohrnstedt, G., S. Kitmitto, B. Ogut, D. Sherman, and D. Chan. *School Composition and the Black—White Achievement Gap.* (NCES 2015-018). U.S. Department of Education, Washington, DC: National Center for Education Statistics, 2015. http://nces.ed.gov/pubsearch. Retrieved March 2018.

46 U.S. Department of Education. Use of Technology in Teaching and Learning. https://www.ed.gov/oii-news/use-technology-teaching-and-learning. Retrieved April 2019.

47 Zimmerman, Eli. The Current State of Education Technology and Where it is Going. EdTech Magazine. https://edtechmagazine.com/k12/article/2018/12/current-state-education-technology-and-where-it-going-infographic. Retrieved April 2019.

48 Ibid

49 Ibid.

50 Sutcher, Leib, L. Darling-Hammond, & D. Carver-Thomas. *A Coming Crisis in Teaching? Teacher Supply, Demand, and Shortages in the United States.* Palo Alto, CA: Learning Policy Institute, 2016.

51 Ibid.

52 Ibid.

53 Data compiled from the American Association for Employment in Education. *Educator Supply and Demand Report 2018-2019.* Sycamore, IL: Author 2019.

54 Ibid.

CPSIA information can be obtained
at www.ICGtesting.com
Printed in the USA
BVHW050255221022
649853BV00001B/1

9 781480 887992